SAUDI ARABIA: ALL YOU NEED TO KNOW

Dr. Nasser Ibrahim Rashid
Chairman, Rashid Engineering
Riyadh, Kingdom of Saudi Arabia
(KSA)

Dr. Esber Ibrahim Shaheen
President, International Institute
of Technology, Inc., Joplin, Mo.
United States of America (USA)

International Institute of Technology, Inc.
IITI Building, 830 Wall St.
Joplin, Missouri 64801 U.S.A.

The Saudi flag bears the inscription: "There is no god but God; Mohammed is the Messenger of God."

Library of Congress Cataloging-in-Publication Data

Rashid, Nasser Ibrahim
  Saudi Arabia : All You Need To Know / Nasser Ibrahim
Rashid, Esber Ibrahim Shaheen.
      p.   cm.
  Includes bibliographical references (pp. 331-340) and
index.
   ISBN 0-940485-02-8
  1. Saudi Arabia   I. Shaheen, Esber I.
DS204.R37   1995
953.8—dc20   95-5829

Table of Contents

Preface

Progress in the Kingdom of Saudi Arabia has brought a fascinating transformation, propelling the Kingdom from years of dormancy to a modern nation, a model of growth and achievement. The Kingdom continues to command world attention and interest for many reasons: first and foremost, it floats on a sea of oil with proven reserves exceeding 260 billion barrels, constituting over 26 percent of all the proven oil reserves of the world. Saudi Arabia, a Moslem moderating force with its Holy Shrines in Mecca and Madina, is the focal point for over one billion Moslems in the world who face Mecca in their prayers five times a day. This is a revered spiritual position which will go on until the end of time. Recently, when the blitzkrieg invasion of Kuwait sent shock waves across the world, Saudi Arabia was in the "eye of the storm"—Desert Storm. It instantly became the center of action in the Theater of Operations; with the support of the United Nations and key countries around the world, it played a pivotal role in liberating Kuwait from the grip of tyranny. All this and more generated an avalanche of interest in this prosperous Kingdom and its central position in the New World Order.

Despite all this, evil forces of envy and greed are busier than ever in their campaigns of distortion and disinformation against the Kingdom. This avalanche of "tabloid journalism" is written by people differing in moral values and objectivity. We have read several of these "negative" writings reflecting a coordinated smear campaign, and found it essential and necessary to write this book to give the true picture about the Kingdom as seen by fair, objective people and not by its blind sworn enemies.

We, as well as many just and objective people are annoyed by this vicious campaign of utter lies and innuendos, and we decided to do something about it, enabling everyone to read and see firsthand and judge for themselves. Let the word of truth ring loud and clear! Let the pictures of yesterday and today tell the fascinating story of miraculous progress in the Kingdom of Saudi Arabia, and how the House of Al-Saud dedicated their energies, wisdom and genuine compassion for the benefit of their people and goodwill to mankind. Character assassination, blatant lies and falsifying history were ingrained in the evil minds of these so-called "writers," who brazenly attacked the credibility, authenticity and integrity of great writers and scholars of the era of Ibn Saud such as Amin Rihani, Fouad Hamza, John Philby and others. Their aim in discrediting the House of Al-Saud is to begin by dismantling the foundation erected by the founder of the Kingdom, Ibn Saud, whose undisputed leadership makes him one of the great people of this century. In order to tarnish the image of the Kingdom, this vicious campaign takes a stab at safety and security in the land, in the name of human rights when the death penalty and other just punishments are meted out to drug traffickers and criminals according to Islamic Shari'a, the law of the land which is based on the Holy Qoran and Sunna of the Prophet. In this regard, a distinguished Saudi scholar and diplomat, recently said: "It is our duty to set the record straight. The death penalty for drug traffickers and hard core criminals is a badge of honor for us, because we uphold Shari'a and we treasure law and order."

To quench the thirst for the latest information and knowledge about the Kingdom, a single, up-to-date and unique book covering the entire spectrum of Saudi life and history was needed. Thus, the book "Saudi Arabia: All You Need To Know" was designed to fill this basic need. It is very encompassing and up-to-date. Vast experience in Saudi Arabia gained through several decades and from writing two other books: "King Fahd and Saudi Arabia's Great Evolution" (in English and another version about progress in the Kingdom in Arabic) and the voluminous documentary book: "Saudi Arabia and the Gulf War," were all put to good use while researching and writing this latest book. While exhaustive, this new book combines good organization and technical insight with an interesting, easy-to-read style. Chapters are very comprehensive and profusely illustrated. This book satisfies the need for a single source of information about a Kingdom which is highly regarded throughout the world, and looked upon with interest and sometimes envy. While this book does an excellent job of fulfilling the need for a single source of information about a very broad topic, bear in mind it is not an encyclopedia, although the topics are wide and diverse.

The First Chapter *"Geography and Climate,"* acquaints the reader with the terrain and weather in the Kingdom of Saudi Arabia. The terrain is described by crisscrossing the Kingdom from the Eastern Province going to Najd and then West to Hijaz, then North to the great Nafud Desert, along the Tapline, then Southward to Dahna and Rab'a Al-Khali, reaching into Asir. The varied climate is described so the reader can comprehend the weather conditions throughout the year.

Chapter Two deals with *"History of the Arabs and Arabia."* The background history defines the Arabs and major tribes of Arabia. Then it touches on the Arab Empire from its height to its decline, reaching to the Arabs of modern time. It also describes Saudi ancestors and puritanism, along with the rise of Abdulaziz and the conquests of Riyadh through the long struggle for unifying the Kingdom. Throughout this vivid description, the traits and superior qualities of Abdulaziz are described, shedding light on how his teachings and qualities of wise leadership live on through his children, especially since not a square inch of the territory came to Abdulaziz without a struggle. His children were taught to deal with difficulties and learned about the hardships of life firsthand from their legendary father. This chapter concludes with a description of the relations between Ibn Saud, Roosevelt, and Churchill.

The Third Chapter describes *"Government."* The modern government of Saudi Arabia is responsible for spectacular progress in the Kingdom and continues the mission of Abdulaziz by carrying on with a banner of justice and goodness toward mankind. The rulers since Abdulaziz are briefly described along with the era of King Fahd Bin Abdulaziz. Historic constitutional reforms are presented. A list of various Saudi government ministries and autonomous agencies is given. The policy of moderation practiced by the Saudi leadership on the national level, in the Arab and Moslem worlds, and the decisive leadership exercised during the Gulf War for liberating Kuwait are described. The government policy of moderation on the international scene leads to a special topic on U.S.–Saudi relations and an oil policy that seeks stability in oil prices and growth for the economies of the world. The great performance of the oil sector during the Gulf War was well acknowledged by General Schwarzkopf who said "The skill and speed with which you were able to react to this crisis attests to your efficiency and organizational skills. We at United States Central Command are very proud of your success in meeting the enormous challenges we faced." Saudi Arabia has deep concerns for the health of the global economy and for world oil markets and supplies. It is "a major stabilizing force in the oil market." This chapter concludes with a discussion of benevolence to the world as exercised by the Saudi leadership and the Saudi people. The goodwill of the Kingdom and its generous contributions cross many borders around the globe.

Chapter Four deals with *"Islam,"* especially since Saudi Arabia is the birthplace for Islam. The Five Pillars of Islam are described along with the great conquests of Islam. Information of interest to the Moslem and the non-Moslem reader alike is also given. The Haramein are also described, especially since in that spirit of custodianship the official title preferred by King Fahd became: "Custodian of the Two Holy Mosques." A section on extremist Islamic fundamentalists concludes the chapter and distinguishes between those who practice the true spirit of Islam and those who, in their extremist and violent behavior, are alien to the true spirit of the Holy Qoran.

The Fifth Chapter is a penetrating treatise on the incredible story of progress experienced by the Kingdom of Saudi Arabia. Entitled *"Progress in a Modern Kingdom,"* it contains detailed, up-to-date information on the great leap forward which propelled the Kingdom into its current prominent place in the sun. The whole spectrum of progress is covered; touching on education, oil and minerals, commerce, funds to foster development, transportation, communication, water and agriculture, industrial evolution, housing and the expansion of the Haramein, health, social justice and youth welfare. After over half a century of fueling this gigantic developmental process, Saudi Arabia has not depleted its oil resources. On the contrary, they skyrocketed from about 3 billion barrels in 1949 to over 260 billion barrels today, and more is yet to be discovered. The discovery of oil in 1938 propelled the Kingdom into a new position of prominence and dynamically changed its history. In light of all these changes, the priceless atmosphere of safety and security that one feels upon touching Saudi soil, continues to prevail. Law and order in the Kingdom will continue to play a unique role in promoting and safeguarding a thriving business atmosphere.

The Sixth Chapter covers *"Modern Cities and Interesting Sites"* in the Kingdom. Several interesting areas in the fourteen provinces are described and several of the major cities including Riyadh, in the center of Najd; Dammam, and Dhahran in the Eastern Province; Hail in the north; Mecca and Madina in the Hijaz; Abha, Najran and Jizan in the south, along with a number of other interesting cities flourishing in the Kingdom. Among these are Taif, Yanbu, the archaeological sites at Mada'in Saleh, Al-ola, Tabouk, Skaka, Buraida and a number of other cities that have become more familiar since the Gulf War.

Chapter Seven on *"Doing Business in Saudi Arabia"* describes the necessary and latest information on this subject. The truly free market economy, which is very much nourished and encouraged by the Saudi leadership, creates a healthy atmosphere for doing business and encouraging international trade. Recent events in the Gulf prompted the world community to repel aggression in the region and helped strengthen a healthy global business atmosphere. Saudi and International Arab Chambers of Commerce are listed. Reduction in public service fees; Saudi-U.S. trade relations; Saudi imports and exports are all described with supporting tables and figures. The Kingdom's annual budgets between 1983 and 1993, along with major allocations for 1993, are presented. Policies for bidding and contracting are described to help the businessman in his search for doing business in the Kingdom. This description leads to the private sector, joint ventures–agents and licensing. Performance requirements and settling of disputes, along with customs, shipping regulations and taxes, help in rounding out the information needed by a businessman. Detailed information may be obtained from other sources as necessary. This chapter concludes with basic information about Shari'a, which is the law of the land derived from the Holy Qoran. The information rendered in this chapter will acquaint the businessman with Saudi requirements and regulations relating to both business and industrial development. Those desiring to do business in Saudi Arabia will find a warm, pro-business environment.

Chapter Eight dealing with *"Practical and Beneficial Information"* gives details on relevant background information, along with some special tips which will refresh the reader's memory and direct the traveler into the Kingdom. The following items are covered: visa requirements; Saudi offices in the U.S., the United Kingdom, and Saudi Diplomatic Missions around the world; information about the host country, travel tips, customs, travel plans, transportation, communication, area codes and telephone numbers for certain Saudi cities and for countries and certain cities around the world. Also: time zones relative to Riyadh; working hours; health; Islam; adapting to a different world; friendly talk; hospitality; cultural differences; education; women, and finally the do's and don'ts. Observing these helpful guides prior to and during a trip to the Kingdom will make a trip memorable and an enriching experience.

Chapter Nine covers *"Useful Arabic."* This gives the reader familiarity with the Arabic language. Knowing the alphabet and the way the letters appear in writing will help the curious and the interested to satisfy their curiosity. Speaking, writing, and reading a few words in Arabic should break the ice and give a favorable impression to those you are dealing with. The Arabic alphabet and some basic conventions along with some rules and examples in Arabic are described. Other topics include time and date, customs, changing money, hotels, post and telephone, shopping, oil business, construction, conversing and being friendly, sightseeing, personal encounters, while at the restaurant, medical attention, emergencies, taxi and car matters.

Appendices contain much useful information and deal with diverse topics. Among these are conversions you will need, the Islamic calendar, a glossary of useful words, a detailed list of pertinent references, useful tables on average monthly temperatures for certain Arab cities and more. All this adds to the enrichment and vast informational impact of this most enlightening book.

> Dr. Nasser Ibrahim Rashid,
> Riyadh, KSA
> Dr. Esber Ibrahim Shaheen,
> Joplin, MO. USA
> January, 1995

Acknowledgements

The authors express their appreciation to the Royal Embassy of Saudi Arabia, its Cultural Mission and its Information Office in Washington, D.C. Everyone contacted was happy and eager to help. Personnel at the Ministry of Information in the Kingdom made available to us everything we requested in our research. We are deeply grateful to them for their kindness and cooperation. Data from the Saudi Arabian Monetary Agency (Sama) was also helpful in our work.

Sincere appreciation and special gratitude are due Mrs. Shirley King who worked hard with loyalty, devotion and patience while typing several rough drafts. She was always encouraging and excited about her contribution. The good advice and dedicated work offered by the late Professor G. E. Ray, certainly helped in improving the quality of this book. Dedication and hard work were also exhibited in their help during the writing of our books: *"King Fahd And Saudi Arabia's Great Evolution,"* and *"Saudi Arabia And The Gulf War."*

Chapter 1

Geography and Climate

Geography

Area and Borders

The Kingdom of Saudi Arabia is a vast land occupying an area of 865,000 square miles, equivalent to about 2.23 million square kilometers. It is approximately equal to the size of the United States of America east of the Mississippi River; or one third the size of the entire continental United States of America and roughly equal to all of Western Europe. The Kingdom occupies four-fifths of the Arabian Peninsula. The latest census taken in the early nineties indicates that Saudi Arabia's population is about fourteen million. Three fourths (or 10.5 million) are native Saudis, and the balance are expatriates who came from all over the world to work in the Kingdom.

Most of the land is arid desert with steep mountains near Taif. Mountains are encountered in other parts of Arabia including the Asir region along the southern portion of the Red Sea. Its coastline is 1,174 miles (1,899 kilometers) on the Red Sea and 341 miles (549 Kilometers) on the Arabian Gulf.

The Kingdom is located in southwestern Asia and bordered by the Red Sea on the west and the Arabian Gulf on the east. In the north, it is bordered by Jordan, Iraq, and Kuwait.

The Gulf of Aqaba, extending north of the Red Sea, becomes the strategic waters surrounded by Saudi Arabia, Jordan, and the Sinai Desert.

The Arabian Peninsula stretches a distance of 1,400 miles (2,254 Km) extending from the Gulf of Aqaba in the north and connecting through Bab Al-Mandab with the Gulf of Aden in the south. The distance (stretching east to west) between the northern portion of the Red Sea and the Arabian Gulf is about 750 miles.

However, the southern part of the Red Sea is far more distant, about 1,200 miles to the Gulf of Oman in the east. On the south the Kingdom borders Yemen. On the east it borders a number of Gulf countries. These are Kuwait, Bahrain, Qatar, United Arab Emirates and Oman. The Arabian Peninsula borders the Arabian Sea (an extension of the Indian Ocean) on the south and east. The Red Sea separates the Peninsula from Africa and places such as Egypt, Sudan, Eritrea, Ethiopia and Djibouti which overlooks the Gulf of Aden and Somalia. The Arabian Gulf separates the Kingdom from Iran.

One of the major regions of the Kingdom includes the *Eastern Province* on the Arabian Gulf. It was once called the Province of Al-Hasa (100 miles wide and only 800 feet in altitude) after the Oasis in which the former capital Hofuf lies. This area is famous for its massive oil reserves, the largest in the world. In the Eastern Province, the coastline along the Arabian Gulf extends from Qatar to Ras Al-Khafji, a distance of nearly 300 miles (483 Km). Along the northern boundaries, the distance from Ras Misha'ab to the Gulf of Aqaba is 850 miles (1,369 Km). Along the southern boundaries, the distance from the Arabian Gulf to Maydi on the Red Sea is 800 miles (1,288 Km). From the shores of the Arabian Gulf a gentle rise takes place until the plain reaches an elevation of 2,000 feet at the Ad-Dahna desert (pronounced Dhana) which is 35 miles wide (56.4 Km). There it begins to slope to the Najd Plateau (meaning highland in Arabic), where Riyadh, the capital city of Saudi Arabia is located.

Najd

The heartland of Saudi Arabia is Najd, which is located west of Dahna. It is about 200 miles wide. An important agricultural area on the plains toward the east includes Al-Kharj. The Najd plateau elevation averages 4,000–6,000 feet, dropping to 2,000 feet at Dahna which faces the Arabian Gulf. The Najd plateau extends to the south reaching Wadi Al-Dawasir and then down to the border of the Rab'a Al-Khali. The plain of Najd extends for nearly 900 miles (1,449 Km) stretching beyond Hail, reaching to the Iraqi/Jordanian borders. There are a number of mountainous areas in Najd. The Nafud Dune ridges extend northward until they join what is known as the Great Nafud. There are also a number of marshes in the Najd plateau. These are remnants of the inland waters which existed in the ancient geological periods.

From Najd to the Eastern Province the land is interrupted by some occasional escarpments and small hills. It is also dotted here and there with some oases. However, the region, just like the rest of Saudi Arabia, is mostly arid and rugged.

Tihama

From Najd on westward, the mountain range continues to rise in height reaching 9,000 feet in elevation at some locations. At the western foot of these mountains, a narrow plain is formed called Tihama, hugging the entire coastline of the Kingdom. It is here where we find the region of *Hijaz* (which means barrier in Arabic). This historic region is home to the two holy cities of Islam, namely Mecca and Madina. It is also home for the important commercial city of Jeddah, gateway to the pilgrimage and home of a large seaport and King Abdulaziz International Airport. The Hijaz includes the city of Taif, which is the summer capital of the Kingdom, well known for its moderate and soothing summer months.

This narrow plain along the Red Sea is about 45 miles (72.5 Km) wide in the south, then it narrows gradually to 30 miles (48 Km) in Jizan. When it reaches Al-Wajh, the width becomes only 10 miles and remains so all the way up to the Gulf of Aqaba. This Tihama coastal plain is known for its marshlands and lava fields.

The range of high mountains which parallel this coastal plain is broken by a number of valleys and wadis (dry river beds). Most important among these are Wadi Himbah, Wadi Yanbu, and Wadi Fatima. Wadi Atwad and Bisha are well known in the region of *Asir*. Since the range of mountains is very steep along the western edge, the flood waters wash the silt to the coastal plains; thus the land becomes a bit more fertile for agriculture and grazing.

While the highest mountains are in the southwest with peaks over 9,000 feet (2,744 meters), they gradually decline to 8,000 feet west of Mecca and then 4,000 feet west of Mahd Al-Dahab, then to 3,000 feet at Madina. The range extends further to the north.

Nafud

In the north one finds a vast expanse of desert sand known as the *Nafud* or Great Nafud, covering an area of nearly 22,000 square miles (57,200 square kilometers), and reaching close to the Jordanian border.

The northern part of Saudi Arabia existing between Nafud, Jordan, and Iraq is part of the great Syrian Desert. It is a very rugged terrain made of gravel plains, lava beds, and rock. This plateau reaches an elevation of about 900 feet (274 meters). It is an interesting, varied terrain where ancient trade routes connected the Mediterranean with Central Arabia and passed through Wadi Sirhan and Al-Jawf Oasis.

Just south of Nafud is Jabal Shammar district, with Hail as its capital. The name of Shammar is derrived from the well-known tribes in the northern region.

The famous pipeline (30–31 inches in diameter) known as *Tapline* was used to carry crude oil a distance of 1,068 miles (1,719 Km) from Saudi Arabia to the port of Sidon in Lebanon for access to the Mediterranean Sea. It moved along the northern frontiers parallel to the borders with Kuwait and Iraq, stretching the entire length of the borders and beyond crossing Jordan, Syria and Lebanon.

Several years ago, crossing a stretch along the Tapline between Saudi Arabia and Jordan was an experience never to be forgotten: travelling one hundred kilometers (62 miles) of hostile desert, mainly traveled by trucks. The road was unmarked and very difficult to follow. On approaching the Jordanian border, the fine desert sand (almost like quick sand) gave way to a geological change where black rocks about six inches in size and smaller were spread everywhere on the flat desert. Progressively, these rocks were left behind as the desert bids farewell!

Today, paved roads and various communities have been established along this line. These include Qaisumeh, Shu'bah, Hafr Al-Baten, Rafha, Ar'ar, Badanah and Turaif. This region became the Center for the Theatre of Operations for liberating Kuwait during the Gulf War. This massive pipeline was finally shut down for a number of reasons, notably the direct accessibility to the Red Sea through a new, gigantic oil east-west pipeline crossing Saudi Arabia and linking the oil-rich Eastern Province with the newly-built

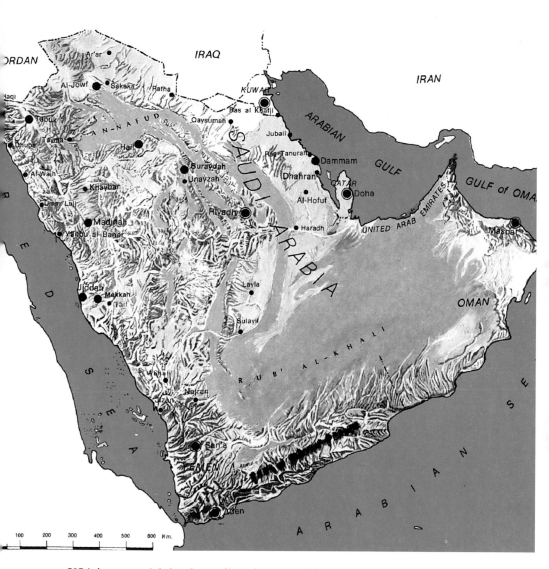

KSA is a vast rich land equaling the area of the USA east of the Mississippi River, or the entire area of Western Europe.

The varied landscape of the Kingdom of Saudi Arabia is nestled with fascinating deserts, hugged by steep mountains, bathed with the warm waters of the Arabian Gulf and the Red Sea, blessed with Holy Mecca and Madina, and last but not least it floats on a sea of oil.

industrial city of Yanbu on the Red Sea, and from there on through the Suez Canal to the Mediterranean Sea.

The Oases of Jawf and Skaka are located southwest of Badanah (an old pumping station for the Tapline). Beyond this, the great depression of Wadi Sirhan provided (from earliest times) access to Jordan, Syria, Palestine, and Lebanon. The Qasim region is located southeast of Jabal Shammar. The towns of Buraydah and Unayzah in this region are well known for their entrepreneurial people who traded between India and Egypt. The Sudair (pronounced S'dair) district is located in southeast Qasim. Al-Majma'a is the capital of Sudair.

Dahna and Rab'a Al-Khali

A large arc of sand extends all the way from the east of Nafud down to Rab'a Al-Khali in southern Arabia. The middle of this arc, 800 miles long (1,288 Km) is Dahna, which is a long narrow belt of fine sand connecting the Great Nafud with the vast Empty Quarter (Rab'a Al-Khali in Arabic). This territory, the size of Texas, is the largest desert in the world. Although it is a harsh terrain, mapping and oil exploration there have been accomplished. It is about 750 miles (1,208 Km) in length and the maximum width is about 400 miles (644 Km). The area covered by this immense stretch of desert is about 250,000 square miles (650,000 Km^2), which is larger than Holland, Belgium, and France combined. It is dotted with beautiful sand dunes and low level sandy mountains with varying heights from 450 feet (137 m) to 850 feet (259 m). Known as the Empty Quarter, it is mostly uninhabited except for some bedouins venturing into the area after trickles of rain give life to a few bushes sprouting here and there.

Asir

On the southwest, the Rab'a Al-Khali is bordered by Asir. Its name means "difficult and rugged" in Arabic. This region consists of a stretch of mountains along the southern coast of the Red Sea. Asir is well-known for its terraced land and greenery since it receives a good bit of rain compared to the other provinces in the Kingdom. The spectacular coastal highlands of Asir rise sharply with their igneous rock to elevations in excess of 9,000 feet (2,744 m) and then plunge down into the terraced green and luscious fields of cultivated valleys, in sharp contrast with the encroaching desert sand. Asir extends for about 230 miles (370 Km) along the Red Sea and nearly 200 miles (322 Km) inland. The slope of the mountains is more gentle east of Hijaz where they gradually give way to the central Najd uplands, which is a large plateau varying in height between 5,000 feet (1,524 m) in the west to about 2,000 feet (610 m) in the east.

Climate

The climate is in general hot or very hot. Along the coastlines, it is also very humid. The interior, being especially dry, makes the heat somewhat tolerable. Along the coastline, high humidity makes the weather uncomfortable. However, air conditioning brings much comfort and is widely used throughout the country. The summer months are very hot. In the spring and fall, the weather is mostly pleasant. Desert areas have cool nights and sunny, balmy days. It is a great delight to see the very bright stars or the brilliant moon at night. The central and northern areas experience temperatures which fall below freezing at times. Ice and snow are rare except in the highest regions. (See Tables for temperatures in certain Saudi cities, certain Arab cities and a useful table for temperature conversions. Certain numbers have been rounded off).

The Shamal Wind is famous for the sand storms it brings from the northern desert. It frequently whips up sand storms in its path. It comes alive in February, March, and again in the early summer; it can blow for days at speeds reaching 30 miles per hour. On occasions sand storms fill the atmosphere and cause discomfort and poor visibility. They last from one to three days and often are cleansed by a rain storm. Rainfall is infrequent in the Kingdom. At times there will be no rainfall in the Empty Quarter for as many as ten years.

The mountains of Asir could experience an average of 20 inches of rain per year. Rain in this region is affected by Monsoons of the Indian Ocean which affect the southern fringes of the Arabian Peninsula and the Sudan Depression. The Dhahran, Khobar, Dammam area may experience an average of three inches of rain per year; at times the average may be seven inches or less than one inch. Eastern Province rainfall begins in November or December and continues intermittently until the end of May. On many occasions, rain comes in torrential downpours causing flash floods and many areas become drenched with excessive amounts of rain.

Water

Artesian water is found trapped under impervious rock at various locations in the Arabian Gulf region. When a well is dug, the water rises in the hole. The Oases of Hasa and Qatif have a good supply of this water, obtained through the centuries from the wells dug into the water-bearing strata. Even the bottom of the Gulf has fresh water springs. The sand covered areas of the coastal region have many sweetwater seepages. Today, water desalination is bringing abundant water supplies to the entire population of the Kingdom. West of the Dahna sands, where the elevation above sea level ranges between 700 (213 m) and 1,200 feet (366 m), water is rather scarce. When wells are dug between 500 feet (152 m) to 800 feet (244 m), reaching the water table, the water is pumped to the surface, but in many instances it is brackish. It has a high salt content and would not be fit for human consumption without treatment. Between the igneous rocks of Central and Western Arabia and the Dahna sands, water is found at the foot of the long and gradual slopes. At the eastern watershed of the escarpment of Tuwaig runs an underground water supply which is used for irrigation work at Kharj. Water is fairly abundant in the mountainous regions of Hijaz. This water supports agricultural works and wildlife.

The Kingdom has no permanent rivers or lakes. When it rains, the wadis flow and sometimes flood. After a few days they dry up. However several dams and reservoirs have been built to take advantage of the rain when it comes. While the terrain is harsh and dry, oases, water wells, desalination, reservoirs, the occasional rainfall and a generous support from the government, all make the desert bloom around cities, communities, dwellings and agricultural centers. Despite all this, the climate remains very hot in the summer, where day temperatures can reach 100 to 115 degrees Fahrenheit (37.8°C–46.1°C). The average maximum and minimum daily temperatures for a year range between 101°–65°F (38°–18°C) for Jeddah and 108°–48°F (42°–10°C) for Riyadh, and 90°–70°F (32°–21°C) for Dhahran. See the following table for various average temperatures.

As a whole, the weather in Saudi Arabia is very pleasant from

September to January. The summer resort of Taif, has low humidity in the summer and comfortable day temperatures around 70°–75°F (21.1°–23.9°C).

Temperatures in Certain Major Saudi Cities

City	Yearly Average Temperature	
	°F	°C
Jeddah	82	28
Mecca	87	31
Taif	73	23
Madina	83	28
Yanbu	82	28
Qurayat	68	20
Turaif	66	20
Hail	73	23
Riyadh	79	26
Dhahran	80	27
Abha	65	18

Average Temperatures for Jeddah, Riyadh and Dhahran

Jeddah

Month	Mean Temp.	Avg. Daily Maximum Temp. °F	Avg. Daily Minimum Temp. °F
January	74	92	55
February	75	93	59
March	78	100	61
April	82	104	62
May	85	104	66
June	87	111	70
July	90	107	75
August	90	105	75
September	88	105	73
October	84	106	64
November	81	96	65
December	76	91	59
Annual	82 (28°C)	101 (38°C)	65 (18°C)
Years	6	6	6

Riyadh

Month	Mean Temp.	Avg. Daily Maximum Temp. °F	Avg. Daily Minimum Temp. °F
January	63	88	28
February	68	95	34
March	75	103	32
April	85	111	50
May	92.5	113	59
June	97.5	122	67
July	101	125	64
August	101	122	68
September	97.5	115	61
October	86.5	110	48
November	74.5	98	36
December	68	90	31
Annual	84 (20°C)	108 (42°C)	48 (10°C)

Dhahran

January	60	69	52
February	63	71	54
March	69	78	59
April	78	88	69
May	88	99	77
June	94	107	82
July	97	108	85
August	96	108	85
September	92	104	80
October	84	95	73
November	74	84	65
December	64	73	55
Annual	80 (27°C)	90 (32°C)	70 (21°C)

Chapter 2

History of the Arabs and Arabia

Arabia was the heartbeat for the flourishing civilizations between Egypt and Mesopotamia. Its history goes far back into the year 7,000 B.C., where people in the Eastern region developed trading ties with the Ubaid culture in the north. Arabia was known as the "Cradle of Civilization."

The southwestern and southern regions were known to the Greeks and the Romans as "Arabia Felix," or "Happy Arabia"–prosperous and considered a major source for frankincense and myrrh.

This region also was a focal point for the trade in silk, ivory, spices for flavoring as well as preserving food, and other goods on their way to the Mediterranean countries. Trade through the Indian Ocean was brought by ship to Arabia where ships unloaded at Aden. From there, transportation was mainly by land to markets in the Western Mediterranean, Egypt and Mesopotamia.

Southern Arabia was the only part of the Peninsula that was agriculturally self-sufficient. The people imported some luxury items, but never foodstuffs. This was possible because of their ingenuity in irrigation. They designed systems to catch run off waters from the infrequent rains that occasionally flooded the wadies.

Who Are the Arabs?

Stretching from the Atlantic Ocean to the Arabian Gulf, Arab land occupies more than five million square miles (thirteen million square kilometers), and it is the richest in oil and gas compared to any country in the world. Twenty-eight percent of this land lies in Asia, and the other seventy-two percent is in Africa. Nearly eighty-five percent of this great mass is desert, under which lie massive quantities of oil and gas.

Two different groups of Arabs lived in the Arabian Peninsula. One was mainly nomadic, roving the huge deserts that extended between the Euphrates River and the center of the Peninsula. The other group were the inhabitants of the southern portion, namely, Yemen. Usually the nomadic group were referred to as the Arabs.

Prior to the birth of Islam, the Arabs were the nomads of Jazeerat al-Arab, meaning the "island of the Arabs," a great portion of which is today *Saudi Arabia*. Many of these people moved northward into the Fertile Crescent that includes countries such as Syria, Jordan, Palestine, Lebanon and Iraq. The migrants mingled with the old civilizations of the Babylonians, Assyrians, Phoenicians and Hebrews.

The harsh environment brought about its own strong laws that characterized the structure of tribal lives. Mere survival depended on the unity and protection of the tribes. A system emerged where a family or a tribe were held responsible for acts of anyone belonging to the family or the tribe. Judgement was swift and severe: eye for an eye, life for a life. The individual crimes were kept in check because of the harsh punishment that followed and the lasting vengeance that took place. Tribal disputes were settled from time to time by an arbitrator being a "wise man" or an authority. At times these disputes provided a good excuse for a raid or "ghazou," aimed at the enemy and his possessions.

With the harsh life of the desert, the Bedouins depended heavily on the camel, drinking its milk and using it for transportation. The major diet came from the dates, fruits of the palm trees. In this environment the fighting mood was a chronic mental condition for the Bedouins and raiding was one of the few manly traits. During the pre-Islamic Period, some tribes practiced the "ghazou" without any mental anguish. It was a sort of national sport and blood was shed in desperate situations. The weak tribes could buy protection by paying the stronger tribes a certain fee called "khouwwah." Despite the many evils of ghazou, the Bedouin within his laws of friendship was a loyal and generous person. The poets and writers of the time sang the praises of hospitality, enthusiasm and manliness.

Severe competition for water and pasture was the main cause for conflicts that split the desert people into fighting tribes. However, the consciousness of being helpless in the face of a very stubborn and rugged nature contributed to the feeling of need for the duty of hospitality. To refuse a guest the courtesy, or to cause him harm after being accepted as a guest, was considered a very serious offense.

The dawn of the twentieth century substantially diminished the number of true nomads or Bedouins in the Kingdom. Much of the Saudi rural population lives in farm villages and oasis settlements. Since the early sixties many nomads and semi-nomads chose this way of life or moved into urban areas where they found work in the oil business or other thriving industries. Tribal distinctions became blurred in large population centers across the land. Old tribal strife vanished once the unified country was born again under the leadership of Al-Saud. Nevertheless, the tribe, which is an extension of the family, continues to have a mystique of its own reflecting national loyalty and political identity.

F. Hamza, an advisor to the Royal Court during the time of Abdulaziz, states that accounting for tribal origin is not an easy task by any standard. Nevertheless, he specifies five strata in identifying the various tribes. These are:

1. *Tribe (qabila in Arabic)* such as A'naza.
2. *Group (Al-Batn)*, for example Dana Wa'el and Dana Moslem from the groups of A'naza tribe.
3. *Division (Al-Fakhz)*, such as children of Ali and children of Souleiman from the division of A'naza groups.
4. *The Clan (Al-Faseela or Al-A'asheera)*, such as Al-Doghman.
5. *Family (Al-Raht)*, for example Al-Sha'alan.

The following table and map lists the major tribes of the Arabian Peninsula.

It was in this cradle of old civilizations that three of the world's greatest religions were born: Judaism, Christianity and Islam.

Before the birth of Islam there were Arab Jews and Arab Christians as well. They still form a minority in the Arab land. With the spread of Islam and the great Arab conquests, the Arab Empire became a melting pot. An Arab may be short or tall, white or black, blond or brown, dark or blue-eyed. He may be of Assyrian, Berber or Phoenician origin. The Arabic language and the Moslem religion are both strong unifying factors. In modern days, an Arab may be defined as any person whose native language is Arabic.

Tribes of Arabia

A'abd Shahab (Bani)
A'alkam
A'Anazah
A'dwan
A'ed
Alm'a (Rijal)
A'mrou (Bani)
Ashraf
A'tiyyah
Bahela
Bakr (Bani)
Balahmar (Ahmar)
Balasmar (Asmar)
Bali
Bani Bashar & Sharif
Baqoum
Bariq
Bina (Al)
Dawasir (Al)
E'eys (Banou)
Fadhl (Al)
Fahm (Banou)
Ghamed
Hajer (Bani)
Harb
Hareth (Banou Al)
Hilal (Banou)
Houtheil
Houwaytat
Ja'ada (Banou)
Jahadila
Jouheina
Jouna (Banou)
Khaled (Banou)
Khath'am Bakr Bin Wael
Khouza'a
Lam (Banou)
Malek (Bani)
Manasir
Mas'oud (Ibn)
Mismer (Al)
Moudhar

Mougheid
Mounjiha (Al)
Mountafiq
Mourra (Al)
Mousa (Al)
Mouteir
O'man
Ou'beida, Roufeida &
   Jarema
O'ujman
Qahtan
Qana and Bahr
Qarn (Banou)
Qoureiniyya
Qeis
Rabi'a
Rabi'a and Roufeida
Reish (Al)
Reith
Sa'ad (Banou)
Sakhr (Banou)
Salim (Bani)
Sanhan
Shadida
Shahr (Bani)
Shahran
Shammar
Shamran
Sirhan
Soubey's
Souhoul
Taghlib
Tamim (Banou)
Thaqeef
Wadi'a
Yam
Zahran
Zalem (Banou)
Zeid (Banou)
Zo'b
Zoufeir

Sources: 1. Hamzah, F. "Heart of the Arabian Island" in Arabic, pp 131–137, Modern Library of Al-Nasr, Riyadh 1933, 1968.
2. Al-Hoqail, H. "A treasure of Geneology and a store of Literature" in Arabic, Safir Printing, Riyadh, 12th Printing, 1993.

Tribal Map of the Arabian Peninsula

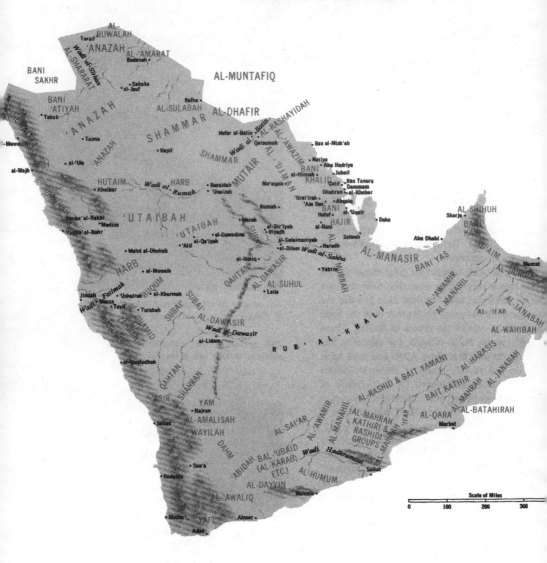

The Arabs achieved prominence and greatness with the rise of Islam.

While the Arabs were the heirs to an ancient civilization, they also excelled in effectively using and improving upon the Greek and Roman civilizations. They in turn played a dynamic role in transferring to the European nations the newly-born civilization, which had benefited from all the ancient ones preceding it. This transfer ultimately led to the awakening of the Western world by setting a steady pace toward Renaissance. During the Dark Ages of Europe, the Arabs contributed to the progress of humanity more than any other people of the time.

Prince Charles of England stated in a speech delivered at Oxford on October 27, 1993, ". . . if there is much misunderstanding in the West about the nature of Islam, there is also much ignorance about the debt our own culture and civilization owes to the Islamic world. It is a failure which stems, I think, from the straightjacket of history which we have inherited. The medieval Islamic world, from Central Asia to the shores of the Atlantic, was a world where scholars and men of learning flourished. But because we have tended to see Islam as the enemy of the West, as an alien culture, society and system of belief, we have tended to ignore or erase its great relevance to our own history. For example, we have underestimated the importance of 800 years of Islamic society and culture in Spain between the 8th and 15th centuries. The contribution of Moslem Spain to the preservation of classical learning during the Dark Ages, and to the first flowerings of the Renaissance, has long been recognized. But Islamic Spain was much more than a mere larder where Hellenistic knowledge was kept for later consumption by the emerging modern Western World. Not only did Moslem Spain gather and preserve the intellectual content of ancient Greek and Roman civilization, it also interpreted and expanded upon that civilization and made a vital contribution of its own in so many fields of human endeavour–in science, astronomy, mathematics, algebra (itself an Arabic word), law, history, medicine, pharmacology, optics, agriculture, architecture, theology, music . . . Islam nurtured and preserved the quest for learning."

Truly, the distinct entity of the Arabs did not clearly manifest itself and assert its prominent position until the birth of Islam. (See Chapter 4 for the great conquests of Islam).

The Vanishing Arab Empire

The great Abbasid Dynasty, which lasted nearly five hundred years, was declining toward the latter part of its rule. By the time the *Mongol* General Hulagu Khan tore down Baghdad in 1258, the Caliph was kicked to death, and after 800,000 people died in the streets, the empire which had begun to decline after the death of Horoun Al-Rashid in 809, was finished.

In a speech at Claremont in Southeastern France on the 26th of November, 1095, Pope Urban urged the faithful to "enter upon the road to the Holy Sepulchre, wrest it from the wicked race, and subject it." By the spring of that year, nearly 150,000 men, mostly Franks and Normans, had answered the call and met at Constantinople. With the depressed economy and the poor social conditions in France, Lorraine, Italy and Sicily, the carrying of the cross was, essentially, a relief and not much of a sacrifice.

When the Crusaders departed, the Mongols or Tartars coming from the highlands of Central Asia, attacked the Arabs mercilessly and caused destruction and devastation. Between the years 1220 and 1227, Genghis Khan and his men terrorized and destroyed many communities in Iran. By the year 1258, the Mongols' terror reached Mesopotamia. Baghdad was ruined and the Abbasid Caliphate was destroyed. One hundred years later Timurlane and his armies reached Syria and burned its major cities. During the barbaric attacks by Hulagu Khan, beautiful libraries and works of art were burned and thousands of inhabitants were massacred. The Mongols continued the destruction in various areas in Mesopotamia and also in Syria. The great system of irrigation which remained in this region to make it fertile and prosperous for many years also was ruined. The blow was devastating and beyond imagination.

The Mongols were finally stopped in Asia Minor, where they were challenged by the rising power of the *Ottoman Turks,* who had invaded Asia Minor in the Thirteenth Century A.D. and received a grant of territory from a weakened Sultan. By the year 1453, the Turks extended their rule to Constantinople, and around 1566 their Empire had expanded to include the entire Arab World and beyond. They ruled the Arabs in the name of Islam for many centuries. The basis of the Sultan's Policy was: *divide and rule.* He turned Moslem against Christian, Sunni against Shi'a, Kurd against Armenian. This was a dark period in Arab history. In 1683, the Ottomans were repulsed outside Vienna and this was the beginning of their slow decline. Their Empire ended in 1918 after the defeat of Turkey, which had entered World War I on the side of Germany.

The Ottoman Empire was like the Roman's in the sense that it was essentially militaristic and dynastic in character. The major objective was not the welfare of the subjects, but the welfare of the governing state as represented by the Sultan. These subjects were of many nationalities, encompassing the Arabian, Iraqis, Syrians, Berbers, Armenians, Slavs, Kurds, Albanians and Greeks, with many creeds, languages and various ways of life. All of them held by the power of the sword. The Ottomans clearly distinguished between Moslems and Christians and encouraged differences even between Moslem Turks and Moslem Arabs. They played one Christian sect against another, very much along the lines of divide and rule. The seeds of decay were right within its structure from the beginning.

Their major decline, a pathway that was long and very tortuous began with their second attempt on Vienna, Austria, in the year 1683. The Turkish expansion into Europe ceased. After that, the Turks had the problem of holding on to what remained under their rule.

The centuries of Ottoman rule are regarded by the Arabs today as the dark period in their history. It is indeed astonishing that such dynamic and creative people were held politically dormant and socially stagnant for such a long time. The end to this period of stagnation came with the rise of the Arab Nationalist movement in the latter part of the nineteenth century. This process was culminated by joining forces with the Allies in World War I, and with the eventual end of Turkish rule in 1918.

At the beginning of this century, Great Britain became the dominant force in this region. King Abdulaziz Al-Saud, known in the West as Ibn Saud (more details follow), used his political genius to gain the necessary help in liberating those parts of Arabia under Turkish rule and foreign influence. While Great Britain and France were determined to limit the Arabs to self-rule under their domination, the United States of America declared its support for self-determination. Good relations were established with the U.S. and careful diplomacy was used to avoid antagonism with the British.

King Abdulaziz Al-Saud was a legendary leader, truly known as the father of his country, which by 1932 was unified as the Kingdom of Saudi Arabia.

Oil discovery and production by 1938 added to the strategic and spiritual importance of this land, the birthplace of the Prophet and guardian to the Holy Moslem Shrines. Saudi Arabia is the heartbeat of the Arab world, the spiritual center for all Moslems of the globe, and the energy giant with undisputable worldwide moderating force and influence.

Arabs of Modern Time

The tremendous impact of Arab oil and world energy needs has brought greater awareness and importance to the Arab world as a whole, especially the oil-producing nations. Almost over-night, news about oil took prominence, and the migration of world technologies toward the Arabs has indeed reached a high point.

With the importance of Arab oil, especially the massive oil re-serves of Saudi Arabia, came economic power and special atten-tion to the Arab cause that had been neglected for many centuries.

The Arabs need Western technology and the West is in equal need of their oil. Without it, many of the Western industries and economies would suffer severely or collapse outright. Thus, a very interesting equation has developed in the past few years, where Arab interests and Western interests must logically and ultimately lead to a common base of mutual benefit and understanding.

One of the thorniest points in Arab matters, as far as the inter-national community is concerned, has been Western insensitivity to a major issue, namely the Palestinian question, and the refugees' dilemma. World peace cries for a just and permanent so-lution to this problem which is at the core of Middle East conflicts.

King Fahd with his wise leadership and political valor devised ingenious ways to help revive the latest peace process initiated by the administration of President George Bush. This coupled with serious American peace initiatives, should clear the way toward an acceptable compromise. Peace accords between Israel and the Palestinians were signed in Washington D.C., on September 13, 1993. They are a step in the right direction toward a just and com-prehensive settlement. (More details are covered in Chapter 3).

However, much destruction has taken place in the span of a

few years. The Middle East has been wracked by bickering differences, wars, and the creation of nearly four million Palestinian refugees. This has resulted in a great burden that has settled upon and choked many nations of the region. One nation that suffered the most in recent times from the aftermath of creating these refugees, is the once fascinating and beautiful country of Lebanon, best known as "the land of milk and honey" and the "Switzerland of the Middle East." It was a beauty crowned with majestic nature where the air smelled of goodness and delight, an ancient land that was a shining example of tolerance among many religions and nationalities. Unfortunately international intrigue, hatred and division in the Arab world brought an ugly civil war that tore the country apart. The result has been the transformation of Beirut, formerly known as the Paris of the Middle East, into the world capital for tragedy and terror.

The Tripartite Committee for bringing peace to Lebanon was made of King Fahd of Saudi Arabia, King Hassan of Morocco and former President Benjadid of Algeria; it culminated with the Taif Conference which became the foundation for ending the Lebanese Civil War. In the early 90's and under the good leadership of Mr. Rafiq Hariri, Lebanon began healing from its deep wounds.

It is imperative that the United States should exercise its unique position of leadership by helping this region gain peace and tranquility. Such a policy will be beneficial not only to the parties concerned but to world peace and the entire world community.

Throughout the Arab world there is action on many fronts to modernize and build. Saudi Arabia, for example is a nation with great wealth and deep religious traditions. Under the wise leadership of King Fahd, progress in every walk of life is mind-boggling. Because of its just and swift rules, this country is one of the safest on earth. The Kingdom is carrying out an industrial and educational evolution of far-reaching consequences. To attract personnel with needed know-how, pay is lucrative and living quarters are similar to any suburban American community.

Billions of petrodollars have been pouring in and massive industrialization programs are under way. In this atmosphere of Arab renaissance, the West, especially the U.S.A., can make a great contribution in leadership and technology that will be beneficial to all.

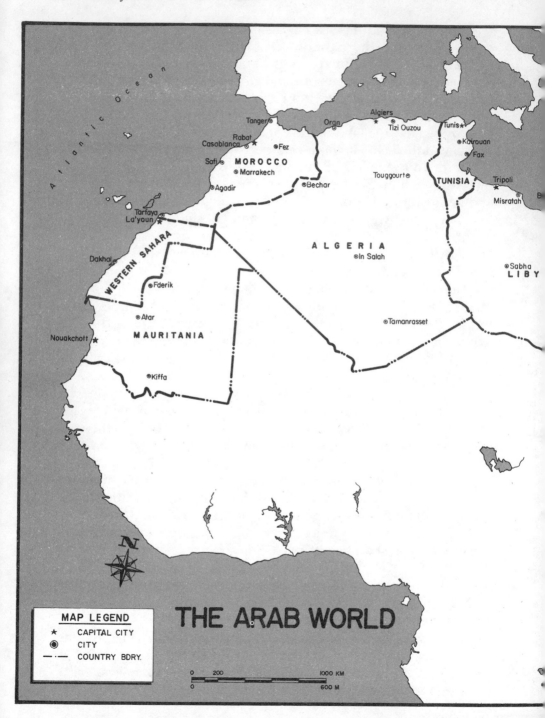

THE ARAB WORLD

MAP LEGEND
★ CAPITAL CITY
◉ CITY
—·— COUNTRY BDRY.

0   200   1000 KM
0   600 M

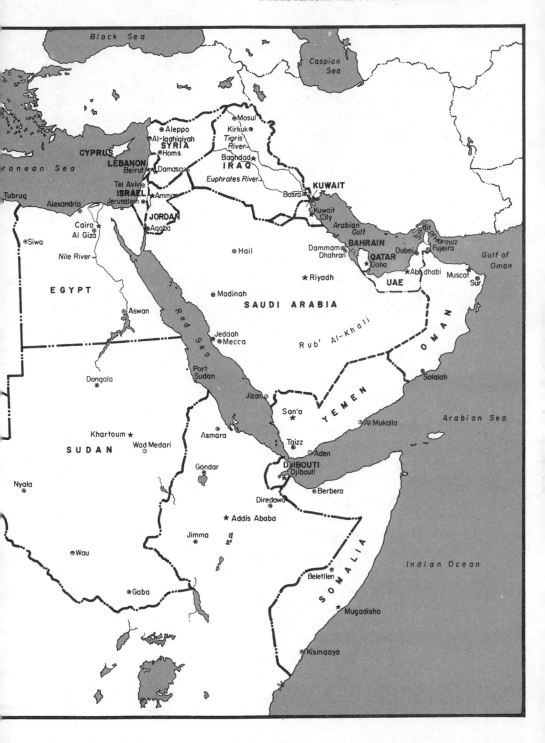

The modern Arabs remain divided into many independent nations. They yearn for Arab unity and a single Arab nation from the Atlantic Ocean to the Arabian Gulf; but this remains largely a dream. Saddam Hussein of Iraq tried to exploit these dreams by occupying and terrorizing Kuwait on August 2, 1990. The World was literally up in arms against him, and the Coalition Forces, under the U.N. umbrella, finally dealt him a devastating defeat. By February 27, 1991, his army fled Kuwait demoralized and humiliated. The Gulf War came on the heel of the Iran-Iraq War. It caused serious divisions and cracks in Arab solidarity. During these two wars and in their aftermath, extremist *Islamic Fundamentalism* gained momentum and brought with it polarization and terrorism; but the voices of justice and moderation shall prevail. Terrorism is basically alien to the mainstream Arab tradition and to the tolerant Moslem religion of the Arabs. These winds shall fade away, for the Arabs are God-fearing people, who have a deep respect for Western technology, great pride in their heritage, and much affinity for justice and hospitality.

Saudi Ancestors and Puritanism

Present Saudi ancestors came from the Qatif region and settled in the historic community of Diriya in the middle of Wadi Hanifa in the northwest corner of Riyadh. Saud Ibn Mohammed Ibn Moqrin ruled Diriya from 1720 until his death in 1725. Then, *Mohammed Ibn Saud* became the ruler for nearly forty years, extending from 1725 until his death in 1765. During this period the title of Imam was adopted for Al-Saud.

With the fall of the Arab Empire, Moslems lost the drive and enthusiasm for practicing the faith of their ancestors. Erroneous practices and behaviors veered away from the religious simplicity originally preached by the Prophet Mohammed. While Islam was still strong in the Hijaz, it became weak and diluted in other parts of Arabia. Certain settlements of Najd were practicing and teaching Islam. Also at Uyaynah, which was not far from the main Saudi settlement of Diriya, people were practicing Islam.

The rule of Mohammed Ibn Saud coincided with the rise of a religious cleansing under the leadership of *Sheikh Mohammed Ibn Abdulwahhab*. He was born in 1703 (1115 A.H.) in Uyaynah and was from the Banou Sinan tribe. His family was deep-rooted in the knowledge of Islamic Shari'a (law) and they sent him to several Islamic cities to continue his religious education.

His father was a learned and generous man. He was a judge and the author of many writings relating to religious matters. He himself taught his bright son and was the first to acknowledge that he often benefited from him in forming his decisions. The son was precocious and finished the study of the Qoran by the age of ten. His father said: "Before he was twelve, he had attained maturity and I had him married."

The son studied law under his father as well as benefiting much from the teachings of Imam Ahmad Ibn Hanbal. He traveled to Hijaz seeking knowledge and also to Basra where he studied the Hadith and read many books on the art of language. Aside from reading in Basra, he also preached the Unitarian faith. "To Allah alone is worship. We walk in the light of a Wali, imitating his example; but we pray only to Allah." His earnest preachings started after he moved with his father from Uyaynah to Huraimala. He preached against the false worship and the idolatrous practices by many. Then he wrote his first book entitled "The Book of Unitarianism."

Sheikh Ibn Abdulwahhab enthusiastically advocated the return to the simple message of the Qoran and the Great teachings of the Prophet Mohammed. His call gave moral basis for unifying the Arabian Peninsula under the House of Al-Saud. The words Wahhabi and Wahhabism were sometimes applied to the followers of this religious leader. His call (Da'wa in Arabic) should never be viewed as a separate sect. Therefore, the words Wahhabis, Wahhabist or Wahhabism are unacceptable. Initially, these preachings were not well received at home and, in 1744, Ibn Abdulwahhab was forced to leave his hometown. He had to move southeast about twenty miles to a community called Diriya. The Amir's wife, a wise woman, and his brothers, along with an ardent disciple named Ibn Swailem, all appealed to the Amir for protection and alliance with Mohammed Ibn Abdulwahhab.

The Amir of Diriya, Mohammed Ibn Saud, went along and formed an alliance to spread the faith and unitarianism across the land. The founding of Saudi Arabia was a culmination of the coupling and fusion of Sheikh Ibn Abdulwahhab's call with Saudi family leadership, which remained a dedicated champion of this religious correction. This relationship flourished and was cemented through intermarriages. They became strong allies in a mission of true Jihad seeking purity in Islam and unity of the nation.

This alliance has endured nearly two and a half centuries since it was contracted in the year 1744 A.D. (1157 A.H.). At that time Mohammed Ibn Abdulwahhab was about forty-two years of age. With the great Saudi support, his mission, or Da'wa, spread like wildfire, covering every part of Arabia from Yemen and Asir up to Jabal Shammar and across to Hasa and on down to Oman.

The Sheikh died in 1792. By then, his call had reached as far south as the *Rab'a al-Khali (Empty Quarter)*. While the south and east of Arabia accepted this effort, the Hasa region, especially the oasis of Qatif and Hofouf, did not submit and were defeated in battle. By now the Saudi State had extended its domain to cover most of the Arabian Peninsula. Such vast expansion of the puritan Islamic call became worrisome to the Ottoman Empire in Constantinople. The Pasha of Baghdad appealed to the Ottoman authorities for help in crushing it. His requests were initially ignored since its strong influence was underestimated. However, the loss of the Holy cities, which meant a loss in prestige and income, made the Ottoman government more decisive in undermining the progress of the Saudi State. The viceroy in Cairo, Mohammed Ali, was asked to take the necessary action. He did, and the first expedition was led by the viceroy's son around 1811. Modern weaponry was of no practical use against the special tactics of the desert tribesmen. Although Mecca and Madina had fallen, the stiff resistance displayed by the people of Arabia forced Mohammed Ali himself to come and lead the military campaign. Reinforcements came under Ibrahim Pasha, another son of Mohammed Ali.

The courageous defenders were shaken by the death of their leader Saud in 1814. By 1814–1818, his successor Abdullah had retreated to Diriya. Ibrahim Pasha, the Egyptian leader reached Najd in 1818. He bombarded and ravaged Diriya until it was turned to ruins. The town fell in that year after an arduous struggle and siege. Abdullah, the Saudi chief, was taken to Constantinople and executed. Despite this major debacle, the Saudi House regained political power over central Arabia and Islamic fervor gained new momentum. Abdullah's uncle, Turki, organized his troops and vowed to oust the Egyptians from Najd. He established his rule in Riyadh because Diriya had been destroyed. He moved on to reconquer Najd and the Eastern Province. The Egyptian garrison was harassed and attacked until it was forced to transfer to Hijaz.

Turki warned against political oppression of the people, but internal tension and squabbling led to his assassination in 1834, by a family rival. His son Faisal took up the reigns of the government and ruled for the years 1834–38 and 1843–65. Although Faisal suffered some early defeats from the Egyptians, he later re-established Saudi rule in Najd and the Eastern Region of Arabia. His strong supporters in these military feats were led by Abdullah Ibn Rashid of Jabal Shammar in the Northern Region of Arabia.

Mohammd Ali decided to bring Arabia into his own sphere of influence around 1834. He supported a rival claimant to Saudi leadership: Khaled Ibn Saud (ruled between 1840–41), a cousin to Faisal who had been imprisoned in Egypt since Abdullah's capture some twenty years earlier. Faisal was a token prisoner for the Egyptian forces, who then occupied Najd and Hijaz and directed the functions carried out by Khaled. However, they overextended themselves in a number of areas and Mohammed Ali had to withdraw in 1840.

Faisal escaped from Egypt in 1843 and regained his position of leadership. Like his father, Turki, he did his best to bring law and order to the land. He died in 1865 and the rivalry between his sons brought on a civil war that lasted for many years. All the stability and cohesion built during Faisal's era was in shambles due to this conflict that erupted between his sons: Abdullah (1865–71, 1875–89) and Saud (1871–75). This provided a window of opportunity for the Turks to occupy the Eastern Region in 1871.

When the rule of Saud, son of Faisal, was established, anarchy was dominant in the region. After his death in 1875, Abdulrahman (1875, 1889–91), the younger brother of Saud and Abdullah announced his succession. Abdullah regained power after one year and then ruled until he died in 1889, when Abdulrahman became the ruler again. Disputes between sons and brothers caused serious damage and distractions that led to challenges from the growing power of the Rashids, who had been placed into power by Al-Saud in the Hail area, governing the Northern Province of Arabia named Jabal Shammar.

Abdulrahman, Faisal's youngest son, was finally forced out of Riyadh. By then, much of Najd was under the control of Mohammed Ibn Rashid. In 1891 the house of Rashid appointed a governor and established a garrison in Riyadh. Leaving the city of his ancestors, Abdulrahman and his family were exiled to Kuwait where they became the guests of the ruler Moubarak and the Kuwaiti people. A bright young man of the family was an eleven-year-old son named *Abdulaziz*, who, in the years to come, would become the founder of the Kingdom of Saudi Arabia. The Rashid successor was a man of minor administrative talent. He governed harshly and succeeded in alienating the tribes under his rule, thus paving the way for the eventual recapture of the region by its just rulers Al-Saud. This was achieved through the sheer courage, superb genius and daring leadership of Abdulaziz, known in the West as Ibn Saud.

Abdulaziz and the Fascinating Story of Capturing Riyadh

Born at the Amir's Palace in Riyadh on December 2, 1880, Abdulaziz had a rendezvous with destiny! His mother, Sarah Al-Sudeiri, died in Riyadh in 1910. When Abdulaziz was barely eight years of age he learned to use the sword and the rifle along with jumping on a horse while moving. He was taught to cope with difficulties, especially the severe conditions normally encountered in the desert. He was taught patience and was trained to exercise self-control. Abdulaziz grew to be tall and handsome.

In the year 1890, when Ibn Rashid conquered the city of Riyadh, Salem was appointed its ruler and Abdulrahman was permitted to live in one wing of the castle. Salem had devised a plot requesting that all the family of Abdulrahman be present at a meeting while having in mind a sinister plan to slay them all at one time. However, Abdulrahman took his sword as well as his men as a precaution. Before Salem could execute his murderous plan, he himself was slaughtered. A young man present at the time was Abdulaziz who learned a lesson about intrigue and bravery. He was sitting in the lap of a big man who protected him from becoming a victim. Abdulaziz was to say later in life: "I learned here that I should be the first to hit when I am exposed to danger."

Preferring not to fall as a prisoner or become a victim, Abdulrahman gathered about twenty of his supporters and his family along with some food supplies and left Riyadh in the darkness of night. The party moved on southward looking for shelter in the desert. After a short time, they divided into two groups: one made of his wife and some servants went to Bahrain, while the other group remained with the father and headed south. For a brief period, the family was in Bahrain and then Qatar. Finally, permission came for the Saudi family to have refuge in Kuwait, where they would remain in the hospitality of the ruling family Al-Sabbah for nearly ten years.

When Abdulaziz reached twenty years of age, he was over six feet tall, a giant of a man! It became clear that he was gifted with qualities of greatness which destiny rested upon his shoulders.

In 1922, the noted author Ameen Rihani met for the first time with then Sultan Ibn Saud. He was fascinated and deeply moved by the sheer greatness of this man. In his tent, by candle light, he described his spontaneous impressions:

"I have now met all the Kings of Arabia and I find no one among them bigger than this man. He is big in word, gesture and smile, as well as in purpose and self-confidence. His personality is complex . . . The shake of his hand and the way he strikes the ground with his stick proclaim the contrary traits of the man . . . He gives you the report about yourself and then pats you on the back telling you that he knows better. He gives you at the first meeting a bit of his mind and his heart, without fear, without reserve . . . He knows himself as well as he knows his people. Hinna 'l-Arab (we are the Arabs)! The man in him is certainly bigger than the Sultan, for he dominates his people with his personality, not with his title . . . strange, indeed! I came to Ibn Saud with an unburdened heart, bearing him neither hatred nor love, accepting neither the English view of him nor that of the Sherifs of Al-Hijaz. I came to him in fact with a hard heart and a critical mind, and I can say that *he captured my heart at the first meeting.*"

Leopold Weiss wrote in the Atlantic Monthly of August, 1929: "Ibn Saud is very tall and possesses superb virile beauty . . . Anyone who meets him is at once impressed by his smile–a charming, understanding, and inexpressibly sweet smile and one cannot but love him."

Newsweek issue of May 12, 1934 said about Abdulaziz:

"A broad-shouldered, enormously powerful man of 54, the King towers over most of his subjects. But he stands before them bare-legged and unshod, wrapped in a plain brown and white Arab robe with intricate gold work on the collar. His jet-black eyes, sometimes spectacled, size up the caller shrewdly. But Abdulaziz likes men who talk up to him, and seldom takes offense."

After his famous meeting with the American president Franklin D. Roosevelt, Time magazine reported on March 5, 1945: "At 65, he is justly called Servant of the Almighty, strong as a lion, straight as a scepter. He is, beyond cavil, the greatest of living Arab rulers."

His deep affection for his family was one of his most lovable and admirable traits. His love and admiration for his sister Noura was something to be treasured. She was a very capable woman who helped in managing the palace in Riyadh. Her influence over Abdulaziz was powerful. Charging with his men, his battle-cry was: "Ana akhou Noura"–"I am the brother of Noura." His love, compassion and respect for family life was unique!

While in Kuwait, his character was developing and his resolve was hardening. Not having all the luxuries of life added more to his resiliency, which gave him more strength and patience. In due time, all these virtues helped him greatly in grasping the opportune moment to reclaim the kingdom of his ancestors.

In the latter part of 1901, Abdulaziz left for Riyadh with forty men from the Al-Saud family and their supporters, along with twenty more followers. He led his weary and tired men to the northern fringes of the Empty Quarter, where he spent several months hoping to recruit more support from the local tribes. Support was not forthcoming and he grew impatient in his wait, especially since life was difficult for his men under the harsh conditions of this barren expanse of sand dunes. Being true and dedicated to his religion, he fasted with his men during Ramadan. On the twentieth of Ramadan, Abdulaziz moved with his party of sixty men; his destination-Riyadh. On the third of Shawwal, the following month, he continued his trip to the outskirts of Riyadh. He and his men were moving at night hiding behind rocks and sand dunes by day. They were finally within an hour and a half walking distance from Riyadh. They hid between the trees until the fall of dusk. That night Abdulaziz told his companions that he was determined to enter the city and conquer it. Whoever wanted to go with him was welcome, and whoever was reluctant should stay. He moved on, with seven of his men. He told the rest around nine o'clock at night, that "by dawn if you do not receive a word, you should run for your lives, because we would have all been killed; and if God grants us success, whoever wants to join us, God be with him."

Abdulaziz moved with the company of his seven men toward the heart of Riyadh with the purpose of taking Fort Musmak–residence of the appointed governor, Ajlan. However, the city had a defense wall surrounding it. Abdulaziz and his men cut a palm tree and used it as a ladder to climb the wall. Some houses were near the outside wall of the castle. One of these was inhabited by Jouwaisir, a cattle merchant, known to Abdulaziz. He knocked on the door and a woman answered: "Who is it?" Abdulaziz answered: "I am sent by Amir Ajlan to buy him two cows from Jouwaisir." The woman said, "You should be ashamed of yourself . . . Does anyone knock on a woman's door at this time of night unless he had bad intentions? Go away." Abdulaziz said, "you be quiet! In the morning I shall tell the Amir and he will rip Jouwaisir apart."

When Jouwaisir heard the threat, he opened the door and Abdulaziz was able to enter the house and get information about Ajlan. Abdulaziz held the man and threatened him not to make a move or he would be killed instantly. While the women were gagged and quieted in a cellar, the cattle dealer fled. Abdulaziz and his men had to enter another house to be able to reach the house where Ajlan's wife lived. In the second house they found a man and his wife. They tied them up with the bed clothing, gagged the wife and threatened them with death if they made any sound.

Abdulaziz waited for a short time to see if the fleeing cattleman alerted the city. Luckily, he did not, then he sent word to his brother Mohammed, who was stationed in the palm groves to bring the rest of the men for support.

Ajlan's wife had a two-story house, so they had to step on each other's shoulders to reach the roof of the second story. After reaching this house they forced the roof door open, crept quietly, and seized the servants one by one. Finally they reached Ajlan's bedroom. Ibn Saud had his rifle and another man followed him with a candle.

They found two persons in bed, but Ajlan was not there. Two sisters were in bed. One of them was Ajlan's wife. While they jumped, screaming, he told them, "Enough! I am Abdulaziz." They were threatened with death if they did not cooperate and remain quiet.

It was learned from them that Ajlan left the fortress after the morning prayer and normally returned to this house. The wife, her sister, and the servants were all locked up. The rest of Abdulaziz's men were brought in from the house next door. All the men settled down around two o'clock in the morning. They drank Ajlan's coffee, ate some dates and prayed, while wondering and thinking about the next step. The decision was to wait until morning when the big gate of the fortress would open and Ajlan would come out. Four men were to stay in the house to cover the group with their rifles. After sleeping about an hour or less, dawn was approaching. Abdulaziz got up and prayed. The plan was to surprise Ajlan as he entered the house.

With the sunrise of January 15, 1902, Ajlan was coming out of the main gate of the fortress and he had about twenty men with him.

When Abdulaziz's eye focused on his enemy, the sight was too much for restraint! Abdulaziz had a gun with one bullet in it. He could not wait any longer. He charged out of the door and moved on to surprise and attack Ajlan. When Ajlan's bodyguards saw Abdulaziz they ran for the fortress gate, but it was already shut. So they moved through a small postern gate two feet high, designed so that a man could enter head first, thus exposing himself to the sword if he was undesired. Ajlan was left alone to face the onslaught of Abdulaziz. He drew his sword to strike Abdulaziz, who covered his face with his arm and fired his rifle point-blank and heard the sword fall to the ground. Ajlan, injured, plunged into the postern gate. Abdulaziz caught his legs and tried his best to keep him from going in. Ajlan's man inside pulled his arms. He then kicked Abdulaziz in the stomach with a strong kick, that nearly fainted him. Abdullah Ibn Jiluwi, a cousin of Abdulaziz, threw a spear at Ajlan but missed! The spear went through the gate of the fort. The steel point is still imbedded in the wood until this day.

In the confusion, the defenders did not slam the postern gate shut. Abdullah Ibn Jiluwi threw himself into the hole and wiggled his way through. The defenders were too confused to kill him as he was going with his head first. Other followers of Abdulaziz moved in, and threw the main gate open. Abdulaziz's men were outnumbered at least two to one, but they moved through the courtyard and towers of the fortress in a bloodthirsty fight that ended in slaughtering many of the defenders. Ibn Jiluwi finally shot Ajlan and killed him with one bullet.

The following is an account by Abdulaziz, who reminisced in later years: "He made at me with his sword, but its edge was not good. I covered my face and shot at him with my gun. I heard the crash of the sword upon the ground and knew that the shot had hit Ajlan, but had not killed him.

He started to go through the postern gate, but I caught hold of his legs. The men inside caught hold of his arms while I still held his legs. His company was shooting their firearms at us and throwing stones upon us. Ajlan gave me a powerful kick in the side so that I was about to faint. I let go of his legs and he got inside. I wished to enter, but my men would not let me. Then Abdullah Ibn Jiluwi entered with the bullets falling about him. After him ten others entered. We flung the gate wide open, and our company ran up to reinforce us. We were forty and there before us were eighty. We killed half of them. Then four fell from the wall and were crushed. The rest were trapped in a tower; we granted safe-conduct to them and they descended. As for Ajlan, Ibn Jiluwi slew him."

Ajlan's guards were surprised and demoralized with the loss of their leader. They lost the will to fight. Abdulaziz went to the center of the area and declared "There is no sense in further resistance." He promised to save their lives if they give up the fight. The battle was over. At this moment of victory one of his men went to the highest point in the fort and declared "The rule is for God! and then to Abdulaziz Ibn Abdulrahman Al-Saud. You are in his safety and guaranteed security."

The capture of Riyadh paved the way for a holy struggle that eventually led to the founding of a great nation, a spiritual center for all Moslems of the world, and a great economic power whose impact is felt throughout the globe, making it the epicenter for justice, safety, wisdom and an abundant source of energy. This closely-knit union is one of the most cohesive ever known in history. One would hardly realize, remember or recognize the recent past of division, disintegration and lawlessness.

The Long Struggle to Achieve Unity

The struggle for unification was long and arduous. Since Abdulaziz Ibn Mit'ab Ibn Rashid was preoccupied by warfare against Kuwait, he delayed his counterattack against Abdulaziz until late in the fall. His campground was at Hafr Al-Batin. He did not give the situation in Riyadh the weight and importance it proved to deserve, so he waited to act until it was too late. Abdulaziz rebuilt the defenses of Riyadh and the city was fortified and prepared to withstand adverse conditions of attack or blockade. His father came back from Kuwait and was placed in charge of the city, while he moved on to unify the nation. Abdulaziz did not come by a single square foot of Arabian territory without fighting for it. Every war he fought, he made a religious war, a war for a principle. His idea finally took the form of welding the destructive and endlessly warring Bedouins of Central Arabia into a cohesive unit. He assured them peace and security the likes of which they had never seen before.

With his charisma, great charm and dynamism, Abdulaziz won the hearts and help of people from southern Najd. By the time Ibn Rashid decided to move on south, he did not attack Riyadh directly, but made a move on Al-Kharj. Abdulaziz was waiting for him in an ambush and when his army advanced, a fierce battle raged on. Ibn Rashid retreated to Hail. Winning this battle was a great moral victory, uplifting the spirit of Abdulaziz and his men. His rule was established in the city of Riyadh and southward on to Rab'a al-Khali. Being very proud of these achievements, his father acknowledged his son's heroism and effective leadership. He abdicated the title of Amir, and bestowed upon Abdulaziz the authority over the Emirate. The father retained the title of Imam.

Abdulaziz Ibn Mit'ab Ibn Rashid was master of most of Central Arabia at a time when his name-sake, Abdulaziz Ibn Saud, was still growing and devising his plans in Kuwait–hardly known to the people in Najd or Hail.

Abdulaziz always set the superb example for his followers and fighters. After a blockade by Ibn Rashid around 1904, Abdulaziz told his fighters:

"Ibn Rashid has been defeated. We need to go outside the town and execute a different plan of action."

They were happy to hear this and they went out for the next

plan to soon find out the truth of his motive and the fact that Ibn Rashid was not really defeated. He ordered them to move on to another target! They were hesitant because they were tired and hungry. They did not have food or water. It was late in the day and they had to cover about twenty miles of distance. To lift their spirits, Abdulaziz made a short speech and said:

"I am one of you and like you! You walk and I walk. You are barefoot and I, by God, will not have a shoe on. And this is my shoe and this is my camel!"

He said this and he walked in front of them barefoot. The troops were moved. They walked on behind him with devotion and determination toward their next target.

Toward the end of May, 1904, Ibn Rashid organized an army strongly supported by Turkish troops and their heavy armaments. The Turks were concerned about the expansion of Abdulaziz; because he was a friend to Mubarak, the ruler of Kuwait who, in turn, was a friend of the British. Moving from the town of Buraidah in al-Qasim, Abdulaziz led his force to meet the advancing forces of his enemy. In the heat of the battle the Turks and Ibn Rashid were defeated. Many of them fled for their lives!

The controversies continued and hostilities led to another showdown which took place near Buraidah on April 14, 1906 (18 Safar 1324 A.H.). This was the decisive historical battle of *Rawdhat Muhanna.* The two forces of Ibn Saud and Ibn Rashid were locked in fierce fighting; there was no apparent gain in the afternoon and by sunset each returned to his camp. Ibn Rashid did not sleep much that night! He moved from one section of the camp to another, rallying his troops and making preparations for the next round of battle. Before dawn, in the pitch of darkness, his senses betrayed him when he thought he was still in a corner of his camp; unlucky for him! He was in the camp of Abdulaziz Ibn Saud. He was urging the people to battle, thinking they were his men, but these were the men of Adulaziz who recognized his voice and slaughtered him with a hail of bullets. He was killed instantly! (His successor was Mit'ab Ibn Abdulaziz Ibn Rashid).

Violent death was almost a way of life for the rulers of the House of Rashid, for some time to come. Brothers, cousins, and other relatives were engaged in a mayhem of murder, revenge and bloodthirsty campaigns.

This was practically the beginning of the end for the contest between Abdulaziz Al-Saud and the Rashids. It took four years and three months after the capture of Riyadh.

The struggle for unifying the land was steady, supported by dedication, determination, wisdom, and sheer courage. Following the historical battle of Rawdhat Muhanna, the successors of his opponent were in disarray and confined to the northern portion of Najd, while the central and south of Najd were under the solid control of Abdulaziz. Problems cropped up frequently. Whenever one was settled, another or many more popped up. By 1908, Sherif Hussain was appointed by the Turks as the Amir of Hijaz. A brother of Abdulaziz, named Sa'ad, was captured by him. He held the brother as a hostage until Abdulaziz was pressured to acknowledge Ottoman authority along with recognizing the hegemony over Qasim. However, as soon as his brother was released, this Ottoman control was deleted.

From Bedouins to Ikhwan

Abdulaziz devised an ingenious plan to settle the nomad tribes. By doing so, he reasoned, a great service would be rendered to the people and a stronger union would result. Once the Bedouins were settled, some differences which developed between warring factions would be minimized or eliminated.

While Bedouins were living as nomads, moving from one point to another in the desert simply by folding their tents and moving with their herds, allegiances swayed easily from one side to the other, especially since the harsh life of the desert made them suspicious in general. However, when settled in a certain way of life, this would become impractical. Their former way of living with shifting loyalties brought with it only reprisals and severe consequences through the loss of personal belongings, homes and agricultural settlements.

Since possessions are very dear to the heart of man and especially the Bedouin, Abdulaziz thought settlements should help in stabilization, allegiance, and improving the socioeconomic standard of the people. Abdulaziz devised the *Hijra Plan* for settling the Bedouins. This became the focal point of his long-range planning.

Hijra meant an agricultural oasis settlement. Here, the Bedouin settled to a peaceful and fruitful life. Mud houses replaced tents.

The Bedouin was better able to protect himself from the seering heat in the summer and from severe cold in the winter. The inhabitants of the Hijra were taught basic methods of agriculture and were given seeds.

Artawia, the first farming settlement of the Ikhwan, was established in 1912. Many other agricultural settlements were established all over the realm of the Arabian Peninsula. Their number totalling 122 during the life of King Abdulaziz.

Basic Islamic teachings were stressed. Religious teachers were sent to teach the tribesmen and preach the new approach. This effort met with tremendous success. Learned religious leaders were delegated to lead the Hijra settlements. The settled Bedouins were known as *Ikhwan*, which means brethren.

A powerful force was ready and available to carry its holy mission of unifying the nation. By 1912, this force of Ikhwan reached eleven thousand. By 1916 all the Bedouin tribes were ordered to become part of the Ikhwan and also to pay Zakat as all Moslems should. With the religious fervor of the Ikhwan, the genius and great courage of Abdulaziz, the wars of unification became truly Holy Wars that would with time overcome the enemies and their selfish desires in keeping the country divided and torn in a state of anarchy and lawlessness. The beliefs were strong in austerity, purity of Islamic concepts and the founding of an Islamic society that practices decency and justice. However, some of the concepts were primitive and their zeal sometimes bordered on fanatic extremism. Abdulaziz, with his genius and vast experience, was able to cope with the situation and make successful use of their enthusiasm and religious zeal. When asked about how he kept the Bedouins under control, he answered "We raise them not above us, nor do we place ourselves above them. We give to them when we can. We satisfy them with an excuse when we cannot. When they go beyond their bounds we make them taste the sweetness of our discipline."

The Ulama, men of religious knowledge were a power that held the Sultan and his people together. They were a medium of control, and seldom meddled in politics. Their main concern was to uphold the five pillars of Islam, namely: the Shahadah (there is no God but God–and Mohammed is his prophet), five prayers a day, the Zakat, fast of Ramadan and the Hajj.

Ending the Contest with Al-Rashid

When Saud Ibn Abdulaziz Ibn Rashid was the Amir of Hail, a powerful woman named Fatimah Sibhan was a power behind the throne. All her servants were loyal and protective. She was able to direct the rule for many years, overcoming the powerful storms emanating from the Ikhwan of Abdulaziz Ibn Saud. For nearly fifteen years, Fatimah Sibhan was the veiled power in Hail, which earned her the hatred and bitter enmity of Ibn Saud's fighters. After many years, Saud Ibn Abdulaziz Ibn Rashid was to join the fate of his other three brothers and was killed by a claimant to the throne named Abdullah Ibn Talal who did not survive since the protective and loyal servants of the Amir also slaughtered Ibn Talal in the melee.

Abdullah Ibn Mit'ab, grandson of Abdulaziz Ibn Rashid, became the ruler. It did not take him long to surrender, and become the honored guest of Abdulaziz Ibn Saud in Riyadh. However, the Ikhwan continued the siege of Hail which refused to surrender! The last Amir of Hail was Mohammed Ibn Talal, who was a brother to the murderer and murdered Abdullah. He thought he would be able to consolidate the House of Rashid and bring back old glory. He held on for three months, but the overwhelming power of Abdulaziz was devastating. The last chapter of Hail was closed and sealed with a disastrous siege of famine, fire, and bloodshed.

Abdulaziz conquered the Rashid headquarters of Hail on November 2, 1921 (29 Safar, 1340 A.H.), thus ending a long dispute and competition. After three months of blockade, the city of Hail gave up the rebellious fight. This long rivalry between the two Houses was finally put to rest. The domain was extended north and west of Hail. This consolidation of territory took place in 1923.

Abdulaziz was always generous in victory. After the fall of Hail, he prevented the troops from any looting. The hungry people were fed from his army's supplies. Surviving members of the Rashids were taken to Riyadh, where they lived at his expense and as his personal guests.

Some military officers in the Rashid army were taken into the army of Abdulaziz. In fact two captains, who refused to be bribed at the gates of Hail during its siege, were promoted. The man who was in charge during the final stand at the fortress became the father-in-law of Abdulaziz. Also the widow of Saud Ibn Rashid be-

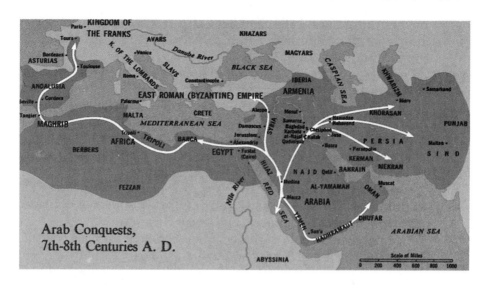

Arab Conquests,
7th-8th Centuries A. D.

Saudi ancestors settled in the historical community of Diriya on the outskirts of Riyadh.

The harsh desert strengthened the good traits of Abdulaziz.

The end of Ajlan was the beginning of a new era under the formidable unifying power of Abdulaziz.

The decisive battle of Rawdhat Muhanna spelled the end of a strong competition.

Ibn Saud and his fighting men on their holy mission for unification

The conquest of Fort Musmak paved the way for liberating Riyadh and sent a powerful beacon for lighting the long struggle to unify the land.

The Murabba'a–Historic Palace of Abdulaziz in Riyadh

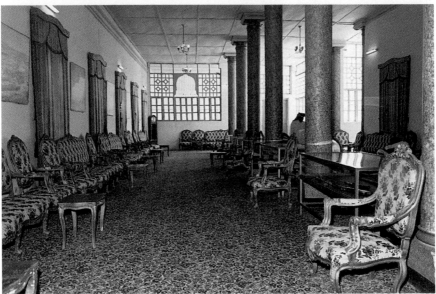

The hall where Abdulaziz held his legendary majlis at the Murabba'a
Castle in Riyadh.

Prince Mohammed Bin Fahd with King Fahd (top) and holding Majlis.

King Ibn Saud celebrating the sailing of the first oil tanker on May 1, 1939 (11.3.1358 A. H.)—A new era of prosperity was born.

The meeting of King Ibn Saud and President Roosevelt on February 14, 1945 was a historic foundation for good American–Saudi relations. A "Special relationship" was born.

Sir Winston Churchill meets with His Majesty King Ibn Saud in Fayyoum, Egypt (February 17, 1945)– on the heels of a meeting with President Roosevelt. Years later, he wrote of the King: "My admiration for him was deep . . . he was always at his best in the darkest hours."

came the wife of Abdulaziz, who adopted her children. The powerful institution of marriage certainly helped to foster the peace and strengthen a relationship of loyalty.

At a Majlis in Riyadh, the last ruler of Hail sat right next to Sultan Abdulaziz who said, "You of the House of Rashid, all of you, are as dear to me as my own children. You live here as I live, neither better nor worse. Your clothes are like mine, your food is like mine, your horses are even better than mine. No. Wallah (by God)! There is nothing in the palace that you may not have. Will any one of you say if he has ever desired anything that is under my hand and did not get it? And you, Mohammed Ibn Talal, it was your own stupid actions that forced me to treat you as a prisoner. Wallah, Billah (by God)! All the time you were held, I was in grief for you-in grief, Wallah! as if for my own son. Be loyal as I am friendly and any ill that befalls you will stir my heart before my tongue to your help. You are now one of my own house. All the resources of defense, which in time of danger I use to protect my Harem, my children, and my people will be put in force to protect you-to protect all of you of the House of Rashid."

The sultan's speech was effective and sincere. In fact, some of the people who heard him were moved to tears. With his compassion, tolerance, and generosity, Ibn Saud gained the hearts of the Rashids, who remained loyal to him throughout his entire life. This faithful loyalty carries on to his family and it is certainly reflected in the cohesive unity witnessed today in the Kingdom of Saudi Arabia.

Hijaz

The Turks appointed Sherif Hussain as the ruler of Hijaz in the western region and as guardian of the Holy cities of Mecca and Madina. He was essentially a tool of Turkish policies in that vital part of Arabia. However, he turned against the Turks in World War I and succeeded in throwing them out of Mecca and Jeddah. His foresight was limited and he was lacking in leadership and dynamism. A British agent named T. E. Lawrence, who was known as Lawrence of Arabia, filled in the void and helped in providing some wisdom and leadership. In order to achieve his goals, Lawrence used his wits. He also used Abdullah and Faisal, the two sons of Sherif Hussain along with British money and the

British political stamina gained through centuries. While the revolt gained some strength, it was never an expression of Arab aspirations. Indeed, it was a reflection of British might and
Lawrence's desire. The fallacy of such policy, which did not respond to Arab aspirations, contained within it the ingredients for
its own destruction. Sherif Hussain had bigger ambitions of becoming a King of all Arabia and thus his demands from the British
became rather disturbing. The promises made by the British did
not take into account the powerful rising star of Abdulaziz.

The treaty concluded between Ibn Saud and the British at the
Uqair Conference helped in controlling the tribes on the borders
with Trans-Jordan and Iraq. The British also asked that Ibn Saud
keep out of the coastal territories of Oman, Kuwait, and Qatar. In
return, Ibn Saud would receive an annual stipend of sixty thousand British pounds. In 1923, shortly after the treaty, the monetary
aid was stopped in a unique British way. They did not clearly
specify their motives. Once the treaty became null and void, Ibn
Saud could have attacked Oman, Kuwait, and Qatar. Instead of
doing so, his guns and ferocious fighters were poised to liberate
Taif, Mecca, Madina, and Jeddah. Around that time, the ruler of
Turkey, Mustafa Kamal, ended the Caliphate and with this act the
Ottoman Sultanate disappeared. In March, 1924, Sherif Hussain
took advantage of this situation and proclaimed himself as Caliph
and thus became the King of the Arabs and Caliph of all Moslems.
These big titles did not do him any good. In fact, shortly thereafter, they helped in accelerating his downfall. His action provided
another conflict with Abdulaziz and the end result was disastrous
for Sherif Hussain.

Abdulaziz and the Ikhwan were not allowed to make the pilgrimage to the Moslem Holy Shrines while they were under the
grip of Sherif Hussain. They were all eager to capture Hijaz and
dismantle the rule of the Sherif. Within six months after the breakdown of the Kuwait Conference, a massacre in Taif took place on
September 3, 1924. Sultan Bin Bijad terrorized the inhabitants,
since Abdulaziz was not on the scene in Taif. When he arrived,
acts of brutality ceased. However, any efforts to halt the Ikhwan
between Taif and Mecca did not succeed. On October 18, 1924
Mecca was taken and Hussain fled for Jeddah where he was
forced to abdicate in favor of his son, Ali. A long siege followed,
until Madina capitulated on the fifth of December, 1925 and Ali

abdicated on December 19, 1925, while Jeddah fell to the forces of Abdulaziz on the 23rd of December, 1925.

After the conquest of Mecca, Abdulaziz spoke to the piligrims at Arafat mountain and said "We should rise to the good faith God has instilled in us; we should not be divided or have hate because this will be among the reasons for our destruction. They are wrong, those who think that some of the western politicians are the ones that have worked to cause our division! By God, no! We tore ourselves as we obeyed the malicious ones among us. But who could tear a nation unified in the word of God and in its deep closeness which is indivisible?"

He also addressed the people in Madina, saying, "I consider your elder as my father, your middle aged as a brother and your young as my son. So be one hand with warmth in your hearts to help me perform the important task which God has rested on my shoulders. In this Arab Islamic land, I am a servant to the religion and a servant to my people. The rule is for God alone."

In 1926, Asir was added to the conquered territories. In 1927, Abdulaziz was crowned King of Hijaz, Najd and its dependencies. A British treaty was signed in Jeddah, in 1927, recognizing the territories conquered by Abdulaziz extending all the way from the Arabian Gulf to the Red Sea.

The Ikhwan leaders grew more zealous, and shortly after the conquest of Hijaz attacked an Iraqi border fort. This attack was a naked challenge to the authority of Abdulaziz, who used his wisdom in every practical way in order to avoid a major conflict with the Ikhwan. They refused to curb their incursions across the frontiers of Jordan and Iraq, and thus grew more overbearing. These raids across the borders were in direct violation of an agreement which had been made with the British at Uqair in the year 1922. Abdulaziz was very patient and in 1928 he called a congress of Chieftains and Ulama to Riyadh, in order to voice their opinion concerning this serious problem. Sultan Bin Bijad and Ad-Dawish did not show up, although all other tribal leaders came. They both were vehement and derogatory in their rebellion against the authority of Abdulaziz. They accused him of being a "heretic" because he made treaties with the "infidels" and made use of "instruments of the devil," such as the telephone, telegraph, automobile, and airplane. At the conference, the Ulama declared that these instruments were permissible by law and indeed most desirable as far as religious practices are concerned. These instruments could increase the strength and knowledge of Moslems. They also declared that by authority of the Prophet of Islam, treaties with non-Moslem nations were very desirable, especially if they brought peace and freedom to the Moslem nation.

A number of skirmishes between the rebels and loyal tribes took place and the patience of King Abdulaziz was wearing very thin. Finally, he crushed the rebellion during the decisive battle of *Artawia*, which was fought in the spring of 1929. The two mutinous leaders surrendered; Bin Bijad was taken to Riyadh and Ad-Dawish, who was wounded severely, was cared for by the personal doctor of Abdulaziz. When Ibn Saud defeated all the rebel leaders, he dismantled the power of the rebellious settlement of Ikhwan. When security was established along the borders, he became the undisputed leader of Arabia. The united land became the Kingdom of Saudi Arabia on September 23, 1932 and Abdulaziz was proclaimed the King.

Soon after, trouble erupted in the Southern Province where Imam Yahya of Yemen captured Najran. He had encouraged liberal tribes to revolt. Saud and Faisal, the two sons of Abdulaziz, led an expedition into the mountains and went on further to capture the port of Hodeida in Yemen. In May, 1934, the dispute was settled and a peace treaty was signed in Taif.

With the end of battles for unity and a nation unified, King Ibn Saud concentrated his efforts on resources and development of the nation. His ingenuity and good luck would strike again! Not only with the water wells he was digging for, but also the discovery of a vastly rich desert underbelly of "black gold–oil, that is."

Roosevelt and Ibn Saud

Franklin D. Roosevelt became the President of the United States of America in March, 1933, shortly after King Ibn Saud declared the unity and birth of the Kingdom of Saudi Arabia in September, 1932. They were both destined to be great men. Both of them sacrificed remarkably in contributing their impressive share for peace and justice in a turbulent world ravaged by war. The Kingdom chose to remain neutral at the beginning of World War II, while the United States also remained neutral for some time, until it was pushed by the surprise Japanese attack on Pearl Harbor. The two leaders had similar philosophies and many common viewpoints. They were also of similar age and both had some physical limitations. President Roosevelt had to use a wheelchair and the King was able to move but with some difficulty; he was not able to climb the stairs because of wounds.

King Abdulaziz admired the fact that President Roosevelt represented a rich, powerful and productive nation that cherished democracy, justice, freedom and dynamism. Roosevelt was a symbol of friendship and hope for many developing nations.

The United States began some political moves into the Middle East during the Versailles Conference for Peace which was held in 1919 on the heels of World War I. The Conference was held after President Wilson's declaration on human rights and self-determination, which was proclaimed by the United States Congress on January 8, 1918.

Although Britain was the dominant force at the time, King Abdulaziz Al-Saud, who is known in the west as Ibn Saud, used his wisdom and political genius to obtain the necessary help for liberating those parts of Arabia which were under Turkish rule. Britain and France were determined to limit the Arabs to self-rule, while the United States declared its support for self-determination, and thus good relations were established with the U.S., but careful diplomacy was exercised in order to avoid any antagonism toward the British.

All these developments were carefully observed by the attentive eyes and ears of Abdulaziz, who foresaw the awakening of a new American giant on the horizon of world affairs. British power and influence on Arab matters were in decline. An atmosphere of understanding and rapport between two great personalities was developing and was strengthened by American ingenuity coupled with the massive oil potential of the Kingdom of Saudi Arabia.

Since the Palestinian problem was getting out of hand by 1936, King Ibn Saud extended his hand of cooperation to the affected Arab countries. His efforts were concentrated on Britain since Palestine was a protectorate under the British. In the meantime, he geared his energies and hope toward the United States, which by now was emerging as a world power and leader.

American oil interests gained momentum with the knowledge that vast oil wealth lay beneath the barren desert of Saudi Arabia.

Because of mutual interests, in 1943 President Franklin D. Roosevelt declared that defending Saudi Arabia was of vital interest to the United States. Through this declaration, the Kingdom became eligible for a lend-lease assistance program. This aid had to be delivered through the British, since they were still a major player in the Middle East. The developing close relationship between Saudi Arabia and the United States was looked upon by the British with caution, suspicion and disapproval.

President Roosevelt invited King Abdulaziz to visit him aboard an American destroyer in the Suez Canal upon his return from the Yalta Conference. Preparation for this meeting was conducted with the utmost secrecy, especially because of the prevalent dangers at that stage of the war. The King left Jeddah at 4:30 P.M. February 12, 1945, aboard the destroyer Murphy, for a historic meeting with President Roosevelt which took place on February 14, 1945.

The Saudi People were bewildered and astonished. Malicious rumors were spread about the King leaving the country, running from his people like Sherif Hussain. Others said he had been kidnapped by the Americans. Of course none of that was true. Ibn Saud was on a mission of peace, honor and justice.

"King Ibn Saud held a reception for officers on the torpedo deck. The entire reception took about ten minutes and we started to withdraw, when he insisted on shaking hands again. We hesitated but Colonel Eddy said, "His Majesty insists . . ." so we shook again. Then Ibn Saud sat back to watch us demonstrate our armament.

We fired depth charges, which rattle the ship, Although Ibn Saud couldn't have expected the terrific jarring that followed, his face was impassive. He didn't blink once but simply nodded reflectively. Ibn Saud showed no effects from the ship's motion."

He invited the officers to dine with him. He showered the entire crew with thoughtful gifts and simply charmed everyone.

As the destroyer neared its destination on the morning of February 14, 1945, out of respect, the royal chairs were turned to face the direction of the president's cruiser.

After two nights and one day, the destroyer Murphy approached from the southern direction. President Roosevelt, out of respect for Ibn Saud, gave his daughter a choice: either to confine herself to her quarters or she could go to Cairo and spend the time shopping. She chose shopping and sightseeing in Cairo, Egypt.

As the destroyer Murphy approached the cruiser, the tent erected on board was flapping merrily in the breeze; King Abdulaziz was sitting in his golden chair with his majestic look and Arabic dress. The President took a birds-eye-view of the destroyer, then wheeled back and waited. At eleven o'clock in the morning, February 14, 1945, the American destroyer Murphy was next to the American ship Quincy, which brought the President from Yalta to the Suez Canal. Ibn Saud along with seven princes and sheikhs came aboard the cruiser. A pleasant informal conversation took place. The meeting was a historic one! Positive impressions from both sides led to better and warmer relations. . . . The atmosphere was very cordial. The meetings were very informative.

King Ibn Saud admired the aluminum wheelchair which was used by the president. Immediately, the president offered the spare aluminum wheelchair as a gift to the King.

A conference for one and a half hours and the dinner was ready! The President took one elevator, while the King took another, to meet in the dining room. While in his elevator, President Roosevelt pushed the emergency red button and stopped the elevator between the decks of the ship and smoked two cigarettes. Although the President was a chain smoker, he did not smoke in the presence of the King at all, out of respect for him and his puritan beliefs!

Thus the meeting between King Ibn Saud and President Roosevelt was very successful on many fronts:

1. Their unique personalities were instrumental in bringing harmony and deep understanding.
2. The Palestinian problem was discussed in detail.
3. The King defended the independence of Syria and Lebanon.
4. President Roosevelt promised that the government of the United States would not carry any basic political change in Palestine without prior consultation with the Jews and the Arabs; nor would the President carry any actions that would be considered hostile to the Arabs.
5. President Roosevelt died two months after this meeting and his promises died with him.

Following the meeting on the fourteenth of February, 1945, King Ibn Saud had other correspondence with the President defending the Palestinian cause with impressive and convincing documentation. On the fifth of April, 1945 he received an answer from President Roosevelt reaffirming his previously stated position.

In a letter dated February 16, 1945, which was sent to William Eddy, the President said "It was for me a most interesting and stimulating experience and I want you to know how fully aware I am of the important part which you played, not only in the arrangement but also, in the conversation itself in making our meeting such an outstanding success."

In a speech President Franklin D. Roosevelt said: "Our conversations had to do with matters of common interest. They will be of great mutual advantage because they gave us an opportunity of meeting and talking face to face, and of exchanging views in personal conversation instead of formal correspondence. For instance, from Ibn Saud of Arabia I learned more of the whole problem of the Moslems and the Jewish problem in five minutes than I could have learned by the exchange of a dozen letters." Shortly before his death, FDR sent in April, 1945 a note to King Ibn Saud saying:

"Your Majesty will recall that on previous occasions I communicated to you the attitude of the American government toward Palestine and made clear our desire that no decision be taken with respect to the basic situation in that country without full consultation with both Arabs and Jews. Your Majesty will also doubtless recall that during our recent conversation I assured you that I would take no action, in my capacity as Chief of the Executive Branch of this government, which might prove hostile to the Arab people."

President Roosevelt died two months after this successful meeting. However, the new Administration did not follow the promises of the Roosevelt Administration.

Ibn Saud, Churchill and the British

After the meeting with President Roosevelt, the King met with Winston Churchill, Prime Minister of Great Britain. When Churchill learned about the meeting between Roosevelt and Ibn Saud, he was "thoroughly nettled. He burned the wires to all his diplomats" desiring to meet with Ibn Saud and others who met Roosevelt.

He was a bit concerned, especially, since the British regarded the Arab world an area where their influence was considered supreme. He revised his plans to meet with these three leaders: King Ibn Saud, King Farouk and Emperor Haile Salassie.

At a reception held by Winston Churchill for King Ibn Saud on February 17, 1945, Churchill said:

"In his own cup, carried from Mecca, he offered me a glass of water from its sacred well, the most delicious that I had ever tasted." Winston Churchill wrote in later years in his book Triumph and Tragedy:

"King Ibn Saud made a striking impression. My admiration for him was deep . . . he was always at his best in the darkest hours. He was now over seventy, but had lost none of his warrior vigor."

Abdulaziz was always careful not to antagonize the mighty power of the British. He was a wise man, but always a man of principles.

He was a man of his word. He always lived up to his commitments and promises. Many times other parties let him down!

According to Philby "Yet, Britain always seemed to be giving him the cold shoulder; and he could not understand why? He could not understand that his own insistence on the incontestable fact of his absolute independence, both in the domestic and in the foreign fields, constituted a barrier that British sympathy could not surmount. Nevertheless, when the second World War broke out, he did not hesitate a moment, in spite of his declared neutrality in the struggle, in showing the direction in which his sympathies lay, though he might have profited by adopting a more equivocal attitude. His neutrality was always formally correct."

"Ibn Saud had an instinctive perception of the right thing to do; and he did it without fear or favor—sometimes to his own embarrassment. Yet there never was the slightest doubt that throughout the war he hoped earnestly for an Allied victory, and was indeed gravely disturbed by the Allied disasters of 1940 and the following year. It was at this time that America became seriously interested in Arabia; a legation was established at Jeddah while a number of President Roosevelt's personal representatives visited Ibn Saud at Riyadh to discuss matters with him and to study the needs of his country. But the cementing of an American political link with Arabia was the outstanding development of these war

years: with far-reaching results, which have completely transformed the social and economical structure of the country within a
single decade."

Abdulaziz was always thoughtful, smart and shrewed in his
dealings with the British. He knew how to handle them despite
their erroneous policies with Sherif Hussain.

Because Saudi Arabia had declared war on Germany prior to
1945, and even though it did not actually do battle, it became eligible to join the United Nations. King Faisal headed the Saudi delegation attending the first meeting in San Francisco. Among the
people accompanying King Faisal was then young Prince Fahd
Bin Abdulaziz, present Monarch of Saudi Arabia. Also, King Ibn
Saud was very instrumental in founding the Arab League in 1945.
He spoke of his efforts and achievements in unifying the Kingdom, he said, "I liberated this Kingdom from foreign domination.
I am a master in it and she is a master herself. So here I united five
countries: Najd, Hijaz, Asir, Hail, and the Hasa; for everyone of
these there were rulers and princes, so I built from it all this nation. I opened in front of the people the doors of life; I prepared
for them the ways for progress and I caught with them the band-
wagon of civilization. We achieved in tens of years what was not
imagined by anyone that we could reach in hundreds of years."

By mid October, 1953, while in Taif, Abdulaziz suffered a heart
attack. Despite his weakened condition and limited activity he insisted on holding his treasured Majlis. By the end of October, he
became seriously ill and was finally confined to his room. At ten
thirty in the morning of November 9, 1953, King Ibn Saud, the
great statesman, desert warrior, father and founder of the Kingdom of Saudi Arabia, was dead. The same day, he was moved and
buried next to his father in Riyadh. His spirit and holy mission are
both alive and well! They go on forever.

A quotation from Gary Troeller in his book The Birth of Saudi
Arabia comes to mind: "For some time now it has been unfashion-
able for historians to speak of Great Men. Yet in the life of his
achievements it would be difficult to resist the conclusion that Ibn
Saud was a great man . . . However, operating within the framework of traditional Arabia and judged by its standards, he stood
the test of greatness."

With a world torn in conflict and strife, be it among nations or in one nation with the populace fighting one another in civil war, the history of Abdulaziz is the shining example for all. His experience is unique and fascinating where lessons of courage, wisdom, and the carving of harmony from the jaws of division and destruction can be a lightening example and a beacon of light for others to absorb and emulate.

Chapter 3

Government

Saudi Arabia is a Monarchy. Its official name is the Kingdom of Saudi Arabia which in Arabic is: Al Mamlaka Al-Arabia Al-Saudia. The Holy Qoran is the constitution of the land and Shari'a, the Moslem law, is based on the Qoran. This was well defined in the Basic System of Government which states that:

"The Kingdom of Saudi Arabia is an Arab Islamic state of total sovereignty. Islam is its religion and its constitution is the Holy Book of God (the Qoran) and the Sunna of His Prophet, peace be upon him; its language is the Arabic language and its capital is Riyadh." Guided by Shari'a, the King is the head of state and Prime Minister. A Council of Ministers is appointed by the King and assists him in formulating and executing his policies. The King is also Commander-in-Chief of the Armed Forces. The ministers and all government agencies are, in the final analysis, all responsible to the top authority in the land, namely, the King, known as the Custodian of the Two Holy Mosques. Recent constitutional reforms relating to the Consultative Council or Majlis Al-Shoura, along with the Basic System of Government all play their important role in shaping and formulating government policies.

The King is assisted by the Crown Prince, or Deputy Prime Minister, and by the second Deputy Prime Minister. The cornerstone in Saudi government policies is the Majlis, an institution whereby anyone can petition Saudi leaders, from the King all the way down to the governors of the various provinces and other leaders of prominence in the government. Thus, the leaders are all accessible to the populace. Stability plays a very major role and is very much treasured by the government and the Saudi people. It is nourished by strict, swift and just application of Shari'a. This approach makes the Kingdom one of the safest countries in the world and the atmosphere is thus very conducive to progress, investment and peace of mind. One of the government's top priorities is to safeguard Saudi traditions and the teachings of Islam, so that all the progress achieved would not infringe or alter traditionally cherished values and practices. The government promotes goodwill, understanding, compassion and unity of the Saudi populace.

Rulers Since Abdulaziz

Upon the death of King Ibn Saud on November 9, 1953, his successor to the throne was his son King Saud. In his youth, he led campaigns in the struggle for unification. He attempted improvements on many fronts, but the financial means were either lacking or deteriorated with time, as did his health. Upon his abdication from the throne, his brother Faisal became the King on 27 Jumada Thani 1384 A.H. (November 4, 1964). In his youth, he contributed successfully to the success of unification campaigns. He visited many European countries and was very much interested in foreign affairs. In 1945, he led the Saudi delegation for the signing of the U.N. Charter in San Francisco, California, USA. Acknowledging the talents of Faisal, Abdulaziz appointed him as his first foreign minister in 1930. When the Council of Ministers was established, Faisal was appointed Deputy Prime Minister. A few weeks later, when Abdulaziz died, Faisal became the Crown Prince, and his ascension to the throne in 1964 paved the way for the initial steps to modernize the Kingdom of Saudi Arabia. For the first time in the Kingdom's history he opened new doors for Saudi women to receive education along the same footing as their male counterparts. He laid the foundation for the first Five-year Development Plan. King Faisal did not live long enough to see the fruits of his labor. He was assassinated on the 25th of March, 1975.

On that date his successor to the throne was his brother King Khaled, a straightforward man who loved the desert and treasured Saudi traditions. He also made his contribution toward the unification of the Kingdom. He was the Crown Prince during the era of King Faisal. King Khaled appointed his brother Fahd as the Crown Prince and First Deputy Prime Minister. He also made Prince Abdullah, his brother, who was head of the National Guard, the Second Deputy Prime Minister. The second Development Plan ended in May, 1980. During his rule, he held the historic Summit Conference of Moslems in Taif and Mecca in 1981. It included 38 nations from throughout the world. In the same year, he initiated the founding of the six-nation Gulf Cooperation Council (GCC). During this time of great strides forward, the economic boom propelled the Kingdom to its rightful place of prominence in world affairs.

King Khaled's right-hand man in carrying out government policies was Crown Prince Fahd. The two leaders made a very successful team. Administrative duties for running the Kingdom were delegated to Crown Prince Fahd. When King Khaled died on June 13, 1982, the industrial evolution and the educational transformation were well under-way. On that day, Crown Prince Fahd became the King of Saudi Arabia.

The Era of King Fahd Bin Abdulaziz

Fahd is a man of great wisdom with decades of vast experience in numerous government assignments and positions. His farsightedness and good policies, coupled with the contributions of his predecessors, brought to the Kingdom great progress, the like of which is unparalleled in the history of mankind. He is regarded as the pioneer and founder of the modern Kingdom of Saudi Arabia. He is the head of the royal family, which numbers about 5,000 people. Like any other group of people, they have their drives, aspirations and problems. Here, the Custodian of the Two Holy Mosques is assisted by the Crown Prince and the Second Deputy Prime Minister.

The practices and policies applied to his immediate family carry over to the larger Saudi family. From here on, it moves to include the Saudi nation as a whole. A truly respected and admired leader of his nation, King Fahd is very active, accessible and popular with his people. He is regarded as the loving father of the entire country. He never misses an opportunity to meet his countrymen. It is in his fiber to meet his people and listen to them to know first hand about their views and problems, their aspirations and desires. For him, justice, moderation, and truth are fundamental and supreme. His impressive administrative capabilities and refined qualities of leadership are the direct result of a vast wealth of experience earned during nearly five decades of public service. He was only 25 years old when he joined the delegation, headed by King Faisal on June 26, 1945, to the founding meeting of the United Nations in San Francisco. He was only 30 years of age when he was sent to represent the Kingdom of Saudi Arabia during the Queen's Coronation in the United Kingdom. He became the education pioneer and first Minister of Education in 1953. He became the Minister of Interior in 1963 and his contributions to internal security in the Kingdom left its impact for many decades. In 1964, when Faisal became the King, he appointed Fahd the second Deputy Prime Minister. The responsibilities for the Ministry of Interior remained on his shoulders. From 1975 to 1982, the running of the daily affairs of government along with national, regional and international policies, all rested on the shoulders of Fahd, in cooperation with and under the guidance of King Khaled. Upon his succession to the throne on June 13, 1982, Fahd received universal national acclaim. His tremendous experience and unique personality played an important role in his being chosen as the King of Saudi Arabia. On this date Prince Abdullah Bin Abdulaziz was chosen as the Crown Prince and the Deputy Prime Minister. Prince Sultan Bin Abdulaziz became the Second Deputy Prime Minister in addition to being Minister of Defense and Aviation.

Fahd is a practical, compassionate man who analyzes a situation from all angles. Time spent in studying a matter prior to decisive action is devoted to cover every facet of the matter at hand. Once this thorough study is done, Fahd acts decisively and logically. His instructions to his associates are to act within Shari'a and let their conscience be their guide. King Fahd examines and follows all important projects relating to the various aspects of the boom and great development of his country. He personally gets involved and participates in reviewing plans, including engineering. He pays attention to the various implementation procedures and various details of a project. He possesses a talent and an obsession with a unique drive to achieve the most for the welfare of his greater family and greatest love: the people; the common men, women and children.

It has become a natural way of life to see this unique man among his people: guiding, exchanging ideas, expressing his views, compassion and wisdom; feeling with them and sharing their happiness or sorrow. In doing so, he feels his innermost desires and emotions for serving the people of his beloved country, the Kingdom of Saudi Arabia. Their education, guidance and welfare are utmost in his convictions and thoughts. For him the true treasure and strength of the country are the citizens. *Human resources* are most valuable. Educating, guiding, training and devel-

oping the Saudi citizen are the positive forces that give tangible results and based upon that, true development takes place on a solid
foundation. All his aides in government and trusted men are in-
structed to make sure that the welfare of the Saudi citizen is kept
foremost in their minds and that they should truly be the civil servants of the people. In this spirit on November 1, 1986, the glorific
titles were placed aside, based on his wish and desire. A Royal di-
rective was issued to replace the term "His Majesty" with "Custodian of the Two Holy Mosques" and to avoid the words "my lord,
magnificent" and other glorifying terms.

From being the education pioneer, to the building of internal
security, the economic boom and vast infrastructure development,
the gigantic improvements of Hajj facilities in Mecca and Madina,
the printing of the Holy Qoran, the continuing dynamic efforts towards new horizons of progress, the liberation of Kuwait, and
many more–this wide spectrum of achievements is now crowned
with King Fahd's evolution of Constitutional Reforms.

Historic Constitutional Reforms

More impressive achievements will thrive under a new umbrella of justice, consultation (Shoura) and security–all inspired
from the Holy Qoran. On the 29th of February, 1992, (26 Sha'aban,
1412 A.H.) the Custodian of the Two Holy Mosques, King Fahd Bin
Abdulaziz made a historic move by announcing basic reforms in-
corporating:

- 83 articles for the Basic System of Government with guarantees for the sanctity of home and personal freedoms.
- 30 articles Governing the Consultative Council (Majlis Al-
  Shoura) which will consist of 60 members and a Speaker.
- 39 articles specifying the Rules for the Provincial System
  governing the various Regions of the Kingdom.

The first article defines the foundation of the Nation, specifying that the Kingdom of Saudi Arabia is a sovereign Arab Islamic
state whose religion is Islam and whose constitution is the Holy
Qoran and the Sunna of the Prophet. These milestone articles cod-
ify governmental protections for personal freedoms and human
rights. They may be looked upon as an extended modern constitution of the Modern Kingdom of Saudi Arabia. Their impact is far-

reaching and certainly befitting and complementing the great progress in the Kingdom.

The Basic System of Government includes important articles relating to general principles and the Monarchy where the rule will be confined to the sons of the Kingdom's founder Abdulaziz Bin Abdulrahman Al-Faisal Al-Saud and grandsons. The most suitable among them will be enthroned to rule under the guidance of the Holy Qoran and the Prophet's Sunna. Also, for the first time, the Basic System of Government spells out that the King is the one who will appoint the Crown Prince and will have the authority to relieve him from his duty by a Royal Order. Basics of Saudi society, economic principles, rights and duties, governmental authorities regarding the judiciary, executive and regulatory branches, monetary affairs, control and general rules are also covered.

The rules governing the Consultative Council will replace the system of the Shoura Council of 1347 A.H. All regulations, instructions and resolutions valid until the implementation of this system would continue until they are accordingly amended. Selected members must be of good reputation, well-educated, well-qualified Saudi nationals by origin and birth. All the rules are spelled out in detail, similar to other parliamentary bodies in the world, but reflecting a true Saudi spirit.

The first article of the Provincial System governing the Provinces of various Regions of the Kingdom specifies the goal to raise the standard for administrative work and development of all parts of the Kingdom. It calls for safeguarding law and order and for the protection of citizens' rights and their freedoms within Islamic Shari'a. Here the articles cover: rules for the Provinces and Emirates, districts and centers, governors (Amirs) of Regions (who report to the Minister of the Interior), oath, responsibilities of the Amir, yearly meeting of the Minister of the Interior with the Amirs (Governors), meeting of the Amirs with the directors, district managers and their appointments, the formation of Provincial Councils in every region or Emirate and various rules and regulations governing these councils.

Former President George Bush sent a message to King Fahd in which he declared "full support for your recent decisions effecting the Kingdom of Saudi Arabia. I know that you have personally worked for a considerable time on these arrangements designed to widen meaningful political participation. I am confident that history will show that you have set your country and your people on the right course, one that will over time increase their security and well-being in harmony with the Kingdom's traditions. That you chose to do so is a testament to your leadership and wisdom . . . you have my great respect."

Another landmark in constitutional and legislative reforms of far-reaching consequences was issued through four Royal Decrees on Friday, August 20, 1993 (3,3,1414 A.H.). The Kingdom entered a new era of historic proportions. The first of these decrees issued by King Fahd deals with Cabinet Bylaws. The Council of Ministers duration will not exceed four years during which, or at the end of this duration, it will be reformulated again.

The King, who is also the Prime Minister, steers the general policy of the Kingdom, guarantees coordination and cooperation between various government agencies and insures coherence, consistence and unity in the work of the Council of Ministers. He also supervises and controls the cabinet, the ministers and government bodies and observes the implementation of rules, regulations and decisions. There are 32 articles covering these basic rules and regulations, including: general provisions, formation of the Council of Ministers, organizational affairs, executive affairs, financial affairs, cabinet presidency and administrative structure of the cabinet.

The second Royal Decree limits Services of Cabinet Ministers to four years, unless a Royal Decree is issued to extend this duration (possibility of an additional two-year extension.) This is a new approach since the previous policy did not limit the time served by Cabinet Ministers. Also this decree specifies the rules and regulations governing the Council of Ministers and their duties.

The Council of Ministers, as the direct executive authority, will have full control of executive affairs and administration (See Saudi Government Ministries and Autonomous Agencies). The Bylaws of the Council of Ministers also stipulates cabinet members must not hold any other government positions unless it is found by the Council to be imperative. Cabinet members cannot purchase or rent government property directly or indirectly and cannot sell or rent their property to the government, nor can they indulge in any financial or commercial transactions. Any violations of these

Simplified Diagram for the Government of Saudi Arabia

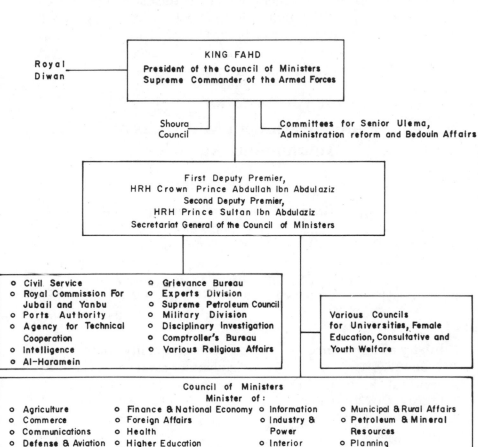

Royal Diwan

KING FAHD
President of the Council of Ministers
Supreme Commander of the Armed Forces

Shoura Council

Committees for Senior Ulema, Administration reform and Bedouin Affairs

First Deputy Premier,
HRH Crown Prince Abdullah Ibn Abdulaziz
Second Deputy Premier,
HRH Prince Sultan Ibn Abdulaziz
Secretariat General of the Council of Ministers

- Civil Service
- Royal Commission For Jubail and Yanbu
- Ports Authority
- Agency for Technical Cooperation
- Intelligence
- Al-Haramein

- Grievance Bureau
- Experts Division
- Supreme Petroleum Council
- Military Division
- Disciplinary Investigation
- Comptroller's Bureau
- Various Religious Affairs

Various Councils for Universities, Female Education, Consultative and Youth Welfare

Council of Ministers
Minister of:

- Agriculture
- Commerce
- Communications
- Defense & Aviation
- Education

- Finance & National Economy
- Foreign Affairs
- Health
- Higher Education
- Housing & Public Works

- Information
- Industry & Power
- Interior
- Justice
- Labor & Social Affairs

- Municipal & Rural Affairs
- Petroleum & Mineral Resources
- Planning
- Pilgrimage & Endowments
- Telegraph, Post and Telephone

- Minister of State and President of Disciplinary Investigation Bureau
- Minister of State and President of Civil Service Bureau
- Minister of State and President of Grievance Bureau
- Minister of State and President of Port Authority
- Minister of State and President of Comptroller's Bureau

- Minister of State
- Minister of State

rules will call for disciplinary action of the council member involved.

The third Royal Decree gives the list of the *Consultative Council members (Majlis Al-Shoura)*. The Chairman, Vice Chairman and Secretary General of the Council are named. The Council is comprised of 60 distinguished members of Saudi society in addition to the Chairman and Secretary General. It must be noted here that 50% of those named to the council were holders of the doctor of philosophy degree. The others were men of distinction and vast experience as well. This makes it amongst the most highly educated consultative or legislative bodies in the world. The duration of service for members of the Council is four years. Majlis Al-Shoura held its first session on December 29, 1993.

Saudi Government Ministries and Autonomous Agencies

Ministry	Function
Ministry of Agriculture and Water Airport Road, Riyadh 11195 Tel.: 401-6666 Telex: 401108 AGRWAT SJ *OR* Fax: 403-1415	Implementation of economic plans and programs for agriculture. Water development. Desalination, irrigation, conservation of scarce water, fisheries, animal resources and locust control.
Ministry of Commerce P.O. Box 1774 Airport Rd., Riyadh 11162 Tel.: 401-2220/401-4708 Telex: 401057 TIJARA SJ Fax: 403-8421	Foodstuff quality control, consumer protection, companies and commercial agents' registration, labeling regulations and standards.
Ministry of Communications Airport Rd., Riyadh 11178 Tel.: 404-2928/404-3000 Telex: 401616 HI-WAY SJ Fax: 403-1401	Design, building and maintenance of road network. Coordination of surface transport including railroads and bus systems.

Ministry	Function
Ministry of Defense & Aviation	Army, Navy, Air Force, Air

Ministry

Function

Ministry of Defense & Aviation
Airport Rd., Riyadh 11165
Tel.: 478-5900/477-7313
Telex: 401188 MDASJ
Fax: 401-1336

Army, Navy, Air Force, Air Defense, construction of military bases, civilian airports and meteorology.

Ministry of Education
Airport Rd., Riyadh 11148
Tel.: 404-2888/404-2952
Telex: 401673 MAAREF SJ
Fax: 401-2365

Provision of free general education in primary, intermediate and secondary schools. Royal Technical Institute, programs for handicapped, antiquities and museums.

Ministry of Finance & National Economy
Airport Rd., Riyadh 11177
Tel.: 405-0000/405-0080
Telex: 401021 FINANS SJ
Fax: 405-9202

Government finance, including budgeting and expenditure of all ministries and agencies. Control of national economic growth. Zakat and income tax. Customs, Central Department of Statistics and National Computer Center.

Ministry of Foreign Affairs
Nasseriya St., Riyadh 11124
Tel.: 406-7777/441-6836
Telex: 405000 MFA SJ
Fax: 403-0159

Political, cultural and financial international relations. Monitors diplomatic relations between the Kingdom of Saudi Arabia and the outside world.

Ministry of Health
Airport Rd., Riyadh 11176
Tel.: 401-2220/401-2392
Telex: 402772 HEALTH SJ
Fax: 402-9876

Health Care and hospitals.

Ministry	Function
Ministry of Higher Education King Faisal Hospital St., Riyadh 11153 Tel.: 464-4444 Telex: 400371 TAALIM SJ or 400860 ALI SJ Fax: 441-9004	Universities and higher learning institutes.
Ministry of Industry and Electricity P.O. Box 5729 Omar bin Al-Khatab Rd. North of Railway Station, Riyadh 11127 Tel.: 477-2722/477-6666 Telex: 401154 INDEL SJ Fax: 477-5451	Development of the Kingdom's industrial infrastructure and power projects. Foreign capital investment, industrial licensing, protection and encouragement of national industry, industrial statistics, industrial cities and SABIC.
Ministry of Information Nassiriya St., Riyadh 11161 Tel.: 401-4440/401-3440 Telex: 401461/arinfor SJ 402640 MINMO SJ Fax: 402-3570	Television and radio broadcasts, publication of newspapers, magazines and relations with foreign press.
Ministry of Interior P.O. Box 2933, Airport Rd., Riyadh 11134 Tel.: 401-1944 Telex: 401622 MORS SJ/402811 INFORM SJ Fax: 403-1185	Public security, coastal guards, civil defense, fire stations, border police, special security and investigation forces, criminal investigation and traffic control.
Ministry of Justice University Street, Riyadh 11137 Tel.: 405-7777/405-5399 Telex: 404450 JUSTIC SJ	Administration of Shari'a and provision of legal services for all citizens of the Kingdom.

Ministry	Function
Ministry of Labor and Social Affairs Omar bin Al-Khattab St., Riyadh 11157 Tel.: 477-1480/478-7166 Telex: 401043 LABOUR SJ Fax: 477-7336	Labor relations, manpower planning and general monitoring of employment situation. Labor permits and work visas, labor disputes, inspection, health and safety. Provisions of vocational and on-job training for handicapped. Social development and reform. Social Security.
Ministry of Municipalities and Rural Affairs Nassiriyeh St., Riyadh 11136 Tel.: 441-5434 Telex: 401063 DOMA SJ	Administration of municipalities throughout the Kingdom. Planning of cities and towns. Development of roads and basic infrastructure. Managing and maintaining services to keep cities and towns clean and healthy.
Ministry of Petroleum and Mineral Resources P.O. Box 757, Airport Rd., Riyadh 11189 Tel.: 478-1661/478-1133 Telex: 401615/401058 PTROMN SJ	Administration and development of the Kingdom's oil, gas, oil refineries and mineral resources in conjunction with the General Petroleum and Mineral Organization (Petromin).
Ministry of Pilgrimage and Endowments Omar bin Al-Khattab St., Riyadh 11183 Tel.: 402-2200/402-2212 Telex: 400189/401603 AWQAF SJ Fax: 402-2555	Provision of facilities for the annual visit of pilgrims to Mecca, Madina and other Holy places in the Kingdom. Administration of land controlled by religious trust.

Ministry	Function
Ministry of Planning P.O. Box 1358, University St., Riyadh 11183 Tel.: 402-3462/401-3333 Telex: 401075 PLAN SJ	Design and implementation of Five Year Plans.
Ministry of Post, Telegraph and Telephone Intercontinental Road, Riyadh 11112 Tel.: 463-7225 Telex: 401220 PTT SJ 401020 GENTEL SJ Fax: 405-2310	Development and maintenance of telecommunications and postal services.
Ministry of Public Works and Housing Washm St., Riyadh 11151 Tel.: 402-2268/402-2036 Telex: 400415 MINPUB SJ/401142 ASHGAL SJ Public Works: Fax: 402-2723 Housing: Fax: 406-7376	Supervision, construction and maintenance of Public Sector's projects. Public housing, evaluation of tenders, allocation of contracts and classification of contractors.

Agency	Function
Central Department of Statistics. Off Airport Road Behind Ministry of Finance Bldg., Riyadh 11187 Phones: 405-9638/401-4528 Fax: 405-9493	Collects and publishes miscella- neous statistics.
Customs Department P.O. Box 3483, Riyadh 11471 Phone: 401-3334 Telex: 401626 CSTM SJ Fax: 404-3412; 404-3400	Customs duties.

Agency	Function
Directorate General for Mineral Resources P.O. Box 2880, Jeddah 21461 Phones: 631-0355/631-0357 Telex: 601157 DGMR SJ	Mineral exploration and concessions.
Directorate General of Zakat and Income Tax Off Airport Road Behind Ministry of Finance Bldg., Riyadh 11187 Phones: 401-0182/404-1537 Fax: 404-1495	Tax collection.
General Organization for Social Insurance (GOSI) P.O. Box 2963, Riyadh 11461 Phones: 478-5721/477-7735 Telex: 406743 GOSI SJ Fax: 477-9958	Social insurance agency.
General Ports Authority P.O. Box 5162, Riyadh 11422 Phones: 476-0600/476-0930 Telex: 401783 PORTS SJ	Port development, loading and unloading of vessels, regulations & documents.
Jeddah Seaport (Jeddah Islamic Port) Jeddah 21188 Phone: 643-2552 Telex: 601175 PORTS SJ	Port development, loading and unloading of vessels, regulations & documents.

Agency	Function
Dammam Seaport P.O. Box 28062 (King Abdulaziz Seaport) Dammam 31188 Phones: 833-2500 Telexes: 801130 DAPM SJ 801139 DAPM SJ Fax: 857-9223	Port development, loading and unloading of vessels, regulations & documents.
Grievances Court (Diwan-Al Mazalem) Morabba-Nasseria Street, Riyadh 11138 Phones: 402-1724/402-4398 Fax: 403-4296	Commercial disputes and grievances, corruption, tax disputes and affairs relating to foreigners and their investments within Saudi Arabia.
Saline Water Conversion Corporation (SWCC) P.O. Box 5968, Riyadh 11432 Phones: 463-0503/463-0501 Telex: 400097 TAHLEA SJ Fax: 463-1952; 465-0852	Desalination complex.
Saudia Arabian Airlines (SAUDIA) Airport Road P.O. Box 620, Jeddah 21421 Phones: 684-2000/686-0000 Telex: 601007 SAUDI SJ	National airline.
King Abdulaziz City for Science and Technology P.O. Box 6068, Riyadh 11442 Phone: 478-8000 Telex: 401017 MARKAZ SJ Fax: 488-3756	Research and development, solar energy projects, patents.

Agency	Function
Saudi Arabian Standards Organization (SASO) P.O. Box 3437, Riyadh 11471 Phone: 479-3332 Telex: 401610 SASO SJ Fax: 479-3063	Development, publishing and distribution of standards.
Saudi Basic Industries Corporation (SABIC) P.O. Box 5101, Riyadh 11422 Phones: 401-2033/401-2361 Telex: 401177/400293 SABIC SJ Fax: 401-2045/401-3831	Joint ventures with foreign firms for heavy industries at Jubail and Yanbu.
Saudi Consulting House P.O. Box 1267, Riyadh 11431 Phones: 448-4588/448-4688 Telex: 404380 SCH SJ 403920 ALDAR SJ Fax: 448-1234	Conducts market research and industrial feasibility studies, prepares and publishes data on industrial development.
Saudi Red Crescent Association Al-Dhabab Road, Riyadh 11129 Phones: 406-9072/406-5092 Telex: 400096 HILAL SJ Fax: 405-1566	Emergency health care.
General Electricity Corp. (Electrico) P.O. Box 1185, Riyadh 11431 Phones: 477-2772 (10 lines) Telex: 401393 ELECTRIC SJ Fax: 477-5322	Electricity Planning, consolidated power companies.

Agency	Function
Grain Silos and Flour Mills Organization P.O. Box 3402, Riyadh 11471 Phones: 404-3334/404-4736 Telex: 401780/402580 SAWAMI SJ Fax: 463-1943	Silos, flour mills, wheat importing.
King Faisal Foundation P.O. Box 352, Riyadh 11411 Fax: 465-6524	Non-profit organization.
Meteorology and Environmental Protection Agency P.O. Box 1358, Jeddah 21431 Phones: 651-8887/671-1994 Telex: 601236 ARSAD	Meteorology and Environment.
Presidency of Civil Aviation Off Palestine Rd. East P.O. Box 887, Jeddah 21421 Phones: 667-9000/667-3664 Telex: 601093 CIVAIR SJ	Overflight and airports.

Agency	Function
Royal Commission for Jubail and Yanbu P.O. Box 5864, Riyadh 11432 Phones: 479-4444 (20 lines) Telex: 401386 JABEEN SJ Fax: 477-5404	Construction of industrial complexes' infrastructure at Jubail and Yanbu.
Saudi Arabian Monetary Agency (SAMA) P.O. Box 2992, Riyadh 11461 Phone: 478-7400 Telex: 400350/351/352 SAMA SJ Fax: 441-1384	Central Bank.
Saudi Fund for Development P.O. Box 5711, Riyadh 11432 Phones: 477-4069/477-4071 Telex: 401145 SUNDOQ SJ Fax: 464-7450	Development projects loans to foreign countries.
Saudi Industrial Development Fund (SIDF) P.O. Box 4143, Riyadh 11491 Phone: 477-4002 Telex: 401065 SIDFUND SJ Fax: 479-0165	Loans to Saudi or Saudi/foreign joint industrial ventures.
Saudi Arabian Agricultural Bank Omar bin Al-Khattab St. P.O. Box 1811, Riyadh 11126 Phones: 402-3911/402-3934 Fax: 402-2359	Purchases agricultural equipment, seeds, animals, provides loans to Saudi farmers.

Agency	Function
The Real Estate Development Fund Address: P.O. Box 5591, Riyadh 11433 Phone: 477-5120/403-3817 Telex: 400955 RDFUND SJ Fax: 479-0148	Provides loans to individuals and organizations for private or commercial real estate projects.
Islamic Development Bank Head Office: Jeddah P.O. Box 5925 Jeddah 21432 Phones: 636-0011/636-0054 Telex: 601 137/601407 ISDB SJ Fax: 637-1334	Development of Islamic projects.
Saudi Railroad Organization Dhahran Airport St. P.O. Box 92, Dammam 31411 Phone: 871-2222 Telex: 801050 SARAIL SJ	Runs Dammam-Riyadh railroad.
Presidency of Youth Welfare P.O. Box 965, Riyadh 11421 Phone: 401-4576 Telex: 401081 SPORTS SJ Fax: 401-0376	Sports complexes, cultural and folkloric clubs, boy scouts.
Civil Service Commission Washm St., P.O. Box 18367, Riyadh 11114 Phones: 402-6900/402-6934 Telex: 401445 CIVIL SJ Fax: 403-4998	Staffing policies throughout the public services. Undertakes staff recruitment & training programs.

Agency	Function
Institute of Public Administration (IPA) P.O. Box 205, Riyadh 11411 Phones: 476-1600 (10 lines) Telex: 401160 IPADMN SJ Fax: 479-2136	Revises & implements educational, pre-service & in-service training programs for Saudi civil servants.
General Presidency for Girls' Education Television St., Riyadh 11192 Phones: 402-9877/403-2500 Telex:.403160 EDUCATS SJ Fax: 403-9570	Responsible for all aspects of female education from primary level through higher education.
Civil Defense (Ministry of Interior) Airport Road, Riyadh 11174 Phones: 479-2828/478-3372 Telex: 401416 MADANI SJ Fax: 478-0846, 477-6579	Protecting, relieving, saving & putting out fires caused by natural catastrophies.
National Guard P.O. Box 9799, Riyadh 11423 Phone: 491-2400 Telex: 401064 NATGRD SJ Fax: 491-2824	Internal security.

Source: Royal Embassy of Saudi Arabia, Commercial Office, Washington, D.C., 1993.

The fourth Royal Decree deals with rules, regulations and duties concerning Majlis Al-Shoura. The Bylaws of the Consultative Council include, in Section One, the jurisdictions of the Chairman of the Council, the Vice Chairman and the Secretary-General. Section Two covers the plenum of the council. The Third Section covers meetings and the Fourth deals with committees. The Fifth Section governs voting and the issuance of decisions, while the Sixth Section governs general rules. There are a total of 33 articles in this chapter.

The Second Chapter gives a list of the rights granted to the members of the Consultative Council and their duties. This contains six articles dealing with membership, salary, an annual leave of 45 days and vacation matters. Members of the Council must show objectivity and neutrality in all activities of the Council. A member should not raise at the Council any personal matters or issues which may be detrimental to the general interest. The Third Chapter deals with organization of financial and employment affairs of the Council and it comprises ten articles. The Fourth Chapter is covered in five articles dealing with various methods of investigation, trial and procedure for members of the Shoura Council.

On the 22nd of August, 1993, the Custodian of the Two Holy Mosques stated that it was difficult to choose 60 members for Majlis Al-Shoura, especially since there are thousands and thousands of highly qualified Saudi citizens to fill such positions. With the limited duration for serving on the Council, many other Saudis will have the opportunity to serve their country in this distinguished consultative body. The King also stated "Consultation is not new for the Kingdom. It was one of the foundations on which the Kingdom was based since its establishment. The Shoura has now been placed in a modern organizational framework. I am always pleased to know of the opinions of the citizens and benefit from their views and expertise. I feel great pride for the achievements of Saudi citizens today. . . In the sciences and arts in comparison with the situation several years ago."

These four Royal Decrees complemented others which were pronounced back on February 29, 1992. Their combination ushered the Kingdom into a new era of reform and achievement. They were all lauded by distinguished statesmen and scholars, not only from the Arab and Islamic worlds, but from throughout the rest of the world as well. These decrees prove to be the best answer to the disinformation campaigns which are spread from time to time by malicious media forces against the peace-loving Kingdom of Saudi Arabia and its Islamic practices. These reforms will strongly serve the interests of the Saudi people under the umbrella of the Islamic faith. The system as a whole could be considered as a model for other Islamic and Arab countries to follow and emulate.

In regard to Saudi governmental reform, President Bill Clinton of the United States wrote King Fahd and said "the Kingdom's national day is a suitable occasion at which we must mention again and again the significance of your efforts towards the development and strengthening of governmental bodies through the establishment of the Shoura Council and other political reforms which you have announced."

Policy of Moderation

On all fronts, the Kingdom of Saudi Arabia follows a policy based on the Holy Qoran, wisdom, farsightedness, and moderation, where, according to the King and the Crown Prince: "Human rights are meticulously maintained. Man's dignity is protected, and in no circumstance or for whatever cause, would we permit it to be compromised." These fundamentals encompass national, regional, international, oil and humanitarian policies.

National Policy

The executive and legislative branches of the Saudi government are represented by the King, the Council of Ministers, and the Consultative Council or Majlis Al-Shoura along with the new rules governing the provinces. Several government agencies work with twenty ministries to help smooth the functioning of the Saudi government which executes its authority as inspired by Shari'a, based on Islam. The basic national policy of the Saudi leadership is to uphold Islamic law, support political moderation, economic stability, and develop the vast resources for the benefit of all Saudi citizens. Compromise, moderation, a strong sense of justice, and consensus are basic to the stability of the country. In formulating the general policy, the King is advised by the Council of Ministers, his advisors, and the Majlis Al-Shoura. The welfare of the citizen is uppermost in the mind of the Saudi leadership. A former United States president once said "The Saudi rulers were able to preserve an acceptable balance between delivering material advantages of a non-modern state and at the same time preserving the proper religious commitment. They also offset their absolute authority with a remarkable closeness to their subjects." Saudis are visited in the four corners of the Kingdom. In fact, the whole system of government moves along with the King and thus becomes more accessible and closer to the citizens of the nation. The King addresses the needs of citizens of all walks of life, including students at various universities. Ideas and thoughts are exchanged, covering all topics of mutual interest. These meetings take place in a friendly, casual, and relaxed atmosphere at different intervals of the year. The leadership responds to the requests and desires of the populace in a loving and understanding manner like a father, a friend, or an older brother. This creates confidence, hope, and endears the leadership to the heart of the Saudi population. All this leads to stability in the country which was well described by the American University (in Saudi Arabia–A Country Study): "The essentially stable political system could be attributed to the absence of history of colonization, the wisdom of King Abdulaziz and his successors, and the powerful force of Islam as a political instrument."

The Kingdom has indeed been blessed with a wise leadership dedicating all its energies and drive to prosperity at home and peace abroad. Coupled with phenomenal oil reserves in excess of 260 billion barrels, the largest oil production and largest oil exports in the world, the Kingdom earned a distinguished position of leadership and moderation not only in the Arab and Moslem worlds but also in the international community as well. The Custodian of the Two Holy Mosques and his leadership team are not only men of achievements on the national and regional scale, but through their moderation and sense of justice, they also helped propel the Kingdom into its rightful place among the family of nations.

The Arab and Moslem Worlds

The Kingdom of Saudi Arabia is a prominent and active member of the Gulf Cooperation Council (GCC). Founded in May, 1981, the Council includes: Bahrain, Kuwait, Oman, Qatar, Saudi Arabia and the United Arab Emirates. GCC enhances and encourages educational, social, economic and military cooperation. It played a very significant role during the *Gulf War for liberating Kuwait* from the grip of Saddam Hussein. The relationship between GCC members was further strengthened during this war which began with the occupation of Kuwait on August 2, 1990 and ended with its liberation on February 27, 1991, through a worldwide effort manifested by the Coalition Forces and supported through several United Nations resolutions. Under occupation, the Kuwaitis were stripped of their passports and their identification papers, in a campaign to cause confusion and strip Kuwait of its legitimate population. Saudi authorities were waiting to receive their Kuwaiti brothers and sisters, mainly at the border town of Khafji. Saudi hospitality, compassion and graciousness to their fellow Kuwaiti Arabs was exemplary. Governor of the Eastern Province, Prince Mohammed Bin Fahd, exhibited valor, wisdom and courage during the Gulf War. As the Governor of the gateway to Desert Shield and Desert Storm, also being inspired by his father's guidance and wise leadership, he contributed impressively in steering this strategic gateway on a safe path commanding world attention and respect. He did his utmost to alleviate the agony and suffering of the Kuwaiti refugees. Sites for processing human waves of Kuwaitis were established. Food, water, lodging and medical supplies were made available overnight! The fear was genuine that Saddam Hussein, by stripping these refugees of their proper documents, would infiltrate the Kingdom with a number of his terrorist groups. So, the job was not an easy one for the Saudis to screen the flood of refugees to separate the undesirable implants of terrorism sent by Saddam and his occupying force in Kuwait. However, efficiently and meticulously, without ever losing sight of the ordeal that the unfortunate refugees had been exposed to, Saudi authorities, on direct orders from King Fahd of Saudi Arabia and the Saudi government, moved with speed and professionalism in processing the multitude of refugees to alleviate their fear and ease their pain. In a short time, thousands and thousands of Kuwaiti refugees were on their way to the four corners of the Kingdom, from the Eastern Province in Dammam and Dhahran to the Western Hijaz in Mecca, Madina and Taif, and from the north in Tobouk to Asir in the south and especially to the heart of Najd in Riyadh. Homes and hearts of the Saudis were opened to receive their destitute brothers and sisters coming from Kuwait. Some Kuwaiti refugees went on to Bahrain where they were welcomed; some were offered free housing, others stayed at hotels paid for by the Kuwaiti Embassy, a few more went to other Gulf countries who also helped the Kuwaiti refugees.

During the boom days of the late 70's and early 80's the Kingdom embarked on a development program which built a great infrastructure, from super-highways to massive airports; from huge air bases, good schools, universities and hospitals, to housing projects which constituted a surplus of hundreds of multi-story apartment buildings in the four corners of the Kingdom. With the flood of Kuwaiti refugees, hotels, private homes, and these large buildings built during the boom for Saudi families with limited income, were filled overnight. The great infrastructure and thousands of residential dwellings became very valuable indeed during the occupation and the liberation of the state of Kuwait. The generosity of the top leadership and the Saudi populace brought compassion and care to all Kuwaitis, who felt in Saudi Arabia as if they were in their own Kuwaiti homes. They were indeed most welcome and best cared for! All their needs for food, lodging, medical services and other necessities of life were made available to them by the Saudis, free of charge and with a great spirit of care and love. For some time, Saudi authorities paid monthly cash allowances as expense money for every family.

The Kuwaiti government in exile was operating from the summer resort town of Taif in Saudi Arabia. The Amir of Kuwait and his Crown Prince and Ministers were conducting Kuwaiti governmental affairs and making urgent contacts with world leaders seeking desperate help for the salvation and liberation of their lost land. Their government was treated with the utmost dignity and respect. Whatever their needs may have been, they were fulfilled by the Saudi host. Many of their business transactions and governmental functions were again operational from Saudi Arabia, with the help and full cooperation of the Saudi government and people. With the help of Saudi newspapers and their presses, a number of Kuwaiti newspapers and magazines began their publications again from Saudi Arabia. Kuwaiti children joined their Saudi brothers and sisters in the schools and universities of Saudi Arabia, at no cost to them. This parade of goodness and care goes on and on, to touch every walk of life and every need the Kuwaitis may have had. Loyalty and gratitude at their best! That is what the Saudis have propagated and exhibited everywhere. They were true friends of their Arab Kuwaiti brothers. They were a true friend in need!!!

Cooperation and a strong relationship were also exhibited during the eight year war between Iran and Iraq which started in September, 1980. As a prominent member of the *Arab League*, the Kingdom stresses the policy of non-interference in the internal af-

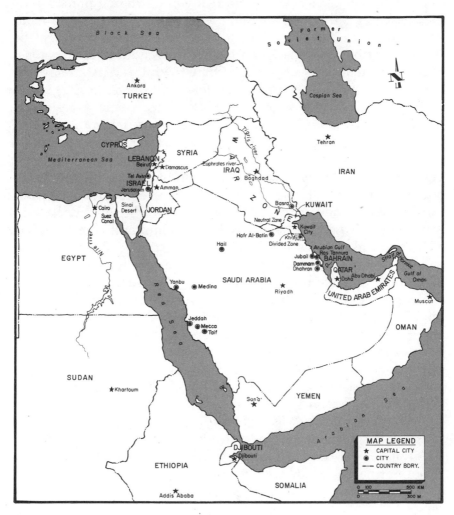

WAR ZONE AND
SURROUNDING AREA

fairs of other countries, while at the same time not permitting any nation to interfere in its internal affairs. Peace and goodwill in the world along with brotherhood and solidarity among Arab and Moslem nations are preached and practiced by Saudi leadership. The Kingdom exercises every effort toward bringing understanding, peace and tranquility among fraternal nations in the Arab world. Strong efforts have taken place in the past to bring rapprochement between Syria and Jordan on a number of occasions. Explosive situations were defused by Crown Prince Abdullah under the leadership and guidance of King Fahd. A ticking bomb which developed in a dispute between Morocco and Algeria was defused by the Saudi leadership. More recently, when the ruler of Iraq occupied the peaceful state of Kuwait, the Kingdom followed every possible means to bring about a peaceful solution to the flagrant violation of international law and brutal occupation of an innocent Arab state. However, all these peaceful efforts did not bring results from an obstinate aggressor who dug deeper in Kuwait. The Kingdom, being the just nation that it is, marshalled all its political energies and resources to the rescue of the people of Kuwait. In this regard, and building on the mountain of goodwill that has developed through the years, the entire family of nations came to the defense of the Kingdom and geared its might toward the liberation of Kuwait from the grip of Saddam Hussein. Literally, King Fahd knocked on every door for peace, he said, "We have made every possible effort at all levels . . . we knocked on every door for peace and followed every path for fraternal dialogue and understanding. (But Saddam Hussein) refused to listen to the voice of reason."

Moving across the vast expanse of the Arab land, you sense the peaceful gestures, the moderating force and economic might of the Kingdom of Saudi Arabia. Always a dialogue is sought and a hand-of-peace is extended to all, no matter how difficult the circumstances may be and how deep the wounds may have become!

The *Palestinian problem* was and remains a central and important Arab issue for the Kingdom. From the days of Abdulaziz, the founder of the Kingdom, Saudi Arabia was always strongly dedicated, "steadfast, unswerving, and unflinching," on the Palestinian issue. Many wars, destabilization, human suffering, and terrorism were the bitter fruits of this difficult and intractable problem. The Kingdom always professed moderation and justice for all concerned. Saudi Arabia with its policy of moderation, deep convictions, a strong economy and international diplomatic stature, supported the Palestinian people in defending their legitimate right to self-determination and the establishment of a national home, so that all people in the region would live in peace and harmony. As far back as September, 1982, Fahd, then the Crown Prince, devised an eight-point peace plan. He originated a creative plan to solve the difficult problem that defied solutions and brought many wars inflicting tragedy and causing destabilization in the region. This became the well-known Fahd Peace Plan. It was articulated during the twelfth Arab Summit Conference in Fez, Morocco. This is the only peace plan which received unanimous approval by the Arab nations. The Fourth Article of the Fahd Peace Plan addresses the reaffirmation of Palestinian rights to self-determination, the exercising of their inalienable national rights under the leadership of the PLO (Palestinian Liberation Organization)–their legitimate and sole representative; and compensation to every Palestinian not wishing to return home.

Despite the disappointing position taken by some Palestinian leaders during the Gulf War, the Kingdom remained true to its basic mission and honorable principles. Fresh from a victory in the Gulf and liberation of Kuwait, it marshalled all its political forces, international credentials and political might to give impetus and momentum for the peace process. It urged and coordinated an international effort to push for an international peace conference. In this regard, massive efforts were made in cooperation with former President George Bush of the United States of America and his Secretary of State James Baker. The support and understanding of the former Soviet Union and its former President Mikhail Gorbachev were sought. Finally, in cooperation with world leaders and the five permanent members of the United Nations Security Council, an international peace conference was held in Madrid, Spain on October 30, 1991. It was co-chaired by the United States of America and the former Soviet Union. It was attended by former President George Bush and former President Gorbachev, along with the representatives of the Israelis, the Palestinians, the Syrians, the Jordanians, the Lebanese and a host of other Arab nations as observers. This was a great step forward towards paving the road for a just and comprehensive peace between the Arabs and the Israelis. The peace conference continued its meetings in the capital of the United States of America, Washington, D.C. for several sessions. Secret sessions between the PLO and Israel were held for several months in Oslo, Norway. The world was astonished and relieved to hear of a historic compromise. Finally, on September 13, 1993, the new President of the U.S.A., Bill Clinton, invited the representative of the Palestine Liberation Organization, Yasser Arafat; the Prime Minister of Israel, Yitzhak Rabin; the Foreign Minister of Israel Shimon Peres, and a representative of the Russian Republic, along with a long list of dignitaries, among them former Presidents George Bush, Gerald Ford, Jimmy Carter, the former Secretary of State James Baker and several other worldwide figures, to Washington, D.C. to sign the peace accord. This historic mutual recognition peace accord was signed between the Palestine Liberation Organization (PLO) and the Israeli representatives. It was further strengthened by serious discussions in Cairo. In the first implementation of this accord, the Gaza Strip and the West Bank city of Jericho have been relinquished to the Palestine Liberation Organization which will be responsible for security and for running both of them in a limited self-rule arrangement. Down the road, further steps will take place toward settling the problem. The signing of this accord and the shaking of hands between two former enemies and arch antagonists was a historic step indeed, paving the way no matter how arduous and long the trip may be, toward a just and permanent peace between the Arabs and the Israelis. Once the Palestinians had signed this accord it became much easier and more practical for the Arab nations involved to solve their disputes with Israel. The very next day Jordan signed an understanding with Israel and serious peaceful negotiations culminated in a peace treaty which was signed on October 26, 1994. Positive moves toward peace continue between Israel and the affected Arab neighbors. While all these are positive steps in the right direction, the road ahead remains tough and arduous. Many disappointments will occur, but major steps toward peace have certainly been made.

To give the accord a breath of life and a chance for success, the co-sponsors of the Middle East Peace Process, the United States of America and Russia, convened a donors conference in Washington, D.C. The goal was to raise three billion dollars from the wealthiest nations of the world to help in financing the Palestinian self-rule in the West Bank and Gaza Strip. The Kingdom of Saudi Arabia hoped that the agreement signed between Israel and the PLO would lead to a permanent, just and comprehensive peace based on Security Council Resolutions 242 and 338 and the principle of land for peace along with total Israeli withdrawal from Arab territories. After all the wars, death and destruction, this understanding did become a reality on September 13, 1993, when the PLO and Israel signed their accord. The fine contributions of Saudi leadership are befitting a peaceful, loving nation like Saudi Arabia, which desires to live in peace and harmony among all nations of the world and especially the nations of the region.

One of the side-effects of the Arab/Israeli conflict was the *Lebanese civil war* which raged on for sixteen years. This tragedy has received deep concern and special attention from the Saudi leadership. The Kingdom has exercised tremendous effort in every possible way to bring the warring factions to peaceful terms and to offer humanitarian and economic aid to all Lebanese. During the Israeli invasion in June, 1982, which devastated most of Southern Lebanon and Beirut itself, all Lebanese and Arabs looked to Saudi Arabia for decisive leadership to stop the Israeli onslaught. The Kingdom immediately contacted the United States of America and used its good offices in cooperation with President Ronald Reagan who also used his power to stop the Israeli invasion. The high regard for King Fahd and the moderation of Saudi policy through the years which cemented Saudi-American relations, all helped in stopping this war and in saving Lebanon from the inferno that was engulfing large parts of the country and its capital Beirut. The invasion was stopped, and King Fahd with his team worked tirelessly with deep devotion and enthusiasm to stop the civil war. He made many emotional appeals to the Lebanese to stop this war of agony, devastation, and human tragedy. He once said to the warring factions "In the name of all that is Holy, all that we and they have in common, the bonds of faith and language, the bonds of blood and soul, we appeal to them to turn over a new leaf in their relations." The former Lebanese Ambassador to the Kingdom of Saudi Arabia, Dr. Zafer Al-Hasan said "King Fahd who played a major role in halting the bombing of Beirut during the savage Israeli invasion, has been pursuing efforts with influential, international and Arab circles to help Lebanon restore its independence, security and stability. All the Lebanese people greatly and proudly appreciate this stand." This benevolent attitude of the Kingdom toward the Lebanese Republic is strengthened and deepened by feelings of brotherhood. King Fahd, Crown Prince Abdullah, the Second Deputy Prime Minister Prince Sultan, and their men including Prince Saud Al-Faisal–the Foreign Minister and Prince Bandar Bin Sultan, the Ambassador of the Kingdom to the United States of America, all made genuine efforts toward a ceasefire in Lebanon and for bringing peace to the war-torn land. The Kingdom worked tirelessly through its good offices in Syria to help bring diverging views and warring factions closer together. The love and sacrifices for Lebanon and the Lebanese people stems from the Kingdom's deep convictions and beliefs in achieving friendship and unity among the people. This policy is carried further into the family of the Arab nation. It has always supported legality and a unified, independent Lebanon, free from all foreign domination.

The endless civil war of devastation that tormented the Lebanese people became intractable despite many efforts to bring it to an end. Finally, and after many efforts by a Tripartite Arab Committee and the international community, King Fahd succeeded in inviting and bringing to the Kingdom the remaining members of the Lebanese Parliament to discuss their differences. The Kingdom sponsored this gathering which became known as the Taif Accord of 1989. An official at the Lebanese Embassy in Riyadh said "The Taif agreement, which was reached after hard work and long discussions has restored hope for a bright future for Lebanon." He also stated that the personal mediation effort and commitment of King Fahd toward ending the Lebanese dilemma made the national reconciliation accord possible.

Former U.S. Ambassador to Saudi Arabia, C. W. Freeman said "We look forward to new successes for our cooperation in the years to come. In Lebanon, we both consider it essential that the Taif agreement, which is a monument to Saudi Arabia's diplomatic skills, be fully implemented so that Lebanon may enjoy national reconciliation and a renewal of unity. Similarly, we trust that the vital role that the government of Saudi Arabia has played in nurturing a Middle East peace process of unprecedented promise will bear early fruit." King Fahd and his team used all possible efforts and convincing powers to help ease the differences that had built up between the Lebanese with the passage of sixteen years of civil war. After lengthy meetings lasting for a month, and arduous efforts by King Fahd and his team, the *Taif Conference* led to a peaceful compromise. Developing better understanding of mutual interest and benefits with Syria, the Taif Conference paved the way toward ending the Lebanese civil war and solving the massive problems which resulted from the devastation and years of conflict. The civil war ended, Lebanon is healing and on the healthy road to recovery. A great credit goes to King Fahd, the Saudi leadership, the Saudi people, and the good offices used with Syria to bring about peace in Lebanon. All this has been done with the great efforts and blessings of King Fahd and the Kingdom of Saudi Arabia. The Lebanese people, not only in Lebanon but in the four corners of the globe, are very grateful for this man in particular and the Saudi people as well. The Lebanese Ambassador to the Kingdom, Z. Hamdan gratefully acknowledged the Saudi role in bringing peace to Lebanon. He said "Saudi Arabia plays a very important role in the Arab and Islamic worlds in general and in helping Lebanon in particular. King Fahd has played a significant role in the past, and because of his personal efforts we are enjoying security, stability and a return to normalcy in Lebanon. We in Lebanon believe the Saudi role is historic, and we, the Lebanese, will never forget that, generation after generation." During a visit to the Kingdom in April, 1993, the President of Lebanon E. Hrawi stated "The peace and security Lebanon now enjoys are the results of the Taif agreement . . . we owe a great debt of gratitude to King Fahd."

Concerning the ravaging civil war in Yemen, King Fahd and Crown Prince Abdullah declared in their joint address to pilgrims on May 22, 1994: "When we review the current situation in sisterly Yemen, we feel profound sorrow for the deteriorating conditions there. We expressed our frank and brotherly attitude on 24th Zul Qi'dah, 1414 A.H. when we called on the parties to the conflict to appeal to reason and logic and place the interests of Yemen and its people in the forefront of their priorities.

We have said so, and we will confirm it time and again, since Yemen's security and stability are to us far more important than they are to any other party. Stability in Yemen is in our interest."

Next to the Arab World, the *Moslem World* occupies a position of importance and religious sharing. Saudi Arabia is an active, dynamic, and founding member of the Organization of Islamic Conference (OIC). The organization strives to support Islamic unity and causes, while putting forth the necessary effort to bring about peace and harmony among the Moslem nations. Being the birthplace of Islam, Saudi Arabia considers this as its greatest contribution to mankind. Nearly two million Moslems from around the globe make the Hajj, or Pilgrimage, to the Holy places in Mecca and Madina. The Kingdom has become the focal point for all Moslems of the world. This position of prominence is esteemed in many nations, especially the Arab countries, the developing nations, and the Moslem world as well. One billion Moslems today look to Saudi Arabia as the guardian of their Holy Shrines and the spirit of justice and tolerance in Islam.

Atheism as professed by communism around the world, is anathema to the Saudi people. The Kingdom has been steadfast against communism throughout the decades. It supported the arduous struggle for the liberation of the people of Afghanistan from the grip of communist domination. It has done all it could on the moral, political, economic and social scale to support the oppressed people of Afghanistan in their struggle against a communist dictatorship that had led to much destruction and devastation in this Moslem nation. The strong support of the Kingdom along with enormous international pressure, especially from the United States of America, England, France, and other free nations, all led to the defeat of the former Soviet Union in Afghanistan. The communists were forced to withdraw and Afghanistan became free again!

When the various Afghan factions resorted to internecine bloodletting, King Fahd invited the Afghan leaders to meet in Saudi Arabia. He used his influence and good offices in mediating the deep divisions between the various Afghan groups, who were earlier a solid front in their victorious struggle against communism and Soviet occupation. Early in 1993 the Afghani warring factions signed a reconciliation accord in Mecca, Saudi Arabia. In a joint address to the pilgrims delivered on May 22, 1994 (11 Zul Hijja, 1414 A.H.), King Fahd and Crown Prince Abdullah stated: "with hearts brimming with grief and pain, we keep track of the worsening situation in Afghanistan. Conditions have deteriorated in Afghanistan . . .

All this did happen because what has been going in

Afghanistan has disfigured the image of Islamic Jihad waged purely for Allah's pleasure and projected it in an other light, that of subservience to certain individuals, loyalty to this or that faction or group and involvement in the struggle between sons of the same creed and the same country."

Crown Prince Abdullah stated the bedrock policy of the Kingdom when he said, Saudi Arabia is "a factor for reconciliation between Arabs and Moslems. It has called for reconciliation and worked to preserve it, and has always worked to promote the interests of Arab and Moslem peoples."

The human tragedy in Bosnia-Herzegovina cries for a just solution. King Fahd was the first world leader who declared his steadfast support for this unfortunate land. He was on the side of justice and squarely against the abhorrent ethnic cleansing. Since the beginning of Serb aggression, compounded with Croation attacks, Saudi Arabia supported the besieged Moslems politically and financially and continues to send humanitarian aid.

At the end of the 1993 Pilgrimage and on the occasion of Eid Al-Adha, King Fahd and Crown Prince Abdullah issued a joint statement addressed to the one billion Moslems around the globe. The Bosnian tragedy was very much on their minds. They said "The second tragedy which gives rise to much concern is that which is now unfolding on the soil of Bosnia and Herzegovina. We have exerted, and continue to exert uninterrupted efforts with prominent leaders in the world to end the tragedy of the helpless Moslem people of Bosnia who have suffered so much at the hands of the Serbs. The fact that the world community is still wavering with regard to taking a firm stand against the Serbs will aggravate the tragedy and may lead to the extermination of the people of Bosnia-Herzegovina. That hesitation undermines the credibility of the international community to support justice and right and stop aggression. The Islamic states have expressed their position at the meeting of foreign ministers of the Organization of Islamic Conference (OIC) in Jeddah (December, 1992) and subsequent meetings and world forums. We are continuing our efforts in consultation with everyone because we believe the catastrophe is more serious than anyone can imagine . . . wiping a Moslem state off the map would confront the world with problems the like of which it has never faced before. The Serbs better keep this in mind; other countries too are well advised to do likewise. For its part, the United Nations ought to take the necessary measures to avert such a terrible fate. Otherwise it would have, historically speaking, to share with others the burden of the consequences. Such consequences could fan the fire of extremism and contribute to instability everywhere in the world.

The ideal solution to the Bosnian crisis is to recognize the right of the Bosnian people to set up a state based on peace, justice and security in this part of the world. The next move is to reestablish peaceful coexistence, mutual understanding and rapport. . . . The people of Bosnia-Herzegovina have the right to exist and maintain their independent identity and to form, together with their neighbors, an integrated region."

Prince Bandar Bin Sultan, Saudi Ambassador in Washington, D.C., addressed a U.S. Central Command Conference (CentCom) and brought up the Bosnian human tragedy. He said "While the world worries about this misperceived threat, a Moslem population in Bosnia, the last remnants of Islam's presence in Europe, is on the verge of extinction. How can we explain to our people in Saudi Arabia, watching western media report on Bosnia's slaughter and horror, that the product of a new democratic and free world ends in ethnic cleansing in the heart of Europe? Honest and simple Moslem men and women in our country and beyond are convinced, right or wrong, that the Bosnians were being abandoned because they were Moslems. It is hard to persuade them otherwise. And here I must honestly say that we are still hopeful that the U.S. position will yet evolve positively, especially compared to the badly-flawed European position."

The President of Bosnia-Herzegovina gratefully acknowledged the Kingdom's support. In a message to the Saudi Monarch, he said "I have found it a suitable opportunity to affirm that the people of Bosnia-Herzegovina will always remember your stand and the Saudi peoples' sympathy toward their tragedy."

Moslem nations around the world accord the Kingdom a position of respect and reverence because of its genuine policies of peace, goodwill, and justice.

When Sudan was struck with famine, Saudi Arabia was there to give a helping hand. Nearly 200 flights of cargo jumbo jets and giant military transport planes carried loads of food, medicine and tents.

When Somalia was devastated by anarchy and famine, Saudi Arabia rushed to the rescue with food and medicine along with

Saudi personnel to help in bringing law and order to a lawless and dangerous environment. On one occasion, Prince Sultan Bin Abdulaziz, Second Deputy Prime Minister and Minister of Defense and Aviation, addressed Saudis serving in Somalia under the U.N. flag encompassing forces from 25 nations. He said "You cooperate with Arab Moslem and international forces to serve a greater goal, namely to restore hope and love and deliver food and medicine to our Somali brothers."

King Fahd and Crown Prince Abdullah call for the true spirit of Islam stressing amity, brotherhood, tolerance and cooperation. "Certain countries have made a habit of referring to Islam as though it were the force that is going to destroy human civilization, change the face of the earth and force mankind to slide back into medieval times. We in Saudi Arabia wonder at this highly biased line of thinking and mode of belief. Our astonishment grows even more as we find that certain societies are exaggerating and accepting personal interpretations and faulty conclusions that are very close to naked enmity to Islam and Moslems. In such societies, talk about Islam and Moslems has taken a sinister turn that endangers the interests of all and threatens to widen the gap between our countries and peoples." They also called on Moslems to "exert great efforts to allay the fears of other countries and peoples and correct their misperceptions. It is also our duty to reassure them through our dealings that the extremism of a few is alien to Islam. The religion of Islam respects man's humanity. Islamic Shari'a, with its inherent sense of justice and tolerance, its respect for man's dignity and the protection of his rights, and its readiness to put to good advantage man's capabilities and talents, is in a position to provide humanity with practical solutions to many problems and crises. In Islam, there is no room for racism, factionalism, ethnocentrism nor sectarianism. Instead there are justice, equality and tolerance, the same three pillars on which the Kingdom of Saudi Arabia was founded and to which it is now striving to give more force in every aspect of life in line with the eternal guidance of the Holy Qoran and its illustrious tenets. . . Saudi Arabia has repeatedly called on the Islamic nation to have a united will and agree on common objectives . . . the teachings of the Holy Book and the Prophet's Sunnah call for amity, brotherhood, tolerance, cooperation and mutual support in all fields free from violence and brutality, both being incompatible with the Islamic creed."

As a mighty economic power of goodwill and moderation, an oil giant, and a regionally geopolitically strategic nation, the Kingdom occupies an important and unique role in the "New World Order."

The International Scene

The cornerstone of Saudi policy is to safeguard the Kingdom's independence and protect it from any aggressor along with guarding the Haramein, which are the Two Holy Mosques of Mecca and Madina. Saudi foreign policy includes respect and adherence to the United Nations Charter; cooperation with peoples of the world toward the establishment of peace, welfare, and stability for mankind; peaceful co-existence and cooperation with Arab and Islamic nations, and the non-interference in the internal affairs of other nations. In this regard King Fahd said "We will never interfere in the internal affairs of other countries and will never allow anyone to interfere in our domestic affairs."

The Saudis are very proud of being a founding member of the United Nations Charter which was signed in San Francisco, California USA, on June 26, 1945. On the heels of World War II, high hopes were pinned on the League of Nations for preventing violence and warfare. Then Prince Faisal, later to become King, signed the Charter on behalf of Saudi Arabia. He was accompanied by the sons of Abdulaziz: Prince Fahd and Prince Khaled. Both became Kings of Saudi Arabia. Addressing the delegates, Faisal said "In such a moment as this, we should not forget the resolute efforts of Franklin Delano Roosevelt for the cause of peace, and for his farsighted action in initiating this Conference." When Fahd became the King of Saudi Arabia on June 9, 1982, he asserted to the nation that Saudi Arabia is active "within the framework of the United Nations, its agencies, and committees. We are committed to its charter. We reinforce its endeavors." The United Nations is considered as "a safety valve trusted and respected for the preservation of international peace and security." according to Saudi Foreign Minister Prince Saud Al-Faisal. He went on to say, "Saudi Arabia stands up against any action that attempts to weaken it or replace the authority of international law with instruments of force and the means of terror." The Kingdom actively participates in various organizations and functions of the

The Kingdom of Saudi Arabia is not only blessed as the birthplace of Islam, and the country with the most massive oil reserves in the world, it is indeed a land of good fortunes for having a wise, compassionate leadership that places the welfare of the people among its top priorities— What a precious lesson for many leaders in this turbulent world.

In the serenity of the desert.

King Fahd and King Hassan II of Morocco.

King Fahd and President George Bush—giant symbols of a great "special relationship."

King Fahd and a Lebanese Delegation.

King Fahd and President Ronald Reagan.

This photo was taken during King Fahd's historic visit to the United States
of America in February, 1985.

United Nations. Its generous financial contributions speak well for the Kingdom's dedication to the U.N.'s success and welfare. In this, Saudi Arabia ranks among the top of all nation donors of the world.

Saudi Arabia strongly supports self-determination and economic development for the nations of the world. It strongly and enthusiastically supports the World Organization, the United Nations Educational, Scientific and Cultural Organization (UNESCO), the United Nations International Children's Educational Fund (UNICEF), as well as other organizations.

The Kingdom strives energetically towards good relations with peace-loving nations of the world. There is deep mutual interest and strong relations with the United States of America, the European community, Japan and the countries of the developing world. The Kingdom did not have any diplomatic relations with the communist world. It is strongly anti-communist because of communism's atheistic ideology and designs for world domination. After the fall of communism, new relations were established with the new Russia and former Soviet Republics.

The gigantic oil reserves of the Kingdom and its tremendous potential in mineral resources, along with its strategic holy position as the birthplace of Islam, all make the Kingdom of paramount importance to Western democracies and others in the world community. The wheels of industrial progress depend greatly on the strategic oil supplies from Saudi Arabia. Friendly relations of unique and specific importance to the Kingdom exist and are continually strengthened with the United States of America, Britain, France, Japan, West Germany and other countries of the European community, plus the Arab and Moslem worlds as well.

The *Gulf War* was ignited by Saddam Hussein when his army ruthlessly occupied the state of Kuwait, despite its peaceful policies as defined by its ruler. The Amir of Kuwait, Sheikh Jabir Al-Ahmad Al-Jabir Al-Sabbah defined Kuwait's peaceful and fraternal mission. He said "Kuwait lives under the protection of Islam as its religion, Arabism as its homeland, co-operation as its strategic path, tolerance as its motto, fraternity as its guidance, consultation as its modus operandi, justice as its rule, progress as its responsibility and peace as its goal." A nation with such a peaceful mission did not deserve the brutality and mutilation dished out of

Baghdad as documented by several sources and later witnessed by General Norman Schwarzkopf who stated in his historic briefing from Riyadh on February 27, 1991 "There was a very, very large number of young Kuwaiti males taken out of the City (Kuwait City) within the last week or two. But that pales to insignificance compared to the absolutely unspeakable atrocities that occurred in Kuwait in the last week. They are not a part of the same human race, the people that did that, that the rest of us are. I've got to pray that that's the case."

The mettle of the Kingdom was manifested in the historic decision taken by King Fahd. After extensive consultation with President Bush and world leaders, and after several appeals to Saddam Hussein to withdraw from Kuwait, the leadership of Saudi Arabia rose to the occasion and challenge! It exhibited tremendous valor and bravery in standing up to defend the security of the Kingdom of Saudi Arabia and to guard its people against the imminent danger poised on the borders of the Kingdom . . . all along, King Fahd being the dynamo in devising meticulous plans for exploring all possible peace avenues, but in the meantime amassing an enormous force backed by the entire world community to bring about the liberation of the State of Kuwait. King Fahd and the generous and courageous Saudi people were of one voice in their stand against tyranny and occupation, against the devastation and destruction of a brotherly nation. The official silence of Saudi Arabia which was in itself a wise move, did lull the aggressive aims of Saddam Hussein so that he would not be excited in any way nor antagonized into placing his operation into the next mode for executing his plan to occupy the Eastern region of Saudi Arabia along with his allies from the south, north and west to bring about the dismantling of the Kingdom. The time had come, after the long days and nights that King Fahd spent consulting with world leaders to secure all possible support, and much of it was urgently needed, to confront this overwhelming force amassed against the borders of his beloved Kingdom. The silence had evaporated! The King had spoken. He took a courageous stand. The world would see and realize anew that the Kingdom throughout its history stood on the side of right not might, for justice against tyranny and oppression. The world was very quick to rise solidly in support of the Kingdom, because of its policy of moderation and justice.

The good deeds of Saudi Arabia paid handsomely during the tragic occupation of the peaceful state of Kuwait. In a narrative account to his people, King Fahd stated on November 27, 1990 (10 Jumada the first, 1411 A.H.) that the world stood on the side of justice. "For example, if we took a poll to know who amongst the countries of the world, stood on the side of the Kingdom of Saudi Arabia, from East to West, South to North, I believe that it would be all countries of the world: Islamic countries in Asia–more than 450 million–and in Africa the same number and in the Middle East, the European countries, North and South America. What is important is–why did all nations of the world stand with the Kingdom of Saudi Arabia and Kuwait? They stood with us because we are right.

Add to this that the will of God made the entire world stand with Kuwait whose capabilities have been pillaged and its integrity had been desecrated. You all have witnessed the situation. We don't just say it lightly. But we have seen it on television, we heard it from people. Never in history has an Arab nation invaded another Arab nation. As for whoever is seeking a solution, he should ask the question to President Saddam Hussein!"

Here is what some key world leaders have said:

"We have tried in vain to avoid the war and fighting. I had sent him (Saddam Hussein) about twenty-seven appeals to withdraw to enable us to seek a cease-fire . . . Today, we are very much concerned about the Iraqi people in the same way we are concerned about the Egyptian and Saudi people and mankind at large. We never like to fight with each other. Whenever I sent an appeal to Saddam Hussein, in return I received many insults."–President Hosni Moubarak of Egypt.

"The history of this century shows clearly that rewarding aggression encourages more aggression . . . I am convinced not only that we will prevail, but that out of the horror of combat will come the recognition that no nation can stand against a world united. No nation will be permitted to brutally assault its neighbor."–Former President George Bush of the U.S.A.

"Time is running out for Saddam Hussein. Either he gets out of Kuwait soon or we and our allies will remove him by force and he will go down to defeat in all its consequences . . . this man is a despot and a tyrant and must be stopped."–Former Prime Minister Margaret Thatcher of England.

"If Iraq really wants to avoid the worst, it must now openly declare and show in its actions that it is leaving Kuwait . . . This is not Vietnam. This is not Afghanistan. This is extremely dangerous . . . Let no one hope to undermine this unity to drive a wedge between us."–Former President Mikhail Gorbachev of the former Soviet Union.

"Not one gesture, not one word from the President of Iraq has given us a glimpse, a hope of reconciliation." President François Mitterrand of France.

On January 30, 1991 after the launching of the air war for liberating Kuwait, King Fahd said "On this occasion, I would like to express my sincere thanks to our friends who did not hesitate in responding to the Kingdom of Saudi Arabia's call for help from the Arab countries, the Islamic countries, and friendly nations. I, hereby, repeat what I had said before that the Arab States and the Islamic countries and our friends in the United States, Britain, and France have offered the largest striking force which could be offered at this time, be it ground, air or marine forces. A number of countries from Europe and other parts of the world have also offered what they could offer including the fleets which we witnessed today, whether in the Arabian Gulf waters, the Mediterranean Sea, or the Indian Ocean." He continued to say that the occupation of Kuwait by Iraqi forces was "A prelude to the occupation of Saudi Arabia and possibly other countries."

In the war of liberating Kuwait, Coalition Forces performed exceptionally well. All Saudi Forces, under the command of Prince Khaled Bin Sultan, met the acid test and contributed their admirable share, as witnessed by General Norman Schwarzkopf who said "First of all, the Saudis over here on the east coast did a terrific job. They went up against the very, very tough barrier system; they breached the barrier very, very effectively; they moved out aggressively; and continued their attacks up the coast."

As a crowning to victory in the Gulf and liberation of Kuwait, an important symbolism is worthy of note. Samir Shihabi, former Saudi Arabia's Ambassador to the U.N., was elected in September, 1992 as the President of the U.N. General Assembly. The global respect for the Kingdom, along with the courage and stature of President Hosni Moubarak of Egypt, played an important role in electing an Arab from Egypt as the Secretary General of the United Nations.

Among all the countries of the world, the Kingdom certainly treasures Saudi-American relations.

U.S.-Saudi Relations

The one special relationship of paramount importance is certainly that between the Kingdom of Saudi Arabia and the United States of America.

W. B. Quandt, an authority on foreign policy from the Brookings Institution said "Because Saudi Arabia sets atop the largest and most easily exploited reserves of petroleum in the world, it inevitably is being drawn into the center of international politics. What the rulers of the Saudi Kingdom do or fail to do can have many severe consequences. What happens in this little known country is therefore of concern to statesmen, bankers, businessmen and strategists throughout the world. "As far as American interest in this special relationship, Quandt continues "for Americans, the stakes involved in the U.S.–Saudi relationship are particularly great. No country has benefited more from relations with Saudi Arabia than the United States. American oil companies have made enormous profits. American businessmen have had a disproportionate share of the Saudi market."

American-Saudi relations trace their origin back to over six decades, to the days of Abdulaziz, when Americans were granted the preferential right to explore for oil, water and minerals. When oil was finally produced in good quantities in 1938, a new era of Saudi-American relations began. A strong foundation for this special relationship was born from the historic meeting of King Abdulaziz with President Roosevelt.

The first was a visionary ruler of an emerging Kingdom at the heart of the Islamic world, the latter a determined leader of a nation at war. Their meeting was in February, 1945. After the historic meeting with the Allied leaders at Yalta, Roosevelt met King Abdulaziz aboard the U.S.S. Quincy in the Suez Canal. This bedrock relationship built on mutual interest and cooperation has grown through the years and remains a strong one.

Oil supplies from Saudi Arabia are strategically very important to the prosperity of the United States of America, as well as Europe and Japan. The Kingdom remains the largest customer for American products in the Arab world. It is the sixth largest market for U.S. products on a worldwide basis. Saudi investments in the United States help strengthen and invigorate the American economy. According to the United States Department of State, in its background notes on Saudi Arabia, this conviction is expressed in this manner: "Coupled with its vast mineral wealth, Saudi Arabia's strategic location makes its friendship important to the United States in the Middle East. Saudi Arabia's leaders value close and friendly relations with the United States." Thousands of Saudi students study for higher education in the United States and more than 30,000 Americans live and work in the Kingdom. The backbone of the five-year development plans is supported by the strong infusion of brain power of Saudis who graduated from top American universities.

Saudi Arabia and the U.S. share a basic and common concern about the security of the region and its orderly progress. Consultations on various international economic and development programs continue. Former president Jimmy Carter put it this way: "Almost invariably, when I was president, I felt that our own basic goals were compatible with those of the Saudi Arabians and that they were inclined to be helpful whenever possible." He continued by saying "They prefer stability between existing regimes, compromises when Arab unanimity is at stake, peace in the region and political orientation toward the West."

A special relationship has been strengthened through many decades beginning with President Roosevelt and moving on to Presidents Eisenhower, Kennedy, Johnson, Nixon, Ford, Carter, Reagan, Bush and Clinton.

H. Laskai, British political scientist and economist, said in essence that Saudi Arabia is stable because no significant part of the population feels permanently excluded. Ambassador Newman states that this is true of Saudi Arabia, and that it is the only country in the vast region which really operates that way. Newman admires the great progress achieved under the development plans. He takes special pride in the fact that former Minister of Planning and now Minister of Petroleum & Mineral Resources, Hisham Nazer, was a former student of the Ambassador.

When King Fahd assumed power in the Kingdom, Newman was so impressed he declared "I saw that his Majesty met with everybody in all the provinces in order to establish this system of multifaceted contact, that is the secret of his success." Another former U.S. Ambassador to the Kingdom J. G. West, once said "I was impressed by their warmth and hospitality and the friendly feeling that existed between the leaders of their country and the United States."

An important meeting between President Ronald Reagan and then Crown Prince Fahd in 1981 took place during the North-South Summit in Cancun, Mexico. When King Fahd visited President Reagan in Washington, D.C., in February, 1985, his principal message was "The United States of America has a responsibility to make use of its powerful influence and to make a strong effort for achieving peace between Israel and the Arab neighbors, through a just solution to the Palestinian question." King Fahd declared "The Palestinian question is the cause of instability and turmoil in the region. I hope, Mr. President, that your administration will support the just cause of the Palestinian people."

Prince Bandar Bin Sultan, in the summer of 1993, said the Kingdom has a "strong, vested interest in strengthening the understanding and the bonds between the Moslem world and the West. We broke with the past and went to the Madrid Peace Conference and into the multilateral talks to resolve the outstanding regional issues between Israelis and Arabs. We are hopeful that a just, comprehensive peace could be achieved based on U.N. Resolutions 242 and 338 and will result in achieving peace for land, the legitimate political rights of the Palestinian people and security for all states in the region. It would be a setback for all of us to seek to repair the international order in one arena while it comes apart in the Balkans. Politics being what it is, we would have far more political ground at home on behalf of a regional settlement on Arab-Israeli matters if there were to be greater Western concern for Bosnia."

In the same spirit of justice and common interests in their message of Eid Al-Adha, in the summer of 1993, King Fahd and crown Prince Abdullah stated "We have been monitoring the peace process, and feel that some fundamentals will ultimately lead to peace. In the forefront of these is the clear and candid acceptance by all of the principle of exchanging land for peace in accordance with (UN Security Council) Resolutions 242 and 338 which guarantee the legitimate rights of the people of Palestine and guarantee security and peace for all . . . although the previous nine rounds of (peace) talks have not led to an agreement on a number of substantial points so far, the fact that the dialogue is continuing affirms that there is a common understanding that there is no other alternative for peace. . . . The facts of history demonstrate beyond the shadow of a doubt that conflicts and wars do not achieve either victories or gains. The Israelis must come to understand that expansionist policies are no longer acceptable to the world community and that the security guarantees they have so often talked about cannot be achieved as long as the Israeli occupation of the land and their policy of hegemony and domination are continued. Such guarantees will be achieved only under peaceful coexistence between the neighboring states and peoples. . . . The peace which we all seek will leave the door wide open for real and comprehensive stability which all peoples have been longing for and which we all should cooperate to achieve."

The second generation of the Saudi Royal Family carries with pride the torch of this special relationship. During the official dedication of King Abdulaziz Chair in Islamic Studies at the University of California at Santa Barbara on January 29, 1992, Prince Mohammed Bin Fahd, Governor of the Eastern Province declared "We in the Eastern Province were hosts to more than half a million troops from 23 nations. The courage and discipline of the American fighting men and women were greatly appreciated by us. We hope those events have brought us closer together."

This gratitude was also evident when Prince Bandar Bin Sultan stated to a conference sponsored by the U.S. Central Command (Centcom) in the summer of 1993 "To be here is to acknowledge an appreciation and to reaffirm a partnership. After Desert Storm, we have become bonded in a unique way . . . . we were both—you on this end, and the societies of the GCC (Gulf Cooperation Council)—tested in the military campaign against the aggression of Saddam Hussein. You were steadfast, you came in style and did order's work. We, for our part, stood our ground, we did not dodge the crisis, and we fought side-by-side. We got to know one another a good deal better after the ordeal was behind us." He went on to say "But those of us who have cast their lot with you for so long—and did so even when it was not fashionable in our sector of the world to be friends of America—know that there is no substitute for American engagement and leadership. Bosnia demonstrates the continuous need for American leadership in Europe. You are also needed to help keep the peace in Asia . . . (and) in the waters of the Gulf, to protect critical commerce of all the world, to sustain the balance of power and to keep the flow of oil to the world uninterrupted."

From the American realm, the new generation was no less eloquent in its dedication and devotion to the special relationship. On the Kingdom's National Day, September 23, 1993, President Bill Clinton of the U.S. said in a letter to King Fahd "I consider the Kingdom of Saudi Arabia to be a very close ally among the community of nations and a promoter of stability in the Middle East. Your effective rule that has lasted for 11 years is evidence of your dedicated efforts towards an ever-increasing role of the Kingdom in international relations." The depth of American-Saudi relations was earnestly, devoutly and affectionately expressed by C. W. Freeman, former U.S. Ambassador to Saudi Arabia when he spoke of the "profound friendship," historically enjoyed by the two countries in "leading the international effort to combat and reverse Iraqi aggression in Kuwait and the threat this posed to the countries of the Gulf Cooperation Council. . . . As the American people prepare to celebrate their 216th year of independence, the 30,000 Americans who live and work in this Kingdom will reflect upon the events which have taken place here over the past few years. They will be thankful for the strong and enduring friendship between the people of Saudi Arabia and the United States. . . . For the past nearly three years, I have had the high honor to serve as Ambassador of the United States of America to the Kingdom of Saudi Arabia and as President Bush's personal representative to the Custodian of the Two Holy Mosques King Fahd Bin Abdulaziz. During that time, under the impact of events and of wise leadership in both of our countries, our nations' commitment to each other's well-being has been tested, and it has survived and strengthened."

As he prepared to leave the Kingdom, he emotionally expressed confidence that "our friendship and cooperation will remain sound. For it is a friendship which is the sum of the strength of each of the countless personal bonds that exist between the Saudi and American people–from the highest levels of leadership to the ordinary citizens of both countries. I know, for I have become part of this fabric of abiding friendship. I may be leaving the Kingdom of Saudi Arabia, but the Kingdom, its King and other leaders and its people, can never leave my heart."

Oil Policy

Saudi Arabia followed a policy of support for the international economic community within a practical mission of moderation. Its policy and leadership, toward world oil production within the Organization of Petroleum Exporting Countries, were very instrumental in protecting the stability of world industries and economies.

The proven oil reserves in Saudi Arabia now stand over 260 billion barrels; this is more than twenty five percent of the world's crude reserves. In October, 1993 the Kingdom surpassed Russia and became the number-one oil producer and top exporter of crude oil and natural gas liquids in the world.

Oil discovery and production by 1938 added to the strategic and spiritual importance of this land, birthplace of the Prophet, and guardian to the Holy Moslem Shrines. Saudi Arabia is the heartbeat of the Arab world, the spiritual leader for all Moslems of the globe, and the energy giant with undisputable worldwide moderating force and influence.

Throughout the world and, especially, in the Organization of Petroleum Exporting Countries (OPEC), the Saudi voice has been a vibrant voice for moderation and stability. On May 6, 1991, Hisham Nazer, Minister of Petroleum and Mineral Resources said "Our oil policy should not be viewed apart from the overall conceptual framework of planning. As owners of at least a quarter of the world's oil reserves, we have to take the long term view, for Saudi Arabia will be producing oil when many other fields would have gone dry. Short term aberrations in the oil market will spring forth every now and then. One has to be flexible and efficient enough to meet them head on. Saudi Arabia is not deflected by them to lose sight of the long term goal of market stability and a comprehensive integration of the oil industry . . . our joint venture with Texaco (Star Enterprise), in the United States, and other upcoming joint ventures around the world will give us the downstream linkages which will contribute to the stability of the market. Our control of our own tanker fleet will add further to the integration process.

(Saudi Arabian Marketing and Refining Company (Samarec) was merged in June, 1993 with the largest oil company in the world, Saudi Aramco. It was recently acknowledged by the allies during the Gulf crisis when it kept the allied war machine fully oiled). Let me quote just one example from a letter I received from General Schwarzkopf about Samarec," "The skill and speed with which you were able to react to this crisis attest to your efficiency and organizational skills. We at United States Central Command are very proud of your success in meeting the enormous challenges we faced."

In Aramco World, issue of September–October, 1993, A. Clark said, ". . . in 1990 when nearly 4.6 million barrels per day of oil production vanished from world oil markets in the wake of the Gulf crisis and the subsequent international embargo on crude from Iraq and Kuwait, between August and the end of that year, in a remarkable effort, Saudi Aramco was able to boost its output from 5.3 million barrels per day to 8.5 million barrels–a 62 percent increase–to help stabilize the market. Oil prices, which had ballooned to more than $40 a barrel, quickly retreated; an energy crunch was avoided that could have seriously harmed an already shaky world economy." He went on to say, "Today, Saudi Aramco has a global marketing organization with subsidiary offices in New York, London and Tokyo–and sells directly to more than 50 refiners worldwide. It owns a tanker fleet. And it has made big investments in refineries and product-distribution networks, including thousands of gasoline stations, in the United States, South Korea and the Philippines.

This "downstream" expansion effort aims to "protect and potentially increase the market share of Arabian crude, maximize the revenues from the sale of Arabian crude, and provide secure outlets through strategic alliances with refining companies in our major markets," says Abdallah Jum'ah, executive vice president of international operations.

Saudi Arabia has deep concerns for the health of the global economy and for world oil markets and supplies. At a conference held in Houston, Texas in February, 1993, Minister of Petroleum and Mineral Resources Hisham Nazer stated "Saudi Arabia is a major stabilizing force in the oil market. We have endeavored over the years to assure the world of secure oil supplies and stable prices. We are investing billions of dollars to increase our production capacity to assure the world of adequate supplies in the years ahead. We are building a state-of-the-art shipping fleet to guard against oil spills. We are upgrading our refineries to supply a cleaner barrel to the market. We are investing in downstream joint ventures all over the world to develop an integrative process which will add to both security and stability."

Benevolence to the World

Saudi Arabia's generous financial contributions speak loudly of the Kingdom's dedication to the United Nations success and progress. The Kingdom ranks fifteenth in its contributions among the more than one hundred and eighty member nations. It ranks tenth in terms of per capita contributions.

The goodwill of Saudi Arabia and its generous contributions cross many borders around the globe. Its compassion, generosity and help stretches from Turkey and Bangladesh to the earthquake victims of Yemen and Mexico, volcano and flood victims of Columbia, Moslems and Christians of formerly war-torn Lebanon, to the famine-stricken nations of Africa such as Sudan and Somalia, the ravaged and destitute people in Bosnia-Herzegovina, and other peoples in need around the globe.

According to the Royal Embassy of Saudi Arabia in Washington, D.C., and other sources, assistance offered by the Kingdom of Saudi Arabia to developing nations in the period 1973–1989 in the form of grants and easy development loans through bilateral, regional and international channels amounted to $59.47 billion, (5.45% of the Kingdom's GNP), with 58% of that total given as grants. Seventy developing nations have benefited from this assistance: 38 in Africa, 25 in Asia, and seven in other regions of the world.

The Kingdom occupies second place of donor nations after the United States when the absolute size of assistance is considered. In the period from 1982 to 1986, the Kingdom ranked fourth among the donor nations in the world. In terms of the percentage of donations to GNP, the Kingdom ranks first. In 1988, the percentage was 2.8%. That is more than seven times the 0.36% for the industrial nations.

Among the OPEC members, the Kingdom occupied first place, with Saudi assistance representing 79% of the total OPEC aid package in the period 1980 to 1987. In 1989, that percentage rose to approximately 90%. The percentage of grants, monetary and development loans offered by the Kingdom ranged from 55% to 60%. These included several interest-free long-term loans that might reach up to 25 years with a 10 year grace period.

The less developed nations have been awarded special attention by the Kingdom in view of the harsh economic conditions they faced. The Kingdom meant from the beginning to make most of the aid package to these nations in the form of grants. Many loans were forgiven including seven and a half billion dollars to Egypt. The volume of direct loans amounted to approximately $5 billion, benefiting 26 developing nations.

Loans made by the Saudi Development Fund (1976–1989) amounting to $7.34 billion benefitted 60 nations and financed development projects for social, health and human services such as roads, water, railways, education, culture, and other infrastructure projects. The percentage of grants was 55% with a repayment period of 25 years and service charges ranging from 2.5% to 3%.

The United Nations Conference on Trade and Development stated that the average official aid offered by the Kingdom in 1973–1981 represented 7.7% of its GNP, and for the period 1981–1987, the percentage of Saudi aid was 3.16% of the GNP. This percentage exceeds by far the 0.07% officially set by the United Nations as percentage of development aid to GNP of donor nations.

On the international level, the Kingdom contributed to the programs and organizations of the United Nations, enabling them to carry out their various human, social and development programs. The Kingdom is a principal contributor to the resources of a large number of regional and international development organizations, contributing no less than 20% of the capital of 12 of these organizations, notably the OPEC International Development Fund, the Islamic Bank for Development, the Arab Bank for Economic Development in Africa, the African Development Bank, the African Development Fund, the Arab Fund for Economic and Social Development, and the International Fund for Agricultural Development. Furthermore, the Kingdom undertakes an active role in supporting international financial institutions. In addition to its growing contribution to the group of the World Bank and the IMF (International Monertary Fund), the Kingdom provided huge loans in the past few years to the two institutions adding to their ability to respond to the growing needs of the developing nations. In addition, the Kingdom has recently decided to participate in financing the programs of structural reform undertaken by the IMF, thus contributing $200 million to provide additional financing to the impoverished nations targeted to benefit from such programs in view of their acute financial problems, deterioration of their balance of payments and the increasing burden of their foreign debts.

Regarding the African nations in particular, the Kingdom's assistance totaled more than $17.4 billion in the period 1973–1989, of which $10.114 billion were grants representing 59% of the total aid to these nations. The rest, $7.3 billion, was offered in the form of very easy loans with no conditions attached. African nations below the Sahara enjoyed a considerable share of the Kingdom's attention in recent years in view of the dire need that required immediate consideration. The Kingdom was at the top of the list of nations that rushed to confront the drought problem that has plagued Africa since 1981. The Kingdom contributed a total of $430 million as non-refundable grants to be used for drilling wells and in rural development in the Sahel countries. These grants were also meant to alleviate the impact of the drought through increasing water and food supply in other affected areas, and helping find solutions to the problems of the refugees. The Kingdom is committed to contribute $100 million to the World Bank Program in the countries of Africa below the Sahara.

The extensive aid given to Iraq prior to the occupation of Kuwait amounted to a staggering figure of nearly twenty six billion U.S. dollars, distributed as follows:

Aid Given to Iraq

Item	Amount in U.S. Dollars
Non-remitted assistance	5,843,287,671.23
Soft cash loans	9,246,575,342.46
Development loans	95,890,410.95
Transport & Military Supplies	3,739,184,077.66
Oil assistance	6,751,159,583.00
Industrial products for reconstruction of Basra	16,772,800.00
Amounts due Saudi Arabian Basic Industries Corp. (Sabic)	20,266,667.00
270 trucks, tractors, trailers and other vehicles	21,333,333.50
Total	25,734,469,885.80

Saudi Arabia was also very generous to Jordan. The massive aid of approximately 6.7 billion U.S. dollars to a small nation helped prop King Hussein's government and financed many vital projects in Jordan. This is illustrated as follows:

An Example of Aid Granted by the Kingdom of Saudi Arabia (Approximately 6.7 Billion US$ to Jordan)

Breakdown:

		U.S. Dollars	
(A)	*Free Aid:*		
	(1)	4,340,000,000	up till 1980
	(2)	509,000,000	Military Aid
	(3)	414,570,000	Budgetary Aid Covering Deficit and Oil Supply
	(4)	275,428,000	Social and Health Aid
	(5)	214,285,000	Aid for the Government of Jordan 1990
	(6)	107,143,000	Economic Aid 1990
	(7)	214,285,000	Economic Aid 1991
	(8)	160,000,000	Oil Supply (March 1984)
(B)	*Loans:*		
	(1)	100,000,000	Cash loan 1981
	(2)	50,000,000	Cash loan 1989/1990
	(3)	41,000,000	Loan for Oil Supply
	(4)	23,142,000	For Al-Aqaba Port Expansion 1977
(C)	*Loans Provided by Saudi Development Fund:*		
	(1)	48,714,000	Amman Water Supply Project
	(2)	20,034,000	Aghwar Irrigation Project
	(3)	23,965,000	For Vocational Secondary Schools
	(4)	20,000,000	To finance road Construction (Zarah-Ghor)
	(5)	28,000,000	Al-Hussein Electrical Project
	(6)	7,500,000	Al-Aqaba Electrical Project
	(7)	25,708,000	Al-Aqaba Electrical Project
	(8)	11,000,000	Al-Hasakah Railroad
	(9)	17,500,000	Al-Aqaba Industrial Port
	(10)	20,000,000	College of Medicine
	(11)	14,245,000	Al-Aqaba Water Supply
	(12)	9,428,000	Irbid Industrial City
	(13)	11,428,000	Road Construction South of Aqaba
	(14)	11,428,000	Al-Zarga River Basin Development
Total		6,773,875,000	

Another country benefiting from the benevolence of Saudi Arabia is Sudan. The total aid received by this country was nearly three billion dollars as shown:

An Example of Aid Granted by the Kingdom of Saudi Arabia (about 2.7 Billion US$ to Sudan)

Breakdown:

		U.S. Dollars	
(A)	*Free Aid:*		
	(1)	359,000,000	Petroleum Aid, up to 1991
	(2)	418,000,000	Military Aid
	(3)	572,000,000	Support for Sudan's Economy and other social and humanitarian endeavors
(B)	*Loans:*		
	(1)	1,049,620,000	Cash loans
(C)	*Development Loans:*		
	(1)	26,340,000	Water Project to Rahd
	(2)	25,490,000	Hyya-Kasla Road
	(3)	9,800,000	Port Sudan Airport
	(4)	4,410,000	Development of West Safana
	(5)	9,110,000	Satellite Communication
	(6)	6,340,000	Communication Network
	(7)	1,170,000	Ministry of Education
	(8)	23,180,000	Niala-Kas-Zalingi Road
	(9)	32,920,000	Sikr Canana
	(10)	4,190,000	Rahd Agricultural Road
	(11)	15,560,000	Rebuilding Al-Jazirah
	(12)	29,410,000	Building Sugar Plants
	(13)	18,900,000	Rebuilding Al-Jazirah (second loan)
	(14)	11,730,000	Supporting the Agricultural Sector
	(15)	9,600,000	Equipment for Sudan's Railway
	(16)	14,530,000	Building Sugar Plants (second loan)
	(17)	50,000,000	Covering Monetary Deficits in Development Projects
Total		About 2.7 Billion	

In addition to this, humanitarian aid is substantial. As an example, in August, 1988, an aerial bridge of nearly 200 planes and several ships carried badly needed supplies to the Sudanese people. Add to this many Islamic and humanitarian initiatives personally undertaken by King Fahd and the Saudi citizens in support of the Sudanese, and you will realize the magnitude of this aid offered by the Kingdom, in line with its policy of compassion and goodwill.

Neighboring Yemen had vast numbers of their countrymen working in Saudi Arabia. Their cash remittances helped prop their economy for decades. When a devastating earthquake hit Yemen, Saudis came forth with compassion and care providing tents and blankets for the homeless, medical supplies for the injured and food for the hungry. Through the years, the Kingdom was generous in contributing needed aid for social programs, building utilities, urban projects, and the reconstruction of the area damaged by earthquake.

During every Pilgrimage season and on the occasion of Eid-Al-Adha or holiday of sacrifice, thousands of sheep and some camels and cattle are donated by the Pilgrims and then slaughtered and processed for distribution to the needy throughout the world. This humanitarian project began in 1983 (1403 A.H.). Between 1983–1992 (1403–1412 A.H.), more than four million head of sheep and 25,000 camels and cattle were distributed to needy Moslems around the globe. First installments were shipped by air to refugees in Sudan, Djibouti and Afghanis in Pakistan. During the Pilgrimage season of 1993, more than half a million processed and refrigerated head of sheep were sent to more than twenty three nations including Egypt, Sudan, Jordan, Syria, Lebanon, Somalia, Pakistan, Bangladesh, Djibouti, Mauritania, Senegal, Gambia, Sierra Leone, Guinea, Tchad, Bourkina Faso, Mali, Niger and other countries. In 1992, 410,556 head of sheep were processed, of which 109,070 were distributed to the needy in Mecca and to the Pilgrims, while 301,486 sheep were shipped to the needy in twenty-three nations of the world.

Presently the Kingdom allocates five percent of its gross national product for foreign aid. It is very active in the international monetary fund and contributes extensively to the stability of financial organizations around the world. The total aid for Arab development totaled 6.3 billion dollars in 1990, the year the Gulf War began. Ninety-nine percent of this aid came from three Gulf countries: 59% from Saudi Arabia, 26% from Kuwait and 14% from the United Arab Emirates. In addition to the enormous monetary aid and humanitarian supplies, Saudi Arabia practices numerous other gestures of goodwill. For example, the Holy Qoran is printed in Madina and millions of copies are distributed free of charge to Moslems around the globe.

Also on January 19, 1992, Prince Mohammed Bin Fahd Bin Abdulaziz, Governor of the Eastern Province, inaugurated the King Abdulaziz Chair for Islamic Studies at the University of California at Santa Barbara. It is intended to promote understanding of the Islamic world–one billion strong–and to build new bridges of understanding between Islam and the West. Prince Mohammed, a proud graduate of this university, generously supported the establishment of this Chair. It is a timely Chair which will contribute its share toward the spirit of cementing Saudi-American relations. Similar Chairs were also established. They shall shed the true light on the Islamic culture which is tolerant and just at the core. This came at a critical time when many voices of extremism are trying to dominate the Islamic World and spread terror and destruction. These fundamentalist extremist forces are truly alien to the true meaning and spirit of Islam and they will fail! Islam means peace. Moslems greet others by saying "Assalamou Aleikom" or peace be upon you.

On the tenth of June, 1993, Harvard Law School received five million dollars from King Fahd to establish the most extensive program for the study of Islamic Law.

According to R. C. Clark, Dean of Harvard Law School, "This is an historic step forward in many ways and for many people. Scholars and students, practitioners and policy makers–all will benefit immeasurably. With one-fifth of the earth's population living in the Islamic world, it is imperative that study of the highest quality be devoted to Islamic law. The foresight and generosity of King Fahd ensure that the world will always have at Harvard Law School a center for serious, objective academic study of this vital field."

The president of Harvard University, N. L. Rudenstine said "This exceptionally generous gift is a very important event for Harvard. We are strongly committed to strengthening our research and education in the broad field of Islamic studies, and this gift will make a vital contribution to our scholarship and teaching about the Islamic world. The Law School effort will be greatly enhanced by this gift, as will many students and scholars throughout the whole university community."

In this regard, the custodian of the Two Holy Mosques King Fahd and Crown Prince Abdullah stated on may 22, 1994: "Our contributions to the promotion of Islamic studies are not confined to Arab and Islamic universities. Other beneficiaries include some of the major universities in the world such as America's Harvard University, Johns Hopkins University, Duke University, Shaw University, Colorado University, Howard University, the American University in Washington, De Paul University, Syracuse Institute, the Middle East Institute in Washington which showed interest in Islamic studies and assigned a chair and a centre for this purpose, not to mention the Islamic universities in Malaysia, Niger, Uganda, Pakistan, Sudan, Palestine, Algeria, Sri Lanka, Morocco and Indonesia. Scholarships have also been given as part of manpower development plans."

The Honorable and humanitarian role of Saudi Arabia was best summarized in a joint message to the Pilgrims given by King Fahd and crown Prince Abdullah. ". . . There were also those who called for the redistribution of wealth with a view to securing equality between the rich and the poor and who would insinuate, whenever they referred to Saudi Arabia explicitly or implicitly, that the Kingdom had failed to do what it should–in their opinion–have done in this respect. We wish that these critics had given as freely and generously to the cause they claimed to espouse as the Kingdom has since it received Allah's Bounty in plenty.

The Kingdom of Saudi Arabia has spent thousands of billions of its income on charity. It has given a great deal to developing and sisterly countries in a spirit of genuine and brotherly cooperation, keeping all the time a low profile and never trying to play up its role in this connection. So many are those by whom the Kingdom stood in joy and adversity, in private and in public.

The Kingdom has often taken the initiative to give relief aid to victims of natural disasters in various countries. It has been doing all that as part of its duty under the umbrella of Islamic brotherhood and in compliance with a saying by the Prophet-peace be upon him–which states that Moslems are like a structure in which the various parts reinforce one another . . . It must be clear by now that the Kingdom has satisfied the requirements specified by the rules of Islam many times over."

The Saudi government has been very generous at home and abroad. It is a benevolent monarchy led by a compassionate leader who seeks counsel not only from his capable cadre of Ministers but always takes into account the welfare of every Saudi citizen. The foundation for the government is Islamic law.

The strength of this monarchy emanates from Islam and its dedication to moderation, a strong sense of justice, and its willingness to seek consensus from its people. The King is a monarch who has and continues to establish understanding and closeness to his citizenry. He is a father figure and a ruler at the same time. The focus of this monarchy is peace at home and abroad, compassion for mankind and prosperity for all its people.

Chapter 4

Islam

One of the great religions of the world is Islam. After its birth, it spread like wildfire. Today, there are more than one billion Moslems around the world. The word "Islam" in Arabic means "submission," that is submission to God, "Allah" in Arabic. The followers are called "Moslems," meaning "those who submit" to God.

Islam is the cornerstone of Saudi society. Saudi Arabia is not only an economic world power, it is the focal point for all Moslems of the world, who must face Mecca, in their prayers, five times a day. Since Islam is not well understood in the West and since it directly affects the lives of one fifth of the world population, it is imperative that we clearly describe this religion for the benefit of anyone interested in it or in Saudi Arabia.

Birth of Islam

The Prophet Mohammed, peace be upon him, was born in Mecca around the year 570 A.D. He is the last of all prophets of God, who included Abraham, Moses and Jesus. His family, Qoureish, was the ruling tribe, but he was an orphan in childhood.

The Prophet was a man of truth and generosity who disliked the degradation of society. He enjoyed meditation in the Hira cave, located near the top of the "Mountain of Light"–Jabal Al-Nour in the vicinity of Mecca. It is here, at 40 years of age, he received the first revelations from God. The year was 610 A.D. and the Angel Gabriel carried the divine message to the Prophet. Preaching God's message was not accepted by many in Mecca, especially the mighty and powerful. There were many pagans at the time who saw a threat from Islam, the new montheistic religion. The believers were persecuted and harassed.

To avoid an assassination plot against him, the Prophet and his followers emigrated to a town 260 miles to the north known as Yathrib, later renamed as Madina. The year of migration was 622

A.D., which constituted the first Hijra year (1 A.H.) in the Moslem Calendar. Moslems controlled Madina in 625 A.D. By the year 629 A.D. the Prophet and his followers reentered Mecca and the idols in the Ka'aba were destroyed without bloodshed.

Ka'aba or the house of God is located in Mecca. It is a cube-shaped stone building, fifty-foot high, with the sacred black stone fixed outside in one of its corners. Moslems around the world face Mecca in their prayers, because the Grand Mosque (Al-Masjid Al-Harām) that contains the Ka'aba is in Mecca. The Ka'aba is draped in black and gold material which is traditionally renewed annually. It is the House of Worship which God commanded Abraham and Ishmael to build over four milleniums ago. God ordered Abraham to summon people to visit the Ka'aba. Today, the pilgrims respond by declaring "Labbeika Allahomma Labbeik," meaning "At Thy Service, O'Lord." Its black cornerstone was cast down by God to Adam after he was removed from the Garden of Eden. This is a symbol of God's reconciliation with mankind. Islam became dominant in Mecca, Madina and shortly thereafter throughout the Arabian Peninsula. The words that descended from God were gathered into various chapters called Souras. They constituted what is known as the *Holy Qoran*, (also known as the Koran) which in Arabic means recitation (from the verb qara'a meaning to read or recite). The Qoran is the cornerstone of the Moslem faith. It is the Moslem Holy Book, which in time became the greatest pillar of the Arabic language and Arabic literature. Beyond any doubt, the Qoran contains the finest and truly most imaginative prose of any literature in any time.

The Holy Qoran is considered as the constitution of the Kingdom of Saudi Arabia, and the law of the land or Islamic law is *Shari'a*. It is derived and based on the Qoran. The Sunna and Hadith are complementary to Shari'a. *Sunna* or "way" to be followed by a Moslem, entails the practice, deeds, sayings and traditions of the Prophet. Next to the Qoran, it is the second authority for all Moslems. The *Hadith* is a true report of what the Prophet said, did, or approved as related and preserved by his companions. Other sources of the law include: ijtihad by highly authoritative religious scholars–progressive reasoning by analogy, ijm'a–consensus, Qias–analogy. But everything must be according to the pronouncement and spirit of the Qoran. The five pillars of Islam must be fulfilled by each Moslem during a lifetime. These are:

1. *Shahadah* or witness and profession of faith, that there is only one God and the Prophet Mohammed is His Messenger. Basic in the Moslem faith is the call to the worship of one God, namely: "there is no God but God and Mohammed is the Messenger of God." The Arabic equivalent is: Shahadat an La Ileha Ila Lloh! Mohammed Rasoul Lloh.

2. *Salah* or performance of prayer. In their prayers, Moslems, individually or in groups face Mecca five times a day at dawn, noon, mid-afternoon, sunset and early evening. The prayer is conducted in the Arabic language and led by a person chosen by the group. While it is recommended to perform prayer in a mosque, however, it can take place elsewhere.

3. *Zakat* or the payment each year of two and a half percent of one's net worth. This money goes to help the needy and the poor.

4. *Siam Ramadan* or fasting by every Moslem during the holy month of Ramadan. Fasting takes place from dawn or first light until sunset. During this period, one must not eat, drink, smoke, or carry on sexual activity. People who are sick, the elderly, pregnant women and those who are traveling may be excused and should make up the days missed at a later date in the year. Those physically incapable must feed sixty needy persons for everyday of fast missed. Fasting is regarded as a healthy exercise making people more sensitive to the sufferings of the needy. Moslems break the fast with a light meal called "iftar" or break–fast. Communities and streets become alive at night. Everyone is usually in a festive mood. The nights of Ramadan are marked with religious activities, including long periods of prayers (Tarawih) performed after the last prayer of the day (Salat Al-Isha). One of the major holidays is Eid Al-Fitr which marks the end of Ramadan. Celebrations go on for four days. It is a happy time especially for children who traditionally receive clothing, toys and other gifts.

5. *Hajj* or pilgrimage to the holy city of Mecca must be undertaken by every capable Moslem at least once in his/her lifetime. The person must be physically and financially in shape to perform this task. The Hajj is a very moving, spir-

itual experience. It is the ultimate highlight in a person's religious life. Over two million pilgrims come from Saudi Arabia and the four corners of the globe. This massive religious gathering is carried out in an orderly and humble manner. Each person is draped with a simple white cloth called ihram. All are equal under God as class distinctions and varied cultures all dissipate during this holy occasion.

The Pilgrimage is characterized by the orderly movement of several masses of people. The logistics and management of these movements are mind-boggling indeed! The Saudi Government, under the leadership of The Custodian of the Two Holy Mosques King Fahd, met this challenge by the most sophisticated network of walkways, bridges and tunnels, complete with a multitude of services. These include hygienic bathrooms, cold water distribution, health care, guides, food distribution, and a secure environment. Major gigantic gatherings in the world such as the Olympics, major rallies and major conferences are all dwarfed when compared with this religious procession.

The Hajj rituals are the same as the one (and only one) performed by the Prophet centuries ago. The conclusion of the Hajj is marked as the second major holiday for all Moslems: Eid Al-Adha or Feast of Sacrifice. Sheep and goats are slaughtered as a sacrifice and their meat is donated to the needy across the world. Gifts, pleasantries and a jovial mood prevail during the Eid of good wishes and goodwill.

Great Conquests of Islam

Islam spread into the northern countries: Palestine, Syria, Iran, Iraq, and also to the south into Egypt. The great political success of this new religion, establishing itself next to the Byzantine and Persian empires, is very startling indeed, since the followers of the Prophet were poor, both in numbers and material resources.

The Moslem religion nourished its believers and Bedouin followers with a great zeal, especially at a time of feuds and wars between the neighboring empires in the North and East. The Roman Empire had succumbed long ago and its successor, the Christian Byzantine Empire at Constantinople, was continually engaged in warfare with the Sassanid of Iran (Persia). These devastating wars, heavy taxation and disregard for the local population, along with sectarian differences in the never-ending theological debates in the Christian world, created a very ripe atmosphere to change the rules and open the gates for the Moslem newcomers.

These differences among the Christians were very acute, to the point that on some occasions persecuted minorities opened the gates of Byzantine cities to the Moslems. The lightning speed with which Islam developed with great impact on life and culture in the area extending from China to Spain, is indeed one of the most remarkable features of the history of mankind.

After the death of the Prophet Mohammed at the age of 63, the leadership passed on to Abou Bakr, who was the first caliph or "Khalifa," meaning Successor. His most brilliant general was Khalid Ibn Al-Walid, who led the Arab drive to break the Byzantine and Sassanid Empires. As the Arab army moved forward, the number of Moujehidine swelled by large conversions to Islam. The Byzantine army was defeated at the Yarmouk River in 636 A.D. Iraq and Persia fell between 637 and 650. The city of Jerusalem fell in 638 and Egypt was conquered in 641. Conquests continued for a century until the Arab Empire extended from China to France, giving a unique feature in history, the likes of which, in vigor and lightning speed, has never been duplicated.

The Caliphate was first in the *Oumayyad* family "Al-Oumaweeyyeen," from the Qoureish tribe, and their rule was centered in Damascus. Rivalries later developed and resulted in dividing the Moslem religion into Sunni and Shi'a (Shi'ite) sects. After the murder of the third Caliph Outhman, his cousin Ali, who was a son-in-law to the Prophet, became the fourth Caliph. Mouaweeia, the governor of Syria, accused Ali of complicity in the murder of Outhman and finally gained the Caliphate after Ali was assassinated.

With this came the major division in the Moslem faith: the Sunni, who believed that the Caliphate was an elective office, and the Shi'a, who believed that the heirs of Prophet Mohammed, namely his daughter Fatima and her husband Ali, were entitled to the Caliphate.

One more attempt was made to wrest the Caliphate for Ali's son, Hussain. But he and his followers were murdered at Karbala, Iraq, in October, 680 A.D. The most important Shi'a Shrines are at

Karbala and Al-Najaf in Iraq. As the division spread, Moslems were divided into several sects.

The Oumayyad dynasty was finally overthrown in 750 A.D. by the descendents of Abbas, an uncle to the Prophet. The *Abbasid* dynasty ruled from Baghdad until its shattering by the Mongols in 1258. Prosperity reached its greatest peak during the Caliphate of Horoun Al-Rashid (786–809).

It was during the two decades of the rule of Horoun Al-Rashid that the Arab Empire distinguished itself with significant achievements in mathematics, medicine, astronomy, art and philosophy. Translations in these fields flourished, and the works of Greeks, Romans and Persians were adapted, improved upon with innovations and later transmitted to the West when Europe was still in the Dark Ages.

In 1097, the *Crusaders* from Europe began their invasion of Syria. This was done in the name of defending Christianity and the Holy Land. They held Jerusalem from 1099 until its recapture by Saleh Eddine (Saladin) in the year 1187. The Crusaders–with trading, commercial, and religious motives–felt the strong influence of Eastern civilization; a civilization which helped bring about the European Renaissance. They also left their impact on a segment of the people in the Middle East. By the year 1299, the last Christian stronghold had fallen. The conquering of the two empires of the time, namely, the Sassanid and the Byzantine, was achieved with high speed. The first real setback for the Arabs and their conquests came from North Africa at the hands of none other than the Berbers, who were much like the Arabs.

The Berbers were nomads who did not like either city dwelling or luxury living. Their features were of the Caucasian type. Some of them slender and tall, others dark or blond and blue-eyed. For nearly one thousand years, beginning in 1200 B.C., the Berbers were ruled by the Phoenicians, who founded the Carthage state, based on Carthage near the city of Tunis in present-day Tunisia.

The Phoenicians were succeeded by the Romans after the destruction of Carthage in 146 B.C. The Roman rule remained for nearly 650 years and was followed by the vandals of the Byzantine Empire. Although there was disparity under the Byzantine rule, a small number of the people of North Africa became Latin-speaking Christians. The large majority of the people did not assimilate with the Roman culture. This was in contrast to the population of Western Europe. The Arabs took some time to subdue the Berbers and bring them under their empire. When this was done, it was done with great success. Where the Romans had failed, the Arabs succeeded in assimilating them as completely as could be. This was due mainly to the natural affinity in culture and way of life which existed between the Arabs and the Berbers, coupled with the vast power already mastered by the Islamic religion. Many of these facts have been reported by the Arab historian, Ibn Khaldoun, who was a native of Tunis.

Ultimately, Christianity was replaced by Islam, and Latin was replaced by Arabic in the entire North African area which had been under the Roman influence. The Latin and Greek populations of the cities left for Spain and Italy. The Berbers continued to use their own language after they had adopted Islam as their religion. By the year 714 the entire countries of Spain and Portugal were in the firm grip of Arab hands. Three years later their armies broke through the Pyrénées into the fertile land of France. At this point their advance was halted. Although they continued to carry on some raids and establish temporary colonies, the weather of Northern and Central Europe was never what the Arabs really desired.

Prior to Islam great Arab poetry was written. It gave an insight into the Arab character, depicted the most impressive features of Arab tradition: enthusiasm, hospitality and deep emotions. However, some of the finest Arab poetry was authored during the Abbasid era when Baghdad reached the apogee of its glory under the Caliph Horoun Al-Rashid, from the year 786 to 809, and his son, the Caliph Al-Mamoun (813–833).

A large number of mosques and government palaces with many beautiful gardens and pavilions were all about. Baghdad was known as a city of pleasure; "the Paris of the Ninth Century." The Golden Age of the Arabs brought to civilization skills in art, philosophy, science and a great culture, all of which enlightened many civilizations that followed. Several Arab cities prospered, and became centers of luxury and wealth, among them Baghdad, Basra, Cairo, Alexandria, Damascus, and Aleppo. One should never forget the fine contributions made by the Arabs in medicine, poetry, algebra and chemistry. Arab ingenuity created new inventions and improved on previous civilizations. Through translations of many works of science, art, literature and technology, the Arabs not only put to good use the knowledge that existed before them, they have also kept the torch of wisdom and knowledge burning–a torch that enlightened Europe during its Dark Ages.

Interesting to Know!

- The Fatiha or opening chapter of the Qoran is recited at the beginning of every prayer. It reflects the essence and true spirit of Islam. Here is its meaning in English:
  "In the name of Allah, Most Gracious, Most Merciful. Praise be to Allah The Cherisher and Sustainer of the Worlds: Most Gracious, Most Merciful; Master of the Day of Judgement. Thee do we worship, And Thine aid we seek. Show us the straight way, The way of those on whom Thou has bestowed Thy Grace, Those whose (portion) Is not wrath. And who go not astray."

- The call to Prayer:
  "God is most great. God is most great.
  God is most great. God is most great.
  I testify that there is no god except God.
  I testify that there is no god except God.
  I testify that Muhammad is the messenger of God.
  I testify that Muhammad is the messenger of God.
  Come to prayer! Come to prayer!
  Come to success (in this life and the Hereafter)!
  Come to success!
  God is most great. God is most great.
  There is no god except God."

- Islam is one of the great religions preaching justice, tolerance and goodness to one's fellowman. It tolerates other beliefs and during the conquests of Islam, minorities were treated fairly and justly. When the Caliph Omar entered Jersusalem in 634 A.D., freedom of worship was guaranteed to all. The Christian Patriarch Sophronius invited Omar to pray in the Church of the Holy Sepulchre, but he prayed outside its gates, fearing that his followers might build a mosque at the church site if he prayed inside. Indeed, one was built right on the land where he prayed.

Justice in Islam is supreme. The Qoran says (60:8–9)*:

"Allah forbids you not, With regard to those who Fight you not for (your) Faith Nor drive you out Of your homes, From dealing kindly and justly With them: For Allah loveth Those who are just.

Allah only forbids you, With regard to those who Fight you for (your) Faith, And drive you out Of your homes, and support (Others) in driving you out, From turning to them (For friendship and protection). It is such as turn to them (In these circumstances), That do wrong."

- Moslems revere Jesus and believe that he is one of the greatest messengers of God just like Abraham and Moses. They believe that Jesus is the son of Virgin Mary, not a Deity or the son of God.

Here is what the Qoran says about Virgin Mary (3:45–47):

"Behold! the angels said: "O Mary! Allah giveth thee Glad tidings of a Word From Him: his name Will be Christ Jesus, The son of Mary, held in honor In this world and the Hereafter And of (the company of) those Nearest to Allah;

He shall speak to the people In childhood and in maturity. And he shall be (of the company) Of the righteous.

She said: "O my Lord! How shall I have a son When no man hath touched me?" He said: "Even so; Allah createth What He willeth: When He hath decreed A matter, He but saith To it, 'Be,'" and it is!

And Allah will teach him The Book and Wisdom, The Torah and the Gospel."

The Qoran tells us about what Jesus said relating to his miracles (3:49):

"I have come to you, With a Sign from your Lord, In that I make for you Out of clay, as it were, The figure of a bird, And breathe into it, And it becomes a bird By Allah's leave: And I heal those Born blind, and the lepers, And I bring the dead into life By Allah's leave; And I declare to you What ye eat, and what ye store In your houses. Surely Therein is a Sign for you If ye did believe;"

In this spirit, following is the Vatican II's Declaration on the Relationship of the Church to Non-Christian Religions:

---

* The first number, for example, 60 indicates the number of Soura in the Qoran. The following numbers such as 8–9 are verses number 8 and 9 in Soura number 60.

"Upon the Moslems, too, the Church looks with esteem. They adore one God, living and enduring, merciful and all-powerful, Maker of heaven and earth and Speaker to men. They strive to submit wholeheartedly even to His inscrutable decrees, just as did Abraham, with whom the Islamic faith is pleased to associate itself. Though they do not acknowledge Jesus as God, they revere Him as a prophet. They also honor Mary, His virgin mother; at times they call on her, too, with devotion. In addition, they await the day of judgment when God will give each man his due after raising him up. Consequently, they prize the moral life, and give worship to God especially through prayer, almsgiving, and fasting.

Although in the course of the centuries many quarrels and hostilities have arisen between Christians and Moslems, this most sacred Synod urges all to forget the past and to strive sincerely for mutual understanding. On behalf of all mankind, let them make common cause of safeguarding and fostering social justice, moral values, peace, and freedom."

Islam is very protective of women's rights and a Moslem marriage is a legal agreement based wholly on the Qoran. While divorce is uncommon, it is permitted only as a last resort, because the sanctity of marriage is a cornerstone of family life. The Prophet said: "Of all things permitted by law, divorce is the most hateful in the sight of Allah." The Qoran allows one to marry more than one wife and a maximum of four at one time, only on the strict condition that the husband treats them perfectly fairly, justly, and equally. It is proclaimed that if you want to be just and you won't, you will marry one wife. Here are some relevant translations from the Qoran as they relate to women:

4.19. "O ye who believe! Ye are forbidden to inherit Women against their will. Nor should ye treat them With harshness, that ye may Take away part of the dower Ye have given them,–except Where they have been guilty Of open lewdness; On the contrary live with them On a footing of Kindness and equity If ye take a dislike to them It may be that ye dislike A thing, and Allah brings about Through it a great deal of good.

4.128. "If a wife fears Cruelty or desertion On her husband's part, There is no blame on them If they arrange An amicable settlement Between themselves.

And such settlement is best; even though men's souls Are swayed by greed. But if ye do good And practice self-restraint, Allah is well-acquainted With all that ye do."

65.1. "O Prophet! When ye Do divorce women, Divorce them at their Prescribed periods, And count (accurately) Their prescribed periods: And fear Allah your Lord: And turn them not out Of their houses, nor shall They (themselves) leave,

Except in case they are Guilty of some open lewdness, Those are limits Set by Allah: and any Who transgresses the limits Of Allah, does verily Wrong his (own) soul."

- The Qoran stresses equality among humans and racism is detested by Moslems:

49.13. "O mankind! We created You from a single (pair) Of a male and a female, And made you into Nations and tribes, that Ye may know each other not that ye may despise (Each other). Verily The most honoured of you In the sight of Allah Is (he who is) the most Righteous of you. And Allah has full knowledge And is well acquainted (With all things)."

The Haramein

Maintaining the Haramein, or the Holy sites in Mecca and Madina, is considered as an honor and a duty. Thus, in this spirit of custodianship, the official title preferred by King Fahd became: Custodian of the Two Holy Mosques. Since Saudi Arabia is the focal point for all Moslems of the world, special attention has been given to large and comprehensive expansions of the Holy places. To make the pilgrims' journey to Arabia a safe spiritual experience, mammoth projects have been completed. The number of pilgrims has increased at an average annual rate of 6.3 percent, reaching over two and a half million today. Hajj is considered the largest single human gathering in the whole world.

Twenty tunnels have been dug into the mountains, nineteen bridges and fly-overs for pedestrians were built, along with the construction of one hundred kilometers of multi-lane road network to ease traffic in the Hajj area. Large reservoirs were built to store the water needed by the pilgrims. More than forty pilgrim cities with information centers and guides were built in various parts of the Kingdom to help accommodate the guests.

Further expansion of the Two Holy Mosques, complete with

all needed services, was begun in 1986. These expansions eventually increased the capacity of the Prophet's Mosque in Madina from 28,000 to over a quarter of a million worshippers. The great Mosque in Mecca was enlarged to accommodate nearly one million worshippers.

Madina is also the site of state-of-the-art facilities where the Holy Qoran is printed in millions of copies and distributed to various Islamic centers throughout the world; in most cases as a gift from the government of Saudi Arabia. Printing is done by safe hands, guaranteeing that the Holy Qoran will be safeguarded from revisions by any enemies of Islam. Also King Fahd expressed his desire to pay for rejuvenating Al-Aqsa Mosque in Jerusalem. This makes the Custodian of the Two Holy Mosques, the first Moslem leader in history to complete the gigantic steps of expansion and maintenance in Mecca and Madina. This project, together with the construction of the tunnels, fly-overs and other necessary services to bring comfort, peace and smooth transportation to millions of pilgrims, as well as the expansion of the Two Holy Mosques, will perhaps be considered in history amongst the most important achievements of King Fahd and his predecessors. These gigantic steps are befitting the Kingdom's position as an honorable guardian of the Holy Places, and a leader of the Moslem World. History will undoubtedly engrave in golden letters these good deeds of King Abdulaziz and his sons.

Extremist Islamic Fundamentalists

This fundamentalist extremism is alien and contrary to the Qoran and the spirit of Islam. During the aggression committed by the Iraqi regime against Kuwait and humanity between August 2, 1990 and February 27, 1991, Saddam Hussein appealed with great manipulation and zeal to the extremist Moslem Fundamentalist forces which were festering in the Moslem world. These forces, while small in number within the Arab world, were vociferous and strong on zeal, but lacking in principle and compassion to fellowmen, be it in the Moslem religion, or men of other religions of the world. These extremists were numerous in Iran. After the Iranian Revolution of 1979, the world was witness to their fanaticism and their message of hate for their fellowmen.

Such forces gained momentum in some parts of the Arab land.

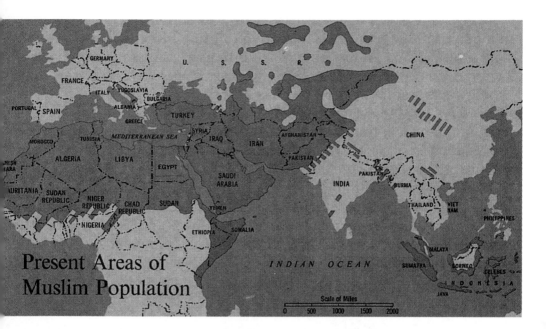

Present Areas of
Muslim Population

A mosque along the shores of the Red Sea is one of thousands gracing the four corners of the Kingdom.

The Fatiha or opening chapter of the Qoran is recited at the beginning of every prayer. It reflects the true spirit of Islam.

Two personal copies of the Holy Qoran belonging to Abdulaziz, founder of the Kingdom of Saudi Arabia.

The Custodian of the two Holy Mosques is the first moslem leader in history to carry the gigantic steps of expansion and maintenance in Mecca, Madina and Jerusalem. This project, together with the construction of the tunnels, flyovers and other necessary services to bring comfort, peace and smooth transportation to millons of pilgrims, along with the expansion of the two Holy Mosques, will perhaps be considered in history among the most important achievements of King Fahd and his predecessors. These gigantic steps are befitting the Kingdom's position as an honorable guardian of the Holy Places, and a leader of the Moslem World. History will undoubtedly engrave in golden letters these good deeds of King Abdulaziz and his sons.

Tunnel network in Mecca

Pilgrims in Arafat (Mecca)

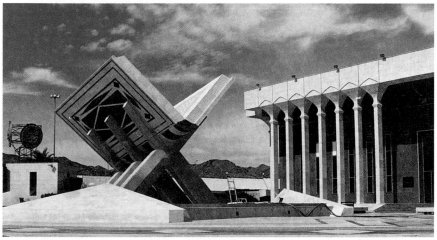

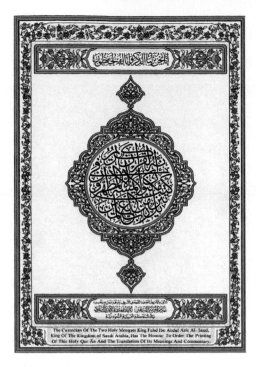

Madina is also the site of state-of-the-art facilities where the Holy Qoran is printed in millions and distributed to various Islamic centers throughout the world; in most cases as a gift from the Custodian of the Two Holy Mosques. Printing is done by safe hands guaranteeing that the Holy Qoran will be safeguarded from revisionists.

Al-Aqsa Mosque in Jerusalem is the third holiest shrine of Islam. It is being rejuvenated, restored and preserved along with two other historic mosques. The good deeds and generosity of the Custodian of the Two Holy Mosques gave the breath of life to this worthy project.

For example, in Algeria, on the Western flank of the Arab world in Africa, these forces were increasing in number and the moderate leadership of the former President of Algeria, Chadli Benjadid, was paying close attention to these developments. Despite their strong influence, the Algerian leadership tried to steer a moderate course. However, Benjadid has since resigned and genuine fears remain about continued serious violence ignited by extremist fundamentalists.

The buildup of these extremist forces and their increasing influence on the masses were worrisome. They were sympathetic to Saddam Hussein, certainly far more than their extremist brothers in Iran; but they were blind and insensitive to the fact that Kuwait was ripped and raped by a ruthless dictator. Their double standards were an injustice to the good spirit of Islam.

They turned a deaf ear and closed their eyes to the atrocities committed against the innocent people of Kuwait. They forgot about the mothers that were raped and lost their children, the fathers who have been abused and tortured and the children that have been brain-washed then tortured and some of them killed. All these are human beings! They are fellow Moslems. The Moslem religion preaches goodness, decency, justice and tolerance! Any such abuse, torture, and ruthless aggression are all condemned by the religion of Islam and the Ulama of Islam who are faithful to the true spirit of Islam.

While this extremism was bordering on terrorism, more recently it became identical to terrorism itself. Criminal activities reached new peaks in Egypt, not only against the moderate leadership of President Mohammed Hosni Moubarak, but against the innocent population and against innocent tourists from abroad. Many people were being killed, injured, or maimed and their properties destroyed, all in line with the fraudulent use of the good name of Islam. This extremism reached other lands including Libya, Afghanistan, Sudan and the United States of America. The latest act of terrorism in 1993, was foiled but was planned and engineered by extremist Islamic fundamentalists. The plan was to destroy the United Nations building, the Tunnel Bridge and cause other damage. In April of 1993, the World Trade Center in New York with a population of fifty thousand was truck-bombed by fanatically inspired extremists who were identified and arrested. Several innocent people were killed; thousands suffered from injury and smoke; billions of dollars were lost in destroyed property and lost time. The moderate Moslem regimes of the world and truly devout Moslems suffered extensively from the extremists' act of terrorism.

Prince Charles, who is the Prince of Wales and first in line to the British Throne, stated in a speech delivered at Oxford Center for Islamic Studies on October 27, 1993: "To many of us in the West, Islam is seen in terms of the tragic civil war in Lebanon, the killings and bombings perpetrated by extremist groups in the Middle East, and by what is commonly referred to as 'Islamic Fundamentalism.' Our judgement of Islam has been grossly distorted by taking the extremes to be the norm. That, ladies and gentlemen, is a serious mistake. It is like judging the quality of life in Britain by the existence of murder and rape, child abuse and drug addition. The extremes exist, and they must be dealt with. But when used as a basis to judge a society, they lead to distortion and unfairness . . . The guiding principle and spirit of Islamic law, taken straight from the Qoran, should be those of equity and compassion. We need to study its actual application before we make judgements. We must distinguish between systems of justice administered with integrity, and systems of justice as we may see them practiced which have been deformed for political reasons into something no longer Islamic."

Islam is the cornerstone for Saudi life. Truly one of the greatest religions, Islam is practiced by nearly one fifth of the world's population. Since its birth it has remained strong and thriving. Like other great religions of the world, Islam is based upon the universal ideals of truth, honesty, justice, tolerance and goodness.

Prince Charles further stated ". . . If the ways of thought found in Islam and other religions can help us in that search (for a wider, deeper, more careful understanding of our world), then there are things for us to learn from this system of belief which I suggest we ignore at our peril."

Chapter 5

Progress in a Modern Kingdom

The incredible story of Saudi Arabia's emergence is a most interesting and fascinating story indeed! From dormant centuries to the most phenomenal development, the Kingdom proudly joined the family of modern nations. In the past two decades, the meteoric ascent of Saudi Arabia has been truly astonishing. A quantum leap forward propelled the Kingdom into its current prominent place in the sun. It has become an outstanding model of growth and progress. The spectacular achievements realized by the Kingdom are truly amazing, especially what has been accomplished in the span of a few years. One cannot help but be fascinated by the great progress that has been realized. Saudi Arabia floats on a sea of oil with proven reserves in excess of 260 billion barrels. The massive income from this great resource was wisely used and invested, bringing with it modernization and an economic boom.

The farsighted leadership of Saudi Arabia dedicated its abundant energies towards making the dream of modernization come true. This leadership was truly the pioneer and the heartbeat of this phenomenal process. Education and industrialization reached a peak during the golden era of King Fahd and his team of dedicated Saudis.

Education

Building blocks for education began several years ago when the first Minister of Education was appointed in 1953. He was Fahd Bin Abdulaziz, the present King of Saudi Arabia. He pioneered in establishing the educational system of the country. He had the foresight, determination and deep dedication to develop education in the Kingdom. He knew that without education the dream of progress and development would not be realized. He said "One of our objectives is to see that the fast-moving wheel of education will maintain its momentum and that the level of education will be improved both qualitatively and quantitatively." According to the King, "An enormous responsibility falls on the shoulders of our young . . . since they are the pillars of construction at present and the mastermind of further development in the future."

Saudis are genuinely concerned with the health of their citizens from birth to death. They provide excellent free medical care for all. Prenatal care is among the best in the world. In addition to hospitalization and medical attention, if a mother is employed during her pregnancy, she will continue to receive full pay for two months.

As the newborn grows and reaches five years of age, he or she will go to kindergarten for a year and at six years of age will start their formal education. He or she will spend six years in elementary school, three years in intermediate school and three years in the secondary school. All their education, books and supplies are free. Schools in the Kingdom adopt the modern approach to teaching. Emphasizing Islamic values begins at an early age.

Boys and girls have equal opportunity to acquire the ultimate in good education. Both have their separate schools that are well equipped and properly staffed. Those who do not succeed in school may choose to work in an enterprise compatible with their capabilities and interests.

Once the young men or young women graduate from high school they may choose to be among students attending seven universities in the Kingdom. Both have equal opportunities for higher education.

At colleges and universities students receive various allowances, including free housing, books, scientific trips, clothing, over $300 per month for expenses, as well as complete medical care.

A student may apply for a scholarship to study abroad, especially for certain specialties. Those working for some organizations, agencies or ministries may improve their status and know-how by studying abroad at their employer's expense. At one time those studying abroad numbered about 10,000 in the U.S.A., over 5,000 in Britain, over 1,000 in West Germany, and a few more throughout the western world. With the dawn of Saudi colleges and universities, these numbers have naturally declined. In 1994, around 3,500 students went abroad for higher education; most of these headed for the U.S.A.

Benefits include: monthly salaries, book allowances, expenses for scientific trips, yearly repatriation to the Kingdom and complete medical care. Superior achievements are rewarded by extra bonuses. If illness befalls the Saudi citizen, he or she will be treated with care. A student studying abroad receives $1,100 every six months for medical care. A couple will receive $2,200 every six months. In either case the government will pay for such extra medical attention as operations or other emergencies.

Saudi women today seek to enrich their knowledge and study for higher degrees. If they are employed, say with the Ministry of Education as an example, their studies may be sponsored by their employer. They will receive their full salary while seeking higher education. Young women are honored, respected and encouraged in their search for better education.

Several separate educational institutions exist for women. Institutes of Commerce and Banking, Teacher's Education, College of Pharmacy and Medicine, just to name a few. Women tend to shy away from disciplines normally dominated by men, such as civil engineering, mechanical engineering, petroleum engineering and other similar professions.

Within a decade, the numbers of students, schools, and those working in them have doubled many times. For example, the number of elementary schools in the academic year 1975–76 was 2,414; in the year 1984–85 it increased to 4,413 schools. The total number of schools reached 16,584 in 1988–1989. In 1994 this number reached nearly 17,500.

In 1930, there were only 2,300 students in the whole country. Between 1970 and 1983 (1390 A.H.–1403 A.H.) the number of students at various levels of education increased from nearly 400,000 to 1.8 million. The enrollment of girls increased from less than 200,000 to 700,000 in that period. In the span of a very few years, education for women became available in over 800 communities, covering every village and city in the Kingdom of Saudi Arabia. In 1994, women are approaching the 50% mark on all fronts. The Kingdom had only 226 schools and 30,000 students in 1951. In 1994, the number of male and female students in different stages of education is around 3.3 million. Females are claiming their educational share. The academic year of 1988–89 had 1.16 million student females, out of a total student population of 2.65 million.

About half of the colleges and institutes in Saudi Arabia offer scientific studies and have a total Saudi teaching staff exceeding 12,000. The number of students registered at the University level increased from 8,000 in the year 1970–71 to 122,100 in 1989–90 and to 132,827 in 1991–92. In the academic year 1994–95, the number of students at Saudi universities is in excess of 135,000. By the year 1984, the total number of male and female students graduating from these institutions of higher learning exceeded 50,000. While in the academic year 1991–92 alone the number of graduates was 16,262. By 1994 nearly 50,000 were studying at teacher training colleges and technical training institutes.

When King Fahd became the first Minister of Education in 1953, the total number of students was still very meager. He once reminisced and said "I remember when I became Minister of Education there was only one secondary school in the Kingdom, in Mecca. The total number of students attending schools in Saudi Arabia at the time was only 35,000." Today, the Kingdom prides itself on a fine system of education, covering the whole spectrum from primary, intermediate and secondary, to technical and vocational schools, colleges and universities.

Only male students are admitted to technical institutes, secondary vocational or commercial schools and to the agricultural institutes. There are also secondary commercial schools and higher institutes for financial and commercial sciences. The fields covered are: accounting and finance, administration, secretarial work, banking, purchasing and sales, collection and cash matters. Day classes are held for regular students and evening classes for working people.

There is also training in the technical area of agricultural education. Such training takes place, for example, at the model Technical Agricultural Institute in Buraidah, that was established in 1977.

The necessary manpower for different trades is trained at various institutes, such as the Health Institutes where the level of training is between the elementary and secondary stages. These institutes train such assistants as statisticians, nurses, technicians, x-ray technicians, surgical operations assistants, health supervisors, laboratory technicians, assistant pharmacists and nutrition assistants. Nursing schools, like the Health Institutes, are for both males and females.

The Ministry of Municipal and Rural Affairs directs some

Technical Assistant Institutes. These include: surveying, foremanships of construction, water and roads, architectural drawing and health supervising. Graduating students work in municipalities or in technical and engineering offices. There are also Tailoring Centers, Postal and Telecommunication Institutes and Arabic Language sections at Islamic University.

The Institute of Public Administration is an autonomous government agency mainly for training civil servants. Programs include: seminars for top executives; training programs in accounting, personnel administration, computer and secretarial work; training programs in various fields such as computers, financial controls, typing, hospital administration and legal studies; English programs for civil servants who are sent abroad for training, or for those who need the English language in their daily work.

The vocational and pre-vocational training centers prepare the necessary skilled and semi-skilled manpower needed in industry. Vocational specialties include: automechanics, auto-body repair, refrigeration, air conditioning, plumbing, painting, electricity, radio-TV, welding, construction, carpentry, metal works and more.

The Instructors' Institute was established in 1980 to train qualified instructors for the vocational training centers including various governmental departments and agencies offering certain specialty training. Training of teachers is directed by the Ministry of Education or the Presidency of Girls' Education.

The first two Junior colleges for men-teachers were established in 1976 in Riyadh and Mecca. Five more colleges were built the following year in Dammam, Madina, Abha, Russ and Taif. Junior colleges for women-teachers were established in 1979 along similar lines as the junior colleges for men teachers.

Special Education Programs for the physically or mentally handicapped include: Al-Nour Institute for the Blind, Al-Amal Institutes for the Deaf, Institutes for the Mentally Retarded and Adult Education for Eliminating Illiteracy.

Gigantic steps are being taken to eradicate illiteracy through educational programs for the elderly. Literacy educational programs are conducted in various corners of the Kingdom in schools, scout camp, institutes, libraries and sports arenas. Total expenditures for these programs exceeded two and a half billion dollars.

It is noteworthy to learn that the student-faculty ratio, around fifteen to one, is among the best in the world. The goal of good quality education has been sought through improvements in curricula, the quality of instruction and the upgrading of the teaching and administrative staff.

Special emphasis is placed on safeguarding religious and moral values along Islamic lines. This has been the core of educational development from a humble beginning in 1949 when the Shari'a College was established, to the great achievements in education crowned by good universities in the four corners of the Kingdom.

The Holy Qoran urges followers to "seek knowledge from the cradle to the grave." The Saudi Arabian society is based on the teachings of Islam, which decrees a high value for education to develop human potential. A very good, close relationship between home life and school environment contributes to the family structure, which is at the heart of Saudi life.

Since Saudi Arabia has the commitment for building a future based on industry and a good level of technology, nearly 70% of all foreign workers eventually will be replaced by Saudi citizens that have been well educated and prepared for their jobs. Of course, this requires not only the levels of education just described but an active program of higher education as well.

Institutions of Higher Learning

Colleges, universities and technical institutes strive to develop Saudi human resources. They were given the responsibility to train specialized manpower and carry on scientific research and development. The Ministry of Higher Education oversees policies in 82 colleges and institutes of higher learning in Saudi Arabia. It was allocated 31% of the budget for the 1980–85 plan for education (2.5 billion dollars). Another 120 million dollars was shared by The Saudi Arabian National Center for Science and Technology, known today as King Abdulaziz Center for Science and Technology (Kacst) and The Institute of Public Administration (Ipa). Kacst designs Saudi policy in science and technology. It renders its assistance to the private sector and carries on applied research independently and jointly with other international organizations. It also grants awards for research, and one of its added functions is coordination of the activities for government agencies research centers and scientific organizations. The latter trains current and potential government employees. It also provides consultation to a number of governmental departments and agencies.

The *Presidency for Girls' Education* encompasses the Undersecretariat for Girls' Colleges. It supervises and manages institutes of higher learning such as the College of Education for Girls in Riyadh which was established in 1970, the College of Education for Girls established in Jeddah in 1974, Mecca in 1975, and the Higher Institute for Social Work in Riyadh, 1975, the College of Arts in Riyadh, 1979, plus the College of Arts and Sciences in Dammam, 1979. Three Colleges of Education for Girls were opened in 1981 in Madina, Buraidah and Abha. In 1982 another College for Education was opened in Tabouk.

There are seven major universities spreading over sixteen campuses and covering the entire Kingdom. Three of these place emphasis on Arts and Sciences, three others are of a specialized type. The Ministry of Higher Education supervises six of the universities while the seventh, the Islamic University, is supervised by the Council of Ministers.

Following is a brief description of these **universities:**

King Saud University (KSU) was established in Riyadh in 1957. Its majestic campus was newly built in Diriya, on the outskirts of the nation's capital. Currently it accommodates more than 30,000 registered students. It is a tribute to the great faith in education espoused by the country's leaders, especially the Custodian of the Two Holy Mosques. The basic mission of the university is to disseminate knowledge and build citizens of the future for the Kingdom. Traditions and religious heritage are intertwined in this process of dissemination.

An inspiring educational atmosphere is supported with good faculty from many parts of the world. Various faculty with a particular expertise are available for consulting to the ministries and agencies of the government. They make a valuable contribution to the development plans. Seminars and conferences are held by the university. Scientists, medical doctors, engineers and men of learning interact with the student body and the faculty. Various sports, cultural and social activities are also a part of university life.

In 1961 fifteen students graduated from the university. In 1981 the total number of graduating males and females was over 5,000. By the academic year 1992–93 the total number of students graduating was over 26,000. In 1957, King Saud University had only twenty-one students and nine professors. The campus today accommodates more than 30,000 students.

The University prides itself with many colleges. These are: Literature, Science, Administrative Sciences, Pharmacy, Agriculture, Engineering, Education (in Riyadh and Abha), Medicine, Dentistry, Medical Assistance Technology, Medicine (in Abha), Agriculture (in Kasim), Commerce and Administration (in Kasim), and the college of Arabic Language. The Bachelor's degree is granted to graduates from these colleges: Agriculture, Education, Engineering and Pharmacy. The campus also includes a teaching hospital for medical students. It is King Khaled University Hospital, which has a capacity in excess of 870 beds. Lodging for faculty, personnel and students can accommodate a population of nearly 45,000.

Islamic University at Madina is an international institution for Islamic studies established in 1960. It has five colleges with eleven different branches, which include the college of Shari'a, colleges relating to the Qoran and religious studies and the college of the Arabic language. The student body of approximately 7,000 students comes from all over the world, covering 105 nationalities which constitute 80 percent of all students.

The university hospital cares for the health needs of the university community. Studies continue year 'round and the programs require four academic years of nine months each. Postgraduate schools offer the master's and doctor's degrees.

King Fahd University of Petroleum and Minerals (KFUPM) was established in 1963. It was previously known as the College of Petroleum and Minerals (CPM). Classes began in 1964 with 67 students and a total faculty of fourteen. Programs were progressively developed to cover a number of disciplines both in the areas of Applied Engineering and Engineering Science. The first graduation ceremonies were held June, 1972 in Dhahran, home of the University. The college became the University of Petroleum and Minerals (UPM) in 1975 and on December 25, 1986, the University was renamed King Fahd University of Petroleum and Minerals (KFUPM). The University has several colleges including Engineering Science, Applied Engineering, Sciences, Computer Science and Design, Business Administration, Environmental Design, and Graduate Studies. The number of students at KFUPM was 3,047 in

1980–81. By the academic year 1990–91, the number of students was nearly 5,000. In 1993–94 the number exceeds 6,500.

The university recruited good Saudi faculty and other professors and scholars from around the world. It has also incorporated in its programs innovative techniques in education, research and public service.

In its quest for excellence, KFUPM is also assisted and advised by a consortium of distinguished American universities such as: Massachusetts Institute of Technology (MIT), Princeton University, University of Michigan, California Institute of Technology, Mississippi State University, Texas A & M University, Colorado School of Mines, University of Rochester and Milwaukee School of Engineering. The consortium committee meets at least twice a year, both in Dhahran and in the U.S. It acts as a visiting-type accreditation committee which evaluates achievement and academic performance. It gives specific recommendations covering curriculum, research and laboratory work. Standards of the Accreditation Board of Engineering and Technology (ABET) are strictly observed.

The *Research Institute* is a branch of King Fahd University of Petroleum and Minerals. Research is undertaken for industry, the general public and the government. It covers various fields from petroleum and gas technology to energy resources, geology and minerals, environment, water resources, economics and industrial development, meteorology, along with standards and materials. By 1994, the Research Institute had already conducted hundreds of research projects. The first Arab Astronaut, Payload Specialist Prince Sultan Bin Salman, aboard the American space mission Discovery, conducted a series of six different experiments specifically designed by a team of engineers and scientists at KFUPM.

This fine University with its mission of superior achievements in education, technology transfer and human resources, has earned its place amongst all universities of the world, especially those in the Middle East. Fortune Magazine called it "A Jewel of a University on Arabian Sands."

King Abdulaziz University (*KAU*) located in Jeddah, was founded by Saudi businessmen in 1967 (1387 A.H.). The rapid development of the university prompted its founders in 1971 (1391 A.H.) to petition the government so that operations would come under its realm. The College of Economics and Administration was the first college at the University, and began instruction with 60 males and 30 females in 1967.

On August 8, 1971, the university became a public institution under the wing of the Kingdom. The colleges of education, Shari'a and higher studies at Mecca, established in 1949, became part of King Abdulaziz University. As of 1981 (1/7/1401 A.H.), the branch in Mecca became an independent institution under the name of Umm Al-Qora University.

The university campus covers an area of 400 acres in the northeast corner of Jeddah and has ten colleges granting degrees up to the Ph.D. level. These include: the Colleges of Economics and Administration, Arts and Humanities, Education (in Madina), Physical Education, Engineering and Applied Science, Environmental Design, Medicine and Medical Sciences (supported by various departments and a university hospital with over 800 beds), Dentistry, Earth Sciences, Institute of Applied Geology, Institute of Meteorology & Arid Lands Studies, and Institute of Oceanography. Separate and equally well-equipped facilities have been established for women. Parallel courses are taught for men and women.

The total number of students for 1983–84 was 14,403. Among them were 10,243 males and 4,150 females. Of these 3,255 students were non-Saudis and the balance of 11,148 students were Saudis. By the 1989–1990 academic year the number of students enrolled at KAU was 22,474 and those graduating were 1,465. About 28,000 students are currently studying at the University.

Like many other university campuses, residential quarters are made available for students, staff, faculties and their families. Future capacity for the whole campus will be as high as 40,000.

Imam Mohammed Bin Saud Islamic University (IMU) was founded in 1974 (1394 A.H.). The Council of Ministers defined its basic mission. It became an annex to the scientific institute known as the Riyadh Ilmi Institute, built in 1950. Thirteen colleges were progressively added including: College of Shari'a, Arabic Language, Higher Judicial Institute, Faculty of the Basics of Religion, Institute for Islamic Call, Faculty of Social Sciences, the College of Shari'a and Basics of Religion in Abha, and Qasim in 1976. Also, a College for Arabic Language and a College for Social Studies were added in Abha and Qasim; an Institute for Islamic Call in Madina and a College for Shari'a and Islamic Studies in Hasa. It has a branch for teaching Arabic to foreigners and also a branch for teaching English to students at the university.

Completion of four academic years are needed for graduation with a Bachelor's degree. Two academic years are required for the Master's program and the Doctorate degree may be earned in two to four years after registration of the dissertation topic.

The university has six branches outside the Kingdom at Ras Al-Kheima, Mauritania, Djibouti and Somalia. The Arabic language is being taught in Indonesia and Japan. The number of students totaled 16,134 in 1983–84. Those pursuing graduate studies numbered 2,725. For the five-year plan ending in 1982–83, 6,232 students graduated from the university and a cumulative total of 14,970 for the academic year 1989–90. The student body was 19,525 in 1992–93.

King Faisal University (KFU) was founded in 1975. Instruction began at that time with 170 students in four basic colleges: the College of Agriculture, Veterinary Medicine (in Hasa), Construction and Planning and the College of Medicine and Medical Sciences in Dammam. A branch for girls' education and a college of Business Administration were later established. The number of students is presently in excess of 7,000.

Academic activities in the various colleges are complemented by applied scientific centers that strengthen the educational process at the university. These include: centers for agriculture, animal science, research facilities, libraries and King Fahd University Hospital in Khobar with nearly 400 beds.

KFU has agreements with various American universities, including Harvard, Cornell, Rice, Texas A & M and others to help in the progress and development of academic programs.

Umm Al-Qora University (UQU) was founded in Mecca in 1981. The university includes the Faculty of Shari'a and Islamic Studies which has existed since 1969 and the Faculty of education in Mecca that began in 1952. For a period, both were under the Ministry of Education (1971–1972), then became a part of King Abdulaziz University prior to becoming part of Umm Al-Qora University. The student body numbers over 14,000.

Since 1981, the university expanded on many fronts including College of Shari'a and Islamic Studies, Education, Applied Science and Engineering, Arabic Language, Education in Taif, College of Da'wa and Basics of Religion (Da'wa and Osoul Al-Deen).

Since 1983 two other colleges have been added: the College of Social Sciences and College of Agricultural Sciences. Many centers for research and related endeavors are very active at the university, including a center for computer science and television education.

On the 23rd of November, 1993, King Fahd issued a Royal Decree defining an evolving new system for higher education which became effective shortly thereafter. The new system comprising 60 articles dealt with university senate decisions, academic council, college administration, principals and undersecretaries, college departments, the teaching staff and the financial system. A higher education council became the supreme authority in higher education except military. The various university councils will now be allowed to accept donations, endowments and grants in addition to money earned from research work and services rendered to other agencies and organizations.

Universities in the Kingdom seek excellence in education in their respective missions and endeavors. All have made great progress. Indeed, an era of renaissance is taking place reflecting giant steps forward in reviving Arabic contributions to science, technology and society.

Education and training are the foundation for developing human resources–the "most precious resources of the nation" and the dynamo for carrying the torch and continuing the mission of impressive achievements in Saudi Arabia. This phenomenal progress is briefly portrayed in the following pages.

Phenomenal Progress

When you compare Saudi Arabia of the early seventies with the Kingdom of the early eighties and nineties, you will certainly be overwhelmed by the mind-boggling progress and dramatic development that has been realized in record time. It is like a dream come true! If one is acquainted with Saudi Arabia, and lets his imagination take him back to the days of Abdulaziz, one will then realize the fantastic effort, blood and sweat that were intertwined and enmeshed in modernizing this great mass of desert. Imagine the magnitude and vast impact of this progress. Keep in mind that only a few years ago, introducing the telephone and telegraph required the ingenuity of Abdulaziz to convince the populace that certainly this machine is not "an instrument of the devil."

The pace of development has moved at an accelerated rate since the mid-seventies. At center stage was the dedicated support and wisdom of King Fahd, keeping the goals high and on target. His vast experience through the years converted dreams into actions and deeds. From the time of his predecessors to his golden era, he has been the man of long-range planning and dynamism.

King Fahd once said "Our goal shall always be–God willing–to maintain the equitable distribution of wealth among all of the citizens and to promote the welfare of every Saudi, no matter how remote his village or how far his city is from the centers of construction and industrial activity." In his goals and dreams, Fahd was enthusiastically supported by a dedicated team of government leaders, ambitious Saudi businessmen, competent Saudi engineers, and a multitude of professional experts from across the world who all helped in a massive process of technology transfer and efficient use of the best talent available to mankind.

In the mid-seventies, the wisdom of optimizing the use of economic opportunities brought a torrent of financial support that was sorely needed to extract reality out of big dreams. The wise decision was to produce all the oil that could be beneficially sold on world markets, to help ease the shortage of oil while also generating hard cash for internal development. At the time, loud voices were strongly supporting and promoting the view that oil is more valuable left underground. The voices urged that only the minimum amount of oil should be pumped and sold. If this policy had been adopted, a historic economic opportunity would have been lost forever. As events moved on and in the present day oil glut, such theory and voices have been proven totally wrong. The foresight of Fahd prevailed and the golden opportunity presented in the oil markets was wisely seized–the revenue was well spent for modernization and industrialization. The dream of King Fahd "to maintain the equitable distribution of wealth among all the citizens" was realized in a remarkably short time, truly unparalleled in the history of mankind.

Development and modernization were based on scientific and well thought out five-year plans. Each of these plans had definite objectives that were defined in accordance with the specific requirements of the economy and basic social entity, so that the

Saudi citizen could enjoy a prosperous and stable way of life. The first five-year plan began in 1970 and others continue to this day. Progress in the Kingdom has covered all sectors of the economy. On previous pages, achievements in education were described. Here, other aspects of this miraculous progress are presented.

Oil and Minerals

First oil exploration rights were given to a British company in 1923. However, this concession was not renewed in 1933 since it was not executed. Exploration rights were given to the Standard Oil Company of California (Socal) in the same year. The Dammam Dome was tested in the summer of 1934 because this structure is similar to the one in Bahrain, but initial tests were not fruitful. In 1936, Well Number Seven was drilled but drilling was halted for awhile and then resumed in the fall of 1937. This resumption proved to be a decision of good fortune for the history of the Kingdom of Saudi Arabia and the company exploring for oil. At a depth of 4,272 feet, oil began gushing in substantial quantities and with it a bright future for the Kingdom and the world was indeed unfolding. This well was completed in March, 1938, several years after the drilling of Dammam Number One. The Arabian American Oil Company (Aramco) was founded and in the early eighties it became a wholly owned Saudi company, known as Saudi Aramco. Initially revenues from oil were meager because development of the oilfields was hampered due to World War II. While oil revenues were only around four million dollars initially, by 1948 production increased substantially and the revenue from oil reached eighty-five million dollars. King Ibn Saud began to realize his ambitions and dreams for development, progress, and the welfare of his people. He wisely used this great resource for the benefit of his people and for initiating development programs, building roads, schools, telecommunications, medical facilities, and much more; thus laying the foundation for the massive developments which took place in later years (See Chapter Three for oil policy).

In 1994, the proven oil reserves of the Kingdom of Saudi Arabia are in excess of 260 billion barrels; the natural gas liquid reserves are in excess of 180 trillion cubic feet, and the natural gas reserves are in excess of 121 trillion cubic feet. All this added sub-

Educating and training the leaders of tomorrow is a cornerstone of
Saudi educational policy.

Seven major universities spreading over sixteen campuses across the Kingdom–seek excellence in education for developing human resources – the "most precious resources of the nation" – the dynamo for carrying the torch and continuing the mission of impressive achievements in the Kingdom of Saudi Arabia.

Classroom instruction and first graduation ceremonies at College of Petroleum and Minerals, CPM (now KFUPM) June 1972–"A jewel of a university on Arabian Sands," according to Fortune Magazine.

King Fahd National Library is not only a masterpiece of architectural design, it is rich (over 364,000 units) with a large volume of books, audio & visual matter and rare documents. Its impressive educational role is a symbol of the pioneering mission of excellence carried by other major libraries in the Kingdom.

SAUDI CRUDE OIL PRODUCTION

(BILLION BARRELS)

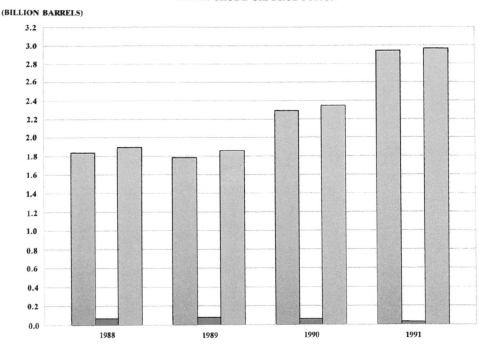

Source: Sama

WORLD DEMAND FOR OIL

(Million Barrels p/d)

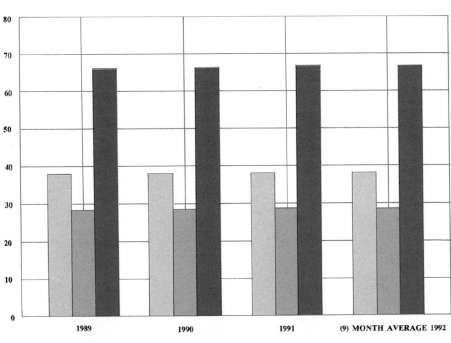

Source: Sama

Ras Tanura Petroleum Terminal

The incredible story of Saudi Arabia's emergence from dormant centuries to the most phenomenal development is one of the most fascinating stories of modern times. Its meteoric ascent is depicted in several photos which reveal a facet of this miracle.

WORLD CRUDE OIL PRODUCTION

(Million Barrels p/d)

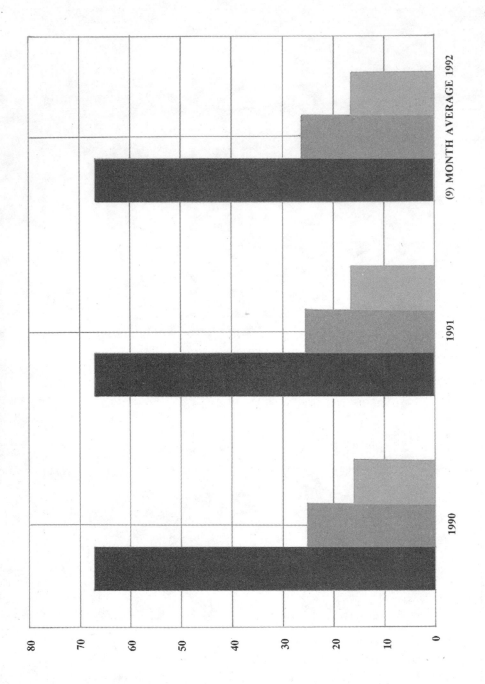

TOTAL WORLD TOTAL OPEC TOTAL OECD

WORLD OIL SUPPLY AND DEMAND

	1994		1993			
	2nd qtr.	1st qtr.	4th qtr. (Million b/d)	3rd qtr.	2nd qtr.	1st qtr.
SUPPLY						
OECD						
U.S.	9.30	9.35	9.57	9.46	9.55	9.83
Canada	2.27	2.30	2.27	2.30	2.16	2.09
North Sea	5.26	5.19	5.09	4.57	4.28	4.34
Other OECD	1.46	1.42	1.37	1.43	1.43	1.42
Total OECD	18.29	18.26	18.30	17.76	17.42	17.68
NON-OECD						
C.I.S.	6.99	7.19	7.43	7.56	8.04	8.28
China	2.94	2.91	2.94	2.89	2.93	2.88
Mexico	3.17	3.20	3.22	3.16	3.15	3.10
Other non-OECD ..	8.57	8.48	8.43	8.28	8.18	8.20
Total non-OECD, non-OPEC	21.67	21.78	22.02	21.87	22.30	22.46
OPEC	27.31	27.33	27.18	27.30	26.66	27.42
TOTAL SUPPLY	67.27	67.37	67.50	66.93	66.38	67.66
DEMAND						
OECD						
U.S. & Territories ...	17.73	18.06	17.95	17.66	17.03	17.24
Canada	1.64	1.69	1.69	1.71	1.61	1.64
Japan	5.07	6.20	6.56	4.79	5.04	6.14
France	1.81	1.91	1.97	1.77	1.86	2.03
Italy	1.75	1.88	2.07	1.81	1.71	1.92
United Kingdom ...	1.79	1.86	1.86	1.80	1.73	1.82
Germany	2.89	2.84	3.00	3.01	2.82	2.78
Other OECD Europe	5.03	5.22	5.37	5.20	4.81	5.05
Australia & New Zealand	0.91	0.89	0.91	0.87	0.89	0.87
Total OECD	38.62	40.55	40.38	38.62	37.50	39.49
NON-OECD						
China	3.15	3.12	3.10	3.00	2.90	2.78
C.I.S.	4.70	5.32	5.35	6.15	5.60	6.33
Other non-OECD ..	20.08	20.32	20.22	19.16	19.35	19.58
Total non-OECD ..	27.93	28.76	28.67	27.31	27.85	28.69
TOTAL WORLD DEMAND	66.55	69.31	69.05	65.93	65.35	68.18

Source: Department of Energy, DOE International Petroleum Statistics Report, Oil and Gas Journal, January, 1995.

RESERVES AND PRODUCTION FOR CERTAIN COUNTRIES

Country	Oil Reserves as of Jan. 1, 1995 (billion barrels of oil)	Oil Production 1994 (million b/d)	Gas Reserves (billion cubic feet)
Algeria	9.20	0.75	128,000
Angola	5.41	0.54	1,800
Australia	1.62	0.53	19,606
Bahrain	0.21	0.11	5,295
Brazil	3.80	0.67	4,852
Brunei	1.35	0.16	14,000
China	24.00	2.95	59,000
C.I.S. (former U.S.S.R.)	57.00	6.99	1,997,000
Columbia	3.40	0.46	7,882
Ecuador	2.01	0.38	3,800
Egypt	3.26	0.89	19,290
Gabon	1.34	0.33	500
India	5.78	0.62	24,967
Indonesia	5.78	1.33	64,388
Iran	89.25	3.57	741,609
Iraq	100.00	0.52	109,500
Kuwait	94.00	1.85	52,400
Libya	22.80	1.37	45,800
Malaysia	4.30	0.64	68,000
Mexico	50.78	2.68	69,675
Neutral Zone	5.00	0.39	1,000
Nigeria	17.90	1.93	120,000
Norway	9.42	2.50	70,912
Oman	4.83	0.80	22,248
Qatar	3.70	0.41	250,000
Romania	1.61	0.14	12,290
Saudi Arabia	260.00	7.82	185,400
United Arab Emirates	98.00	1.84	188,400
United Kingdom	4.52	2.50	22,248
U.S.A.	22.96	6.64	162,415
Venezuela	64.48	2.46	130,400

Sources: Oil and Gas Journal, Department of Energy, Ministry of Petroleum and Minerals, Sama.

stantially to the strategic and spiritual importance of the Kingdom. Imagine, back in 1944 Aramco only produced 20,000 barrels of oil per day! It had reached a peak in 1980 when Saudi Aramco's oil production was nearly 10 million barrels per day. Today, Saudi Arabia produces over 8 million barrels per day and is capable of producing over 10 million barrels per day when needed. Saudi Aramco produces 95 percent of the Kingdom's total oil production and manages 98 percent of Saudi petroleum reserves. It is worthy of note that Saudi Aramco has discovered more oil than it has produced by far. It is certainly the world's largest oil producer and exporter.

A massive system was designed and built to gather associated gas (gas produced along with crude oil) from the various areas of Saudi Aramco's operations. This is known as the Master Gas System (MGS). It has contributed substantially to the industrial development programs in the Kingdom of Saudi Arabia. Associated gas is processed and fractionated for use by Saudi Aramco and large numbers of Saudi industries. The recovered ethane is a basic feedstock which is supplied to the petrochemical industries in the twin industrial cities of Jubail and Yanbu. Propane, butane and natural gasoline, which are also produced in this system, are exported to a number of countries around the world. Instead of flaring associated gas just to get rid of it, it was recovered efficiently and became an additional national source of raw materials for the thriving petrochemical industry. It has also become a good source of energy for power plants to generate electricity, and for home use across the Kingdom. This master gas system also included the building and operation of a pipeline to deliver natural gas liquids and ethane to Yanbu on the Red Sea, where a fractionation plant and a terminal for exporting natural gas liquids were built. The fractionation plant made available feedstock to the petrochemical industry and fuel gas for the Royal Commission Power Plant. Necessary gas was also supplied as an energy source for the desalination plant of the Saline Water Conversion Corporation and for Petromin refinery. Since the oil discovery at Dammam Number Seven in 1938, more than sixty oil and gas fields have been discovered.

World demand for oil is on the increase, averaging over 66.6 million barrels per day for 1994. For example, crude oil production for Saudi Arabia was in excess of 8 million barrels per day while

Saudi Aramco Proved Petroleum Reserves
(Million Barrels)

Year	Reserves at Beginning of Year	Gross Increase During Year	Annual Production	Annual Net Increase	Reserves at End of Year
1976	107,857	5,384	3,054	2,330	110,187
1977	110,187	3,547	3,291	256	110,443
1978	110,443	5,802	2,961	2,841	113,284
1979	113,284	3,477	3,377	100	113,384
1980	113,384	3,632	3,525	107	113,491
1981	113,491	6,769	3,513	3,256	116,747
1982	116,747	51,022	2,310	48,712	165,459
1983	165,459	2,138	1,597	541	166,000
1984	166,000	1,735	1,435	300	166,300
1985	166,300	1,310	1,110	200	166,500
1986	166,500	2,212	1,712	500	167,000
1987	167,000	1,857	1,457	400	167,400
1988	167,400	86,788	1,804	84,984	252,384
1989	252,384	6,895	1,775	5,120	257,504
1990	257,504	2,628	2,284	344	257,848
1991	257,848	3,557	2,939	618	258,466

Source: Ministry of Petroleum & Mineral Resources, Saudi Aramco Annual Reports and Sama.

Saudi Crude Oil Production
(Million Barrels)

Company Year	Saudi Aramco	Getty	A.O.C.	Total	% Change	Daily Average
1976	3,053.89	29.68	55.71	3,139.28	21.56	8.58
1977	3,291.19	31.96	34.81	3,357.96	6.97	9.20
1978	2,944.13	29.50	56.27	3,029.90	−9.77	8.30
1979	3,376.40	30.11	72.64	3,479.15	14.83	9.53
1980	3,525.30	28.50	70.00	3,623.80	4.16	9.90
1981	3,512.70	27.06	40.13	3,579.89	−1.21	9.81
1982	2,309.44	23.60	33.37	2,366.41	−33.90	6.48
1983	1,596.62	—	—	1,656.88*	−29.98	4.54
1984	1,435.50	—	—	1,492.90*	−9.90	4.08
1985	1,110.00	—	—	1,158.80*	−22.38	3.17
1986	1,711.80	—	—	1,746.20*	50.69	4.78
1987	1,459.20	23.80	22.40	1,505.40	−13.79	4.12
1988	1,830.00	35.20	24.90	1,890.10	25.55	5.16
1989	1,776.10	23.80	48.60	1,848.50	−2.20	5.10
1990	2,284.00	13.90	42.60	2,340.50	26.62	6.41
1991	2,939.30	—	23.70	2,963.00	26.60	8.12

* Including other oil companies.
Source: Ministry of Petroleum & Mineral Resources, Petroleum Statistical Bulletin and Sama.

Production of Refined Products
(Thousand Barrels)

Year	Fuel Oil	Diesel Oil	Gasoline & Naphtha	Lpg	Jet Fuel	Kero-sene	Asphalt & Others	Total
1976	104,528	26,914	61,036	47,021	4,346	8,535	5,081	257,461
1977	98,279	32,116	61,592	57,571	2,054	8,569	6,793	266,974
1978	95,423	37,491	68,001	65,326	202	9,854	7,263	283,560
1979	97,997	34,991	72,566	79,523	248	9,913	9,497	304,735
1980	89,003	44,507	72,316	74,865	359	11,691	9,753	302,494
1981	85,513	54,152	71,149	69,510	190	12,020	11,966	304,500
1982	93,748	66,975	66,853	57,243	1,570	10,244	14,125	310,758
1983	100,855	84,411	75,363	41,334	3,782	11,429	16,610	333,784
1984	97,950	96,143	75,079	51,220	4,612	9,498	14,920	349,422
1985	122,125	110,553	89,546	51,225	9,935	14,223	17,648	415,255
1986	138,325	109,290	109,711	55,050	11,807	18,901	53,152	496,236
1987	152,577	149,129	130,102	7,949	20,572	26,913	14,442	501,684
1988	164,282	161,590	130,539	9,559	15,822	30,947	13,084	525,823
1989	148,348	145,670	124,104	7,909	18,214	29,918	13,437	487,600
1990	183,863	161,660	135,991	7,320	54,369*	—	18,033	561,236
1991	161,700	147,439	128,594	8,380	48,642*	—	22,501	517,256

* Including Kerosene & Aviation Gasoline
Source: Ministry of Petroleum & Mineral Resources, Petroleum Statistical Bulletin and Sama.

Oil Revenue by Source
(Million U.S.$)

Year	Saudi Aramco*	Getty Oil	Arabian Oil	Other Oil Companies	Total	% Change
1976	29,937.3	254.7	559.2	3.6	30,754.8	19.8
1977	35,702.1	263.4	571.6	1.2	36,583.3	18.8
1978	31,609.0	286.6	338.2	—	32,233.8	−11.8
1979	47,588.9	272.0	574.3	—	48,435.2	50.3
1980	82,716.4	469.6	1,280.4	—	84,466.4	74.4
1981	99,196.3	755.6	2,143.3	—	102,095.2	20.9
1982	67,895.8	671.9	1,910.9	—	70,478.6	−31.0
1983	35,701.0	528.5	1,122.1	—	37,351.6	−47.0
1984	29,611.8	434.8	1,423.7	—	31,470.3	−15.7
1985	17,662.5	460.7	199.7	—	18,322.9	−41.8
1986	13,044.6**	384.8	125.4	—	13,554.8	−26.0
1987	—	—	—	—	17,489.3	29.0
1988	16,262.0	210.0	166.0	—	16,638.0	−4.9
1989	—	—	—	—	—	—
1990	30,249.9	198.3	674.0	—	31,122.2	—
1991	—	—	—	—	—	—

* Including Value of Royalty Oil Payments in Kind and Saudi Arabian Government Share in Abu Sa'Fah Oil Field.
** Excluding Participation Profits.
Source: Ministry Of Petroleum & Mineral Resources, Petroleum Statistical Bulletin and Sama.

world usage averaged over 66.7 million barrels per day for the first nine months of 1992. For the same period the average output for OECD (Organization for Economic Cooperation and Development) countries was 16.4 million barrels per day. OPEC's output for this period reached 26.6 million barrels per day which was the highest since 1981. In the meantime, crude oil production for the United States of America declined by 2.2 percent, reaching an average of 9 million barrels per day. The crude oil production for the former Soviet Union declined by 12.4 percent, thus averaging about 9.2 million barrels per day. In May, 1994 it had reached about 7.0 million bpd.

The Kingdom has vast refining capacities and a number of large refineries which not only satisfy domestic needs, but export overseas as well. Oil continues to be the backbone of the Saudi economy and a major source for fueling development and progress in the Kingdom.

Since oil discovery, nearly 75 billion barrels of oil has been produced to fire and bankroll the massive development in the Kingdom. It should be remembered that back in 1946 the Kingdom of Saudi Arabia had a proven reserve of only 3 billion barrels of oil, and in 1959 these reserves were only 50 billion barrels. As mentioned previously, today these reserves stand at over 260 billion barrels, constituting over 26% of the proven oil reserves of the entire world.

The Kingdom is also well endowed with *mineral resources*. The gold mine of Mahd Al-Thahab began operation in 1983. It has a production capacity of 120,000 tons of raw materials per year. Deposits of iron, zinc, copper, phosphates, lead, tungsten and some coal have also been discovered in the Kingdom. Northeast of the city of Najran, raw materials have been estimated at 4.5 million tons, with a content of 1.6 percent copper, 4.7 percent zinc, 1.2 gram-ton gold, and 43.7 gram-ton silver. Exploration also has taken place in the Sukheirat region which is rich in raw materials. Large deposits of iron have been discovered in the Wadi Al-Sawaween area. Coal was discovered in good quantities near Qasim, while phosphate was discovered in the North of the Kingdom.

According to the Saudi Arabian Monetary Agency's annual report 1411–1412 A.H. (1991), "The General Directorate of Mineral Resources conducted, during 1991, operations involving collection of surface samples of gold ore at Umm Shalaheeb deposits, drilling of trenches and map drawing. Exploration activities were also undertaken on gold ore deposits in ultra-base rocks in different areas of the Arabian Shield apart from the search for precious stones, and emeralds in particular.

The Directorate also continued exploration activities through geochemical and geophysical surveys, map drawing and information analysis made at a number of areas such as Jabal Riyadh belt, Hamdha belt, B'ir Hamdan belt North East Abha, and Al-Amar belt in the Arabian Shield. The Directorate also continued exploration of gold ore at A'queeq Ghamid and Bahra area located on Mecca-Jeddah road.

The reserves of gold ore at Al-Sukhaybarat mine are estimated at 8.4 million tons. Annual production of the mine, the utilization period of which is estimated at 12 years, is 1,500 kilograms of gold and silver. Total production of the mine, since the beginning of its utilization on April 30, 1990 up to the end of July, 1992 reached 1,882 kg of gold bullion."

Commerce

The Kingdom of Saudi Arabia has a thriving commerce extensively nourished by the oil sector and strongly supported by a free market economy. In 1991, the number of new companies registered with the Ministry of Commerce was 285. The total number of companies operating in the Kingdom of Saudi Arabia with a license from the Ministry of Commerce reached a total of 7,032 in 1991. In the same year, commercial registrations for individual firms stood at 32,197, while the total of these individual firms with single ownership stood at 314,725. In the same year, the Ministry of Commerce issued 173 licenses for establishing offices which provide professional services. These were issued for various specializations in the realm of engineering, economic services and legal consulting. The total number of these offices reached 2,111, of which 90.1 percent were owned by Saudis, while 8.6 percent were owned by non-Saudis and 1.3 percent were jointly-owned. Foreign commercial agencies registered in 1991 (1411 A.H.) were 348 and the cumulative total reached 3,321. Of these, 17.7 percent were Americans, 15.8 British, 12.8 German, 6.6 French and 6.3 Japanese. This represented 59.2 percent of the total number of registered agencies.

Funds to Foster Development

Those playing a major role in the development process include the Public Investment Fund, the Saudi Agricultural Fund and the Real Estate Development Fund for both projects and power plants. Long-term, interest-free loans, and assistance to private citizens as well as public and semi-public institutions, were extended through these funds.

Saudis with industrial licenses are eligible to receive long-term loans (up to 15 years duration) equivalent to 50% of the total cost of a project. The Saudi Industrial Development Fund (Sidf), established in 1974, was designed to support and promote the development of private industry in the Kingdom. The fund contributed extensively by providing medium-term loans and the necessary advisory services to many local manufacturers. The credit dispersed by the various public financial institutes showed a very steep growth from a miniscule sum of 16 million Saudi Riyals in 1969–70 to the staggering figure of about 26 billion Saudi Riyals in 1983–84. Cumulative credit given by all financial institutions until the middle of 1984 totaled nearly 184 billion Saudi Riyals. These disbursements were gradually lowered since credit needs were reduced. After their peak years, they reached a level of 5.3 billion Saudi Riyals in 1988–89. By early 1993, these financial institutions have provided Saudis and Saudi companies over 245 billion Saudi Riyals or the equivalent of 70 billion U.S. dollars, as long-term, interest-free loans.

Transportation

The building of modern highways, paved and unpaved roads, airports, seaports, railroads, bus transport, telephone, telegraph and postal services were all very essential in providing the basic foundation for development.

Today a road network connects the four corners of the Kingdom with modern expressways complete with various types of interchanges reminiscent of the most modern highways that you will encounter in Western Europe or most of America. In 1970 the total road network was about 17,000 kilometers. In 1990 the Kingdom had 116,511 kilometers of roads both paved and unpaved. The total today is 127,698 kilometers.

While all this was under construction, great care was taken to protect the environment and animals of the desert, be it sheep, goat, camel or others, so crossing paths were provided at various intervals on major highways. Today cities and villages of the country are easily reached by modern roads. These modern roads became very useful to the pilgrims, to the Saudi citizen and his family and especially during the Gulf War for liberating Kuwait in 1990–1991. There are gardens planted and manicured in various parts of this network of highways. Traffic jams around major cities were solved via bridging or bypassing through city belts. Also there are modern roads connecting the Kingdom with its neighbors, such as the road to Yemen and the road connecting the Kingdom with Kuwait. Two roads connect with Jordan. One road connects with Qatar; it extends to the United Arab Emirates and the Sultanate of Oman.

King Fahd causeway, or bridge, connects the Kingdom with Bahrain. On November 11, 1982, the cornerstone of the bridge was jointly placed by King Fahd and the ruler of Bahrain, Sheikh Issa Bin Salman Al-Khalifa. This highway is, essentially, a four-lane highway; two lanes in each direction with one lane for emergency in both directions. It is 25 meters in width and about 26 kilometers in length (15.5 miles). The cost of 1.2 billion dollars was paid by the Saudi Arabian government in line with its policy of increased cooperation and welfare among the Gulf Cooperation Council (GCC). The bridge was technically finished on April 26, 1986, after nearly five years of work.

An ultra modern *rail system* is the only one in the Arabian Peninsula. A major railroad connects Riyadh and Dammam. This system is being expanded and made more efficient through the Saudi Government Railroad Organization. A new dual line connecting the Eastern region with Riyadh has been built. It reduces travel time from seven hours previously to four hours, with stops in Dammam, Abqaiq, Hofouf, Ain Aradh, Al-Kharj and Riyadh. Yet, the number of railroad passengers is modest, increasing from 117,000 in 1970 to 414,000 in 1991. In 1994 the railway system used over 47 locomotives, 2,165 freight cars and 58 air conditioned passenger cars.

The Saudi Public Transport Company, founded in 1979, manages urban and cross-country public transport. A fleet of over nine hundred buses gives a needed service to the commuter and helps in reducing traffic jams and congestion in major cities. It provides efficient transport facilities, comfort and safety for the pilgrims performing the Hajj each year at the Holy places in Saudi Arabia. It contributed its valuable share during the Gulf War.

Twenty-three *airports* connect the four corners of the Kingdom and give easy access to most countries in the world. Three of these airports are international. They are: King Khaled International Airport on the outskirts of Riyadh, King Abdulaziz International Airport near Jeddah, and the International Airport in Dhahran in the Eastern region. The new King Fahd International Airport is located between Dhahran and Jubail at a distance of 36 kilometers (22.2 miles) northwest of Dammam on a site of 528 square kilometers. The first phase is on its way to completion in 1994. When finished, it will be able to handle 16 million passengers and 176,000 tons of freight per year. It is estimated to cost over 7.6 billion Saudi Riyals or 2.03 billion U.S. dollars.

Seaports also play an important role in opening the gates to the outside world through imports and exports. Twenty-one seaports rank amongst the most modern in the world. Leading among these are the Jeddah Islamic Port, King Abdulaziz Port in Dammam, Jubail Commercial Port, King Fahd Industrial Port in Jubail, Yanbu Port and Jizan Port. These ports have a total of 133 piers. The two largest are the Jeddah port and the port in Dammam, having respectively 45 and 39 piers. The expansion of seaports was extensive, having the capability of handling 135 ships at one time. The Jeddah Islamic Port recently received two major awards for its excellent services to international shipping.

Communication

The Kingdom has made impressive achievements in modern communications. Telephone services have received tremendous improvements in quality and reliability. You can call anywhere in the Kingdom and to over 183 countries around the globe. The service is ultramodern. In many instances it far surpasses the best telephone systems anywhere in the industrialized world. The expansion of telephone lines in Saudi Arabia has truly been phenomenal; another expansion is currently underway, reflecting a four billion U. S. dollar contract with AT&T which was announced in May, 1994.

The local network is supplemented with an advanced international network of communication including four earth stations for communication via satellites. *Telex and Fax* services have also expanded and a large network is now in operation giving instant access to the four corners of the globe.

Since the early seventies, the *Postal service* has improved both in quality and reliability. A giant leap forward was realized by introducing the most modern methods and equipment, especially automatic handling and separation of mail, including the zip code and express mail for a number of Saudi cities. Continuous efforts are being made to improve services through training and by making use of the latest advances in technology.

In the field of *information* (television, radio and press), impressive strides have been made. The television studios in Riyadh are among the most modern in the world. The television tower graces the majestic and huge marble building of the Ministry of Information. Two major television stations, one in Arabic and another in English are run by the government. News is televised in Arabic, English and French. The Eastern region of the Kingdom is capable of receiving several stations from the neighboring Gulf countries, including stations from as far away as Iraq and Iran. The Kingdom also has 37 radio transmission stations.

Television programs are also broadcast by the Kingdom to the outside world, especially to the Islamic countries on special religious occasions. The Kingdom is connected to brotherly nations with a network of cables and microwaves. An earth station can receive and transmit from the Arab satellite (Arabsat) which was put into orbit on June 17, 1985. The same year, it was used to transmit the Hajj procession to the Islamic world, live on the air. King Fahd Telecommunications City was inaugurated in 1987. This seventh earth station for reception and transmission is considered to be the largest in the world.

At least three major daily newspapers are published in English as well as over a dozen in Arabic. Some of these have a wide circulation on the international scene, especially Europe and the Arab World.

The Kingdom of Saudi Arabia was in the forefront of exhibitors at the World's Fair for communications and transport, Expo 86 held in Vancouver, Canada. The Kingdom's pavilion was a reflection of its fine achievements in this sector. Visitors to the Fair were very much impressed with the spectacular progress.

Around the same time, the Kingdom was well represented at the International Fair in Paris. The Saudi pavilion was a great success. Among its first visitors was Jacques Chirac, former French Prime Minister, who inaugurated its opening.

The Kingdom takes pride in sharing the story of its modernization and culture with the rest of the world community. In this spirit, the Exhibit of "Saudi Arabia Yesterday and Today" was successfully shown in a number of countries. It was especially well received in 1989–1990 in a number of American cities, including Washington, D.C., Atlanta, Georgia, New York City, Dallas, Texas, and Los Angeles, California, also Toronto, Canada, London, England, Paris, France, Cairo, Egypt, Casablanca, Morocco and Tunis, Tunisia. The Saudi delegation to the World Petroleum Congress, held in Norway, May 29-June 1, 1994, was headed by Ahmad Zamel, Deputy Minister for Technical Affairs, Ministry of Petroleum and Mineral Resources. He welcomed the King of Norway and other dignitaries to the successful Saudi exhibit. Delegates from Saudi Aramco included Faysal M. Al-Bassam, Vice President for Saudi Aramco Affairs, and Yusof Rafie, Vice President for Employee Relations and Training.

Water and Agriculture

The Kingdom gives high priority to water availability. It is a world leader in water desalination. Currently it has 33 *desalination plants* on the shores of the Arabian Gulf and the Red Sea, producing over 576 million gallons of drinking water per day (equal to 70% of drinking water in the country), in comparison to only 5 million gallons per day produced in 1970. Some of these plants also generate electricity as a by-product (3600 megawatts an hour, or 30% of electric generation in the country). Contracts have been signed to raise production to 800 million gallons per day within two years from June 6, 1994.

Acquifers complement other sources of water and are harnessed by digging deep wells which now exceed 4,800 in number.

By 1994, the Kingdom had built nearly 200 *dams*. There were only sixteen dams in 1975. One of these is the biggest in the Middle East, built in the region of Bisha in the southern part of the Kingdom, and will hold 86 billion gallons of water. These dams collect water from the occasional rainfalls and have a storage capacity in excess of 500 million cubic meters.

The special attention given to agriculture is in line with the policy of diversifying the economic base. About half the Kingdom's population lives in rural areas. Many of them work in agriculture. It is strategically important to increase production for an expanding population.

The government encourages farmers by granting them agricultural land and giving interest-free loans. The Agricultural Bank has contributed extensively in this regard. Generous support by the government for the agricultural sector materialized as follows: payment up to 50% of expenses for fertilizer; payment up to 50% of the animal feed; supporting potato production by allowing the farmer to have five tons free and after that paying 1,000 Riyals for every ton with a maximum of 15 tons; equipment for poultry and dairy, absorbing up to 30% of the cost; transport of animals by airplanes, absorbing 100% of the cost.

The Agricultural Bank, the Saudi Credit Bank and the Agricultural Development Fund provided financing to the farmers. For the period 1975–1985 the small and medium-term loans to farmers exceeded 42 billion dollars. In the Five-Year Plan 1980–1985, the government allotted twenty-billion dollars to agriculture. By the end of 1991 the Saudi Arabian Agricultural Bank distributed 34 billion Saudi Riyals (9.1 billion dollars) in interest-free loans to farmers and private Saudi companies.

Between 1975 and 1985, the land under cultivation increased by 1,300%. In this period wheat production increased by 400 times. By 1994, land under cultivation had increased to nearly four million hectares (9.8 million acres). One of the shining achievements in the development plans is the production of wheat. It reached 2.3 million tons in 1986, 3.5 million tons in 1990 and over four million tons in 1994. This is more than twice the amount needed for local consumption. Saudi Arabia, basically a desert land, became an exporter of wheat to several countries in the world.

Poultry and meat production increased threefold. Egg and dairy production doubled. Thus, the Kingdom became self-sufficient in meat, poultry, eggs, dairy products and began to export wheat, dates, certain vegetables and fruits to the international market.

The generosity of the Kingdom extends far beyond its borders. It has granted several million dollars to the International Fund for Agricultural Development (Ifad) to finance projects in nearly 80 developing countries. Millions of dollars were donated to the international food program, along with large quantities of dates and thousands of tons of wheat given to other nations in need.

On November 9, 1984 the Food and Agricultural Organization (Fao) in Rome, Italy, acknowledged these achievements in agriculture by giving an award to the Kingdom's Ministry of Agriculture and Water.

The Industrial Evolution

Saudi Arabia was transformed into a modern industrial state in a record time of nearly two decades. The Kingdom embarked on gigantic projects for massive industrial development. Basic to an industrialization boom is the availability of reliable sources of energy, mainly *electrical energy*. When oil and gas are abundant and within easy reach, and when a coupling is made of the latest international technology with long-range planning, wisdom, dedication and the technology acquired by the natives, then all the ingredients for success are there. That is exactly what is behind the success story of the Kingdom's industrialization and its diversifying of its economic base, so they would not have to depend solely upon oil.

The Saudi government generously supported industrialization. Its goal was to acquire and provide an abundant supply of electric energy for industry as well as all Saudi citizens. The Saudi Industrial Development Fund was very generous in its loans to the various electrical power companies. This provided the impetus for building the necessary power stations. Availability of abundant sources of cheap oil and gas also were a great incentive.

King Fahd gave special personal attention to development projects, especially electrical power generation because electricity is a service of great importance touching the lives of citizens everywhere. His directives were to make electricity available in the cities, villages and distant settlements. As early as March, 1986, King Fahd inaugurated the eighth electrical power station in the capital of Riyadh. It is considered among the biggest electrical generating stations in the world with a production capacity of 800 megawatts, which will increase to 1,000 megawatts. The station covers an area of nearly 600,000 square meters and cost nearly one and a half billion Saudi Riyals. Today, electricity reaches 5,990

One of the many ultra modern shopping centers.

King Khaled International Airport in Riyadh is one of twenty-three airports connecting the four corners of the Kingdom and giving easy access to most countries of the world.

A bounty of agriculture–Saudi Arabia, basically a desert land, overnight became an exporter of wheat to several countries of the world.

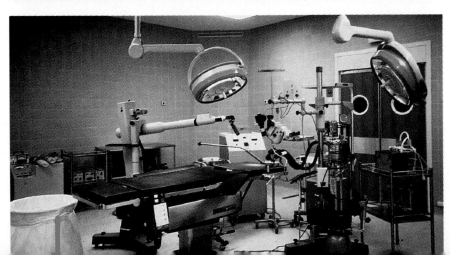

Exhibits of "Saudi Arabia yesterday and today" tell the story of the Kingdom joining the family of modern nations. Millions of people and dignitaries throughout the world witnessed the Kingdom's parade of progress. Prince Salman Bin Abdulaziz, Governor of Riyadh attending one of these exhibits.

The Custodian of the Two Holy Mosques King Fahd Bin Abdulaziz meets the captain of the Saudi Arabian national soccer team as the General Presidency of Youth Welfare President Prince Faisal Bin Fahd looks on.

cities, villages and hijras in the Kingdom. Between 1985–1988, domestic consumption of electricity increased by 23%. In 1991, industrial consumption reached nearly 17,000 million kilowatt-hours which represented about 28% of the total electric energy consumed.

The phenomenal growth of installed electric capacity increased by an average of 32% per day from 418 megawatts (MW) in 1970 to nearly 14,600 megawatts in 1984. By 1992, electric generation from various electric power companies reached 17,049 megawatts, which is fourteen times higher than what it was in 1975. Add to this 2,825 megawatts of electric generation from certain desalination plants, and the total will reach nearly 20,000 megawatts, serving over two and a half million subscribers.

The expansion of the non-oil sector was equally remarkable. The government played a key role in developing the basic hydrocarbon industries, and the private sector has done its share in building other industrial projects. With abundant energy from oil and electricity along with large income from oil, *manufacturing plants* are being built at an average rate of 45 a year. Between 1970–1984, the number of operating plants rose from 207 to over 1,600, reaching today nearly 2,500.

Saudi Basic Industries Corporation (Sabic) expanded its global distribution network to improve its marketing strategy and wide reach to service customers around the world. It plays an important role in the Kingdom's drive for the industrialization and diversification of the economy. This company was established as a basic umbrella having joint ventures with various companies on a 50-50 basis. Possible partners were recruited based on established expertise. Many American firms such as Mobil, Shell, Exxon and Texas Eastern were all recruited along with a consortium of Japanese firms led by Mitsubishi. Sabic brought into reality eleven basic industries since it was first formed in 1976. These industries include massive projects in the metal sector, fertilizer and petrochemicals. A number of joint-ventures with American and Japanese companies enable Sabic to efficiently present its products to world markets.

Between 1970 and 1991, the Kingdom's Gross Domestic Product (GDP) increased nearly three-fold to 113 billion dollars. Industrialization and the private sector played a pivotal role. The latter's contribution rose from 7.4 billion dollars in 1970 to 38.5 in

1991. The Saudi Industrial Development Fund also played a major role by financing more than one thousand projects at a cost exceeding fifteen billion dollars. Industrial centers were built near a number of Saudi cities such as Riyadh, Jeddah, Qasim, Dammam, Hofouf and Hasa.

In the industrial cities of *Jubail* and *Yanbu*, Sabic ventures were built from ground zero. The Royal Commission for these twin cities was established September 21, 1975 and was responsible for their development. The commission operates as an independent agency directly under the chairmanship of the Custodian of the Two Holy Mosques, King Fahd. These two industrial cities encompass some of the most important industrial complexes in the world today. Jubail is a city on the Arabian Gulf with an area of 400 square miles (1,050 square kilometers) and a worker population of 30,000. It was designed to accommodate 350,000 people. It is projected to have a population around 300,000 by the year 2010. Yanbu, on the Red Sea, has an area of 57 square miles (150 square kilometers), and a population of 18,000. It is designed to accommodate a population of 150,000. About twenty primary industries and four secondary industries are in operation in these cities; others are in the building stage. Petrochemicals, fertilizers, methanol, industrial gases, plastics, iron, steel and many more are produced.

Industrialization in Jubail and Yanbu turned previously wasted gas, which accompanied oil production operations, into a useful resource instead of being wasted and burned just to dispose of it and become an environmental health hazard. Gas fuels the industry and is the major source of feedstock for petrochemicals.

At one time, the mammoth project of the twin industrial cities was employing a skilled labor force in excess of 100,000 people. When the Jubail industrial project was inaugurated in 1977 it heralded a new era in the modern and industrial history of the Kingdom.

Saudi universities conduct applied and scientific research. Substantial support is received from King Abdulaziz Center for Science and Technology (Kacst). It has the responsibility of directing and formulating Saudi Arabia's national science policy. Joint research projects are conducted in cooperation with international scientific centers in the world. Cooperation is being achieved between Kacst and American scientific organizations. An example of this is the Saudi-U.S. program for cooperation on solar energy.

Over thirty separate projects have been undertaken since 1979, for conducting solar energy experiments in the U.S. and the Kingdom.

A major Research Institute (RI), which is an independent center affiliated with King Fahd University of Petroleum and Minerals (KFUPM), has conducted solar research since 1977. This Research Institute, described under Educational Progress, carried on a variety of other research projects responding to the needs and long-range goals of the Kingdom. This impressive institute has the most modern scientific equipment and the latest in computer technology. It has about one hundred laboratories. Since the late 60's, KFUPM scientists have been investigating water desalination, hydrogen production, solar cooling and environmental research.

An agreement was signed in 1983 between the National Aeronautics and Space Administration (Nasa) and Kacst for cooperation in space-related research. This cooperation helped in mapping programs, ground water exploration and sand drift monitoring. The General Electric company was granted a contract to supply and install a remote sensing facility station for the reception, processing and analysis of space photos sent by satellite. New joint research agreements are continually being made. Notable among these is the one with the Canadian National Research Council. Visions, dreams and ambitions become reality as the Kingdom approaches its goal of industrialization and a diversified economic base.

Housing and Expansion of the Haramein

Vast sums of money have been invested in building homes for low income groups. In addition, long-term, interest-free loans are granted to citizens for building their own homes. Apartment buildings have been built by investors. Loans are interest-free and for a long number of years. From 1975 until 1984, 403,000 units were built, out of which 287,000 were built by the private sector with loans from the Real Estate Development Fund. The availability of housing had reached 65 units per 1,000 people in 1989 as compared to only 5 units per 1,000 people in 1980. During the Fourth Development Plan of 1985–90, 285,000 housing units were built. The Ministry of Public Works and Housing, along with the Royal Commission for Jubail and Yanbu, have both built a large number of units. Housing projects specifically built for employees were carried by other government institutions. Leading amongst these are the National Guard, various universities, Ministry of Defense, Ministry of Interior, and some other ministries. Many public buildings possess a unique architecture blending Arab traditions and making ample use of marble.

Saudi cities rank amongst the most modern in the world. If one had the chance of visiting these cities in the early seventies, chances are, he would not recognize them today. One witnesses progress everywhere: going from Hail in the north, the Jizan in the south, or from Jeddah on the Red Sea to Riyadh, in central Najd and on to Dhahran, Khobar and Dammam in the east!

The Ministry of Municipal and Rural Affairs, along with supporting agencies, made large investments in the public utilities sector. Water and electrical networks along with sewage and rainwater drainage systems have been built. Municipal services, construction of beautiful public parks, market centers and streets were completed.

Maintaining the *Haramein,* or the Holy sites in Mecca and Madina, is considered an honor and a duty. Since Saudi Arabia is the focal point for all Moslems of the world, special attention has been given to large and comprehensive expansions of the Holy places. To make the pilgrims' journey to Arabia a safe, spiritual experience, mammoth projects have been achieved. The number of pilgrims has increased at an average annual rate of 6.3 percent, reaching over two million today. Hajj is considered the largest single human gathering in the whole world. Descriptive details have been given elsewhere.

"The Holy Mosque in Mecca (Al-Haram Al-Makki) has undergone colossal expansion, raising its area from 193,000 square meters to 328,000 square meters.

Its courtyards can now accommodate 730,000 worshippers compared to 410,000 worshippers previously. The new expansion has created space to accommodate more than one million worshippers at a time at a cost of SR10 billion.

The expansion of the *Prophet's Mosque* has raised its total area from 16,500 square meters to 165,500 square meters. The new area can accommodate 700,000 worshippers and well over one million during peak times compared to only 38,000 worshippers previously.

Costs incurred by this colossal project amounted to SR30 billion. These two colossal projects rise as a living testimony to the government's keen interest in all that is related to the pilgrimage and the pilgrims, and the care it takes in ensuring the comfort and safety of all visitors.

Costs of the other projects implemented in Makkah Al-Mukarramah and the pilgrimage sites are more than SR4 billion. They include road networks, bridges and tunnels, illumination, tree-planting and water stations."

Health, Social Justice and Youth Welfare

A comprehensive *health care* system has been developed including specialized hospitals equipped with the latest equipment. Some of the specialty treatment centers are for the eye, heart disorders, kidney, burns, tuberculosis and cancer.

King Khaled Eye Specialist Hospital in Riyadh is one of the best equipped and largest hospitals in the world. Resident physicians are pioneers in the eye treatment field. Patients come to this hospital from many corners of the world including Spain, Egypt, England and the U.S. King Faisal Specialist Hospital and Research Center has earned a fine reputation. With a commitment to provide the good medical care for the citizens, the Ministry of Health arranged a surgery exchange program between the well-known Baylor College of Medicine in Houston and the hospital in Riyadh.

Many Saudi students go to the U.S., England, France and Germany for training in medical care. Also the Kingdom has a number of medical schools. The universities with medical degrees include King Saud University in Riyadh, King Abdulaziz University in Jeddah and King Faisal University in Dammam. The Abha district also will have a medical college. King Khaled University Hospital, with a capacity of 870 beds, is a teaching hospital within King Saud University Medical School.

King Fahd Medical City in Riyadh, built at a cost of 533 million dollars, is a massive medical complex that includes four major hospitals for Pediatrics, Maternity, Psychiatry and General care. An estimated staff of 3,000 is housed in a specially built complex. Also included are a burn treatment center and a kidney transplant center.

A number of government agencies and ministries provide medical services for their dependents and also for other citizens.

These are the National Guard, Ministry of Interior, Ministry of Defense and some other agencies that run modern hospitals and health centers for their own personnel.

The Saudi Red Crescent Society complements the Ministry of Health in first aid, accidents and other emergencies. During the Hajj period, health facilities are made available in cooperation with the Red Crescent. About 12,000 doctors, nurses and other medical personnel are ready to treat the pilgrims. Another unique feature of the Saudi Arabian health system is the Flying Medical Corps. In this manner health care is made available to people in remote areas of the Kingdom.

In the fourth Five-Year Plan, the private sector played a larger role in the medical field. Twenty more hospitals were built, along with 1,000 health centers and 100 diagnostic and obstetric centers. The number of professionals and technical personnel increased to 63,452. Stimulated by generous government loans, the private sector now plays a significant role in the health sector. There were 74 hospitals in 1970 with 11,000 beds, 600 clinics, 3,300 nurses and 1,200 doctors. Currently there are more than 254 hospitals with 55,000 beds, 2,500 clinics, 38,000 nurses and 18,000 doctors. The Fifth Development Plan of 1990–1994 provided 500 new primary health centers and 6,580 new hospital beds. New projects will increase the number of hospitals to 292.

A unique charity hospital has been opened on the outskirts of Riyadh. It is designed for treatment and research of leukemia and lymphomas in children. It is known as King Fahd Children's Medical Center and Research Hospital (Kfcmc). Its cost is about one hundred million dollars. The hospital has an intensive care unit of forty beds and is equipped with the best and latest specialized medical technology. The most modern laboratories, support facilities, staff housing and engineering support are provided. Children will be admitted to Kfcmc without regard to ability to pay. Kfcmc will guarantee payment of the cost of treatment for any child without other means of support.

Much of the plan for this hospital was modeled after the well known St. Jude Children's Research Hospital in Memphis, Tennessee, USA. The hospital is designed so that most clinical services are centered around an Outpatient Treatment Center. This charity Research Hospital was founded by Dr. Nasser I. Rashid, co-author of this book, entirely at his own expense after his son Fahd, who was stricken with leukemia, was cured. Dr. Rashid donated this hospital to the Saudi Government. It will be run by King Faisal Specialist Hospital. The welfare of the Saudi citizen is utmost in the minds of Saudi leaders. The purpose is to bring comfort, peace of mind and happiness to the Saudi citizen.

A *social insurance* or employment insurance protects employees. The social services budget in the fourth plan (1985–90) was about four billion dollars, not including social insurance or housing construction. This amounted to four times more than the amount allotted in the first development plan of 1970–75. The government guarantees a proper income in case of disability or retirement. In case of death a proper income should be given to the employees' dependents. Disabled people and others stricken by disasters are afforded a decent standard of living by the government. Pensions are disbursed to these people. In 1962, the upper limit of these benefits was 410 dollars per family. In early 1991 these benefits were 3,000 dollars. While aid for this sector was 3.7 million Saudi Riyals in 1979–80, it became 137.4 million Saudi Riyals in 1989–90. Rehabilitation programs for the physically and mentally handicapped are offered along with various other social services.

The *social security* system fills a basic social need. The total amount given to recipients increased by 33.7% on an annual average, from 41.7 million Saudi Riyals in 1969–1970 to one and a half billion Saudi Riyals in 1983–1984.

The General Presidency of *Youth Welfare* (Gpyw), established in 1974, is a testimonial to the belief that the "Kingdom's most valuable asset is not its massive reserves of oil, but its youth." Its president is Prince Faisal Bin Fahd and his deputy is Prince Sultan Bin Fahd.

King Fahd is President of the Higher Council for Youth. His deep interest in their guidance and upbringing is a natural extension of his love as a father and educator. Programs have been designed to strengthen the minds, morals and spirits of the young. Basic principles of good behavior, adherence to traditions and respect for fellow-man are inherent in many youth activities.

Modern recreational and sports facilities have been built in Jeddah, Dammam, Abha, Hail, Qasim, Riyadh, Al-Khobar, Tabouk and other Saudi cities. Swimming pools, cultural libraries, literary clubs, dormitories, science centers, game centers, arts and crafts also received special attention. The largest urban centers have large sports complexes known as Sports Cities. Presently, there are fifteen of these sports arenas throughout the Kingdom. For example, the King Fahd International Stadium built in Riyadh is an ultra-modern sports facility having a capacity in excess of 80,000 spectators. Its design blends the traditional shape of an Arab tent with the latest high-tech available in the construction business. The seering heat of the sun is blocked through the use of a high strength innovative fabric as a tent cover coupled with the latest technologies. It has a soccer field, running tracks, television studio, a center for the media, various accommodations for athletes, and a huge eating facility capable of accommodating 3,000 people.

Sports are popular, especially soccer and basketball. In 1985, the national soccer team reached a high point by gaining a victory in the Asian Cup. In June 3 of 1989, another victory was won by the Saudi team which was the World Under-16's Championship in Scotland. On October 29, 1993 thousands of Saudis welcomed their victorious soccer team home. They had just successfully competed against five Asian teams at Doha, Qatar to determine the winning team for representing Asia in the World Cup Finals. Saudi Arabia's National Soccer Team finished first. In the summer of 1994 the Saudi National Soccer Team, with the Asian Championship under its belt, vigorously competed in the United States of America for the World Cup and represented the Kingdom with great pride.

The General Presidency of Youth Welfare orients young people and supports their interests. This program provides an overall global policy to ensure gainful use of free time of the youth so they can take advantage of their talents and potential. Strengthening the bodies and imparting in their souls the profound teachings of Islam along with Arab traditions are given priority attention.

Money allotted to Gpyw increased dramatically from 22.3 million Saudi Riyals in 1973–1974 to over 11.5 billion Riyals (3 billion U.S. dollars) in 1990. Recreation and education of the youth are very much strengthened through nearly 200 social and cultural athletic clubs.

These are scattered throughout the Kingdom. Their size reflects the size of the community in which they are located. Under the supervision of Gpyw, the Kingdom has 18 sports federations that plan and organize tournaments and leagues for the youth, including the handicapped. Sports clubs organize teams for more than 200 national and regional yearly competitions.

Sports experts are hired and training programs are offered to ensure the availability of qualified personnel to manage sports arenas and activities. In 1981, a degree program in sports administration and management was established by Gpyw.

Hundreds of local playgrounds have been built where the youth in these neighborhoods play volleyball, tennis, handball or basketball. Over twenty youth sports camps have been established throughout the Kingdom. These are modern facilities equipped with dining and lodging, along with indoor and outdoor sports of various kinds. These camps provide an opportunity for Saudi youth from the four corners of the Kingdom to intermingle and interact with one another. Scouting and camping trips are organized throughout the year.

Cultural programs are also organized. Literary clubs are very popular. Literary and poetry competitions are held in several Saudi cities. The Society for Culture and Arts strongly supports young artists and encourages them to excel. Some of the artistic work is displayed at cultural centers in the Kingdom such as the King Fahd Cultural Center in Riyadh, or shown abroad at exhibits organized by Gpyw.

Scientific hobby groups are formed at certain regional clubs to encourage those who are scientifically gifted. Social responsibility of the youth is much encouraged by the General Administration for Social Activities. Volunteer work is organized where social services are rendered by the youth to the pilgrims or in environmental programs and anti-drug campaigns. Team Spirit prevails and the moral fiber of the youth is enriched and strengthened.

The Gulf Cooperation Council has Deputy Ministers for Youth and Sports who meet on a regular basis to discuss ways and means of cooperation and competition. Prince Faisal is very active in this regard both nationally and internationally. He is an active member of the Olympic Committee. From time to time he makes special visits to get better acquainted with what other youths are doing on the international scene. The latest practices are sought, studied, sometimes adapted and adopted. Faisal Bin Fahd responded to an invitation by the chairman of the Nobel Peace Prize to visit Norway and the city of Stockholm. He met with top leaders of the country and visited sports and recreational facilities along with other youth centers. He closely observed the various programs and sports centers, always seeking ways to improve, innovate, implement and bring new ideas for Saudi youth who are the Kingdom's treasure and its bright hope for the future.

The procession of impressive achievements goes on. While Saudi Arabia is a modern nation in every sense of the word, it continues to seek the best talent in the world and actively seeks joint ventures with experienced and proven companies, be they from Japan, Germany, Europe or the U.S.A.

Many world leaders, journalists, politicians, scientists and engineers all around the globe are astounded by this massive modernization. This is recognized and admired on the international scene when one measures words and matches them with deeds.

Diversifying the economic base, modernizing the Kingdom, making most impressive progress in industrialization–all these are a reality. Another reality must be pondered by leaders around the world: namely, the fact that Saudi Arabia sits atop the richest oil reserves in the world. After over half a century of oil production that fueled this gigantic development process, Saudi Arabia did not deplete its oil resources. On the contrary, they skyrocketed from about 3 billion barrels in 1949 to over 260 billion barrels today, and more is yet to be discovered.

This is coupled with the priceless atmosphere of safety and security that one feels upon touching Saudi soil. Crime is the lowest among all nations of the world. This is truly the envy of many; especially those who are true to their conscience; those who treasure the good inner feeling of security that mankind longs for, but much of the time is deprived from experiencing or harnessing.

A western writer said "The crime rate remains relatively low and would be considerably lower if there were no foreign workers in the country. Violent street crime is almost nonexistent." Law and order in the Kingdom will continue to play its unique role in promoting and safeguarding a thriving business atmosphere.

Chapter 6

Modern Cities and Interesting Sites

Traveling through the Kingdom of Saudi Arabia, one observes flourishing modern cities across the land. They rank amongst the cleanest and most modern cities of the world. If one had the chance of visiting these cities a decade ago, chances are he would not recognize them today. Parks, trees, modern streets, modern buildings and modern services are everywhere.

The Kingdom is divided into fourteen regions known as Provinces, Governorates, or Emriates (The Saudis call them Emirates). All regions of Saudi Arabia have been blessed with miraculous progress. Going from Hail, the bride of the North, to Jizan in the South, or from Jeddah, the bride of the Red Sea on the West, to Riyadh the bride of the desert in central Najd and on to Dhahran, Khobar and Dammam in the East, one witnesses progress everywhere. This parade of progress and great achievements are self-evident and mirrored in the beautiful gardens and polished buildings that dot the desert landscape. A brief description of some cities in the various provinces will give the reader an idea about the basic characteristics of these cities, their regions, and the points of interest.

Province or Emirate	Capital City
Riyadh	Riyadh, ultra-modern capital of Saudi Arabia, in Central Najd
Mecca	Mecca, Holiest city of Islam, in Hijaz
Madina	Madina, second Holy city of Islam
Tabouk	Tabouk, northwest, close to the Jordanian border

Province or Emirate	Capital City
Qurayat	Qurayat, in the northern corner of the Kingdom, close to the Jordanian border
Northern Province	A'r'ar, northern city, very close to the Iraqi border; near the theatre of operations during Gulf War
Al-Jawf	Skaka, west of the Great Nafud desert
Hail	Hail, in Jabal Shammar area
Qasim	Buraidah, on the west edge of the Dahna desert
Eastern Province	Dammam, on the Arabian Gulf, with Dhahran and Khobar, it is a tri-city metropolis; capital of the oil wealth of Saudi Arabia; focal point of Desert Shield & Desert Storm
Ba'ha	Ba'ha, southwest, close to the Red Sea
A'sir	Abha, highlands with terraced luscious green terrain
Jizan	Jizan, city by the Red Sea, facing several islands offshore
Najran	Najran, south on the border with Yemen; hugging the western edge of the mighty Rab'a Al-Khali

Riyadh

This is the capital of the Kingdom of Saudi Arabia. It has undergone a profound transformation since the days of Abdulaziz. This city has witnessed great achievements in development and modernization. It has expanded greatly in all directions and has become a capital city befitting the stature earned by the Kingdom of Saudi Arabia. In 1986 Riyadh celebrated its 50th anniversary as a municipality. The word Riyadh in Arabic means "gardens." Who would believe that in the span of such a few years, Riyadh truly would become a garden spot in the heart of the desert? The transformation that has taken place here is exemplary. Similar transformations have been witnessed in many cities throughout the four corners of the Kingdom.

While Riyadh was only 8.5 square kilometers (3.3 square miles) in 1932, by 1994 it was over 1,600 square kilometers (615 square miles) in area. Its population has expanded from 19,000 in 1918 to over 2.5 million people in 1994. Its climate, between September and March, is pleasant with moderate temperatures. Summers are hot and dry with temperatures varying between 35 and 45 degrees centigrade. Nights in the winter can be cold. Some unpleasant sandstorms come with the north wind, especially in February and March, soon to be washed away by rains which are torrential at times.

Historic landmarks in Riyadh include the famous Fort Musmak, where the fate of Saudi Arabia hung in the balance at the time when Abdulaziz conquered the city and began his long and arduous struggle for unifying the Kingdom of Saudi Arabia. This fort, where the governor ruled, was built in 1865 (1282 A.H.) and is located in the commercial center next to the Emirate of Riyadh. It was liberated by Abdulaziz in 1902 (1319 A.H.). The Fortress has been restored and rejuvenated but kept its historic value and unique design. It remains a distinctive, impressive monument to the past.

Of historic importance also is the Murabba'a Palace, meaning Square Palace; it is located in the center of town. It acquired this name because of its four square towers. It was built about sixty years ago. Part of the Palace was used by the founder of the Kingdom as a home and the rest as the seat of government, where the King held his Majlis and those working with him had some offices. It is a unique old structure, considered as an Antiquity Museum and currently managed by the General Authority of Antiquities of the Ministry of Education.

The historic area of Diriya, known also as Al-Diriya was destroyed by the Turks after a long resistance in 1233 A.H. Saudi ancestors came from the Qatif region and settled in this historical community located in the middle of Wadi Hanifa in the northwest corner of Riyadh. Saud Ibn Mohammed Ibn Moqrin ruled Diriya from 1720 until his death in 1725. Mohammed Ibn Saud succeeded him. His rule lasted nearly 40 years extending from 1725 until his death in 1765. It was he who welcomed Sheikh Mohammed Abdulwahhab who was seeking purity in Islam. The founding of Saudi Arabia was a culmination of the coupling and fusion of this islamic puritanism and Saudi family leadership, which remained a dedicated champion of this islamic cleansing until this day. Thus, Diriya was the Saudi capital for the first Saudi state which ended in the first half of the 13th century A.H. (18th century A.D.). When the second Saudi state was established by Imam Turki Bin Abdullah Bin Mohammed Bin Saud in 1240 A.H., Riyadh became the capital city of the Saudi state, and it has remained the capital of Saudi Arabia ever since.

Jabal or mountain Abou Makhroug, is located in the Malaz area in the center of Riyadh. It is now a park with an interesting landmark, a large rock shaped in an arch. During the time of King Ibn Saud this was used as a recreational area for him and his family, since it was then in the open desert. Also Abdulaziz and his men spent the night here when they were on their way to occupy Fort Musmak.

Other interesting landmarks of modern Riyadh include:

- The Governor's office, known as Qasr Al-Hokm. An ambitious program has been carried out to develop Riyadh's old governor's district into the city's cultural, historical, commercial, and social center.
- The diplomatic quarter is one of the most modern sites in the Kingdom. Most of the embassies and consulates of various countries of the world are housed in this ultra-modern quarter. It is located about five miles (eight kilometers) from the center of the city on an area encompassing seven million square meters (about 8.5 million square yards). It can accommodate 120 diplomatic missions and about 31,000 inhabitants.
- The King Fahd International Stadium which was established by the General Presidency of Youth Welfare in 1988. It is designed in a tent-shaped fashion, from durable and fireproof material. It can accommodate up to 80,000 people.
- The King Khaled International Airport is located about 22 miles (35 kilometers) from the city's center and covers an area of 87 square miles (about 225 square kilometers). It is the largest and most modern airport in the world today.

The unique architectural design incorporates Islamic and Arabic heritage and can accommodate up to 15 million passengers per year.

- Other landmarks of interest include the two universities located in Riyadh; King Saud University and Imam Mohammed Ibn Saud Islamic University.

- The water tower located in the Murabb'a Quarter, near King Faisal street is surrounded by a luscious beautiful garden. The tower is crowned on top with a special restaurant for official guests.

- The television tower is a very impressive landmark of the city of Riyadh. It is located in the middle of the Ministry of Information Complex and has a height of 176 meters (577 feet). It is certainly one of the most prominent features in the city and can be seen for miles.

- The Nasseria Gate is a modern landmark dating back forty years, when it was the main gate to the Nasseria Palace. It was also part of the wall which surrounded this Palace.

- King Faisal Conference Hall, with its distinctive architectural style, is a site for conferences and national gatherings. It is connected with the luxurious Intercontinental Hotel at Ma'zar Street.

- The King Abdulaziz Hall is located in Darat Al-Malik Abdulaziz or Foundation of King Abdulaziz containing his personal library and personal desk. The Foundation has a number of exhibits including mementoes used by the founder of the Kingdom; the two Holy Qorans he used while praying and other personal belongings such as coins, weapons, hand fan, watch, compass, notes, cars and other interesting items. It also gives an interesting pictorial account of Saudi history and development, especially during the era of Abdulaziz.

- There are several modern parks, first class hotels and good restaurants in Riyadh.

- King Fahd Library, located on Mecca road in the Olaya district, contains the most modern library facilities. The majestic white marble building incorporates Islamic architecture with a modern blend. The Library covers an area of 58,000 square meters.

- King Abdulaziz Library is rich with many books in science, arts and history. Several depict the history of Saudi Arabia.

- Riyadh has museums; leading among them is the Museum of Antiquities and Folklore Tradition. It is located in the Shemeisi Quarter. Various halls in the museum are rich with exhibits depicting the various development stages of the Kingdom beginning with the early days to the Islamic era.

- Several parks dot the landscape of the city. In 1987 (1407 A.H.), a zoo was enriched with several species of animals. It is considered as the largest of its kind in the Kingdom, covering an area of 134,000 square meters (160,000 square yards). It is dotted with gardens, playgrounds, rest areas and small man-made lakes.

- There are many shops in Riyadh and many shopping centers with merchandise from all over the world. Many of these shops have some of the most beautiful jewelry that one could find. Prices are also very reasonable. Beautiful modern buildings are scattered throughout the city. Many government Ministries are eye-catching with their impressive building designs. The Gulf Fly-Over Bridge is a fine example of engineering design. It is also a major landmark in the city.

Among the scientific centers in Riyadh one counts: the King Abdulaziz City of Science and Technology (Kacst); King Fahd Security College, affiliated with the Ministry of Interior; King Abdulaziz Military Academy and King Faisal Air Force College, both affiliated with the Ministry of Defense and Aviation, and King Khaled Military College, affiliated with the National Guard.

Several hospitals are located in the city. Among them are the King Fahd Hospital, King Fahd Medical City, King Faisal Specialist Hospital and Research Center, King Khaled Eye Specialist Hospital, and King Fahd Children and Medical Center (KFCMC), which is the only specialized hospital for children's leukemia and other types of cancer outside the United States of America.

The city of Riyadh also has an industrial area called Industrial City, covering an area of 450,000 square meters (540,000 square yards). Another industrial city was set up covering an area of 21 million square meters (25.2 million square yards). Several products are manufactured here.

One of the main attractions in the city of Riyadh is *Jenadriyah*,

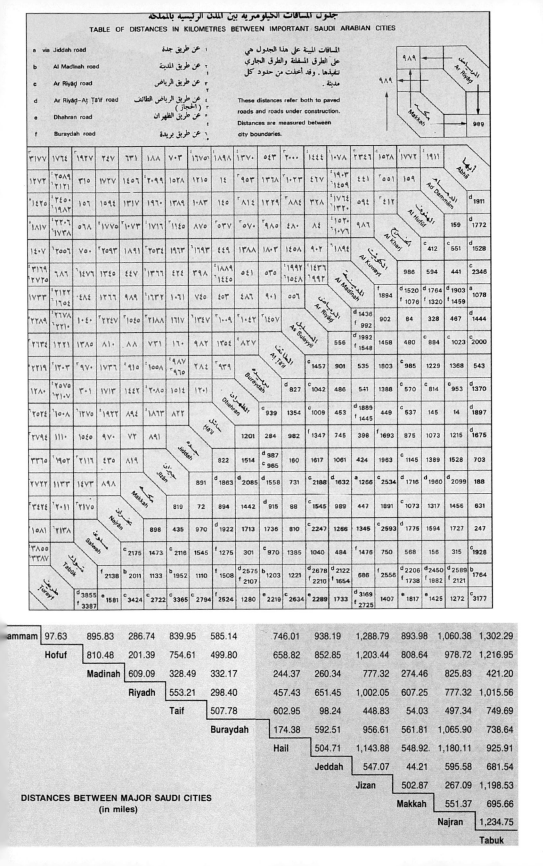

جدول المسافات الكيلومترية بين المدن الرئيسية بالمملكة

TABLE OF DISTANCES IN KILOMETRES BETWEEN IMPORTANT SAUDI ARABIAN CITIES

a — via Jiddah road — عن طريق جدة

b — Al Madinah road — عن طريق المدينة

c — Ar Riyāḍ road — عن طريق الرياض

d — Ar Riyāḍ-Aṭ Ṭa'if road — عن طريق الرياض الطائف (الحجاز)

e — Dhahran road — عن طريق الظهران

f — Buraydah road — عن طريق بريدة

المسافات المبينة على هذا الجدول هي على الطرق المسفلتة والطرق الجاري تنفيذها . وقد أخذت من حدود كل مدينة .

These distances refer both to paved roads and roads under construction. Distances are measured between city boundaries.

DISTANCES BETWEEN MAJOR SAUDI CITIES (in miles)

اشارات التحذير والخطر
DANGER AND WARNING SIGNS

منعطفان أوضما يمين
Double Bend. The
First to the Right

منعطف يمين
Right Bend

منعطف خطر أو منعطفات خطر
Dangerous Bend or
Dangerous Bends

طريق منزلق
Slippery Carriageway

اشغال
Road Works

اخفاضات
Uneven Road

تقاطع طرق بدون افضلية
Intersection with a
Non-Priority Road

تقاطع طرق بدون افضلية
Intersection with a
Non-Priority Road

طريق ضيق
Carriageway Narrows

ممر مشاة
Pedestrian Crossing

ممر اطفال
Children Crossing

مقطع سكة حديد غير محطور
Level-Crossing
Without Gates

مركز إسعاف
First Aid Station

انتبه - طريق أفضلية
Priority Road Ahead

مستشفى
Hospital

الاشارات الاجبارية
PROHIBITORY AND MANDATORY SIGNS

منوع الدخول لعموم السيارات
No Entry for all
Motor Vehicles

منوع المرور لكافة السيارات
No Entry for
all Vehicles

منوع المرور على الاتجاهين
Closed to all Vehicles
in Both Directions

قف - جمرك
Stop-Customs

منوع التجاوز
Overtaking Prohibited

نهاية التحظير خطر التجاوز
End of Prohibition
of Overtaking

منوع الاتجاه إلى اليسار
Turning to the Left
Prohibited

تحديد السرعة
Speed Limit

نهاية منطقة تحديد السرعة
End of Speed Limit

وجهة السير
Direction
to be Followed

قف
Stop

مواقف انتظار مؤقت
Restricted Stopping
or Waiting

موقف
Parking

منوع الوقوف
No Parking

محطة بنزين
Benzine Station

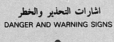

Conference Palace in Riyadh

Conference Palace in Taif

Dhahran of yesteryears.

KFUPM in Dhahran of today.

Khobar (Eastern Province) of yesteryears in the early seventies.

Khobar (Eastern Province) of today. Photos cannot lie, they speak for themselves.

which is the National Heritage and Cultural Festival, held every year in the vicinity of Riyadh. This two-week festival is managed and organized by the National Guard under the guidance of Crown Prince Abdullah. It is the finest cultural event in the entire Gulf. Thousands of people come to this festival from all corners of the Kingdom of Saudi Arabia, the Arab world and the Islamic world as well. It is located about thirty miles northeast of central Riyadh. The annual festival is held in May. It begins with the fascinating camel races and then a banquet featuring presentations of Saudi literature and culture. Colorful dancers, with their swords, demonstrate the national Saudi dance known as Ardah. Folk songs and music from the various regions of the Kingdom are exhibited. These performances are repeated every evening during the festival. Nearly five hundred writers, scholars, and poets attend sessions relating to poetry and literature. Seminars covering various topics from children's art to Islam and the Western world are given. These cultural events strengthen the understanding and pride of the younger generation in their heritage. Art exhibits take place during this festival including drawings by Saudi children. A book fair is included and Saudi history is portrayed in photographs and old documents. Artisans and craftsmen show their trade and workmanship. At the souk, traditional handi-crafts, jewelry, and old items are exhibited. Special exhibits are sponsored by various ministries, agencies, and the fourteen provinces. The old and the new are portrayed side by side. Also exhibitors from the Gulf Cooperation Council participate in this festival.

Jeddah

This is a great commercial city on the Red Sea. It is the gateway for pilgrims coming from all over the world to visit Mecca and Madina during the Hajj season. The climate is pleasant and moderate between September and March. The summer months are hot and humid with temperatures reaching 45 degrees centigrade. The city area is 1,200 square kilometers (463 square miles). The city had a population of 30,000 in 1947, and in 1994 it has close to two million inhabitants. Jeddah has a beautiful Corniche along the Red Sea, with many parks and recreational facilities. A promenade along the shores is a very pleasant experience. The sunset is a great sight to see. It is soothing and inspiring to observe the reflections on these shores. The city's coastline extends for over eighty kilometers (fifty miles).

One of the impressive landmarks of Jeddah is King Fahd Fountain, which is a beautiful sight day or night. It is considered the tallest fountain in the world. The water rushes upward to a height of 260 meters (853 feet).

Jeddah has been well known for decades for its bustling economic activity. It is a very active trading and shipping center. Goods coming to the Kingdom are mainly shipped via Jeddah on the Red Sea or Dammam on the Arabian Gulf. The Islamic Port of Jeddah is the largest seaport in the Kingdom. It has played an impressive role in handling the vast tonnage of materials used during the development boom years. Also, not long ago, Jeddah was the center for foreign missions to the Kingdom prior to their transfer to the Diplomatic Quarter in Riyadh. King Abdulaziz International Airport replaced the old Jeddah airport in order to accommodate the ever increasing numbers of pilgrims who flood the city during the Hajj season. The airport is located on an area of 105 square kilometers (40 square miles). It has three air terminals, namely the international terminal, the domestic, and the terminal for pilgrims. This large airport has the capacity of handling more than ten million passengers per year.

Several beautiful pieces of architecture and parks dot the city by the shore. Jeddah has been known for many years as the bride of the Red Sea. It is a strategic location for three continents, namely, Asia, Africa, and Europe. It is the important gateway to the Holy cities of Mecca and Madina. It has several hospitals with advanced medical facilities and it is the seat for King Abdulaziz University.

Historically, after the capitulation of Jeddah on December 23, 1925 (1344 A.H.) and after a long siege, the modern history of Saudi Arabia began as Abdulaziz was well on his way to founding a cohesive union. Jeddah has several old traditional structures with unique Hijaz architecture; the Nasif House is one such building of much interest to newcomers.

Dammam, Khobar and Dhahran

Not long ago, these were three distinct towns in the Eastern Region along the Arabian Gulf. During the development boom modern highways and urban expansion essentially connected the three communities and they became one large metropolis. This Eastern Region has a moderate climate between September and March. Summers are hot and very humid, with temperatures reaching 43 degrees centigrade. The combination of heat and humidity make the weather rather uncomfortable during the summer months of June, July and August. Dammam is the capital of the Eastern Province. It is only a few minutes from the centers of Dhahran or Khobar. The total area of the three cities is 718 square kilometers (277 square miles). Their combined population is over half a million, with an annual growth over 3.5 percent. The Qatif oasis with its artesian wells is only a short distance from this tri-city area.

King Abdulaziz seaport of Dammam was built mainly to handle the import of oil exploration equipment. This area was and remains the hub for oil operations in the Kingdom of Saudi Arabia. This famous seaport handles a large portion of the imported commodities and equipment reaching the Kingdom. It is the second largest port in the Kingdom, after Jeddah Port. Thus, Dammam is certainly a major shipping area also. Crude oil is loaded on giant tankers at Ras Tanura, not far from Dammam.

The modern railway system connects Riyadh with Dammam via Hofouf and Abqaiq. This new line shortened the distance between the two cities to four hours travel. It is a very comfortable railway system. Goods coming in containers to the Dammam seaport and destined for the Central Province in Riyadh may be directly moved to the Customs Terminal which was built in Riyadh to facilitate customs clearance. This was achieved by the General Railway Corporation.

There are other important oil cities in the Eastern Province, such as: Ras Tanura, 90 kilometers (57 miles) distance from Dammam; Abqaiq, 90 kilometers (57 miles) from Dammam. Dammam is about 380 kilometers (237 miles) from Riyadh, only 23 kilometers or 15 miles from Qatif.

King Fahd International Airport is located about 50 kilometers (31 miles) from Dammam and about 64 kilometers (40 miles) from the industrial city of Jubail. This is the largest airport in the Kingdom covering 760 square kilometers (93 square miles). The first phase of construction was completed in 1993.

Since the early 80's this metropolis has experienced fabulous growth. From a very humble beginning in the midst of a hostile desert, the area has been transformed into one of the most modern in the world today. Seeing this area before the development boom and after the reign of Prince Mohammed Bin Fahd, who is the Governor of the Eastern Province, one would not believe the transformation that has taken place in such a short period of time. Beautiful parks, modern highways, modern buildings and a clean environment, all bear witness to this great development. Among the impressive projects is the Corniche for Dammam and Khobar along the shores of the Arabian Gulf. This corniche has become one of the most beautiful shores in the world today. The area of Half Moon Bay has been developed as a beautiful tourist and recreational attraction. Here, the blue water of the Gulf is an inspiration and a sight to see, with abundant sunshine, beautiful sand dunes and lovely environment. The development of beautiful beaches, motels, chalets and other needed facilities with camping grounds and moorings for boats all add to the attraction and pleasure of the shore. King Fahd Park in Dammam is the largest in the Kingdom with an area of 273,000 square meters (2.9 million square feet). Beautiful trees, flowers and shrubs add to the luscious green environment.

Dammam is the home for two colleges of King Faisal University. One of them is Medicine and Medical Sciences and the other is for Architecture and Planning. Prince Mohammed Bin Fahd Awards for Excellence in Education are given in Dammam every year around April. It is an important event in the Eastern Region for encouraging students to excel in education. This Eastern Region has good health facilities and several industries. Of course, leading amongst them is the oil industry.

Khobar today is a modern city, certainly far different from what it used to be only a few years ago. It has been transformed from a small village to a teaming city on the shores of the Arabian Gulf. Khobar is now regarded as a commercial center for the tri-city area. It has many shops with consumer goods from all over the world. In the old days Khobar harbor was used to bring goods and needed equipment for the oil industry via small ships. Goods imported from Bahrain used to be unloaded at Khobar. It is still functional with small ships, a passenger lounge and a warehouse. However, with the building and expansion of the large port of Dammam, shipping facilities have now been transferred to the capital of the Eastern Province, namely Dammam. The town of Khobar has nearly 100,000 people. Several companies are located here especially since it is so close to Dammam and Dhahran. The beautiful parks at Azizia and Half Moon Bay are only a short distance from Khobar. Many people working in the oil industry live in the Khobar area which helps its economic well-being. King Fahd Bridge or Causeway connects the Kingdom of Saudi Arabia with the state of Bahrain, stretching a distance of 25 kilometers (16 miles).

Dhahran, only ten kilometers (6 miles) west of Khobar, is one of the important cities of this triangle. It was a small desert land back in the early 30's; but has gained importance during the rush for oil exploration, leading to oil discovery in 1938. The Arabian American Oil Company had its headquarters in Dhahran; in 1981 (1401 A.H.) it became Saudi-Aramco, largest oil company in the world and enjoys 100% Saudi ownership. Dhahran was the site for the first international airport built in the Kingdom called Dhahran International Airport. It is also home for King Fahd University of Petroleum and Minerals, located on a beautiful campus of 6.5 square kilometers (2.5 square miles). The massive development of oil operations and great expansions conducted by Saudi-Aramco made Dhahran the most advanced technology center in the Kingdom. Saudi-Aramco is essentially a city in itself with work facilities, housing, mosque, recreational facilities, schools, and a good hospital.

In 1990–1991, this region was very active during the Gulf War for liberating Kuwait. The great infrastructure which was built during the boom years in the Eastern Province became very handy indeed in facilitating the mission of repelling the aggressor and liberating Kuwait. At one time, the region became the focal point for the whole world.

Hail

Capital of the Province of Hail, this historic city is located in the Jabal Shammar or Mount Shammar area. It is 980 meters (3,200 feet) above sea level. The northern region of Hail hugs the Great Nafud desert. The city's population itself is over 119,000, increasing at a rate of 9.9 percent per year. It is well known for its abundant agriculture and rich history. This is the city where the famous man of generosity, Hatem Al-Tayye was born and raised. Among its legendary men of courage and poetry is Antar Ibn Shaddad, the writer of the famous Arab poetry known as Mouallaqat.

The Shammar tribe, a branch of the Tayye tribe, has been living in Hail for several centuries. Thus, the mountains of Hail are named after this tribe. They are called the Shammar mountains or Jabal Shammar. The climate is not severe and temperatures in the summer are below 40 degrees centigrade (104 degrees Fahrenheit). Winter temperatures are on the low side and may reach freezing. The rainy season is normally in the winter, but because of its elevation, the region often receives good quantities of rain in the spring as well. The city is surrounded by about 405 villages and Hijar. The population of the entire region is in excess of half a million. Hail was a busy center for people traveling north or south in the Arabian Peninsula, and a major route for pilgrims coming from Iraq and Syria on their way to Mecca. It was also a transit point for Moslems propagating the faith of Islam.

Hail is linked to other Saudi cities through its airport, located about 10 kilometers (6 miles) from the city. It has a number of major highways. Among them is the Hail-Qasim road extending for 300 kilometers (185 miles). It connects Qasim to Riyadh, a distance of another 650 kilometers (400 miles). Other roads include the Hail-Madina, extending a distance of 530 kilometers (335 miles), and continuing on to Mecca.

All ministries and government agencies have branches in Hail. Eighty percent of the work force in Hail is involved in the rich agricultural sector. The city is rich with antiquities. It has old castles and forts. Ibn Rashid Palace is one of its oldest Fort-Palaces, built towards the latter part of the nineteenth century. Many rocky areas contain ancient inscriptions and drawings. The old Zubaida route passed through the Faid oasis. This is named after the wife of the famous Abbasid Caliph, Horoun Al-Rashid (786-809 A.D.). This old road was built to bring the pilgrims from Iraq to Mecca. The Habashi mountain is rich with old archeology, some of it dating as far back as 4,000 years. About fifty kilometers from Hail, one will find the mountain of Tawarn and the grave of Hatem Al-Tayye is nearby. The modern city has health care centers, sports centers, sports facilities, many beautiful buildings and parks. The whole region has 1,200 Mosques. With all the development in Hail and the region, no wonder the city is properly called the bride of the north.

Mecca and Madina

These are the two Holiest cities of Islam. The ancient caravans and trade fairs were attracted to Mecca centuries ago. Mecca was a major religious center even before Islam. In their prayers, one billion Moslems from throughout the world face Mecca five times a day. This is the site where the Holy Qoran was revealed to the Prophet Mohammed. The Ka'ba and the Holy Mosque are both located in Mecca. There were 360 idols located in the Ka'ba prior to Islam. The Prophet Mohammed, however, threw the pagan idols out of Ka'ba. In 622 A.D., the Hijra year 1 A.H. in the Moslem calendar, persecution led the Prophet to leave Mecca fleeing for his safety and the safety of his followers. The town he fled to was called Yathrib which later became known as Madina. After eight years of Hijra, the Prophet was able to go back to Mecca in the year 630 A.D., thus ending polytheism and idol-worshipping. Every Moslem is supposed to make pilgrimage to Mecca, if capable, once in their lifetime.

Mecca, the Holiest city of Islam, is located in a rugged landscape where mountainous rocks may reach a height of 300 meters (1,000 feet). It is a distance of 45 miles (73 kilometers) east of Jeddah. It is located on a flat mountain plateau, 620 meters (2,046 feet) above sea level. Volcanic rock is spread in the western and southwestern parts of this city covering 50 square kilometers (19 square miles). The climate is moderate in the fall and spring, the winter is mild, but the summer is very hot. Its population is nearly three quarters of a million people. All major expansion has evolved around the Holy Mosque which has always been considered as the center of Mecca. The vast expansion of the Holy Haramein, meaning the Holy Mosque in Mecca and the Prophet's Mosque in Madina, was described earlier in this book. Vast sums of money, in the billions of dollars, were spent on these massive expansion projects. Umm Al-Qora University is located in Mecca. Several health facilities are also in Mecca to help the citizens and the pilgrims.

Today the city thrives with much progress, new supermarkets and first class hotels, super highways with cloverleafs and overpasses. Because of its mountainous nature, Mecca has the most so-phisticated tunnel systems found anywhere in the world. Along with all this modernity, the eternal values of Islam endure and prosper today. Every year two million pilgrims converge on Mecca to fulfill one of their sacred religious duties and make their dream come true.

Madina, located 447 kilometers north of Mecca (255 miles), is the second holiest city of Islam but the first Islamic community. When the Prophet Mohammed emigrated from Mecca, he was well received by the people in Madina who followed Islamic teachings. Madina was the city where Islam began to flourish and expand to people in distant lands. It was initially known as Madi-nat Al-Nabi, city of the Prophet, then it became simply Madina. In Arabic it is also known as Al-Madina Al-Mounawwara, the city of light. The Prophet Mohammed himself helped in building the Prophet's Mosque in Madina. That is where he is buried. The city was part of the old Hijaz which was under Ottoman suzerainty, until it was liberated by King Abdulaziz. It has several architec-tural structures which bear the turkish influence. Under the lead-ership of King Fahd Bin Abdulaziz, the Prophet's Mosque in Mad-ina was expanded and renovated extensively. Sky-scraping minarets rise high above the Prophet's Mosque. Both Mecca and Madina are closed to non-Moslems. The population of Madina has expanded vastly, from 50,000 in 1926 to over half a million in 1994.

Recent expansions of the Prophet's Mosque raised its capacity from 38,000 worshippers to 700,000. The mosque now has four minarets, 72 meters high (238 feet). Six more minarets are being added. Each of them is 92 meters high (304 feet). The number will total ten minarets. There will be 23 entrances to the mosque.

Madina is home for the King Fahd Holy Qoran Printing Com-plex. State of the art printing facilities are used to carefully and meticulously print accurate copies of the Holy Qoran which are then distributed throughout the four corners of the world.

Modern expressways link Madina to the far distant cities and hamlets of the Kingdom. The Mecca-Madina expressway is 420 kilometers (255 miles) long. It connects with the Jeddah-Madina expressway. These are ultra-modern highways of six lanes–three in each direction, and a central section 20 meters (66 feet) wide for future possibilities. The service road on each side is 10.9 meters (35 feet) wide. The Madina-Badr-Jeddah road is 400 kilometers long (250 miles). It moves in a southwesterly direction leading to the industrial city of Yanbu on the Red Sea. The Madina-Riyadh expressway which is 1,000 kilometers long (600 miles) goes through the central region of Qasim, reaching Buraidah and Uneiza. The Madina-Tabouk road is 1,000 kilometers long (600 miles) and moves northward linking highways with Jordan and northern Syria. This national network is complemented by ring roads or loops which circle the city of Madina, thus preventing traffic jams.

Madina is home for Islamic University which has students from over one hundred countries. Saudi students constitute only 20 percent of the entire student body.

Hospitals, telephone service, and other facilities provide the needed services for the inhabitants of the city and the pilgrims during the Hajj season. Water comes from artesian wells and de-salination plants. The desalination plant at Yanbu on the Red Sea provides much of the needed water for the population and the pil-grims.

Madina is very rich with historic sites, especially since it was the first Islamic community from which Islam was propelled and spread around the world. Leading among the historical sites are the Prophet Mosque, the Mosque of Guba, the Qiblatein Mosque, and other mosques. The Sayyid Al-Shahada or master of martyrs area is of historical importance, including the Ohud and Rumat mountains where the historic battle of Ohud was fought between the Moslems led by the Prophet Mohammed against the pagans.

Abha, Najran and Jizan

These southern cities of the Kingdom, wedged between the Red Sea and the Empty Quarter, give another flavor of Saudi life and will help in completing the coverage of the four corners of the Kingdom, north, south, east and west. The city of Abha, located next to Khamis Musheit, is 2,200 meters (7,261 feet) above sea level. Abha is linked with Jizan by a highway, 200 kilometers in distance (124 miles). It is also linked with Najran, a distance of 380 kilometers (236 miles). It is 730 kilometers (453 miles) from Jed-dah, via the coastal road. The Taif road is 562 kilometers (349 miles) long. Rugged Tihama mountain terrain has been tamed by engineering feats manifested in roads and bridges connecting inland Saudi Arabia with the Red Sea coast. The airport is 17 kilometers (10.6 miles) from the center of the city and connects with other airports in the Kingdom.

Rocky hills surround the Abha valley. The climate in the capital of Asir is moderate throughout the year. Summer temperatures do not exceed 30 degrees centigrade (85 degrees Fahrenheit). Winter temperatures could be as low as 5 degrees centigrade (41 degrees Fahrenheit). Asir has the good rainfall which is amongst the highest in the Kingdom averaging about 50 centimeters (20 inches) of water. Beautiful parks have been established in Abha and the surrounding regions. Visitors come from all over the Kingdom to enjoy their time there and the beauty of nature. The Asir National Park was built by the Ministry of Agriculture and Water. It covers an area of 450,000 hectares (1.1 million acres). The city has abundant supplies of underground water supplemented by dams built in different locations in Asir. Among these is the Abha Dam which is 350 meters (1,148 feet) long and 33 meters (115 feet) high. Abha is also supplied with a portion of the desalinated water from the Al-Shaqiq plant on the Red Sea.

Jizan on the southern shores of the Red Sea has mountainous terrain and about one hundred islands offshore. Through the years, deposits of rich land, carried by floods, came from the neighboring mountains and valleys to create fertile plains behind the coastal region. The city is humid in the summertime, temperatures range between 33 and 44 degrees centigrade. In the winter, temperatures range between 17 and 35 degrees centigrade. Steep mountains rise to 11,000 feet (3,354 meters) at the highest peaks. In the mountain areas, the temperatures in the summer range between 16 and 28 degrees centigrade and in the winter 3 and 25 degrees centigrade. The climate along the shore is hot and humid in the summertime, where humidity could reach 90%, while in the mountains it is moderate in the summer and relatively cold in the winter. Slopes are terraced, where fruit trees such as banana and plum are planted. Crops of wheat and barley are grown as well.

The Jizan Province has many mineral springs. One of them, a hot spring, is about 50 kilometers (31 miles) southeast of the city. The Alwagara is located north of Jizan-Al-Kawia Street and the Albuza mineral spring is a distance of 53 kilometers (33 miles) from the city of Jizan. Progress has touched the lives of all inhabitants in the Jizan Province. While the population is one and a half million for the entire province, the city of Jizan has a population in excess of 100,000. The Province is one of the richest agricultural regions in the Kingdom of Saudi Arabia. Oranges, mangoes, grapes, plums, lemons and beautiful flowers are all grown in this region. The city of Jizan has an airport, a seaport and several interesting historical sites.

The city of Najran is the capital of the Province with the same name. This Province extends southward until it reaches the borders with Yemen. Najran is about 1,210 meters (3,970 feet) above sea level. The oasis of Najran is bordered on the east by the vast sands of the Empty Quarter or Rab'a Al-Khali. Its climate is semi-desert and dry. Heavy monsoon rains pour down during the months of March, April and May. The population of this province is less than half a million, with the city of Najran having a population of 60,000 and a growth rate of about 4.2 percent per year. The Najran valley dam is one of the largest in the Kingdom. It has a storage capacity of 85 million cubic meters (3,000 million cubic feet). It is 35 kilometers (22 miles) from the city of Najran. It is 260 meters (850 feet) long and 60 meters (197 feet) high. Najran is a fine desert oasis with a valley rich with silt and lush greenery. Because of fertility and rain, varied crops thrive such as potatoes, radishes, squash and tomatoes, along with beans, wheat, corn and barley. Fruits are also produced here such as bananas, figs, dates, and melons. The orange groves and grapes of Najran are well known in the Kingdom. Dates remain traditional fruit for Najran and other cities around the Kingdom. They are very delicious at harvest time. Richness of soil and availability of well water for irrigation have created a beautiful forest of date palms. A date palm tree may produce up to 140 kilograms (308 pounds) of dates per year.

The trunk of the palm tree has been used for traditional construction of homes in Najran. When mixed with clay, the palm branches are used to build sturdy walls and when intertwined they make fences or shelters. The walls built from thick clay give fresh coolness in the summertime. The palm leaves are braided to make rope and women weave these into mats or baskets. Because of the great role the palm tree has played in Saudi life, it has been included in the Saudi symbol as a sign of prosperity, next to the sword which is the symbol for justice and security. Some unique structures have been built from mixtures of palm, straw and clay. Many have beautiful architectural designs. Multi-storied structures surrounded by walls were built. The ancient Amir Palace, in the center of the old town of Abou Saud, is of much interest and has been restored as a museum by the Ministry of Education.

In the midst of much modernization and fantastic developments, the countryside and even many of the cities, remain a source of great traditions, art, and natural beauty. The modern city of Najran has kept a good balance between its historic traditions and the massive developments that have engulfed the Kingdom and spread to cover Najran as well.

Several other interesting cities flourish in the Kingdom. Among these:

- Taif which is a summer resort area famous for its moderate climate and for its delicious grapes and pommegrenates. It is known as the summer capital of the Kingdom. It is a short distance from Mecca, about 85 kilometers (52 miles) and 900 kilometers from Riyadh (560 miles).

- The industrial cities of Yanbu on the Red Sea and Jubail on the Arabian Gulf were described earlier.

- The famous archaeological sites at Mada'in Saleh, a short distance east of Al-Wajh which is located on the Red Sea, and right next to Al-Ola up in the northwest of the Kingdom.

- The city of Al-Ola, which is in the Province of Madina and 380 kilometers (240 miles) north of it, has many antiquities and it has been mentioned by Jarir and Ibn Rabi'a in the famous Arab poetry known as Mou'allaqat. The city is 1,000 meters (3,280 feet) above sea level and it has a moderate climate with low humidity. Summer temperatures range between 26 and 36 degrees centigrade (79–97 degrees Fahrenheit).

- The city of Tabouk, where the elegance and development of the city is manifested everywhere, is located on the northern side of the Kingdom close to the Jordanian border. The climate is moderate, with summer temperatures ranging between 29 to 41 degrees centigrade (84–106 degrees Fahrenheit) and in the winter, temperatures range between −9 to 17 degrees centigrade (16–63 degrees Fahrenheit). Tabouk is 674 kilometers (418 miles) away from Madina.

- The city of Skaka is in the Jouf Province where the climate is desert-like. It is dry in the summer with an average temperature of 42 degrees centigrade (107 degrees Fahrenheit). It has a relatively cold winter with an average temperature of 8.5 degrees centigrade (47 degrees Fahrenheit). January is the coldest month of the season, and the temperatures could reach −7 degrees centigrade (19 degrees Fahrenheit).

- Buraidah, the capital of the Qasim Province, and its twin city Unaiza are both located in the central region of Saudi Arabia, right on the border with the great Dahna desert facing them on the east. The distance between Buraidah and the Islamic port of Jeddah on the Red Sea is 965 kilometers (600 miles). The distance to the port of Dammam on the Arabian Gulf in the East is 730 kilometers (450 miles). This region has been very important throughout history because of its strategic location as a center for the caravans crossing and moving in the four directions. The climate is a continental desert, and rainfall is scarce. The maximum temperature reaches 41 degrees centigrade (106 degrees Fahrenheit) and the minimum temperature reaches 12 degrees centigrade (54 degrees Fahrenheit). For Unaiza, the maximum summer temperature reaches 47 degrees centigrade (117 degrees Fahrenheit). The minimum temperature in the winter ranges between 0–11 degrees centigrade (32–52 degrees Fahrenheit). Average rainfall is 0.8 inch per year or 20.3 millimeters.

- Other cities have become more familiar since the Gulf War. These include: Qurayat in the northern-most region of the Kingdom; also Turaif, Ar'Ar, Rafha, Hafr Al-Batin, Al-Qaisouma, Al-Khafji. All of these were along the major centers of operation during the war for liberating Kuwait. Also, Ras Tanura, famous for its oil refinery and for the great oil shipments to the whole world, Abqaiq, Hofouf and Al-Kharj. Several other cities and towns are of interest but they are too numerous to be mentioned within the scope of this book.

Chapter 7

Doing Business in Saudi Arabia

Oil discovery in 1938 propelled the Kingdom into a new position of prominence and dynamically changed its history. Saudi Arabia became not only the spiritual leader of all Moslems of the world as the birthplace of Islam, but it was on the road to becoming a mighty world economic power as well. The affluence from oil coupled with wise and farsighted leadership transformed the Kingdom into a very lucrative market for exporting nations around the world, especially the United States of America, the Western countries and Japan. Not long ago, the mention of Saudi Arabia evoked in the minds of most people the vision of vast expanses of hostile desert and nomadic tribesmen. This imagery finally yielded to modernization. Discovered black gold became very important and more vital to keeping the wheels of progress turning, not only in Saudi Arabia but other nations around the globe. Since the early 70's, and especially in the early 80's, Saudi Arabia made a great leap forward and embarked on a great mission of progress which brought about prosperity and tremendous achievements. The business opportunities created in the Kingdom-gateway to the Gulf countries–were indeed immense. They continue until this very day and certainly will thrive well into the twenty-first century.

The truly free market economy, which is very much nourished and encouraged by the Saudi leadership, creates a healthy atmosphere for doing business and encouraging international trade. Recent events in the Gulf prompted the world community to repel aggression in the region and helped strengthen a healthy atmosphere for global business. In June, 1974, the Custodian of the Two Holy Mosques, King Fahd Bin Abdulaziz, then Second Deputy Prime Minister, signed the document which gave birth to the "U.S.–Saudi Commission on Economic Cooperation." To implement this arrangement, a reimbursable technical assistance agreement was signed in February, 1975. Permanent U.S. representation to the commission was established in the capital city of Riyadh. Under this joint commission, cooperation grew extensively in a number of areas including education, technical training, science and technology, solar energy research, transportation, administration and industrialization. Prince Bandar Bin Sultan, Saudi Ambassador to the United States of America in Washington, D.C. said, "The Kingdom of Saudi Arabia is dedicated to the concept of free trade based on competition. There are no foreign exchange controls, quantitative restrictions, or tariff barriers. The long-term objective of the Saudi government's industrial policy is to diversify the Kingdom's economic base and to reduce its dependence on the export of crude oil. Since the early 1980's, the Saudi economy has been moving from the stage of building the basic infrastructure to the stage of production of goods and services. This structural shift, together with the Kingdom's need for American technical know-how and the Saudi government's pursuit of diversification and privatization of the economy, has provided American firms with excellent opportunities to establish a long-term presence in Saudi Arabia. The Kingdom encourages American companies to join with Saudi partners and provides the best climate for joint venture operations in the Middle East."

In less than two decades, the Kingdom had built a massive first-rate infrastructure, certainly adding to the thriving business atmosphere in the Kingdom. The government strongly supports the free market economy and encourages Saudi products, while supporting diversification in the industrial sector, so that the economy will not be entirely dependent on oil. It also invests substantially in developing Saudi manpower and seeing to it that economic cooperation is established on all fronts. In their massive development, the Saudis use Saudi talent coupled with business and technical expertise from throughout the world, especially the U.S., Europe, Japan and other countries. With the shortage of Saudi skilled manpower, recruitment of large numbers of expatriates was and is practiced, and laborers from many Asian countries continue to work in Saudi Arabia at reasonable rates.

Investment incentives are numerous, leading among them the healthy business environment of a rapidly growing free-enterprise economy. The political stability and security are basic for development and investment initiatives. The government extensively supported the industrial sector and gave luring and lucrative incentive packages. According to the Minister of Industry and Electricity, Abdulaziz Al-Zamel, "The whole country is like a free trade zone. There are no currency restrictions, capital moves freely in and out, there are no personal income taxes, there are ten-year tax holidays for manufacturing projects, raw materials and components are imported duty-free and the protection of private ownership is established in Islamic law."

The Secretary General of the Council of Saudi Chambers of Commerce and Industry (See following table for a list), A. Al-Dabbagh said, "The Saudi private sector is in a position to benefit from major changes that have swept through world markets recently. These include global availability of technology, the transfer of technical know-how, the triumphant market economy and the rise of the private sector all over the world."

In late March, 1992, the Custodian of the Two Holy Mosques, King Fahd Bin Abdulaziz decreed large reductions in the cost of utilities and other public services. This will directly help the Saudi citizen, the expatriates and the business atmosphere in the Kingdom. Electricity, water, natural gas, gasoline, diesel, telephone service, commercial registration fees, and passport fees were all re-

Saudi and International Arab Chambers of Commerce

National

Council of Saudi Chambers of Commerce and Industry
Address: Riyadh Chamber of
            Commerce & Industry
            Bldg.
P.O. Box: 16683, Riyadh 11474
Phone: (1) 405-3200/405-7502
Fax: (1) 405-3200 (Ext. 118)
Telex: 405808 MAJLES SJ/406308
            MAJLES SJ

Abha Chamber of Commerce and Industry
P.O. Box: 722 Abha
Phone: (7) 227-1818
Fax: (7) 227-1919
Telex: 701125 SOUTH SJ
Cable: 901126

Al-Ahsa Chamber of Commerce and Industry
P.O. Box: 1519 Al-Ahsa 31932
Phone: (3) 582-0458
Fax: (3) 587-5274
Telex: 861140 HASAGO SJ

Al-Baha Chamber of Commerce and Industry
P.O. Box: 311 Albaha
Phone: (7) 725-4116
Fax: (7) 725-0042
Telex: 731048 CMRCBH SJ

Arar Chamber of Commerce and Industry
P.O. Box: 440 Arar
Phone: (4) 662-6544
Fax: (4) 662-4581
Telex: 812058 TJARYH SJ

Bishah Chamber of Commerce & Industry (Branch)
P.O. Box: 491 Bishah
Phone: (7) 6225544/6225524
Fax: (7) 622-1511
Telex: 933039: South SJ

Dammam Chamber of Commerce and Industry
P.O. Box: 719 Dammam 31421
Phone: (3) 833-5217/832-5218
Fax: (3) 834-5900, 833-5755
Telex: 801086 GHURFA SJ

Hafar Al-Baten Chamber of Commerce & Industry (Branch)
P.O. Box: 984 Hafar Albaten 31421
Phone: (3) 7220986
Fax: (3) 722-0976

Hail Chamber of Commerce & Industry (Branch)
P.O. Box: 1292 Hail
Phone: (6) 532-1060, 532-1064
Fax: (6) 532-4644
Telex: 611086 SHAMMAL SJ

Al-Jawf Chamber of Commerce and Industry
P.O. Box: 585 Skaka, Al-Jawf
Phone: (4) 624-9488/624-9060
Fax: (4) 624-0108
Telex: 821065

Jeddah Chamber of Commerce and Industry
Address: King Khalid St., Ghurfa Bldg.
P.O. Box: 9549 Jeddah 21423
Phone: (2) 642-3535/647-1100
Fax: (2) 651-7373
Telex: 601069 GHURFA SJ

Jizan Chamber of Commerce and Industry
P.O. Box: 201, Jizan
Phone: (7) 317-1519

Al-Majma'a Chamber of Commerce and Industry
P.O. Box: 165 Almajma'a 11952
Phone: (6) 432-1571, 432-0268
Fax: (6) 432-2655
Telex: 447020 GHURFA SJ

Makkah Chamber of Commerce and Industry
Address: Al Ghazzah St.
P.O. Box: 1086 Makkah
Phone: (2) 574-4020/574-5773
Fax: (2) 574-1200
Telex: 540011 CHAMEC SJ

Madina Chamber of Commerce and Industry
P.O. Box: 443 Airport Rd., Madina
Phone: (4) 822-1590/822-5380
Telex: 570009 ICCMED SJ

Najran Chamber of Commerce and Industry
P.O. Box: 1138, Najran
Phone: (7) 522-3738
Fax: (7) 522-3926
Telex: 921066 CHACOM SJ

Qasim Chamber of Commerce and Industry
Address: On Intersection Al-Wehda St. & Alamara St.
P.O. Box: 444 Buraida Qasim
Phone: (6) 323-6104, 323-5436
Fax: (6) 324-7542
Telex: 401060 SINAIA SJ

Riyadh Chamber of Commerce and Industry
Address: Dhahab St.
P.O. Box: 596 Riyadh 11421
Phone: (1) 404-0044/404-0300/ 402-2700
Fax: (1) 402-1103
Telex: 404110 GHURFA SJ
   4010564 TJARYH SJ

Tabouk Chamber of Commerce and Industry
P.O. Box: 567 Tabuk
Phone: (4) 422-2736/422-0464
Fax: (4) 422-7378
Telex: 681173 GHURFA SJ

Taif Chamber of Commerce and Industry
Address: Al-Sadad St. (Wadi Widj)
P.O. Box: 1005 Taif
Phone: (2) 736-4624; 736-3025
Fax: (2) 738-0040
Telex: 751009 TFCHMB SJ

Yanbu Chamber of Commerce and Industry
Address: King Abdulaziz St.
P.O. Box: 58 Yanbu
Phone: (4) 322-4257/322-4258
Fax: (4) 322-6800
Telex: 661036 GHURFA SJ

International

National U.S.-Arab Chamber of Commerce
1825 K Street, NW, Suite 1107
Washington, DC 20006
Tel: (202) 331-8010
Fax: (202) 331-8297

U.S.-Arab Chamber of Commerce (Pacific)
One Hallidie Plaza, Suite 504
San Francisco, CA 94102
Tel: (415) 398-9200
Fax: (415) 398-7111

MidAmerica U.S.-Arab Chamber of Commerce
208 S. LaSalle Street, Suite 706
Chicago, IL 60604
Tel: (312) 782-4654
Fax: (312) 782-4871

Northeast U.S.-Arab Chamber of Commerce
420 Lexington Avenue, Suite 2739
New York, NY 10170
Tel: (212) 986-8024
Fax: (212) 986-0216

Arab-Belgium-Luxemburg Chamber of Commerce
60, Ave. Mingnot Delstache
1060 Brussels
Tel: 344-82-04
Telex: 64108 CCABL

Arab-British Chamber of Commerce
6 Belgrave Square
Longdon SWIX 8 H
Tel: (044) 71-235-4363
Telex: 22171 ARABRIG
Fax: (044) 71-245-6688

Arab Chamber of Commerce and Industry in Germany
Godesberger: Allee 125
Tel: 0228-373637
Telex: 8869665 ARAB D
Fax: 0228-379626

Arab-Swiss Chamber of Commerce and Industry
Route de Florissant 70
P.O. Box 304
CH-1211 Geneva
Tel: (022) 473202
Telex: 427119 CHAM CH
Fax: (022) 473870

Arab-Turkish Chamber of Commerce
149, Ataturk Bulvari
Bankanlikar, Ankara
Tel: 1177700
Telex: 42343 TOBB TR

Camara De Comercio e Industria
Arab-Portuguesa
Avenida Fontes
Pereira de Melo, 19-8
Lisboa-1000
Tel: 547499, 547312, 547371, 547411
Telex: 18816 CCIAP
Fax: 547-411

French-Arab Chamber of Commerce
93, Rue Lauriston
75116 Paris, France
Tel: 553-2012
Telex: 613512 CCFAF

Italian-Arab Chamber of Commerce
Piazzale Delle Belle Arti 6
00196 Roma, Italy
Tel: 360-6901
Telex: 614196 CAMITA I

Maltese-Arab Chamber of Commerce
Auberge San Anton
Vjal De Paule
Balzan, Malta
Tel: 481-707
Telex: MW 993 MACCOM
Fax: 482714

Source: Royal Embassy of Saudi Arabia, Commercial Office, Washington, D.C., 1993.

Reduction in Public Service Fees

	Old Rate, Riyals* Per 1000 KW-hr	New Rate, Riyals Per 1000 KW-hr
3,000 Kilowatt-hours	210	150
4,000 Kilowatt-hours	310	200
6,000 Kilowatt-hours	610	360
Water		
First 100 liters	30	15
Gas		
25 rotl (pound) (11.23 kilograms)	10	7
Gasoline		
One liter	0.534	0.33 (33 cents per gallon)
Diesel		0.10 (10 cents per gallon)
Telephone		
Installation	600	300
Annual subscription	360	150
Local calls	0.05	Free
Annual Commercial Registration Fees		
Holding companies	10,000	1,600
Limited companies	8,000	1,200
Joint stock companies	6,000	800
Individual establishments	500	200
Passports		
Issuing fee	300	200
Exit visa	100	Free

* 3.75 Saudi Riyals = one U.S. dollar

These fees are adjusted from time to time depending on economic conditions.

duced across the board as shown in the table concerning Public Service Fees. According to businessmen and economists these reductions were an expression of faith in the strength of the Saudi economy.

Also, reduction in port service charges amounted to 213.3 million dollars for the first year and reached about one billion Saudi Riyals in the second year (266.6 million U.S. dollars). This reduction helped the import-export business. The operating costs for businessmen and shipping companies and agents were reduced substantially. The head of the shipping committee of the Jeddah Chamber of Commerce and Industry said "Imagine the benefit that will ultimately percolate to the consumer level with the reduction of seaport service charges by 50%. The drop in the cost of importing raw materials, coupled with low operating costs for Saudi manufacturing companies will boost production, thereby increasing supply to the domestic market and boosting exports to foreign markets."

Prior to covering the details relating to rules and regulations for doing business in Saudi Arabia, it will be helpful to give the reader and the potential businessman an example and an idea about the extent of the *Saudi-American commercial relations*. These relations date back several decades up to and prior to the discovery of oil in 1938. Exploration and discovery of vast oil reserves propelled this relationship into prominence. As mentioned before, the foundation rested on the shoulders of two great leaders, namely King Ibn Saud and President Franklin D. Roosevelt. The strengthening of this relationship, based on mutual interest, made it a special and unique one not only economically but politically and strategically as well. In fact, throughout the years, after the discovery of oil and until the present day, the number one economic partner for the Kingdom of Saudi Arabia has been the United States of America, for essentially every year with the exception of two years. Recent events in the Arabian Gulf and elsewhere contributed even more towards nourishing this partnership, which has brought many benefits to both parties on all scales. Other Western and friendly nations have also fared well in their economic and political relationship with the Kingdom.

It is of interest to see the level of U.S.-Saudi trade as exhibited in the following tables, which also include major Saudi imports from the U.S.

Saudi-U.S. Trade (Millions of Dollars)

Year	Exports to U.S.	Imports from U.S.	Balance
1985	2,026.8	4,474.2	−2,447.4
1986	4,054.3	3,448.8	+605.5
1987	4,886.5	3,373.4	+1,513.1
1988	6,236.9	3,799.2	+2,437.7
1989	7,181.3	3,576.0	+3,605.3
1990	9,974.3	4,034.8	+5,939.5
1991	10,978.3	6,572.0	+4,406.3
1992	10,366.9	7,163.3	+3,203.6

Saudi Imports from the U.S. (Millions of Dollars)

Main Commodities	Year				
	1988	1989	1990	1991	1992
Food and Live Animals	382.8	388.8	225.9	240.4	223.6
Beverages and Tobacco	135.9	149.4	186.7	213.9	175.1
Crude Materials (except fuel)	67.6	82.4	0.0	30.8	42.0
Mineral Fuels, Lubricants, etc.	13.7	14.7	0.0	0.0	0.0
Oils and Fats (animal and vegetable)	24.9	27.8	38.5	30.4	25.2
Chemicals and Related Products	241.1	213.1	36.2	93.4	24.5
Manufactured Goods	371.0	378.8	210.8	508.7	1,517.5
Machinery & Transport Equipment	2,080.9	1,798.4	1,255.21	1,656.7	2,552.4
Misc. (manufactured material)	257.4	342.8	41.7	47.4	273.0
Other Articles	0.0	0.0	1,725.8	2,770.7	2,329.9
Special Category	135.1	0.0	115.5	414.1	0.0

Source: Commercial Office, Royal Embassy of Saudi Arabia, Washington, D.C., U.S. Department of Commerce, Bureau of Census, Washington, D.C.

Major Trading Partners of the Kingdom

Year	Country and Rank	Value of Imports (Millions of U.S.$)	% of Total Saudi Imports
1987	1. Japan	3,465	17.25
	2. U.S.A.	3,065	15.26
	3. U.K. ·	1,559	7.76
	4. W. Germany	1,554	7.74
	5. Italy	1,372	6.83
1988	1. U.S.A.	3,535	16.30
	2. Japan	3,479	16.00
	3. U.K.	1,586	7.30
	4. W. Germany	1,573	7.20
	5. Italy	1,404	6.50
1989	1. U.S.A.	3,838	18.20
	2. Japan	3,010	14.20
	3. U.K.	2,150	10.20
	4. W. Germany	1,322	6.30
	5. Italy	1,208	5.70
1990	1. U.S.A.	4,017	16.71
	2. Japan	3,684	15.33
	3. U.K.	2,715	11.29
	4. W. Germany	1,772	7.37
	5. Switzerland	1,581	6.58
1991	1. U.S.A.	5,867	20.00
	2. Japan	3,977	13.70
	3. U.K.	3,271	11.27
	4. W. Germany	2,273	7.83
	5. Switzerland	1,408	4.85
1992	1. U.S.A.	7,459	22.40

Source: Compiled by the Commercial Office, Embassy of Saudi Arabia, Washington, D.C. Also Foreign Trade Statistics 1990 and 1991, Central Department of Statistics. Ministry of Finance and National Economy, Kingdom of Saudi Arabia.

In 1992, the U.S. accounted for 7.5 billion dollars or 22.4% of total Saudi imports of 125 billion Saudi Riyals (33.3 billion dollars). U.S. exports were 78% higher in 1993 than they had been in 1990. On the other hand, Saudi exports to the United States of America were around 10.4 billion dollars in 1992.

Composition of Imports Yearly (Million Riyals)

Commodity Group	1983	1984	1985	1986	1987	1988	1989	1990	1991
Total Imports	135,417	118,735	85,562	70,780	75,313	81,582	79,221	90,139	108,881
1. Live animals & animal products	4,975	4,696	3,911	4,038	4,326	4,278	4,392	4,838	5,613
2. Vegetable products	6,588	8,859	5,036	4,357	4,720	4,789	4,499	3,737	3,610
3. Animal & vegetable oils & their products	426	550	390	318	347	267	212	403	490
4. Prepared foodstuffs, beverages, spirits, vinegar & tobacco	4,597	4,634	3,558	3,203	3,507	3,768	3,461	3,639	4,446
5. Mineral products	3,475	2,912	1,419	907	839	711	727	760	844
6. Products of the chemical & allied industries	5,081	5,245	4,801	4,916	5,838	6,470	5,274	7,232	8,065
7. Artificial resins and plastic materials, cellulose esters, rubber, synthetic rubber	3,501	3,468	2,915	2,810	3,057	3,302	2,943	3,518	4,213
8. Raw hides and skins, fur skins and articles thereof, travel goods and hand bags	504	485	391	377	409	393	374	358	435
9. Wood & articles of wood charcoal, cork & articles of cork and wicker work	2,799	2,094	1,142	868	927	1,403	1,088	1,249	1,564
10. Paper making materials, paper card board & articles thereof	1,600	1,606	1,204	1,148	1,379	1,600	1,349	1,736	1,879
11. Textiles and textile articles	9,056	8,823	7,524	7,303	8,566	8,665	7,754	7,947	9,169
12. Footwear, headgear, umbrellas, sunshade whips, artificial flowers, articles of human hair & fans	920	852	785	740	933	932	975	895	1,194
13. Articles of stone plaster, asbestos, ceramic products, glass & glassware	4,160	3,669	2,637	1,959	1,921	1,965	1,666	1,677	1,846
14. Pearls, precious & semi-precious stones, precious metals, articles and imitation jewelery	4,205	3,605	3,293	1,944	2,135	1,970	3,848	6,213	5,531
15. Base metal & articles of base metals	19,101	14,183	10,277	6,524	6,308	8,133	6,476	7,830	9,931
16. Machinery, mechanical appliances, electrical equipment & parts thereof	36,120	28,409	17,841	14,683	14,415	15,527	14,557	14,777	21,115
17. Transport equipment	19,087	15,916	12,105	9,427	10,190	11,930	14,640	18,471	22,868
18. Optical, photographic, measuring, checking precision medical & surgical instruments & apparatus, clocks & watches, musical instruments, sound records & reproducers & parts thereof	5,279	5,014	3,472	2,949	3,067	3,110	2,927	2,836	3,072
19. Arms, ammunition and parts thereof	13	23	17	28	26	24	21	28	45
20. Miscellaneous manufactured articles	3,613	3,355	2,449	1,983	2,099	2,034	1,773	1,751	2,648
21. Work of art, collection pieces and antiques	317	337	395	298	304	311	265	244	303

Source: Ministry of Finance and National Economy, Central Dept. of Statistics, Foreign Trade Statistics Yearbooks and Sama.

Direction of Exports (Million Riyals)

Region and Country	1984*	1985**	1986**	1987*	1988**	1989**	1990**	1991**
Gulf co-operation council:	5,061	5,191	4,851	5,926	6,134	8,314	11,066	12,043
of which:								
Kuwait	140	292	410	611	912	1,096	746	2,501
Bahrain	4,787	4,221	3,256	4,273	3,763	4,777	6,564	5,836
United Arab Emirates	81	518	428	461	1,172	1,868	3,010	3,193
Other Arab League Countries:	3,915	4,897	2,480	2,129	3,663	3,139	6,528	5,198
of which:								
Jordan	1,324	1,391	479	492	414	109	322	147
Iraq	52	128	169	45	378	612	483	
Yemen	415	811	647	396	882	596	689	309
Lebanon	309	167	60	53	74	73	114	103
Egypt	26	216	24	226	466	528	2,423	3,048
Syria	14	105	49	58	49	45	77	123
Morocco	1,284	655	50	42	230	156	1,144	1,061
Sudan	320	857	384	496	603	565	594	158
Islamic (Non-Arab Countries):	6,960	6,865	2,417	2,846	2,848	3,191	5,916	10,117
of which:								
Pakistan	1,962	1,764	1,000	1,138	1,292	1,157	1,682	17
Bangladesh	179	249	104	218	111	229	311	215
Malaysia	1,295	834	118	182	321	344	297	295
Indonesia	2,712	3,157	255	616	413	439	621	2,301
Turkey	748	785	852	653	667	787	2,838	5,235
Asian (Non-Arab or Islamic Countries):	68,540	44,635	23,446	33,068	30,816	35,839	60,467	60,568
of which:								
Japan	42,130	29,820	15,137	19,205	15,416	18,545	31,559	28,689
India	4,191	3,075	1,101	1,753	2,558	2,571	4,115	4,103
Thailand	2,830	564	167	313	590	940	1,099	885
Singapore	7,041	2,930	2,026	4,296	5,311	6,352	8,917	9,094
Taiwan	6,416	4,651	2,830	3,643	3,955	4,069	5,634	4,968
South Korea	4,067	2,000	1,521	2,700	1,727	2,100	6,254	9,938
Philippine	1,118	1,060	403	642	366	660	2,215	2,016

Direction of Exports (Million Riyals) (continued)

Region and Country	1984*	1985**	1986**	1987*	1988**	1989**	1990**	1991**
African (Non-Arab or Islamic Countries):	547	439	403	386	731	771	1,740	1,767
of which:								
Kenya	456	165	121	65	75	118	233	198
Oceania:	2,261	1,433	758	1,064	1,505	1,554	1,600	2,284
of which:								
Australia	1,891	889	705	802	1,017	1,151	1,166	1,677
New Zealand	370	544	53	243	265	380	434	607
North America:	8,741	5,576	12,658	16,866	20,262	27,750	41,496	42,525
of which:								
United States of America	8,741	5,465	12,393	16,767	19,860	27,437	39,890	40,969
South America:	4,312	4,416	3,012	3,395	3,567	2,477	5,551	4,933
of which:								
Brazil	4,043	3,805	3,010	3,052	3,402	2,452	5,482	4,993
Western Europe:	25,933	23,839	23,969	18,692	21,309	22,651	30,571	37,968
of which:								
Germany	2,327	2,122	2,208	1,152	2,117	927	984	1,009
Holland	2,344	5,742	3,636	5,263	4,955	4,746	7,857	10,802
England	1,914	1,873	2,094	1,337	2,043	1,620	2,664	3,525
Portugal	1,205	1,082	323	709	566	614	607	582
France	5,573	4,984	4,133	2,260	4,530	5,549	7,917	8,203
Italy	5,949	3,754	5,644	3,507	2,907	4,305	5,978	7,675
Greece	1,786	746	1,006	954	500	180	567	1,206
Spain	2,500	764	1,932	2,080	1,443	1,827	2,181	3,563
Eastern Europe:	84	72	152	50	162	327	1,197	1,249
Other Countries	3,440	2,173	231	178	291	228	207	262
Grand Total	129,794	99,536	74,377	84,600	91,288	106,241	166,339	178,914

* Excluding Re-exports
** Including Re-exports
Source: Ministry of Finance & National Economy, Central Department of Statistics and Sama.

A powerful shot in the arm comes from the Saudi-American Business Council which was officially founded on December 30, 1993. The inaugural meeting was held by Saudi-American financial leaders and businessmen on April 28, 1994 in Washington, D.C. One of its basic goals is to strengthen trade opportunities for Saudi-American companies and give valuable up-to-date information in this regard, along with discovering investment opportunities and aiding in technology transfer.

Opportunities abound, especially in light of the massive expansion projects and improvements which are being implemented by Saudi-Aramco; also Saudi Basic Industries Corporation (Sabic) with several plants and many projects. There are tremendous possibilities for more trade and more benefits for all concerned.

Saudi Arabia's Gross Domestic Product (GDP) grew by five percent to 110.2 billion U.S. dollars in 1992, and it accounted for 26.5% of the total GDP for the entire Arab World. According to the Minister of Finance and National Economy M. Aba Al-Khail, the Kingdom spent about nine hundred billion dollars to build a "wide net of infrastructure projects and educational, health and other structures. . ." For 1993 see Budgets and Allocations shown in these tables.

Kingdom's Annual Budgets
(in Billions)

Fiscal Year	Revenues			Expenditures	
	Riyals	U.S. $		Riyals	U.S. $
1982–83	313.4	83.57		313.4	83.57
1983–84	225.0	60.00		260.0	69.33
1984–85	214.1	57.09		260.0	69.33
1985–86	200.0	53.33		200.0	53.33
1987	117.2	31.25		170.0	45.33
1988	105.3	28.08		141.2	37.65
1989	116.0	30.93		141.0	37.60
1990	118.0	31.46		143.0	38.13
1991+	118.0	31.46		143.0	38.13
1992	151.0	40.26		181.0	48.26
1993	169.15	45.10		196.95	52.52

+ Nominal budget, actual expenditures higher due to Gulf War
3.75 Saudi Riyals = one U.S. dollar.

Major Allocations for 1993 (in Billions)

Sector	Riyals	U.S. $
Education (Human Resources)	34.093	9.09
Health and Social Development	14.087	3.75
Municipal Services and Water Authority	6.98	1.86
Transportation & Telecommunications	9.078	2.42
Infrastructure	2.095	0.558
Economic Resources Development	8.93	2.38
Defense and Security	61.636	16.43
Public Organizations	30.69	8.18
Domestic Subsidies	9.167	2.44
Specialized Credit Institutions	8.0	2.13

Source: Saudi Arabia, Newsletter February, 1993 and Saudi Newspapers.

Bidding and Contracting

The government must receive at least three bids for all contracts exceeding one million Saudi Riyals (about 300,000 U.S. Dollars). For construction projects, and in order to increase competition, at least five contractors must be asked to submit their bids. A committee of three or more people from the Ministry of Finance and National Economy or from the government agency responsible for the project must review the bids and award the contracts according to a vote decided by a majority. These bids are open to the public. Companies with the lowest bid and meeting specifications will be awarded the contracts. Normally, the price is estimated by the Saudis and if all bids are significantly larger than what they should be according to these estimates, then the project will be negotiated. This also applies if the lowest bidder does not meet the conditions of the project.

Although most contracts with the Saudi government require a fixed price or lump sum bid, sometimes special clauses may be used on a rare basis. Once a price increase of 25% over four and a half years was allowed.

Tender regulations allow price increases for variations in transportation charges, insurance rates, or the price of raw materials. When all bids exceeded by large sums the cost estimated by government consultants, government agencies have been known to cancel all such bids. The Saudi government insists that bid prices come reasonably close to practical estimates. Contracts in excess of 300 million Saudi Riyals (90 million dollars) are made in U.S. dollars. Contracts less than this amount are paid in Riyals, which are easily converted to U.S. dollars or other foreign currencies. Since January, 1979, all contracts over 100 million Saudi Riyals (30 million dollars) require the personal approval of the King.

Companies bidding on projects supervised or undertaken by various Ministries in the Kingdom must make themselves known to these Ministries or agencies. A list is compiled of these foreign companies and the Ministries or agencies will choose companies from this list to bid on the various projects available at the time. For a company to be properly registered, a questionnaire must be completed in both Arabic and English. Also included must be the latest annual report of the company along with two references and two copies of a list of completed projects. A copy of two recently signed contracts must be included. These documents should be submitted to:

Attention: Director,
Contractor's Classification Committee
Non-Saudi Contractors' Division
Al-Washem Street
Riyadh, Saudi Arabia
(Tel: 966-1-404-3889; 966-1-404-3990)

Small projects of the turnkey-type may be requested, where the offeror will include training of personnel along with completion of the project. Large industrial and infrastructure projects, through various phases, including master plan, management of construction and detailed engineering, all may be awarded to different companies. Normally, the consulting and design phases of a project are conducted by one company, while others participate in the execution of such designs for the final construction of a project. Personnel training and operational management are normally conducted by the construction manager. In awarding contracts, the Saudi government is required by Saudi law to give preference to Saudi companies or to joint-ventures which are more than fifty percent owned by Saudi citizens. Jubail Industrial City contracts for architecture and engineering are awarded only to one hundred percent Saudi-owned companies. When a qualified Saudi company may not be found, then foreigners are awarded the contracts.

However, all bidders must have a local address such as the address of a local representative of the foreign company.

Recently, knowledgeable business sources said:

"The Kingdom of Saudi Arabia is now by far America's largest trading partner in the Middle East, with an estimated 19 billion dollars in two-way trade last year (1991), including 6.6 billion dollars in Saudi Arabian imports from the United States. Saudi Arabia, for its part, is now–by a considerable margin–the largest supplier of petroleum to the U.S. market. Trade and investment are bound to continue to expand as more and more Saudi and American trade delegations explore the opportunities in each other's markets."

With the construction of a gigantic modern infrastructure, the Kingdom gears itself for the future. With a period of consolidation, emphasis is being placed on the private sector to be actively involved in industrialization and services. A prime intention of the government is to encourage the private sector to take initiatives. It will continue to provide basic incentives for development and progress through the various funds.

Saudi Arabia is on the road to becoming the Middle East's industrial high-tech center. The *"Offset program"* is a novel approach for generating industrial investment. This policy requires contractors to reinvest back into the Kingdom a portion of the value of their major contracts. The Saudi government will require the large foreign-owned consortiums that may be involved in defense projects to reinvest up to 35% of the value of their contracts back into high technology service industries in the Kingdom. Also, foreign contractors must subcontract 30% of the value of a government contract to local subcontractors and thus help in revitalizing the local economy.

Diversifying the economy is one of the major policies of modernization and industrialization. "We must stop being just an oil-based economy," says a senior official from the Ministry of Industry. A broad industrial base has been established. It is on the road to becoming much healthier with time. Income from this sector will be on the increase and thus, will lessen dependency on oil. While oil will continue to play a major role in the economy, other sectors will contribute their share. Any lack in technology will be rectified through the tremendous effort of the government and the citizens toward attracting American, European and Japanese companies for joint ventures and for setting up operations in the Kingdom, so that technology transfer will be more accelerated in the years ahead. The private sector will play a major role in all the joint ventures. For example, contracts with the Boeing and General Electric companies will lead to "Offset Ventures" that will help in creating an aviation service industry in the Kingdom; an industry designed to service not just Saudi requirements, but also the needs of their allies in the Gulf Cooperation Council (GCC). Large contracts signed with Britain to the tune of several billion dollars carry with them an Offset Program, much of which will be based and geared towards the aerospace industry. These high-tech areas will increase the need for highly skilled workers who will help in operating these projects and the Offset Ventures that are derived from them.

King Fahd has called upon Saudi businessmen to rise to the challenge and generously invest in the future of the land. As revenue from oil and funding from the government both level off or decrease, the private sector could become a major partner in future development. The fourth Five-Year Plan stresses the importance of this sector's involvement and serious contribution to fueling the nation's economy through diversification. Free enterprise has been a close kin to Arabia from the myrrh and incense days way back in the beginning of history. Early traders of Arabia linked the Arabian Peninsula to the outside world.

Private Sector, Joint-Ventures and Agents

Foreign companies engaged in work with the government of Saudi Arabia are required to have Saudi representation or joint-venture partners in the Kingdom. This is essential for many reasons, foremost among them the fact that a local representative will receive from government officials notices regarding forthcoming projects. The local representative will also do what is necessary so that the foreign company will be on the bidders' list. This local representative or Saudi agent is very familiar with the local situation and can best advise his foreign partners on the most appropriate ways to present a proposal, so that it will have a good chance of success in meeting the requirements. He is also in the best position to represent the foreign company in front of the Saudi client. All foreign companies working in Saudi Arabia must register with the

Ministry of Commerce. However, a consultant hired by a Saudi company to do consulting work with them while visiting the Kingdom on a few occasions, will not have to register as long as no residency or work permit violations are practiced. These consultants are usually in an advantageous position for bids when they fill out prequalification forms regarding public sector projects.

Non-Saudis are not permitted to act as commercial agents in the Kingdom. The commercial agent cannot perform his duties until his name has been included in the register with the Ministry of Commerce. His function is crucial since he is held responsible for the company and personnel he sponsors.

More detailed information in this regard can be obtained from the Department of Commercial Registration, Ministry of Commerce and the Department of Internal Trade, Agencies Section, Ministry of Commerce.

According to Resolution #124, issued by the Council of Ministers on 29-5-1403 A.H., (March 14, 1983) a foreign contractor or a Saudi-foreign joint-venture prime contractor with less than 51% Saudi capital is required to contract not less than 30% of "Public Works Contracts" that require the performance of works, such as construction, maintenance, and operations. Subcontracting should be given to contractors who are at least 51% owned by Saudis who sponsor their own work force. More information regarding this matter may be obtained from the Ministry of Finance and National Economy.

A foreign contractor and his Saudi Agent are governed by Royal Decree number M/2 issued on Mouharram 21, 1398 A.H. (January, 1978). According to this regulation:

1. If a foreign contractor does not have a Saudi partner, then he should have a Saudi service agent.
2. The Saudi agent must be living in the Kingdom and must be registered in the Commercial Register of the Ministry of Commerce which authorizes him to act as an agent for the foreign company.
3. An Agency Agreement governs and defines the obligations and relations between the Saudi agent and the foreign contractor.
4. The foreign contractor pays fees to the agent in return for his services. These fees should not exceed five percent of the cost of the total contract.

5. More than one Saudi agent could be employed by a foreign contractor involved in various types of work. This is done in order to have proper specialization for the corresponding work.

When it comes to local agents, the exception to local representation is only in the sales and services contracts with the Ministry of Defense and Aviation. Here, the use of an agent is definitely forbidden. (A Saudi agent is certainly recommended for companies seeking supply contracts.) For government bidding, a company may be represented only by one agent. Saudi Agency Regulations forbid an agent from representing both the consulting engineer and the implementing contractor in a single contract. This is expressly practiced to prevent any conflicts of interest. Not more than one service agent is allowed for each Saudi project in which a company may be interested. However, a foreign contractor may have more than one Saudi agent doing services as opposed to commercial functions. A Saudi service agent is not permitted to represent more than ten foreign companies.

In choosing an agent or a partner, good care must be exercised to avoid difficulties down the road. Thus, a healthy relationship should be developed and sought in these undertakings.

Licensing

Various licensing regulations exist for a number of cases. It would be beyond the scope of this book to cover these in detail. However, some of the highlights of these licensing regulations and procedures will be covered here.

The Foreign Capital Investment Law governs the investment of such capital. It is allowed to take place in economic development projects excluding petroleum and mineral extraction projects. It is also to be accompanied by foreign technical expertise. The Ministry of Industry and Electricity considers the following as development projects under this law: projects for the development of manufacturing industry; development of agriculture production; health services; provisional services and projects for undertaking contracts. This law allows foreign investors to set up a project either exclusively on their own or as a joint-venture with Saudis. Further information on rules and procedures for this law may be obtained from the Ministry of Industry and Electricity. In

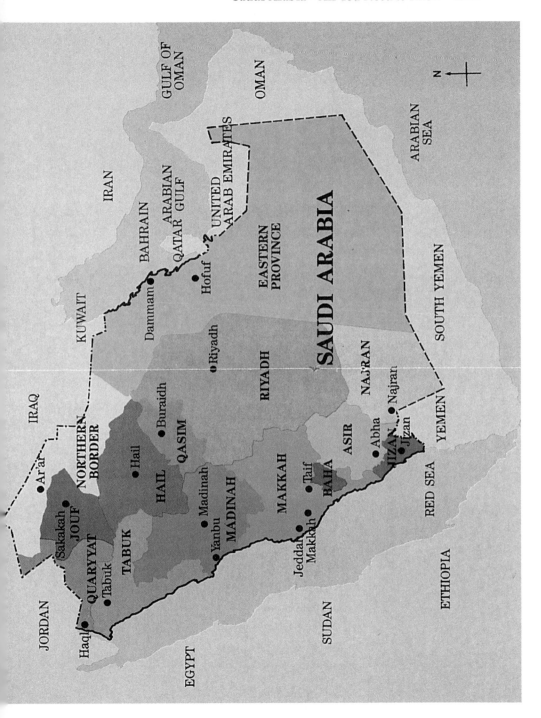

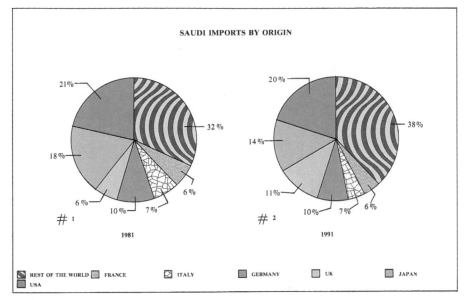

SAUDI IMPORTS BY ORIGIN

1
1981

2
1991

REST OF THE WORLD   FRANCE   ITALY   GERMANY   UK   JAPAN
USA

Source: Sama

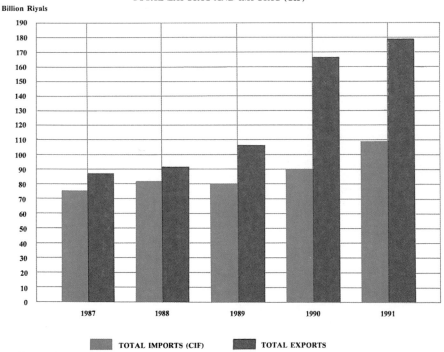

TOTAL EXPORTS AND IMPORTS (CIF)

Billion Riyals

TOTAL IMPORTS (CIF)   TOTAL EXPORTS

Source: Sama

Saudi Arabia is endowed with the largest oil reserves in the world. Oil is the engine for progress. It is the lifeline for world industry. Miraculous progress and a thriving business atmosphere are both fueled by this God-given resource.

Crew of the Discovery Space Mission visiting the Kingdom of Saudi Arabia, and dancing the A'rda in the bottom photo.

Saudi Money.

case the project is considered for license, application finally goes to the Foreign Capital Investment Bureau with all necessary documentation.

"According to Ministry of Commerce resolution 680, foreign firms that do not use a Saudi agent and wish to subcontract for service or supply tenders must register for a license with that Ministry and establish an office in Saudi Arabia.

Foreign firms who are invited to bid on a tender by the Saudi government need to apply for a license and establish an office in the Kingdom only if they are awarded the contract.

Partnerships with Saudi firms are advisable for foreign companies seeking to manufacture in the Kingdom or to provide services. Manufacturing facilities and specific service firms with at least 25% Saudi ownership qualify for the same concessions (e.g. loans, tax allowances, etc.) as wholly-Saudi-owned firms."

Trademarks, patents, and copyrights are all governed by their respective laws and protected according to various regulations and procedures, the latest of which was enumerated in seven chapters which took effect on 15-6-1410 A.H. (January 12, 1990). In fact the Kingdom had recently completed the needed procedures for joining the International Copyright Agreement, which was modified and established in Paris on July 24, 1971. According to M. Al-Khoudheir, director of publications in the Ministry of Information, this agreement had taken effect in the Kingdom on July 13, 1994.

In order to be licensed to practice various professions such as engineering consultants, engineers, lawyers, legal consultants, accountants, etc., certain basic qualifications must be met. Various Ministerial Resolutions specify the requirements and define corresponding rules and regulations. For specific details on licensing, the reader should contact the Department of Internal Trade, Ministry of Commerce in Riyadh.

Performance Requirements and Settling Disputes

The Kingdom of Saudi Arabia requires bid and performance bonds from most foreign companies in the amount of 1% and 5% respectively of the total value of a given contract. Bonds could be in the form of a bank guarantee payable on demand, a certified check drawn on a local bank, or cash. Each guarantee must be approved by a bank in Saudi Arabia, acting as an agent for the foreign bank. A list of acceptable insurance companies has been issued by the government of Saudi Arabia. The limits which each of these insurance companies may underwrite are also specified. "The performance bond is not required for consulting work, service contracts, supply of spare parts, nor for contracts which the government awards for direct purchase–contracts which are less than one million Saudi Riyals in value and do not have to be tendered." In some joint-ventures, the Saudi firm has been persuaded to put up the whole guarantee. The performance bond is reduced on operation and maintenance contracts as work progresses on the project. However, it cannot go below 5% of the value of the uncompleted work. The requirement to post large performance bonds works a hardship on firms new to overseas work, because they may have to collateralize the bond up to 50% of its value. The same is true with the advance payment guarantee. The bond also ties up a firm's line of credit with the bank.

The bid bond is always required, except in the case of a purely negotiated contract where there are no competitors. The performance bond is generally due from the winning bidder within ten days after he has been notified of the award. It is returned to the contractor on final completion of the project, although the contractor remains responsible for defects or collapse of the structure for a period of ten years (unless the structure was not meant to last ten years).

An advance payment of ten percent of the cost of a project may be paid by the Saudi client upon the signing of the construction contract. This advance must be backed by the contractor with a bank guarantee of an equal sum. Also up to 75% of the cost of construction materials will be paid by the government, once they are imported and stored properly so no damage will result from storage. As work progresses, the government will make progress payments of up to 90% on the completed work. The remaining ten percent will be held pending the final delivery of the project, or may be paid against bank guarantees as the work advances. Saudi companies and joint-ventures, where a Saudi partner holds at least 60% of the capital, may be paid in full for the completed work, without requiring a bank guarantee.

When estimating time for completing a project, it is wise for the contractor to allow for work slowdowns and stoppages during major holidays such as Eid Al-Fitr (end of Ramadan) and Eid Al-Adha (end of Pilgrimage).

A provision for settling disputes is always included in contracts. Commercial disputes are generally resolved through personal contacts and negotiations or through the Saudi arbitration system. Arbitration or Grievance Boards have been established in order to settle certain commercial disputes. The Boards render decisions which may be accepted by both parties or could be appealed to the Shari'a court. The Council of Ministers may be involved in solving major disputes.

Commercial disputes come within the domain of the Grievances Court (Diwan Al-Mazalem) Commercial Circuit, as of December 31, 1987. Prior to that date the Committee for Commercial Disputes settled these matters. Regulations governing disputes relating to negotiable instruments are handled by committees established in Riyadh, Jeddah and Dammam. The decision issued by any of the committees can be appealed within fifteen days of its pronouncement. The commercial office of an Embassy of the Kingdom may lend assistance to solving disputes from both parties if they desire this assistance.

While English is widely used in the Kingdom, companies must conduct all their business with the Kingdom in the Arabic language. Tender announcements for each project specify the language of the bid. Most major contracts use the English language. Documents establishing joint-venture or agency representation must be in Arabic in order to be legally binding. In case of any dispute, the Arabic text of any agreement will supersede other languages in front of the legal system.

Customs

Some young national industries are protected through the imposition of 20% import duties on certain imported commodities. However, most consumer goods are duty-free; for example rice, tea, coffee, beans, sugar, barley, corn, cardamom along with livestocks and meat. Other items will have an import duty of 12% of the total cost which includes insurance and freight. Certain items are subject to customs based on their weight, but rates are normally very low. Favorable concessions are given to members of the Arab League. Bilateral trade agreements with certain

Arab states entitle them also to further reductions in customs duties.

In accordance with the Saudi government's commitment to help the private sector, contractors are required to purchase equipment and materials from a Saudi importer or a Saudi manufacturer. Only when such supplies are not available, then contractors are permitted to directly import their needs from foreign sources. Shortages of such supplies may necessitate the importation of most requirements of a given project. Tariff rates range from none to four percent. Certain items which are produced in Saudi Arabia such as aluminum or wooden frames are assessed a tariff of 20%. However, most contracts provide for importing supplies and machinery duty-free. Certain contracts with the U.S. Army Corps of Engineers provided for the Saudi government to pay all the costs for importing needed materials. Re-exportation of trucks and other vehicles in good working order is generally not permitted. Most contractors write off the costs of equipment imported for their construction projects. Goods are normally cleared rather quickly through Customs at various Saudi seaports. Original export documents should be legalized by Saudi Consular authorities in the country of origin. This facilitates customs clearance tremendously.

Shipping Regulations

All commercial shipments to Saudi Arabia must have the following documents: commercial invoice, certificate of origin, a bill of lading or air-way-bill, steamship or airlines company certificate, an insurance certificate when goods are insured by the exporting company and a packing list. In special circumstances, other additional documents may be required. The commercial invoice, certificate of origin and any other special documents must be authenticated and certified in the following order:

- A notary public must notarize these documents.
- A local U.S. Chamber of Commerce must seal and certify them.
- A U.S.-Arab Chamber of Commerce must also seal and certify them.
- The Consul General of the Kingdom in the country of origin must legalize these documents. An original copy is legalized by the Consulate General and returned to the ex-

porter. A copy is kept by the U.S.-Arab Chamber of Commerce. The documents, an original or a copy, must have the hand-written signature of the person who issued such a document. Fax copies of signed documents are not accepted by the Consulate General. Properly prepared documents which are sent by mail should also have a self-addressed stamped envelope. Details on filling the various shipping documents may be obtained from the commercial Attaché's Office in the various embassies of the Kingdom throughout the world. Also, a U.S.-Arab Chamber of Commerce or a U.S. Chamber of Commerce will be helpful in this regard. Manufacturers of the products being shipped and shipping companies will also help in fulfilling the requirements by the Consulate General of the Kingdom.

As mentioned previously, certain exported goods will require special documentation. For example, food products will require a food manufacturer's ingredients certificate and also a consumer protection certificate, along with a price list.

Only male beef or sheep meat fresh or frozen is imported into the Kingdom. More special documents are required for this. These are:

1. A document certifying that an officially–licensed slaughter house was used for the slaughter of these animals in accordance with Moslem religious practices and procedures. This certificate should be legalized by a properly acknowledged Islamic center in the country of origin. Poultry should also have such a certificate.

2. An official health certificate with pertinent information. All meat products shipped must have a health certificate to guarantee freedom from disease.

Other special documents are required for shipping grains, seeds, animal feed, livestock, pets, horses, fruits and vegetables, electrical appliances, etc. An individual shipping a motor vehicle must obtain a certificate from the manufacturer prior to shipping any car for personal use in Saudi Arabia. The manufacturer usually obtains this certificate from the Saudi Arabian Standards Organization (Saso). A student or diplomat with a personal used car is exempted from this requirement.

In general, importing fruits, vegetables, plants, seeds, live animals, and poultry must be approved by the proper Saudi authorities prior to their shipment. All merchandise imported into the Kingdom must be identified with the country of origin, except when it is not possible. The importation of used clothing will require a certificate of disinfection. As mentioned elsewhere, the importation of alcohol and narcotics is strictly forbidden. Also the importation of pig meat is not allowed according to Islamic practices. Firearms, wireless telephones, certain communications systems, sensitive materials and certain publications require a special permit from proper authorities. Shipments of less than $2,000 dollars which are of non-commercial nature and cars imported for personal use, regardless of their value, do not require shipping documents.

Taxes

All income taxes of Saudi and expatriate employees working in the Kingdom were abolished by a Royal Decree on the first of June, 1975. However, Saudi citizens and all Saudi companies must pay religious tax or Zakat at an annual rate of 2.5 percent of profits for companies and on the assessable amount for individuals.

Expatriates, who are self-employed in a private practice, be it lawyers, accountants, doctors or other professions, are taxed on their net annual income as follows: an income of 6,000 Saudi Riyals is exempt from taxation; an income between 6,001 to 10,000 is taxed at a rate of 5%; 10,001 to 20,000–10%; 20,001 to 30,000–20%; an income over 30,000 S.R. is taxed at a maximum rate of 30%.

Certain large projects have been contracted where companies manage to negotiate a special clause exempting them from taxation on profits when in Saudi Arabia. In general, Saudi law requires that all foreign and Saudi companies are subject to profits tax on the profits earned in the Kingdom. Companies with joint-ventures having at least 25% Saudi ownership, and under the provisions of the Foreign Capital Investments Regulations are exempt from income tax for up to ten years. A company's tax status is determined by the tax department of the Ministry of Finance upon receipt of the company's records and activities in the Kingdom. These records are submitted in Arabic and kept in the Kingdom.

U.S. and Saudi accounting procedures are used in auditing companies. Those paying taxes are taxed on their net profit at the following rates: 25% on the first 100,000 Saudi Riyals; 35% on the sum from 100,001–500,000; 40% on 500,001–1 million, and 45% on amounts exceeding one million Saudi Riyals. Different rates are used for companies working in petroleum and hydrocarbon facilities. When a company receives a certificate from the Ministry of Finance stating that the contractor is either exempt from paying taxes, or has properly and satisfactorily paid all the due taxes, then the final payment on its contract will be made. The foreign partner in a joint-venture does not pay zakat. An official form for the financial statement of due taxes must be made no later than the 15th of March, following the end of the fiscal year on December 31.

The Minister of Finance and National Economy, M. Aba Al-Khail stated in May of 1993, that all foreign companies which are actively involved in the capital expansion of various industrial projects in the Kingdom of Saudi Arabia will be exempted from paying taxes on their profits acquired in the Kingdom. Foreign investors will be encouraged to re-invest their profits which come from joint-ventures and this will boost the joint industrial projects. He said, "The prime objective of this decision is to encourage foreign participation in industrial projects and acquire foreign technology. Such exemption will require that foreign capital be used for the development of Saudi industries and it will be applied for a duration of ten years from the date a joint company begins its industrial production."

Shari'a

Commercial and business deals are governed by Shari'a or Islamic law. There are many similarities between Shari'a and Western law. This includes the fact that all people are equal under the law. One is innocent until proven guilty. The burden of proof is placed on the plaintiff. Written contracts have a sanctity and legitimacy of their own. Like the Western legal system, the Saudi system also has appeal procedures. Any claims must be proven and substantiated by two male witnesses perferably Moslems, or one male witness and two females, or one male and the oath of the claimant. Four male witnesses are required in vicious or serious crimes. Character witnesses also may be required to support and verify the reputation of other witnesses. Hearsay is normally not accepted as evidence, while evidence under oath is accepted in case written evidence is not available. It must be noted here that reference to a precedent is not practiced as is the case in the United States. A ruling issued by a judge is not binding on other judges, nor on him in a case which may come up later. Islam forbids interest, but allows management fees and services. Awards for damages are much in line with practicality and far different from what is encountered in the West, especially the U.S. They are certainly much more modest under Shari'a. For example, damages relating to property will be actual sums for repair or replacement of the property. Damages for accidental death are a sum of approximately 35,000 dollars. The loss of the opportunity cost of money is not compensated under Shari'a.

Attorneys and formal written proceedings are not required in typical court proceedings. A defendant being tried for a criminal act cannot delegate his defense to an attorney. The Judge or Qadi seeks the truth from all parties involved in the case. In general, judges will encourage a compromise to solve disputes, but when this fails, a judgement is made. A court close to the home of the defendant will speedily hear the case no matter where the contract was signed. In the same trial both civil and criminal aspects, Private right and Public right, can be judged in the same court and trial. When sentence is imposed by a judge, it is carried out by the official representative of the government such as the Governor of a province. While there are nearly a dozen administrative tribunals responsible for certain regulations of a Ministry or an Agency of the government such as the Committee for the settlement of commercial disputes, committee for settlement of labor disputes, or the grievance board, there is also in the Kingdom a court system which constitutes four levels of Shari'a courts. These include: the most common General Courts having one or more judges, they handle cases of personal, civil, family or criminal nature; Limited Courts having one judge, they handle smaller cases which involve civil or criminal matters. There are also two appeal courts. The highest Shari'a appeal is the Court of Appeals having five or more judges. This court does not have jurisdiction over administrative tribunals or disputes between lower Shari'a courts and another tribunal. The fourth Shari'a Court, known as the

Supreme Judicial Council, concerns itself with matters referred by the Custodian of the Two Holy Mosques, the King. It also considers appeals from various other courts and reviews cases involving death or mutilation which have been rendered by the lower courts. The Amir or Governor of a given Province can use his wisdom and good offices to settle civil disputes. If such an attempt does not succeed, then the matter is referred to a Shari'a court. Chambers of Commerce and Industry in various cities can arbitrate commercial disputes. The Grievance Board, or Diwan Al-Mazalem, includes Shari'a and Secular-trained legal counselors. It is not a Shari'a court; it draws its authority from the Kings' power to administer justice and redress grievances by individuals who allege wrong-doing by the government. This Board has jurisdiction over any complaint which comes to its attention, especially those lodged against government agencies and their administrative regulations.

As one can see from the previous information, the Kingdom is extremely interested in providing opportunities for the creation of both business and industry. To that end, encouragement is given to both nationals and foreign investors interested in helping not only themselves, but the Kingdom as a whole to diversify and continue to grow in the framework of a free market economy. Partnerships between foreign and national investors are encouraged.

The Kingdom has given development a huge boost by such actions as: lowering the cost of utilities and services for everyone, reducing port charges, giving tax breaks, requiring reinvestment of some profits back into the Kingdom and providing easy term-loans.

Certain occupations and projects require licensing in order to operate within the Kingdom. It is imperative that prospective professionals and businesses contact the proper agencies to obtain detailed information necessary for doing business in Saudi Arabia.

The Kingdom provides an exemplary legal system conducive to business transactions. Disputes are settled swiftly and fairly. The Shari'a is the governing force here as well as other areas of Saudi life.

Customs regulations are designed to protect the Saudi business community, while at the same time encouraging foreign trade. Those desiring to do business in Saudi Arabia will find a warm welcoming atmosphere. To be successful, it is imperative that one acquaints himself with Saudi regulations relating to both business and industrial development. Those who plan well and venture into Saudi business will help themselves as well as the Saudi free economy.

Chapter 8

Practical and Beneficial Information

The Kingdom of Saudi Arabia is a very interesting country, enriched by unique traditions and a rich culture. A visitor will be vastly impressed and moved by the miraculous progress achieved in this oil-rich Kingdom. The time spent will be most beneficial if he or she has prepared well for such a trip. No doubt the Kingdom, with its fascinating history dating back thousands of years, being the birthplace of Islam and the richest oil country in the world, is not simply an average nation on this earth. It is very different from wherever you may have originated your trip! In this chapter, we will present many useful hints or tips that will prove very beneficial to the traveler and will certainly help make a trip to the Kingdom a joyful one indeed.

Although the Saudi way of life is different to Westerners, especially Americans, British and French, once the traveler learns certain basic facts about the Kingdom, its religion, culture and traditions, he/she will be better able to enjoy their visit. The following relevant background information along with some special tips will refresh your memories and direct your travel into the Kingdom:

Visa

Prior to entry into the Kingdom a traveler must have a valid entry visa and a valid passport.

To inquire about a visa, contact the consular or visa section of the Royal Embassy of the Kingdom of Saudi Arabia in Washington, D.C., London, England, Paris, France, or other countries where you may be. You may also contact one of the many Saudi Arabian Consulates located in a number of cities around the world. For example, New York, Houston, Los Angeles, etc. If a consulate is not available in the native country of the traveler, a visa can be obtained from an assigned consulate in a country neighboring his own. The American Embassy and the British Embassy are located at Embassy Headquarters in Diri'ya on the outskirts of Riyadh and both have Consulates in Jeddah and Dhahran. Other countries of the world are represented in the capital city of Riyadh and some with Consulates elsewhere. The entry visa is normally good for one visit and for a specific time varying between two weeks to three months. People who enter the Kingdom with an employment visa will need an exit visa upon departure from the Kingdom. A Saudi Arabian citizen or a company must sponsor the entry visas with the exception of the Umra visa (for visiting Hajj or pilgrimage facilities). In the case of business visas, the Saudi sponsor in the Kingdom must send to the Saudi Consulate or Embassy a letter or sometimes a fax/telex signifying this sponsorship.

Those desiring to work in the Kingdom for a given company must add to their application a copy of the signed contract and a letter from the company employing them. Those who have worked in the Kingdom previously must also include with their application a letter of release from the previous employer.

Your travel agent or company can also help in this regard. It is desirable to have multiple entry visas when possible, so the businessman can enter and leave the country as many times as wished during a valid visa. It is recommended that you ask for a three-month or a one-month visa even when you plan to stay only for a short time; you never know what may develop and you may need to stay longer. In this way you avoid the inconvenience of securing another visa. When you receive your passport, check both its validity and the expiration date of your visa. When working in the Kingdom on a regular basis, one will be required to have residency status. If the employee desires to leave, he or she will need an exit visa; many companies and individuals establish proper channels to facilitate visa requirements.

The number of Pilgrims' visas for each country is specified according to agreements reached at an Islamic Conference. Any Moslem wishing to make the Pilgrimage applies to his government for the Hajj visa through a prearranged liaison. Reflecting quotas for each country, Pilgrims come to the Hajj headed by their respective delegations or committees. The quota system is necessary in order not to overburden Hajj facilities beyond their capacities.

To obtain the pertinent information and visa application, write to any Saudi Arabian Consulate or Embassy.

Following are some addresses which will be useful to the traveler. The first group is for the United States of America, the second for London, England, and the third is for Saudi Arabian Missions around the world.

Saudi Offices in the U.S.A.

1. Royal Embassy of
   Saudi Arabia
   601 New Hampshire
   Ave., N.W.
   Washington, D.C. 20037
   Tel.: (202) 342-3800
   Fax.: (202) 337-3233
   Tlx.: 440132 Najdiah
   a) Commercial Office
      Tel. (202) 337-4088
      Fax.: (202) 342-0271
   b) Information Office
      Tel.: (202) 337-4134 or
      337-4076
      Fax.: (202) 944-5983
   c) Medical Office
      Tel.: (202) 342-7393
      Fax.: (202) 337-9251
   d) Visa Section
      Tel.: (202) 342-3800

2. Royal Consulate General
   of Saudi Arabia
   One Westheimer Plaza,
   5718 Westheimer St.
   Suite 1500
   Houston, Tx. 77057
   Tel.: (713) 785-5577
   Fax.: (713) 785-1163

3. Royal Consulate General
   of Saudi Arabia
   10900 Wilshire Blvd.,
   Suite 830
   Los Angeles, Ca. 90024
   Tel.: (213) 208-6566
   Fax.: (213) 208-5643

4. Royal Consulate General
   of Saudi Arabia
   866 UN Plaza
   Suite 480
   New York, N.Y. 10017
   Tel.: (212) 752-2740
   Fax.: (212) 688-2719

5. Saudi Cultural Mission
   2600 Virginia Avenue,
   Suite 800, N.W.
   Washington D.C., 20037
   Tel.: (202) 337-9450 General
   (202) 298-8803
   Fax: (202) 298-8863

6. Saudi Arabian Mission
   to the UN
   405 Lexington Ave.
   56th Floor
   New York, N.Y. 10017
   Tel.: (212) 697-4830
   Fax.: (212) 557-4139

7. Office of the Defense and
   Armed Forces Attaché
   2109 E St., N.W.
   Washington, D.C. 20037
   Tel.: (202) 857-0122

8. Office of the Naval Attaché
   1755 Jefferson Davis Hwy.
   Suite 500
   Arlington, Va. 22202
   Tel.: (202) 692-0340

9. Saudi National Guard
   3000 K St., N.W.
   Suite 320
   Washington, D.C. 20007
   Tel.: (202) 944-3344
   Fax.: (202) 944-3340

10. Saudi Press Agency
    1155 15th St., N.W.
    Room 1111
    Washington, D.C. 20005
    Tel.: (202) 861-0324
    Fax.: (202) 872-1405

11. Saudi T.V.
    1215 Jefferson Davis
    Highway
    #302 Arlington, Va. 22202
    Tel: (703) 685-3800
    Fax: (703) 685-7907

Saudi Diplomatic Missions Abroad

Afghanistan

Wazir Akbar Khan Mena,
(Behind Ministry of Interior)
Kabul
Tel: 25260, 25757
Tlx: 930/59

Algeria

5 Rue Arezki Abri, Hydra,
  Algiers
Tel: 605973, 603243
Tlx: 936/530939

Argentina

Alejandro M. de Augado 2881,
1425 Buenos Aires
Tel: 802-43033375

Australia (and New Zealand)

12 Culgoa Ciruit
O'Malleya T2606, Canberra
P.O. 63 Parran A.C.T. 2605
  Australia
Tel: (62) 862099, 865511
Tlx: 612454 NAJD AU

Austria

Formanekgasse 38, Austria
Tel: 362316/362317
Tlx: (847) 115757 SAUDIA

Bahrain

P.O. Box 1085, Manama
Tel: 727223
Tlx: 9871 NAJDEY NB

Bangladesh

House No. 25, Rd. #10,
  Gulshan Ave.
Gulshan Model Town, Dacca-12
Tel: 600-221/600-222
Tlx: 950/642305 NJDH BJ

Belgium

45, Avenue Franklin Roosevelt
1050 Bruxelles
Tel: 649-2044, 649-5725
Tlx: 846/
64626 NAJDIA B 61600

Brazil

SHI/SUL OL 10–Conjunto 9;
  Casa 20
CEP: 70471–Brasilia-DF
Tel: (061) 248-3718, 248-0793
Tlx: 391/61156 EMAS BR

Cameroon

Quartler Nlongkak, Bastos
  Yaounde
Cameroon
Tel: 223261/222675
Tlx: 978/8336 KN
          8645 KN

Canada

99 Bank St., Suite 901
Ottawa, Ont. K1P 6B9
Tel: (613) 237-4100
Tlx: 389/534285 NAJDIAH
  OTT

Chad

23 Teleksh St. A, Paul Anjamina
P.O. Box 1092
Tel: 3815

Denmark

Lille Strandvej 27,
2900 Hellerup, Copenhagen
Tel: (01) 621-200, 621-370
Tlx: 855/15931 NAJDIA DK

Djibouti

Saoudite
B.P. 1921, Djibouti
Tel: 351645, 350790
Tlx: 994/5865

Egypt

3 Ahmed Naseem St., Giza,
  Cairo
Tel: 728012, 726037
Tlx: 927/92749

Ethiopia

Old Airport Zone
P.O. Box 1104,
Addis Ababa, Ethiopia
Tel: 22087/22625

France

5 Avenue Hoche 75008, Paris
Tel: 766-0206, 727-8112

Germany

Godesberger Alle 40–42, 5300
  Bonn 2
Tel: 379013/16
Tlx: 841/885442 BONN D

Ghana

No. 3 Yiwa Street
Abelenpke, Ghana
Tel: 76820

Greece

71 Marathonodromou St.
P. Psychico, Athens
Tel: 6716913-2-1

Guinea

Landreah–Port B.P. 611,
  Conakry
Tel: 461317
Tlx: 601-2146

Holland

Alexander Street 1g
The Hague 5214 JM
Tel: 070 614-391/070-606-880

India

No. 1, Rino, Road Kilokeri
New Delhi 10014
Tel: 632-081/632-098

Indonesia

Jalan Imam Bonjol 3, Jakarta
Tel: 346-342/346-343
Tlx: 46687 NEJDIAH,
  JAKARTA

Iran

59 Bucharest Ave., Tehran
Tel: 624-297/624-298
Tlx: 088-213828

Iraq

Al-Mansour Mahala #609
  Zeqaq
#1, House 48/1/A
Tel: 5413755
Tlx: 934/213330 NJDIA IK

Italy

Viale Regina Marghenita,
  No. 260
001981 Roma
Tel: 868-161/868-162
Tlx: 843/614186 NJDIAH I

Japan

1-53 Azabu Nagasaka-cho
Minato-Ku, Tokyo 106
Tel: (30) 589-5241/(30) 589-5242
Tlx: 25731 NAJDIAH J

Jordan

Jabal Amman 5th Circle
P.O. Box 2133, Amman
Tel: 81455, 814154
Tlx: 925/21298 NAJDIA JO

Kenya

P.O. Box 58297 Nairobi
Tel: 29501, 29502, 331181

Korea

1/112, Shinmoon-ro-2–Ka
Chongro ku, Seoul
Tel: 725-9263/725-9264
Tlx: 26216 NAJDIAH K

Kuwait

Arabian Gulf Street, Embassy
  District
P.O. Box 20498, Safat
Tel: 253-0728
Tlx: 959/23458 KT

Commercial Office

P.O. Box 20602
Al-Safa, Kuwait 13067
Tel: 314358/318004

Lebanon

Al-Manara-Bliss St., Ras Beirut
Tel: 804272, 804273, 804274
Tlx: 923/20830

Libya

Qourtobah St., Tripoli
Tel: 30486, 30485
Tlx: 929/20950

Malaysia

251, Jalan Pekelilinc, Kuala
   Lumpur
Tel: 425987/425644
Tlx: 784/30795 NAJDIA MA

Mali

Badalabougo, Bamako
Tel: 222-528/223-910
Tlx: 972/408 NEJDIAH
   BAMACO

Mauritania

P.O. Box 498, Nouakchott
Tel: 52665, 52633
Tlx: 935/816

Mexico

Reforma No. 607
Col. Lomas de Chapultepec
   11000
Mexico City
Tel: 520-1531, 540-0240

Morocco

43 Place de l'Unité Africaine,
   Rabat
Tel: 30171, 32794
Tlx: 933/31986 NAJDIAH M

Niger

P.O. Box 339 Niamey
Avenue des Djermakey)
Tel: 72370, 723215
Tlx: 982/5279 NAJDIAH NI
        5299 SAUDIA J1

Nigeria

182 Old Road, Abkoy, Lagos
Tel: 681-053
Tlx: 961/23193

Oman

Falj St. (behind Chamber of
   Commerce), Muscat,
P.O. Box 4411, Ruwi
Tel: 701111, 701840
Tlx: 926/3401 BM NAJDIA
   Muscat

Pakistan

House no. 32, Street no. 18,
   Sector F-6/2, Islamabad
Tel: 820156/820150
Tlx: 952/5671 RESA PK
        54040 NAJDIA PK

Philippines

8th Floor, Insular Life Bldg.
Ayala Ave., Makati, Metro
   Manila
Tel: 817-3371, 817-3372
Tlx: 742/23132 NAJD PH

Qatar

Al-Doha, 3rd Circle Rd.–South
Al-Mountazah Garden
Tel: 427144, 427145
Tlx: 957/4483 NAJDIA DH

Senegal

Rue Berranger
    Ferrauoxmasclary
B.P. 3109, Dakar
Tel: 21-69-28/22-23-67/21-15-57
Tlx: 962/294 NAJDIYAH SG

Singapore

No. 10 Nassim Rd., Singapore
    1025
Tel: 734-5870/734-5879

Commercial Office

Hex 17-03 Liat Towers
581 Orchard Rd.
Singapore 0923, Singapore
Tel: 235-8455/235-8459
Tlx: RS 39199
Fax: 737-4657

Somalia

Makkah Almokarrama St.,
    Mogadishu
Tel: 3817, 8733
Tlx: 999/523

Spain

Pasco de la Habana, 163
    Madrid-16
Tel: 457-1250/457-1254
    457-1258, 457-1262

Sudan

6–10 New Extension St. 29
P.O. Box 852, Khartoum
Tel: 41938, 45051
Tlx: 970/24014
    NAJDIAH SD

Sweden

Banergaten 10 115-22
    Stockholm
Tel: (08) 635775 cons.: 638750
Tlx: 854/14330
    NAJDIAH S.

Switzerland

12 Kramburg Strasse
Berne 3006
Tel: 031-441555/031-441556

Commercial Office

139 Rue de Lausanne
1202–Geneva,
    Switzerland
Tel: 327401/327402

Syria

Abu Rummaneh St.,
    Damascus
Tel: 334914, 334915
Tlx: 924/11906

Taiwan

11th Floor, No. 550
Chung Halao East Road,
   Section 4
Taipei
Tel: 703-5855/703-5910
   703-5755

Thailand

138, Silom Road
Boonmuter Bldg., 10th Floor
Bangkok, Thailand
Tel: 235-2171/233-7942

Tunisia

16 Nahg Al-Namsa Blvd. Tunis
Tel: 280504, 281265
Tlx: 934/

Turkey

Mahatma Ghandi Cad. 93
Gazi Osman Pasha
Ankara, Turkey
Tel: 344-577/344-580/344-581
Tlx: 42456 NJD TR

Commercial Office

Cinnah Cadd. 43/15
Cankaya, Ankara, Turkey
Tel: 393-249
Tlx: 46059 TJRA TR

Uganda

7 Kololo Hill Drive
P.O. Box 7274, Kampala
Tel: 41983/41984/42028
Tlx: 973/0988

United Arab Emirates

SH, Khalifah bin Shakhboot St.
West 17 Villa No. 60,
   Abu Dhabi
Tel: 365700
Tlx: 944/22670 NAJDIA EM

United Kingdom

15 Curzon St., London W1
Tel: 071-917-3000

Commercial Office

154 Brompton Rd.
London S.W. 3
Tel: 071-589-7246

Venezuela

Edifficiousucre–Piso 6
La Floresta–Avenida
   Francisco de
Miranda
Tel: 284-2866, 284-2622
Tlx: 395/29398 SAUDI VC

Yemen

a. Haddah Road, Qadi
   Abdul Rahman
   al-Aryan Bldg.
   P.O. Box 1184, Sana
   Tel: 240429, 240430
   Tlx: 948/2420
b. Khormaksar Soukra'a
   Khormarsar, Aden
   Tel: 23540, 22760, 22437
   Tlx: 956/282

Zambia

5th Floor, Premium House
Independence Ave.,
Lusaka
Tel: 72957, 72956
Tlx: 965/3411 LUSAKA
   ZAMBIA

Zaire

Avenue des Batetela 1054
(opposite Intercontinental),
Kenshasa
Tel: 30782
Tlx: 21541

Saudi Offices in the United Kingdom

1. Royal Embassy of Saudi
   Arabia
   15 Curzon Street,
   London W1
   Tel: (071) 917-3000

2. Consular Section
   32 Charles Street, W1
   Tel: (071) 917-3456

3. Economic Section
   127 Sloane Street, SW1
   Tel: (071) 730-8657

4. Information Office
   18 Cavendish Square, W1
   Tel: (071) 629-8803

5. Commercial Office
   154 Brompton Road, SW7
   Tel: (071) 589-7246

6. Defense Office
   22 Holland Park, W2
   Tel: (071) 221-7575

7. National Guard Office
   18 Seymour Street, W1
   Tel: (071) 486-1224

8. Saudi Press Agency
   18 Cavendish Square, W1
   Tel: (071) 495-0418

9. King Fahd Academy
   Bromyard Avenue, W3
   Tel: (071) 743-0131

The following are beneficial and useful tips for everyone:
- It is a good idea to carry along about twenty passport-size *pictures*. You may be visiting other countries in the region and some may require four pictures per visa. When you arrive you may be asked to furnish a few more pictures.
- When obtaining your visa, make sure to check on *vaccination* requirements. You may be able to get this information from your airline or travel agent. Inoculation certificates may be needed for one or more of the following: smallpox, yellow fever, cholera, typhus. Vaccinations are recorded in

a book, which you should carry during your travel. Inspection is usually strict when there are confirmed cases of cholera, otherwise you may be admitted without any question about vaccinations as has been the case for travelers coming from the U.S. and Europe.

- You may not have any knowledge of the Arabic *language*. It is not that easy to pick up in a matter of a few months because it is very different from the English or French languages. However, it would be wise and very useful for you to try and learn a few phrases, numbers and words, especially for greetings. These will go a long way and leave an everlasting impression, as the Saudis appreciate such gestures and effort. It may open new doors for you and put your counterpart at much ease. The key is to use your few expressions or whatever vocabulary you may have acquired without fear; poor grammar should not hamper your drive. One of the most convenient and pleasant expressions you will want to learn is: "Assalamou aleikom" which in English means "peace be upon you." This is a very popular expression in Saudi Arabia and throughout the Moslem world. The people you are greeting will respond–"Wa aleikomou salam"–which means, "peace be upon you also."

Read About the Host Country

Prior to your departure, it is advisable to read about the history of the country you will be visiting. Having a knowledge of the people, the geography, and history of the host land is very useful in carrying on a conversation with your colleagues and friends. The nationals will certainly appreciate your knowledge about their country. It should not take much of your time.

You may not want to go into great depth, or maybe you would want to acquire additional information from looking through a world almanac and reading just about a couple of pages, but if you read the chapters on Geography, History and Islam, you would be very well prepared for your visit to Saudi Arabia.

Travel Light

When traveling, it always pays to travel light and take only the necessary items. Some people go to the extreme and take with them medicine, cornflakes, toilet paper and the like including bigger items if they are going to the Kingdom to work. They take refrigerators, stoves, televisions, etc. Those who take the most will have the biggest headaches. If you travel light, you will be able to buy many things you need once you reach the country of your destination. The Kingdom has many modern shopping centers and consumer goods abound; in most cases prices are reasonable and many times better than what you may find in other parts of the world including the U.S., Britain, France, or Germany. If you happened to know some people who recently visited or resided in Saudi Arabia, it would be helpful to have their advice. Take only the essentials such as some books, necessary clothing compatible with Saudi traditions and weather conditions and a good simple camera. Those who prefer to take their heavy items with them are usually going to work in the Kingdom and their companies take care of all the transport cost and all the customs. Traveling light is a good practice, whether you are going to be there for a short time or a long duration. During your stay you are going to buy and gather many items, momentos and good bargains, and you will certainly be loaded when you come back.

- Take some *cash* with you, although most of your money may be in American Express or Visa checks. U.S. dollars are universally accepted, so are other currencies be it the British Pound, the French Franc, the Japanese Yen or the German Deutch Mark and others. While many Arab countries regulate their currency and require a declaration of the amount of money one is bringing, Saudi Arabia is a free economy and does not have these controls. While in a number of other countries, especially in the Arab world, visitors are not allowed to take out their local currency except in small declared amounts, the Kingdom does not have any restrictions on converting the Riyal or transferring money outside the country. However, you should clearly respect the rules of the country which are being applied at the time of your visit.

While we are on the subject of money, the monetary unit in the Kingdom of Saudi Arabia is the *Saudi Riyal*. Three and three quarter Riyals (3.75 S.R.) are equivalent to one U.S. Dollar and can be freely traded anywhere in the Kingdom. It is one of the most stable currencies in the world today. The Riyal is divided into one hundred halalas. Five halalas equal one quirsh; 20 quirsh = 1 Riyal. The coins are: five, ten, twenty-five, fifty, and one hundred halalas. The notes are: one, five, ten, fifty, one hundred and five hundred Riyal denominations. The dollar is based on Special Drawing Rights (SDR), so when the SDR per dollar changes, the official rate of the dollar is adjusted, but the rate hovers around 3.75 SR per dollar or 1 SDR = 3.75 SR.

Luggage/Flying

You should be at the airport about one hour before your departure time. The major airline for the Kingdom of Saudi Arabia is called Saudia. It is a world renowned airline with very professional crews and excellent service. Saudia flies from Washington and New York directly to Jeddah or Riyadh. It has flights from all major cities of the world (always ask for excursion and special discount fares–usually booked in advance). Of course, there are a number of other airlines that fly into the Kingdom and you will choose whatever you think is best for you. These include: Air France, British Airways, Lufthansa, Swiss Air, EgyptAir, Middle East Airline, just to name a few. Remember that traveling from the U.S., you are allowed to have two pieces of luggage *weighing* a maximum of 75 pounds each. So on your way from the U.S. to the Kingdom you will be allowed a total of 150 pounds (68 kilograms). However on the way back from the Kingdom to the United States the allowance is different. A tourist class traveler is allowed to bring a total of 44 pounds (20 kilograms) of luggage; first class passengers are permitted to bring a total of 66 pounds (30 kilograms). If you stay in Europe and then continue your trip to Saudi Arabia, you will be allowed only 20 Kg for tourist class and 30 Kg for first class. Remember, when flying from Europe to the U.S. you are allowed the two pieces of luggage weighing 75 pounds each; but leaving from Europe to any other destination, beware that you will be limited only to 20 or 30 Kg, depending on your class. Any excess luggage will cost you at a steep rate if it is to accompany you. If you send the excess baggage by air freight, it will be a lot cheaper. Minor excess weight is usually tolerated. A few kind words always help.

According to IATA regulations, you are not permitted to carry or put in your luggage any restricted or *dangerous articles*. These include poisonous gases, compressed gases such as butane, propane, oxygen, or infectious material like bacteria and viruses; also, explosives, munitions, fireworks and flares. Arms are also forbidden, such as sporting guns, handguns and pistol caps. Other items that must be carefully controlled are lighters and matches which must be carried on the person, and oxidizing materials such as peroxides and bleaching powder, poisons such as cyanides, insecticides, weedkillers and arsenic. Other items that are restricted include: magnetized material, mercury, offensive or irritating materials and large knives and swords. Necessary medicines are permitted. Some may require documentation and proof of doctors' prescription.

Alcohol and pork are not permitted in the country. They are both forbidden according to Islamic teachings. Narcotics are forbidden and anyone peddling or selling dangerous drugs such as heroin, cocaine, marijuana, LSD, etc. may receive the death penalty. In fact, on entry or departure, forms are handed out with the clear warning; it states in red letters: "WARNING: DEATH FOR DRUG TRAFFICKERS." "Trafficking in drugs–either smuggled, supplying, or receiving–incurs capital punishment within the Kingdom." Since the enactment of this law, drug related crimes and trafficking have decreased substantially. Also, one is not permitted to bring with him pornographic material or defamatory books about the Kingdom or Islam.

Customs

While in Customs it always pays to keep your cool and show kindness. A word or two in the language of your host country may help you a good deal. Most likely all your personal belongings will be duty free, but if you have, for example, two or three calculators, you may have to pay customs on one or two of them. Personal items that are used or slightly used have the best chance of going through Customs without any penalties. Whenever some disagreement develops, remember you are a guest in their country, and you should abide by and respect their laws and traditions. Losing your temper or getting in serious arguments will get you nowhere, only compound your troubles. In general, customs' agents are kind and courteous and you should not have any problems bringing all the clothing, items or gifts you desire. Remember you are a guest, it is their country and now you are the foreigner.

In general, you should breeze through as long as you have left the restricted items back home.

Travel Plans

Prior to deciding on the time of travel one must consider weather conditions and holidays. Summer in the Kingdom is very hot, and on the shores of the Arabian Gulf and Red Sea it is not only very hot but it is also very humid. Between June and September, temperatures could reach 115 degrees Fahrenheit. The best time in the Kingdom is between September and January. Between February and June the Shamal wind carries with it violent storms.

Also, there is the holy month of Ramadan. Its specific timing varies from year to year and the Moslems fast from sunrise to sunset. You would be better off to avoid visiting during this month (Check a Moslem calendar each year for that time or check with a Saudi office), but if you have to make the visit it should be okay. If you are in Saudi Arabia during Ramadan, out of respect for their customs you should not smoke, eat or drink in front of a fasting Moslem during the day.

The Hajj or Pilgrimage is usually a very busy time of the year. This is seventy days after Ramadan. Nearly two million pilgrims converge on Mecca and Madina. About one million come from the outside world, and this is one time of the year you would want to avoid.

Air conditioning is very much in use throughout the Kingdom. Pleasant balmy days are witnessed from October to April. In the heart of the Kingdom, for example in the area of Riyadh and surrounding areas, the nights can be chilly, even freezing may be experienced in the mountain areas of Asir.

Transportation

When taking a taxi make sure to find out what it is going to cost before getting in the taxi. Some taxi drivers are very nice, but once you reach your destination their charge may be more than what you expected. Taxis have meters. Make sure that the meter is turned on, or find out exactly what the charge will be to reach your destination; you can bargain with them. Taxi drivers are workers from several different countries, mainly, from the Philippines, Pakistan and India. Some of them are very new to the area and do not know their way around nor do they know much English or Arabic. It pays to examine the taxi driver carefully to be sure that he knows where your destination is. Taxi fares are very reasonable compared to other major cities of the world. Taxis give efficient, good service between the cities and major airports.

Other forms of modern transportation exist in the Kingdom. The Saudi Arabian Public Transport Company (SAPTCO) operates bus service within the towns and runs between larger centers of population. A modern rail service has been introduced to the Kingdom. First class air conditioned carriages run daily between Riyadh and Dammam. Once you are able to get your tickets the journey by train is a pleasant experience. Travel between cities in the Kingdom is comfortable and good on Saudi airlines, which covers essentially all major towns and cities in the Kingdom. A flight between Riyadh and Jeddah takes an hour and twenty minutes and then between Riyadh and Dhahran it takes forty-five minutes. These flights are carried on modern jets with excellent services and good safety records, as well as good departure and arrival time schedules. One could rent a car. All major car rentals exist in the Kingdom and rental fares are reasonable and comparable to fares in other cities of the world. Remember that the cost of gasoline in the Kingdom is far less than it is in Western countries. For example, a gallon of gasoline will cost around thirty cents or less, while in the U.S. it will cost in excess of one dollar, and could be as high as three to four U.S. dollars in other European cities. This lowers the cost of transport in the Kingdom. Employees who are residents of the Kingdom must have a valid Saudi drivers license and visitors should have either a valid drivers license from their home country or an international one.

Traveling Within the Kingdom

Employees of foreign origin and all foreign visitors to the Kingdom must carry with them a letter of consent which is supplied by their employer or a sponsor approving their travel. This is carried along with an official Immigration Registration Certificate allowing them to travel within the Kingdom of Saudi Arabia. Foreigners must register with their respective embassies. Employees in the Kingdom are prohibited from taking another job besides the one given by their sponsor. All those who come during the Pilgrim season to perform Hajj, Umra or visit must leave the Kingdom as soon as these rites are completed.

Communications

The Kingdom of Saudi Arabia has one of the most efficient and reliable telephone services in the world. There is direct dialing to most countries of the world by direct telephone, fax, or telex. The country code for the Kingdom of Saudi Arabia is 966. *Area codes* for major cities and certain useful numbers are shown in this table:

Area Codes for Certain Saudi Cities

Area Code	City	Area Code	City
01	Afif	02	Hada
01	Durma	02	Jeddah
01	Dowadmi	02	Mecca
01	Kharj	02	Obhor
01	Murat	02	Taif
01	Mazahimiyah		
01	Shaqra		
01	Riyadh		
03	Abqaiq	04	A'r'ar
03	Dammam	04	Madina
03	Hafr Al-Baten	04	Qurayat
03	Dhahran	04	Skaka
03	Hofouf	04	Tabouk
03	Jubail	04	Turaif
03	Al-Khafji	04	Yanbu
03	Khobar		
03	Qatif		
03	Ras Tanura		
06	Badayah	07	Abha
06	Buraidah	07	Al-Ba'ha
06	Hail	07	Bisha
06	Majm'a	07	Jizan
06	Qasim	07	Khamis Musheit
06	Azzilfi	07	Najran
		07	Sharoura
		07	Uneiza

The Emergency telephone numbers in the Kingdom are:

		International Information	900
Police	999	Telephone Directory Information	905
Ambulance	997	Telephone Maintenance	904
Fire Department	998	Speaking Clock	961 or 963
Road Accidents	993	Telex Maintenance	930

However, calling from Saudi Arabia to the United States of America you dial 001 then area code and phone number.

In order to dial international calls you should dial the following:

1. The international access code, for example in Saudi Arabia, you dial 00.
2. The code for the country you are calling, for example 1 for the U.S.A. and 44 for England.
3. The city code, such as 1 for London, 1 for Paris, 312 for Chicago, and 1 for Beirut.
4. The telephone number you are calling.

Thus, you should dial these:

Access code from your locale + country code you are calling + city code + telephone number you are calling.

Consult the following Tables for certain international country codes and for certain time zones relative to Riyadh.

Some International Country and City Codes

Algeria 213
  Algiers 2
  Boumerdes 2
  Constantine 4
  Oran 6
  Skikda 8

Antigua 1 809

Argentina 54
  Buenos Aires 1
  Mendoza 61

Australia 61
  Brisbane 7
  Melbourne 3
  Sydney 2

Austria 43
  Vienna 1

Bahamas 1 809
  Nassau 32

Bahrain 973

Bangladesh 880
  Dhaka 2

Barbados 1 809

Belgium 32
  Antwerp 3
  Brussels 2

Bermuda 1 809 2

Bolivia 591
  La Paz 2

Bosnia-Herzegovina
  Sarajevo 71

Brazil 55
  Brasilia 61
  Rio de Janeiro 21
  São Paulo 11

Bulgaria 359
  Sofia 2

Burma 95
  Rangoon 1

Canada 1
  Calgary 403
  Montreal 514
  Ottawa 613
  Quebec City 418
  Toronto 416
  Vancouver 604

Chile 56
  Santiago 2

China 86
  Beijing 1
  Shanghai 21

Colombia 57
  Bogota 1

Congo 242

Costa Rica 506

Cuba 53
  Havana 7

Cyprus 357
  Larnaca 41
  Limassol 51
  Nicosia 2

Czech Republic 42
  Prague 2

Denmark 45

Egypt 20
  Alexandria 3
  Cairo 2
  Ismailia 64
  Port Said 66

El Salvador 503

Ethiopia 251
  Addis Ababa 1

Falkland Islands 500

Finland 358
  Helsinki 0

France 33
  (For Paris dial
  331 + 8 digits.
  For other parts
  of the country
  dial 33 + no.

Germany 49
  Berlin 30
  Frankfurt 69
  Hamburg 40
  Munich 89

Greece 30
  Athens 1

Hong Kong 852

Hungary 36
  Budapest 1

Iceland 354
  Reykjavik 1

India 91
  Bombay 22
  Calcutta 33
  New Delhi 11

Indonesia 62
  Jakarta 21

Iran 98
  Abadan 631
  Ahvaz 61
  Tehran 21

Iraq 964
  Baghdad 1
  Kirkuk 50

Israel 972
  Haifa 4
  Jerusalem 2
  Tel Aviv 3

Italy 39
  Milan 2
  Naples 81
  Rome 6
  Vatican City 66982

Jamaica 809

Japan 81
  Hiroshima 82
  Kyoto 75
  Nagasaki 958
  Osaka 6
  Tokyo 3

Jordan 962
  Amman 6
  Aqaba 3

Kenya 254
  Nairobi 2

Korea (South) 82
  Seoul 2

Kuwait 965

Lebanon 961
  Beirut 1
  North Lebanon 6
  Sidon 7
  Tripoli 6

Libya 218
  Tripoli 21
  Benghazi 61

Luxembourg 352

Malaysia 60
  Kuala Lumpur 3

Mexico 52
  Acapulco 748
  Mexico City 5

Monaco 33 93

Morocco 212
  Casablanca
   (direct)
  Fes 6
  Marrakech 4
  Rabat 7
  Tangier 9

Netherlands 31
  Amsterdam 20
  Delft 15
  Hague 70
  Leiden 71

New Zealand
  Auckland 9
  Wellington 4

Nicaragua 505
  San Marcos 43
  Granada 55

Nigeria 234
  Lagos 1

Norway 47
  Oslo 2

Pakistan 92
  Islamabad 51
  Karachi 21
  Lahore 42

Palestine 972
  (West Bank)
  Jerusalem 2
  Ramalla 2

Peru 51
  Lima 14

Philippines 63
  Manila 2

Poland 48
  Warsaw 22

Portugal 351
  Almada 1
  Lisbon 1

Puerto Rico 809

Qatar 974

Romania 40
  Bucharest 0

Russia 7
  Moscow 095

Saudi Arabia 966
  Dammam 3
  Dhahran 3
  Hail 6
  Jeddah 2
  Mecca 2
  Madina 4
  Riyadh 1
  Yanbu 4

Spain 34
  Barcelona 3
  Cordoba 576
  Granada 58
  Madrid 1
  Marbella 52
  Palma de Mallorca 71
  Zaragoza 76

Sweden 46
  Stockholm 8

Taiwan 886
  Taipei 2

Turkey 90
  Ankara 4
  Istanbul 1

USA 1
  Alaska 907
  Austin 512
  Boston 617
  Chicago 312
  Houston 713
  New York 212
  San Francisco 415
  Tampa 813
  Washington D.C. 202

Zaire 243
  Kinshasa 12

Serbia 38
  Belgrade 12
  Zagreb 41

Somalia 252
  Mogadishu 1

Sri Lanka 94
  Colombo 1

Switzerland 41
  Basle 612
  Berne 31
  Geneva 22
  St. Moritz 82
  Zurich 1

Thailand 66
  Bangkok 2

United Arab Emirates 971
  Abu Dhabi 2
  Dubai 4

Venezuela 58
  Caracas 2

Zambia 260
  Lusaka 1

Singapore 65

South Africa 27
  Cape Town 21
  Johannesburg 11
  Pretoria 12

Sudan 249
  Khartoum 11
  Omdurman 11
  Port Sudan 31

Syria 963
  Aleppo 21
  Damascus 11
  Hama 331
  Homs 31
  Tartous 431

Tunisia 216
  Bizerte 2
  Carthage 1
  Tunis 1

Uruguay 598
  Montevideo 2

Yemen 967
  Hodeida 3
  San'a 2

Zimbabwe 263
  Harare 4

Time Zones for Certain Countries Relative to Riyadh, Saudi Arabia*

Country	Change in Time	Country	Change in Time
Algeria	−3	Malaysia	+4.5
Argentina	−6	Mexico	−9
Australia	+7	Monaco	−2
Austria	−2	Morocco	−3
Bahrain	0	Netherlands	−2
Belgium	−2	New Zealand	+9
Brazil	−6	Nigeria	−2
Cameroon	−2	Norway	−2
Canada	−8	Oman	+1
Caribbean	−7	Pakistan	+2
Cyprus	−1	Peru	−8
Denmark	−2	Philippines	+5
Egypt	−1	Portugal	−3
Finland	−1	Puerto Rico	−7
France	−2	Qatar	0
Germany	−2	San Marino	−2
Greece	−1	Senegal	−3
Hong Kong	+5	Singapore	+4.5
India	+2.5	South Africa	−1
Indonesia	+4	Spain	−2
Ireland	−3	Sri Lanka	+2.5
Italy	−2	Sweden	−2
Ivory Coast	−3	Switzerland	−2
Japan	+6	Taiwan	+5
Kenya	0	Thailand	+4
Korea (South)	+6	Tunisia	−2
Lebanon	−1	United Kingdom	−3
Luxembourg	−2	Upper Volta	−3
		U.S.A. (E. zone)	−8
		Venezuela	−7

* The plus sign means ahead in time and the minus sign means behind. For example if the time in Riyadh is 4:00 P.M., the time in New York, U.S.A. is 8:00 A.M. and thus it is behind by 8 hours. Time differences may slightly vary with the season and the city.

The Kingdom has two major *television* stations. One broadcasts in Arabic, the other in English with a news bulletin given in the French language. The Ministry of Information oversees the television network along with radio broadcasts both in Arabic and several other languages. The Kingdom has seven major newspapers and three of them are printed in English. The Eastern Region of the Kingdom is capable of receiving several TV stations from the neighboring Gulf countries including stations from as far away as

Iraq and Iran. The Kingdom has 37 *radio* transmission stations with 10 television relay stations and 9 mobile television stations along with 5 temporary television stations. Television broadcasts use the European standard called Secam. Since the U.S. uses the Ntsc System, a regular American television will not pick up Saudi TV signals. One can purchase locally multiple system televisions for a reasonable price. A Saudi or European TV recording will not work on a standard U.S. TV unit. One must be careful with electrical outlets. Some are 110 volts and others 220 volts.

Working Hours

Offices of the government are open from 7:30 A.M. until 2:30 P.M. General banking hours are from 8:00 A.M. until noon and from 5:00 P.M. until 7:00 P.M. Private businesses are normally open from 8:00 A.M. until 1:00 P.M. and again from 4:00 P.M. until 7:00 P.M. This corresponds to some morning business hours in the United States. Some of them are open from 8:00 A.M. until 5:00 P.M. While Thursday and Friday are holidays for government workers, most of the time business employees will work until 1:00 P.M. on Thursdays. Markets and shops are open until 9:00 P.M. On Friday they are open at 4:00 P.M. During Ramadan, typical business hours are 10:00 A.M.–2:00 P.M. and 9:30 P.M.–11:30 P.M. All work in the Kingdom must stop during prayer times. Businesses must shutdown during the brief prayer. These prayers are: Al-Fajr (dawn) and the noon prayer (Dhohr), the afternoon prayer (Asr), the Maghreb or sunset prayer and the early evening prayer (Isha). The exact times for these prayers are published in the daily newspapers and they vary slightly during the year. A businessman will be happy to know that there is a good mail service with efficient overnight delivery including services of DHL, Federal Express and the like. Saudis use the metric system for measurement. Expatriates working in the Kingdom do not pay any taxes and Americans working abroad are entitled to a $75,000 deduction when reporting their income to the Internal Revenue Service.

Health

A high priority is given to medical services. A very advanced and comprehensive health care system has been developed. Specialized hospitals have been built and equipped with the world's most up-to-date equipment. Some of the specialty treatments are for the eye, heart disorders, kidney, burns, tuberculosis, cancer, and a host of other diseases, just to mention a few. For example, King Khaled Eye Specialist Hospital in Riyadh is considered one of the best equipped eye hospital in the world. Also, the King Faisal Specialist Hospital and Research Center in Riyadh is considered among the best hospitals anywhere. Others include King Khaled University Hospital, King Fahd Medical City in Riyadh, National Guard and Military Hospitals, Saudi Aramco Hospital and many others throughout the Kingdom. A hospital similar to St. Jude's (a Children's Research Hospital for Leukemia) was needed in Saudi Arabia. The co-author of this book, Dr. Nasser Rashid, using over 100 million dollars of his own money, designed and built the King Fahd Children's Medical Center (KFCMC) in Riyadh, specializing in the treatment of childhood cancer.

Medical doctors in all fields of specialties are available. There are very modern public and private hospitals. Prescription drugs are easily obtained from pharmacies. Sometimes prescriptions with generic names are needed, especially since brand names in the Kingdom may differ from other countries. Many drugs including antibiotics may be obtained directly from the pharmacy without a prescription.

While on the subject of health, you should drink only pure water. It is bought in bottle form most of the time. Some is boiled and cooled before drinking. Also it is advisable and wise to wash all your vegetables in chlorinated water or eau de javel.

Islam

Saudi Arabia is a Moslem country and Islam is its official religion. Shari'a, which is the legal system in the Kingdom is derived from the Holy Qoran and Sunna (teachings of the Prophet Mohammed). The Qoran is also considered the constitution of the Kingdom (See Chapter on Islam). The Holy month of Ramadan during which Moslems fast from sunrise 'til sunset ends with Eid Al-Fitr which is a celebration of the breaking of the fast. The second major religious holiday is the celebration of pilgrimage to Mecca and it is called Eid Al-adha or the holiday of sacrifice. The time for these two holidays changes from year to year depending on the lunar calendar which is 354 days long in contrast to the Gregorian calendar which is based on the solar system and is 365 days long.

A Different World!

The best thing you can do is be adaptable. Your living conditions may vary widely from those in the United States, although the Kingdom has made great strides in the last several decades and the progress is indeed miraculous. The scenery and the nature that surrounds you is also different from your home country. You will certainly find some civilization gap. For Westerners, Saudi society, traditions and culture are indeed different; but you will find many Western ways, Western technologies and consumer goods. Religious traditions dominate every aspect of this Moslem country. As mentioned, shops must be closed during prayer times. Because justice is swift and fair, the country is one of the safest on the face of the earth.

There may be a few cultural barriers for a new arrival until one gets adapted and adjusted to the new way of life. A male visiting a Saudi family will only be in the company of other males. Women will share the company of other women. Saudi women dress very conservatively in black and cover their faces, while other Moslem women in Saudi Arabia dress modestly and cover their body with black dress but they do not have to cover their faces. Saudi men dress in white robes and on official or special occasions they wear on top of it a typical Saudi dress which is very dignified and certainly different from the Western dress. It is called a mishlah or bisht made of light wool and nearly touching the floor in length. It flows gracefully with a gold-thread trim and is rich black or light tan in color. The head is covered with a ghoutra and iqal which are respectively a checkered or white cloth and double ring of black cord to keep the ghoutra stable on the head. Leather sandals are also used. This formal dress is compatible with the searing heat of the desert. At manufacturing plants of the desert and other industrial facilities, Western clothes and hard hats are worn as a measure of safety. When Saudi men go abroad they dress like Western men and conduct business in similar manners. Women are not permitted to drive in the Kingdom. The male companion will be driving her or a chauffer will take her shopping and take the children to the doctor, etc. You may have been accustomed to speedy action and reaction back home, but in the Kingdom the pace is slower when it comes to dealings or handling matters. This is very much in contrast with the mind-boggling speed with which the Kingdom modernized itself in the span of just a few years.

The Kingdom carried out an industrial and educational evolution of far-reaching consequences. To attract personnel with needed know-how, pay was lucrative and living quarters were similar to any suburban American community. The housing continues to be of very good quality and the setting could easily be taken for a southwestern U.S. town. Those working in the Kingdom will end up taking vacations by going back home or visiting a number of interesting countries in Europe, Asia or the Middle East. This helps in rejuvenating the spirit and mind, so they will be ready to start again.

Time Zone

Saudi Arabia is under one time zone which is the equivalent of the Eastern Standard Time in the United States plus eight hours. During the Daylight Savings Time, Saudi Arabia is seven hours ahead of Eastern Standard Time. Of course if you live in Missouri, then Saudi Arabia will be ahead nine hours during Eastern Standard Time and eight hours during Daylight Savings Time. The Kingdom is three hours ahead of the Greenwich Mean Time. During the British summer season, you add two hours only to Saudi time. Thus, you should allow yourself some time to get over jet-lag, since your days become nights and nights become days. It may take from four to seven days to get over the jet-lag. This may interfere with your sleeping habits, but you will adjust and will be able to do your visit and carry on your business.

It is advisable to be punctual and on time, although in many Arab countries, including Saudi Arabia, being on time is not widely practiced. Do not be offended if you have to wait an hour or two.

Diplomacy

Be diplomatic and carry on small talk reflecting what you have learned about Arabic and the history of the Kingdom of Saudi Arabia when you are visiting. This may prove to be a most valuable tool in bringing about a friendly atmosphere with better understanding and mutual respect. Avoid any heated political or religious discussions. If possible, bring some gifts of the latest "in-items" which will be appreciated, not necessarily because of their value, but because of the thoughtfulness carried with them.

It is offensive and disrespectful to place your feet up so your shoes are facing someone. This is true with almost all Arabs! Arabs are warm people with deep emotions, pay great attention to self-esteem, and have high regard for their women's honor and protection.

Hospitality

While Arab hospitality and generosity are well known in history and story books, the Saudis are by far among the most generous and hospitable people in the world. With them these traits are truly legendary! They are traced back to the famous man of hospitality and generosity known as Hatem Al-Tayye. The Saudis are very warm and emotional people. They are friendly and warmly welcome their guests. When invited to a Saudi home, Arab coffee is served with dates, followed by Saudi tea with or without mint. Saudis drink many cups of tea a day. When invited for a dinner, the Saudi host is very gracious and happy to have you in his company. The food prepared for the occasion will feed many times the number of those invited to the dinner table. Several delicious dishes are prepared and you are urged to eat more and more. The dinner table is rich with all kinds of food and the atmosphere is usually jovial and pleasant. The visitor is a guest of honor and he or she is treated in the most respectful and warm way. Males eat in one place, while females eat at another dinner table. Many Saudis will have cooks and other help that stay with them throughout the year. These are expatriates who work in the Kingdom and they come from the four corners of the globe. Many of the cooks are from other Arab countries, Philippinos, Pakistanis, Indians or people coming from Sri Lanka, Thailand, or other parts of the world. At the end of the meal, sweets, tea and coffee are served. The sweets are usually very rich and delicious. A Westerner will not be able to eat much of the rich sweets. It is a Saudi custom and Arab tradition to have lots of food for the visitors. At the end of the meal much of it remains and is served to the helping hands. You can be sure that there will always be a plate of rice with meat. Rice is a very basic Saudi staple. Extending his hospitality, the Saudi makes the visitor feel at home, but in doing so he is also abiding by Saudi customs and culture.

In matters of hospitality, generosity, and safety, the Western man and woman could learn a great deal from their Saudi counterparts. While the host will insist on his guest eating more and more, it does not mean that he is pushing his guest, but his insistence and the abundance of food are indicative of the hosts' hospitality and generosity toward his honored guests. While the dinner may be served on a table as in Western countries and silverware is used, some Saudis may serve the dinner on a huge platter placed over a cover or carpet on the floor. While sitting on the floor backs and elbows are propped with cushions when drinking the tea or eating. While this is different from the Western way, it is still comfortable and interesting. On occasions the Saudis will eat with their hands. The guests can either eat with their hands or use utensils. It is not as hard as one thinks. It is a good idea to practice sitting on the floor with your legs crossed and you would be able to do it like a pro within a short time. Sometimes a large bowl of rice and ribs are served on a big platter. The custom is for one to take a handful of rice with the right hand and roll it into a small ball then eat it. Once dinner is finished, usually late at night between 10:00 P.M. and midnight, all the guests leave. Saudis do not eat their dinner at five or six o'clock in the evening as is the case in a number of Western countries.

Avoid "Bitching Clubs"

It is important for the Westerner living in any Middle Eastern country to keep in mind that there are customs and cultural differences that must be respected. "When in Rome, do as the Romans do," so to speak. The expatriate worker must learn to exercise respect, tolerance, and patience to work within the customs of the host country. A good measure of diplomacy should also be exercised in various situations.

The most serious error committed by some Americans, Europeans and other expatriates working overseas is forming what we call "bitching clubs." A group of disgruntled workers and their wives get together and drink tea, coffee or soft drinks and tear down the place left and right, rehashing everything that goes wrong, and at times not finding what is right with the place. This attitude and behavior, taking place day-in and day-out after working hours, and sometimes during working hours, will ruin your spirit and disturb your outlook on life. Instead of moaning, groaning, and complaining, it pays to look for positive things that exist in the land, and it does pay to socialize with people who are from neighboring areas. Remember one thing: you chose to work in their country! It pays to be humble, kind, respectful, and appreciative of the traditions, accomplishments, and history of the host land. Be respectful to everyone, especially those down the line of hierarchy. Those that are down the steps of the ladder could break the steps or destroy the ladder. You should pay attention to them; a little act of respect and hospitality will go a long way and will be much appreciated.

Sometimes you may become despondent and bothered with bureaucracy or the reluctance of some to make decisions. Use your insistence, convincing power and patience.

There are many instances in which you may get very good service and craftsmanship. You may get your watch fixed while waiting, for a very small fee–perhaps a fifth of what you might pay in the U.S. You may get your glasses fixed very professionally while waiting and, again, at a small cost.

Engineers and workers from the host country are progressively "rolling up their sleeves" and realizing the importance of practical work, maintenance and mechanical repairs. This trend in thinking and feeling is changing rapidly with industrialization. You should take this into consideration when dealing with them. Remember also, that you, being born or raised in America, are influenced extensively by the American way of life; you have been exposed to mechanical things and repairs since childhood. You have tried to fix your bicycle and car many times, and often fixed it for good; nevertheless, it was an experience in the applied approach. While going to undergraduate school, if you did as some of us did, you covered a wide spectrum of jobs ranging from yard work to nursing to tutoring, repairs and selling shoes, etc. All these contribute to your applied approach. Practical engineers are really what people in the developing countries need the most.

Working abroad can be very challenging and very rewarding; the glamour and spirit of adventure associated with it make it a genuinely exciting experience. But take this advice–don't expect too much, be patient, and develop a thick skin. Be adaptable and diplomatic; but stay firm when you have to be. The Japanese proverb is a good guide: "When the storm blows, the wise bam-

boo bends and does not break." Stay adaptable, look for the positive, and don't let frustration overtake you.

It pays to think international! The world community is smaller
than you think. Who knows? A great future may be awaiting you
over the horizon, in a different and fascinating foreign land.

Education

The building blocks of education started many years ago when
the first Minister of Education was appointed in 1953. The minister was Fahd Bin Abdulaziz, the present King of Saudi Arabia. He
pioneered a major role in establishing the educational system of
the country. Education is the cornerstone for the massive achievements that have been realized. Fahd had the foresight, determination and deep dedication to develop education in the Kingdom.
He knew that without education the dream of progress and development would not be realized.

Not long ago there was not one university in the Kingdom. In
the span of a short number of years, seven major universities have
been built. They are operating with good standards.

Today the children in the Kingdom are getting the best possible education. Indeed, recently a new primary or secondary school
was being opened every two weeks all year round. The total
school enrollment is around three million boys and girls. A great
leap forward!

Developing the minds of men and women alike was at the
heart of a success story that met the challenge of development and
modernization in the Kingdom.

While on the subject it should be mentioned here that many
schools are run by various delegations in the Kingdom, such as
the school run by the Indian Embassy and the Pakistani Embassy.
The Saudi Arabian International School (SAIS-R) in Riyadh is a
well known established school, with a student enrollment in the
neighborhood of 2,500 from nearly 45 nations around the world.
The International School has a nursery, a kindergarten, and goes
up through grade nine. The students can continue their high
school education in some schools in Europe, Switzerland or
France where they have boarding schools. In most cases the employees are reimbursed for the education of their children in the
form of an education allowance from their employer. The student
ratio is about twenty-two to one and the teachers, while primarily

American, come from all over the world. The standards are very good. The International School is licensed by the Saudi Arabian Ministry of Education. A school board is elected annually by the parents and it governs the school. An American curriculum is used and English is the language of instruction. The school is well endowed with a good library containing over 30,000 volumes and first class science laboratories and good sports facilities.

Another well-known school is called the Dhahran Academy in the Eastern Province, center of the oil operations in the Kingdom of Saudi Arabia. It also is run under the auspices of the Saudi Arabian International School System. It is an overseas American school helped by the department's Office of Overseas Schools. It is located on the Consulate General Compound and it gives instruction from kindergarten to grade nine. The language of instruction again is English and the Academy is operated along the same line as the International School in Riyadh. Children whose parents are working at Saudi Aramco and some others be it American or other expatriates can attend the Academy. It has over 1,500 students from nearly 40 countries around the world. Again, graduates from ninth grade will finish their high school in Europe or in the U.S. Assistance is rendered by the Overseas School Office situated in the Department of State in the United States where parents can be advised on the choice of schools in Europe or elsewhere so their children can continue their education and obtain their high school diploma and beyond.

Women

Upon his ascension to the throne in 1964, King Faisal opened many new doors for Saudi women. For the first time in the Kingdom's history, women were able to obtain an education along the same footing as their male counterparts, going from kindergarten to the university level. This basic policy has continued to flourish. A very good and close relationship between homelife and school environment contributes to the family structure which is at the heart of Saudi life. This policy was strongly supported and practiced by other Saudi leaders and especially King Fahd, Custodian of the Two Holy Mosques–the education pioneer. Special attention to the education of women has progressively expanded, beginning as long ago as 1960. Since that time the number of girls and women in schools has constantly increased. Of the three million students in Saudi schools today, about 50 percent of them are women. The seven Saudi universities have colleges for women. However, their instruction is separate from men. The number of female students at Saudi universities is now nearly 50% of the student population. The Undersecretariat for Girl's Colleges constitutes a major division of the Presidency for Girls' Education. It specializes in handling higher education for girls. There are over sixty-one colleges in Saudi Arabia. Half of these handle scientific studies and have a total Saudi teaching staff exceeding 10,000. A universal education for women has been the goal and it is now essentially achieved.

A Westerner, coming to the Kingdom for the first time, will be surprised that Saudi women in public are veiled. This is nothing but a simplistic first impression. The Saudis honor, respect, protect, and revere their women. The woman is the central figure of family life which is the very basic essence of Saudi society. While studying or working or even examining items while shopping, the veil is moved aside. In the presence of men who are not closely related to the family, women remain in separate quarters. At first sight one may have the impression that Saudi women do not have as much power as women in the West. This is nothing but a tip of the iceberg, because women in Saudi society are really not only deeply honored and respected but indeed powerful. This is nothing new to Saudi society. Women today are receiving a good education and becoming professionals in many fields and endeavors such as teaching, medicine, nursing and many more. There are banks and other businesses run by women. There are women professors, doctors, writers, editors and broadcasters. Women do not specialize in professions that are normally dominated by men such as mechanical engineering, construction, or combat-ready assignments. Their top priority which is central to the Saudi way of life and tradition is the family. Family matters are private and belong to the family not to the public. You will find that tradition calls for a low-key approach in matters of family, and privacy is very important in the Saudi way of life. Taking care of women and respecting them, protecting them along with their rights is very clearly specified in the Holy Qoran. No man is entitled to take advantage of a woman. If a woman or man is not happy with their marriage, according to Islamic Shari'a they can part company and everyone's rights are protected as dictated in the Holy Qoran. The young children will remain with their mother. As mentioned previously in the chapter on Islam, a man is allowed to marry more than one woman. He can marry four, but if he wants to be just he will marry only one. In modern Saudi society, women are receiving an education on equal footing with men and many are holding equal jobs and earning income, thus becoming more partners with their men who now find it more difficult and impractical to acquire more than one wife. Men marrying more than one woman in Saudi Arabia are few and are becoming more rare. It is certainly becoming harder for a man to keep up to par with his partner and provide for one family without adding more families to his domain. Today the Saudi woman is modern, well-educated, family-oriented and essentially more satisfying and pleasing to her man who will find it unnecessary and burdensome to have another woman for a second wife.

Women are not allowed to drive in Saudi Arabia. The man has the added responsibility of providing for her transport either by having a chauffeur or by driving her himself to help her buy the groceries or take the children to the dentist or doctor or school. The whole policy and tradition revolves around protecting and shielding the woman from the stresses and burdens of life which are faced by men (See chapter on Islam). In general, the family unit is remarkably strong and divorce by Western standards is rare. While in many cases marriages are arranged, boys and girls make their desires and choices known, but they do not marry against the wishes of their parents. Parents are very much respected and honored by their children, as clearly specified in the Holy Qoran. You are not supposed to talk back or treat parents in any disrespectful manner, but treat them with kindness and care.

Today women are providing a great pool for the Saudi work force. A number of them go abroad for further education and have positions in the Saudi government or in international Saudi companies. Many of them are employed by radio and television networks as well. Businesses owned by Saudi women increased by 266% between 1988 and 1993, thus reaching 10,697.

The parents of a girl will discuss the dowery with her future husband who is supposed to provide it. While parents have their say and their word is very much respected, young men and women have the final word in marrying or not. Whenever a marriage does not work, divorce takes place as mentioned in the chapter on Islam. However, divorce is most detested by the Prophet. The end of marriage is never vehement and divisive as one witnesses again and again in the West. Divorces are very private without heartache amongst the parties concerned or their families, or the lengthy public legal battles that rage on in Western societies, where the children become the prime victims of the fights and squabbling that develop with so many pushes and shoves in various directions. This essentially tears not only at the fabric of family, but also at the spirit and heart of the young children who suffer severely and become torn between the two partners. The aftermath, the scars and the price are steep indeed!

Away from the centers of population in the desert, Bedouin society moves on freely. The women here are mostly unveiled and they share the tasks and chores of life with their male counterparts. Bedouin women are free in their movements and their life is not as sequestered as one would find in major centers of population.

This section is best concluded with the impressions of two statesman: Margaret Thatcher, former Prime Minister of England, visited Saudi Arabia more than once and discovered the importance of women in Saudi Society. She expressed that many of them are "highly cultivated, very well educated and well informed. Their influence is greatly underrated in the West and an evening's conversation with them is a highly stimulating occasion." Prince Charles of England said in his speech at Oxford University on October 27, 1993 "The rights of Moslem women to property and inheritance, to some protection if divorced, and to the conducting of business, were rights prescribed by the Qoran fourteen hundred years ago, even if they were not everywhere translated into practice. In Britain at least, some of these rights were novel even to my grandmother's generation!"

Do's and Don'ts

Here are some useful hints of what you should *do* and what you shouldn't do.

- Take a good pair of sunglasses with you. Sun in the Kingdom is very bright.
- It is a good idea to bargain when you are shopping at a

Bazaar or Souk because you can always get things much cheaper than the asking price.

- When you have an Arab guest that you have invited to your home and you offer him a drink or food, ask more than once because most likely he will refuse the first time, which is part of the Arab tradition.
- Learn as much as possible about the history of the country, Islam, and then some Arabic expressions and exhibit this knowledge whenever the opportunity arises.
- Make the gesture to allow your guests or friends to enter first. It is a sign of respect and politeness.
- If you invite a Saudi or other friends to eat out, go ahead and insist on paying the bill. In the Arab tradition, there is no such thing as Dutch treat (or separate checks). Learn from Arab hospitality and generosity; profusely invite your guests and shower them with kindness and make available lots of food and soft drinks–preferably several dishes.
- When in public dress modestly and conservatively. Preferably women should wear a long dress with long sleeves and a scarf on their head.
- The old saying, "When you are in Rome do as the Romans do" is a good one; so "when you are in Saudi Arabia do as the Saudis do." When the Saudis enter a home, most likely they will remove their shoes. It is a sign of respect if you remove your shoes too, although it may not be required.
- No doubt you will see the religious morality police or Moutaw'a who enforce prayer times and the closure of shops in the centers of population during prayer. Be respectful, kind and exercise some patience.
- Respect Saudi traditions, customs, and religious practices.
- Whenever feasible or possible buy a gift which reflects kindness or thoughfulness which you may give to a Saudi friend who will certainly appreciate it, especially if it is made in your home country.
- Be complimentary and have a positive attitude and remember that Saudi traditions are unique and different from those in your home country. So patience is a good virtue. You must respect and abide by Saudi laws which are fair, just and swift.

Here are a number of items which you *should not do:*

- It is very wise for you not to discuss matters of religion and especially criticize Islam or traditions and customs related to Islam, nor criticize in any harsh or impractical manner the government or the system which is followed in the Kingdom. Constructive criticism and fair ideas could be exchanged freely.
- You are forbidden from entering the Holy cities of Mecca and Madina. These two cities can be visited only by Moslems. While in the Kingdom only Moslems may enter a Mosque. They must remove their shoes and leave them prior to entry into the Mosque.
- During the Holy month of Ramadan, where all Moslems must fast all day, it is improper and inconsiderate for anyone to eat, drink, or smoke in public. Out of courtesy you must avoid doing so, while you can do this in the privacy of your quarters or office.
- While you can freely carry on many discussions, it is very wise to avoid getting into heated political discussions.
- Offer food and drinks with your right hand only since the left hand is used for personal hygiene.
- If you admire the possessions of a Saudi, he will most likely insist on giving you whatever you have admired. This can be sometimes embarrassing, so while it is a good idea to offer compliments, you must be careful in your admiration.
- When you and your spouse are in public, it is a good idea not to offer affection. Although you may see Arab men holding hands, it is only a sign of good friendship. The Saudis may shake your hand, kiss you on the cheek, or tap you on the shoulder as a sign of friendship.
- When taking pictures it is wise of you to ask permission from the people whom you wish to photograph. When you are taking a picture of an airport, a base, or a ministry, again it is a good idea to ask the guard in charge for permission, otherwise you may be violating their rules and regulations.
- You must not bring into the Kingdom of Saudi Arabia anything illegal or forbidden as mentioned previously. You are

very clearly warned against bringing any drugs such as heroin, cocaine, marijuana, etc. Drug trafficking in the Kingdom is punishable by the death penalty.

- When a Saudi man is visiting you, you should not insist on him removing his traditional head dress (the Ghutra).

- When Moslems are praying you should not pass in front of them so as not to interfere with their facing of Mecca, and you must not step on prayer rugs.

- When referring to the Moslem religion of the Saudis, you must not call them Mohammedans because they are Moslems, nor should you call them of the Wahhabi sect because there is no such thing in Saudi Arabia. This misnomer has been mentioned in many books in reference to the puritanical movement of Sheikh Mohammed Bin Abdulwahhab who linked this D'awa with Mohammed Ibn Saud back around the year 1744. This coupling of Saudi leadership with Islamic teachings continues until this day. The words Wahhabi or Wahhabism must not be used and they certainly are erroneous and misleading.

- It is improper to stare at Saudi women, or at someone praying, or even at other Saudi men.

- You should not offer your Saudi guests spirits or pork which are both forbidden in Islam.

While the list of useful information is very helpful to the traveler to the Kingdom of Saudi Arabia, it is certainly far from being complete. It is complemented by other detailed chapters which provide in-depth information and which must be read carefully so that the visitor will have a well-rounded education and understanding of the Kingdom of Saudi Arabia. For example, if you are going to do business with the Kingdom or work in the Kingdom, then you will certainly be well advised and interested in reading a detailed chapter about doing business in Saudi Arabia.

If you observe these helpful guides and ideas prior to and during your trip to the Kingdom, rest assured you will have a memorable stay and your trip will be an enriching and certainly successful experience. The superficial images and impressions about Saudis being rich Sheikhs rocking along on camel backs will certainly vanish from your mind. The tremendous progress achieved by the Kingdom while keeping its traditions and culture will certainly astound you!

Chapter 9

Useful Arabic

It is useful to develop some familiarity with written Arabic. Knowing the alphabet and the way the letters appear in writing will help the curious and the interested to satisfy some of his curiosity. Speaking, writing, and reading a few words in Arabic should break the "ice" and give a favorable impression to those you are dealing with.

Arabic Alphabet

There are twenty-nine letters in the Arabic alphabet. They look very different from anything you have seen before. Each letter guards its basic identity, but will appear somewhat differently, depending on its position in the word.

Arabic is a logical language, but is a different and difficult one. It is systematically built from the alphabet with all the familiar rules of grammar. Table 1 shows the various letters and their shapes: (The dotted capital letters in the English equivalent column indicate that actual pronunciation is different in Arabic).

Remember that Arabic is read from right to left, and that most of the letters appearing at the end or middle of a word have little connecting tails attaching them to other letters.

Table 1–Arabic Alphabet

English Pronunciation	English Equivalent
alif	a
ba	b
ta	t
tha	c
jim	j
Ha	H
Kha	Kh
dal	d

Table 1–Arabic Alphabet (Continued)

English Pronunciation	English Equivalent
Thal	th
ra	r
zein	z
Seen	S
Sheen	sh
Sod	Ṣ
dod	Ḋ
Tah	T
thah	Z
Ȧin	Ȧ, Ė, Ȯ, İ
Ġhain	Ġh
fa	*f*.
Ḳaf	Q̇
kaf	K
lam	l
meem	m
noon	n
ha	h
waw	w
La	la
ya	Y

Source: Reference 153

Basic Conventions

Since certain Arabic letters do not have an equivalent in the English language, and some of them are hard to pronounce, a list of the difficult sounds and the corresponding conventions should be of some help to the reader.

Symbol	*Explanation*
Ḣ	When written in capital form with a dot, it indicates a letter which is a good bit stronger than h. It is a sound produced at the lower portion of the throat when the tongue is pressed down, the same as if a doctor has pressed it with a spoon to check the throat of his patient (with this letter you need to be patient). *Example:* Ḣelou–meaning pretty

Kha   A sound similar to clearing the throat when spitting
      Example: Kharab–meaning destruction

A,E,O   This is similar to the sound of a calf calling his mother
        cow.
        Example: Arab   = (meaning) Arabs
                   Eshreen = twenty
                   Oomir   = age

Gh   Close to the sound made when you gargle.
      Example: Gharawm = love (a good word to remember)

Q   Similar to a k-sound, but it is pronounced far back at the
      entry to the throat.
      Example: Qareeb = near

Note that these letters, which are very different from what you
have been used to in the English language, are clearly distinguished by a capital letter and a dot for quick identification.

Some Rules and Examples in Arabic

Delving into detailed grammar will not be our purpose; it is
sufficient and interesting to get familiar with the necessary tools of
Arabic. We shall touch on personal pronouns, verbs, basic signs
for pronunciation, adjectives, plurals, and conclude with some
readings in Arabic.

1. Personal Pronouns

English	Pronunciation
I	ana
you	anta
he	houa
she	hia
it	houa (m)
	hia (f)
we	naHnou
you (plural)	antom
they	hom

Here are some examples on their use with the verb:
to drink = shariba.

English	Pronunciation
I drink	ana ashrab
you drink	anta tashrab
he drinks	houa yashrab
she drinks	hia tashrab
we drink	naHnou nashrab
you drink	antom tashraboon
they drink	hom yashraboon

Note that the key word (shariba) has been conjugated, or twisted around if you wish, but it guarded its originality just as it would in French or English. Don't let the varied forms misguide you. Even if you cannot conjugate, stick to the original word, and with the proper maneuverability, your message will get across. No one will be offended in your twisting of some words and Arabizing others. The most important thing is to get the message across; when you succeed in doing that, it will sound good, no matter what you say or how you say it.

Let us take another verb (to study = darasa) and see how it will change with these pronouns.

English	Pronunciation
I study	ana adros
you study	anta tadros
he studies	houa yadros
she studies	hia tadros
we study	naHnou nadros
you study	antom tadrousoon
they study	hom yadrousoon

Now watch how easy it is to claim possession:
Take the word pencil for example:

English	Pronunciation
pencil	Ọalam
my pencil	Ọalami
your pencil	Ọalamak
his pencil	Ọalamahou
her pencil	Ọalamaha
our pencil	Ọalamouna
their pencil	Ọalamouhom

Note that by adding the i (pronounced ee), this possession was obtained: my pencil, and so on (see following table).

Possessive Case	Pronunciation
my pencil	i (Ọalam<u>i</u>)
your pencil	(Ọalam<u>ak</u>)
his pencil	hou
her pencil	ha
our pencil	na
their pencil	hom

2. Verbs

In English, we speak of the infinitive form as the original word for a verb; in Arabic the masculine third person singular is used. Thus, when we say: to travel, in Arabic we use:

he traveled = sefara

Another example, take the verb: to drink, in Arabic we use:

he drank = shariba

Aside from this, you have the imperative form and two other forms denoting completion and incompletion as illustrated in table 2.

Remember the "core" or original shape of the word and verb; then apply whatever you have learned from the basic symbols, rules, and conversations; then you should be able to get your point across. Note that in the Glossary, you will find many verbs in the present form, such as:

yaktob = he writes
yaḋrob = he hits
These may be changed to:
I write = ana aktob
I hit = ana aḋrob
or get the infinitive equivalent:
he wrote = kataba
he hit = ḋaraba
Flexibility with what you know, mingled with the sign language, are the name of the game.

Table 2–Conjugation

Verb	Past		Present	
	English	Pronun-ciation	English	Pronun-ciation
walk	he walked	masha	he walks	yamshi
	she walked	mashat	she walks	tamshi
talk	he talked	takallama	he talks	yatakallam
	she talked	takallamat	she talks	tatakallam
hit	he hit	ḋarab	he hits	yaḋrob
	she hit	ḋarabat	she hits	taḋrob
sit	he sat	jalasa	he sits	yajlis
	she sat	jalasat	she sits	tajlis
visit	he visited	zawra	he visits	yazour
	she visited	zawrat	she visits	tazour
go	he went	zahaba	he goes	yazhab
	she went	zahabat	she goes	tazhab

Table 2–Conjugation (Continued)

Imperative		Future	
English	Pronun-ciation	English	Pronun-ciation
walk	imshi	I will walk	sa-amshi
walk	imshi	she will walk	sa-tamshi
talk	takallam	I will talk	sa-atakallam
talk	takallami	she will talk	sa-tatakallami
hit	iDrib	I will hit	sa-aDrob
hit	iDribi	she will hit	sa-taDroubi
sit	ajlis	I will sit	sa-ajlis
sit	ajlisi	she will sit	sa-tajlisi
visit	zor	I will visit	sa-azour
visit	zouri	she will visit	sa-tazouri
go	izhab	I will go	sa-azhab
go	izhabi	she will go	sa-tazhabi

3. Basic Signs of Pronunciation

Certain basic signs are associated with the reading of Arabic words, even if they have not been incorporated in the writing. Beginning readers of Arabic will find these signs attached to the words to ease and bring about proper pronunciation.

4. Adjectives

In Arabic, the adjective follows the noun in position and general accents, as you see in these examples:

Good man = rajolon moumtezon

Here are some other examples:

I like delicious grapes =
ouHibbou el-Iinaba el-laziza

Delicious is the property of the grapes.

5. Plurals

In French or English, you add the letter s to the noun, and in most cases you would have obtained the plural. But in other instances, you switch a letter or more, without adding the s and you have the plural. In Arabic you do a good bit of the latter. Take, for example, the word "man":

man = rajol

to make the plural you have:

men = rijẽl

Table 3 shows examples.

6. Definite Article: the

Arabic is unique in its excessive use of the definite article:

the = Al

To the Arab, it seems to be an inherent part of so many words, but to a Westerner, one can do away with it, many times, and without a significant loss. Watch the Als in these words:

The Arabs = Aarab
Nasser = Al-Nasser
Sadat = Al-Sadat
Security = Al-Amn

You can keep them or drop them without a great loss.

Table 3–Plurals

English Singular	Pronunciation	English Plural	Pronunciation
House	beit	Houses	bouyoot
School	madrasa	Schools	maderis
Rich	Ġhani	Rich	aĠhnia
Poor	faĠir	Poor	fouĠara
Library	maktaba	Libraries	maketib
Tiger	nimr	Tigers	noumour
Intelligent	zaki	Intelligent	azkia
Doctor	daktour	Doctors	daketira
Car	sayyara	Cars	sayyarawt
Automobile	Automobile	Automobiles	Automobilet
Moon	Ġamar	Moons	aĠmar
Camel	jamel (in Egypt: (Gamal)	Camels	jimēl
Road	TareeĠ	Roads	ToroĠ
Plant	masnaȦ	Plants	masaneĖ
Friend	sadeeĠ	Friends	asdiĠa'a
Flower	zahra	Flowers	azhawr
Tree	shajara	Trees	ashjar
River	nahr	Rivers	anhawr
Heart	Ġalb	Hearts	Ġouloub
King	malik	Kings	moulouk

Numbers

The numbers used in America and Europe are called Arabic numerals; but the Arabs today use different symbols.

English	Arabic	English	Arabic
zero	sifir	forty	arbĖen
one	waḢid	fifty	Ḳhamseen
two	ithnain	sixty	sitteen
three	thalatha	seventy	sab-Ėen
four	arba-Ȧ	eighty	tmaneen
five	Ḳhamsa	ninety	tis-Ėen
six	sitta	hundred	meeya
seven	sab-Ȧ	two hundred	meetein
eight	thamaniah	thousand	alf
nine	tis-Ȧ	two thousand	alfein
ten	Ȧshra	ten thousand	Ȧshrat alaaf
eleven	Ḣda-Ȧsh*	million	malioun
twelve	Tna-Ȧsh	billion	miliar
thirteen	tlata-Ȧsh		
fourteen	ar-ba-Ȧ-taȦsh		
fifteen	Ḳhams-ta Ȧsh	**Some Ordinals of Interest**	
sixteen	sitta-Ȧsh	first	awwal
seventeen	sabe-Ėta-Ȧsh	second	tani
eighteen	tminta-Ȧsh	last	aḲhir
nineteen	tiseĖta-Ȧsh		(sometimes
twenty	Ėshreen		aḲheer)
twenty-one	WaḢad wa Ėshreen	once	marra
twenty-five	Ḳhamsa wa Ėshreen	twice	marratein
thirty	tlateen	three times	tlat marrat

Time and Date

English	Arabic
The hour	A'sseȦa
Minute	DaǪiǪa
Second	Thania
Morning	SabaḢ
Afternoon	BȦd 'ezzohr
Evening	Masa

Time and Date (Continued)

English	Arabic
What time is it? (What is the hour)	Kam 'esseȦa
It is two thirty P.M.	sseȦa ithnein wa nisf bȦd 'ezzohr.
Twenty till three A.M.	Tlati illa tolt sabaḤan.
Eight o'clock in the evening.	Thamenia mass'an.
Quarter to ten.	Ȧshra ill robĖ
Midnight	Nisf el-leil.
Noon	'ezzohr
Five thirty	K̇hamsa wa nisf (or K̇hamsi w'noss)

Days of the Week	Ayyem el-ousbȮ

In Arabic you use the word *the* before every day of the week.

Monday	Al-ithnein
Tuesday	Al-thoulatha
Wednesday	Al-arbouȦa
Thursday	Al-K̇hamis
Friday	Al-jomoȦa
Saturday	Al-sabt
Sunday	Al-aḤad
What is today?	Ma houa el-yom?
Today is Monday.	Al-yom houa el-ithnein.
We will come over Sunday.	Sanaji li-İndakom el-aḤad.
Friday is the Moslem holiday.	El-jomoȦa Ȯtla lil-Mosleemeen.
We work Saturday morning.	NashtaG̣hel sabeḤ Al-sabt.
This weekend	Hezihi Al-weekend
This day.	Heza Al-yom (or Heza 'nnahar).
Past week	El-osbȮ Al-maḊi.
I will come back tomorrow.	sa-arjȦ G̣hadan.

Months of Year	Ash-hor a-ssana

Some modifications of the English version are sometimes used, such as (Fibrayar) for February, and (Avril) for April in Egypt; also in Algeria, Avril is used for April, and (oot) is used for August (from the French Août and Avril). etc. . . .

January	Kanoon Al-theni (Janvieh) (Yaneyer)
February	Shbat (Fibrayar)
March	Ezar (Mars)
April	Nisan (Avril)
May	Ayyar (Mayo)
June	Houzeiran (Jwan)
July	Tammouz (Yolyo)
August	Eb (oot) (Ogostos)
September	Eiloul (September)
October	Tishreen awwal (October)
November	Tishreen tani (November)
December	Kanoon awwal (December)

This is the month of Ramadan.
In this month, Moslems fast
  during the day and eat
  at night.

Heza shahr RamaḊan.
Fi heza shshahr
  Al-Mouslimun yasoumoun
  fi nnahar wa yakouloun fi
  Al-leil.

January is a very cold month
  in Chicago.

(Janvieh) Kanoun Al-thani
  houwa shahr berid jiddan
  fi ChicaĠho.

I am happy to be here.
The climate is warm here.

Ana masrour (mabsout) hina.
A-ttaQ̇s (Al-Mounekh)
  Ḣarr hina

Come and see us in the fall.
  (the seasons start with the
  word the = Al)
Fall is a good season in
  Saudi Arabia
Fall
Winter
Spring
Summer

TaAa shoufna fi Al-Kharif

Al-Kharif Jameel fi
  Al-Saudia
Al-Kharif
Al-shita
Al-rabi
Al-saif

Customs

When at the Customs, it pays to be patient and courteous. A few words in Arabic are always a plus.

English	Arabic
Greetings, hello	Assalamou ÀlaiKum (literally this means: peace be upon you; it is widely used throughout the Arab world). The corresponding word: *marHaba* may also be understood throughout.

The custom man will answer you by saying,

Hi!	wa ÀlaiKumou ssalam (meaning that: peace be upon you too).
How are you?	Kifak? (in Algeria, the word used is: shHal)
Fine, thank you	MliH, Shoukran
I'm an American	Ana Amriki
I am British	Ana Enkleezi
I am French	Ana Faransi
I am German	Ana Almaani
I am Russian	Ana Rousi
I speak little Arabic	Ana biHki Shwait Àrabi
I like the Arab World	Ana bHobb elbilad elÀrabia
I'm an engineer	Ana mouhandis
I'll stay here for one month	Sa-abQa houna limouddat shahr.
These are personal effects	howdy amtiÀty
They are not subject to customs	ma Àleihom Dariba
Do you have alcohol?	hal maÀaK Khamr
No	la
Where can I change some money?	Wein fini ibdil flous?
There at the bank	hownah fi Al-bank
I need a taxi, if you please	baddi taxi min faDlak
What is the distance to the hotel?	ma hia Almasafa ila Al-hotel? (sometimes fondoQ is used for hotel)
The distance is 30 Kilometers (1 mile = 1.62 kilometers)	almasafa hia talateen kilometer

Changing Money

English	Arabic
Is there a bank at the airport?	Hal youjad bank fi el-matawr?
Yes! It is over there.	NaÀam! howa hounek.
Thank you.	Shoukran (mamnoun).
What is the value of the dollar?	Ma hia Ġeemat addoular?
One dollar is equivalent to 3.75 Saudi Riyals.	Addoular yousaywee 3.75 Riyal Saudi
Saudi Riyals.	rialat saŎudia.
Please change one hundred dollars for me.	Min faḊlak Ġhayyerli (baddelli) miat doular.
Please give me your money-declaration paper.	Min faḊlak Ìtini waraQat tasriH addarawhim.
Here it is.	Hezihi hia (tfaḊḊal).
Do not lose this paper.	La touḊayyeĖ hezihi Al-waraQa.
Keep it.	IḢtafiz biha.
Do I need to declare my money?	Hal yajib an ouKhbir Àn darawhimi (foulousee)
No	La (Kalla)
No! It is not necessary.	La! leisa Ḋarouri (moush Ḋarouri).
Where could I change money in town?	Eina yomkin an ouĠhayyer foulous fi Al-madina?
You can change money at some hotels and banks.	Yomkinak an touĠhayyer foulous fi baÀḊ Al-outelet wa Al-bounouk.
Could I take local currency out of the country?	Hal yomkinouni an aĠhoz darohim Ġhawrij Al-balad?
Yes!	naÀam (eh).
We have a free market.	Ìndana souQ Ḣorra.
Free economy.	Iktisad Horr.
You can bring in all the money you want.	Yomkinak an tajlob eyye kammia tasha'a (tourid) min addarahim.
You can take with you all the money you want.	Yomkinak an taĠhoz maÀak koll ma tasha'a min addrahim.

English	Arabic
Could I change money from individuals or anybody?	Hal yomkinouni (biQdir) an ouĠhayyer (baddil) foulous min el-afrawd aw eyye shaḰhs?
In this country! Yes you can.	Fi heza el-balad! na'am Yomkinak.
In our country you should change only at the banks and hotels.	Fi baladina yajib an touĠhayyer fi el-bounouk wal-outelet faQaT.
Where could I change these dollars?	Eina yomkin an ouĠhayyer ha ddoularat?
Over there at the bank.	Hounek fi Al-bank.
I enjoyed my stay in your country.	Sourirt bi-ziyawrati li-baladikom.
You are welcome.	Ahlan wa sahlan.
Please come back and visit us again.	İmal maḢrouf irjaȦ wa zourna marra tania.
Please give me your money-declaration paper.	Min faḊlak İtini waraQat tasriḢ addarohim.
There it is.	tfaḊḊal.
I lost it.	ḊayyaȦtaha (ḊoȦat).
So long for now.	BḰhotirkom
Have a safe trip.	MaȦ assalema

At the Hotel

English	Arabic
Hello!	MarḢaba!
My name is Tony Brown.	İsmi Tony Brown.
I have a reservation for one. room	İndi Ḣajz li Ghorfa waḢida.
Single bed or double bed?	Bi-sarir waḢad aww sareerein?
Room with double bed, please.	Ġhorfa bi-sareerein min faḊlak.
water.	Ma'a (mayye).
hot water.	Ma'a soḰhn.

English	Arabic
bathroom.	Beit mayye (mirHaḊ), (toilette)
soap.	Sawboon.
radio.	Radio.
television.	Televizion.
telephone.	taleephon.
balcony.	Balcon.
Room with good view of the city.	Ġhorfa wamanzar jameel lil-madina.
Room with good view of the sea.	Ġhorfa wamanzar jameel lil-baHr.
I need a quiet room.	Ana bi-Ha ja li-Ġhorfa hadia'a.
For how long?	kam el-moudda (el-zaman).
I need the room for two days.	Ana bi-Haja lil-Ġhorfa li-yawmein.
one week.	ousbouȮ.
one month.	shahr.
I need a big room for six people.	Ana bi-Haja li-Ġhorfa kabira li-sittat ashḰhass.
How much will it cost per night?	Kam toukallif fi Al-leila?
Are all meals included in the price?	Hal Al-akl daḰhel Ḋimn Al-thaman (Al-hisab)?
No, only breakfast.	la, faQat el-tarweeQa. (Al-Foutour)
Okay! That's fine.	Tayyeb! Heza mleeH.
Please give me your passport.	Min faḊlak İTeeni passporek.
Please fill in this paper.	Min faḊlak Ȧabbi hezihi el-waraQa.
You can go to your room.	Yomkinak el-zehab li-Ġhorfatik.
Please give me back my passport.	Min faḊlak arjİli passporee.
Take it when you leave.	Ḱhozhou İndama tatrok.
I prefer to keep it with me.	oufaḊḊil an aHtafiz bihi.
The room is dark.	el-Ġhorfa mȮtima.
small.	saĠheera.
too large.	kteer kabira.

English	Arabic
noisy.	mouḊijja (fiha Ḋajij).
cold.	berida.
hot.	Ḣarra (saḢina).
Here's another room for you.	Hezihi Ġhorfa thania lak.
We hope you like it.	Na'amal an tȦjibek.
Yes Sir! It is nice.	NaȦam ya sayyidi (ya aḰhee = brother) innaha mleeḢa.
Hello there! (man)	MarḢaban ya rajol.
Would you please bring some	
soap?	Min faḊlak jiblee sawboon?
pillow?	miḰhadda?
bottled mineral water?	Ġanninat ma'a maȦdani?
Would you please bring to my room:	Min faḊlak jib li-Ġhorfati:
breakfast.	tarweeĠa. (fouTour)
lunch.	Ġhada'a.
dinner.	Ȧasha'a.
coca cola.	coca cola.
non-alcoholic beer.	beera bidoon kooḢool.
orange juice.	Ȧasir leimoon.
I need a typist.	Ana bi-Ḣaja li man yaTbȦ Ȧla el-ela el-kateeba.
translator.	moutarjim.
a driver.	saiĠ.
I will leave early tomorrow.	Sa-atrok Ġhadan bekiran (Ġhoudwa).
Please send my mail to this address.	Min faDlak ȧrsil bareedee ila heza el-Ȯunwan.
May I have the bill?	Ȧtini el-Ḣisab (el-fetoura).
You can pay the day of departure.	Yomkinak an tadfaȦ yom e-ssafar.
I need a taxi at 6 A.M.	AḢtej li-taxi asseȦa e-ssedeesa sabeḢan.
Thank you very much for the good service.	Shoukran jazeelan lil-Ḱhidma el-moumtaza.
See you later.	Min shoufak baȦden.

Post and Telephone

English	Arabic
post	**Al-Bareed**
Where is the Post office?	Eina markaz el-bareed?
How far is it from here?	kam yabȮd min hina?
Hi Sir! (brother)	MarHaban ya sayyedi (ya aK̇hee).
I need some air letters to send to the U.S.	Ana biHaja li-makateeb jawiyya li-irseliha li-Ameerka.
How much is each one?	kam thaman koll waḢad.
I need some airmail stamps for the U.S.	Ana biHaja li-TawebeĖ jawwiyya li-Ameerka.
They cost one Riyal each.	Youkallifoon Riyal el-waḢeeda.
Please let me have ten.	Min faḊlak İteeni Ȧshra.
How much does it cost to send an airmail postcard to the U.S.?	Kam youkallif irsel kart postale li-Ameerka bil-bareed el-jawwee.
Please send this box by surface mail.	Min faḊlak arsil heza el-soondooQ bil-bareed el-baḢri.
It is too expensive by airmail.	Ġhali kteer bil-bareed el-jawwi.
When will it reach the U.S.?	Eyye mata yasil li-Ameerka?
I should send a telegram.	Momkin an oursil talleĠhrof.
When will it get there?	Eyye mata yasil hounak.
In one day.	Bi-yom waHad.
That's good! But I should telephone anyway.	MleeH! walekin yajib an outalfin Ȧla eyye Ḣal.
Telephone	**Taleephone**
May I telephone from here?	Hal youmkin an outalfin min hina?
You should go to the second floor	Yajib an tazhab li-ttabeQ̇ el-thani.
We are closing now, please come back later.	Innana nousakkir el-en, min faḊlak irjaȦ baȦden.
But this is urgent (important).	Wa lekin heza mouhimm.

English	Arabic
Okay! come back later.	Ṫayyeb! irjaȦ baȦden.
Hi! (Peace be upon you).	Assalamou Ȧaleikom (marḢaban).
I am Omar Johnson	Ana Ȯmar Johnson
I would like to call this number in Missouri, U.S.A.	Oureed an attasil biheza el-raQ̇m fi Mizzouri bi-Ameerka.
It will cost two dollars per minute.	Sayoukallif ithnain doular biddaQ̇eeQ̇a.
That's fine, thank you!	MleeḢ, shoukran.
Sorry! all lines are busy.	Mouta'assif ! koll el-K̇houTouT mash Ġhoula.
Wait a little.	Intazir Q̇aleelan.
Another hour is gone!	SaȦa ouK̇hra maḊat!
Mr. Johnson! your call is at cabin 6.	ya sayyed Johnson! moukalamatak fi Ġhourfa (cabine) sitta.
Hello!	MarḢaban!
How are you Ahmad?	keefak ya Ahmad?
We have a problem, and we need your advice.	Ȧndana moushkila wa naḢnou biḢaja li-ra'aiak.
What is the problem?	Ma heea el-moushkila?
Hello! Hello!	Alo! Alo!
Ahmad! do you hear me?	Ahmad! Hal tasmaȦni?
Operator! the line is disconnected.	Operator (standard) inQ̇atȦ Al-K̇haTT.
Sorry! You have to wait.	Mouta'assifa! Yajib an tantazir.
We are closing at noon but will open again at 4 P.M.	Sanousakkir zohran wa lekin sanaftaḢ marratan ouK̇hra asseȦa el-rabiȦa baȦd azzohr.
Okay! I will place the call from the hotel.	Tayyeb! Saoutalfin min el-otel.
Operator! please give me the International service at the Post office.	Operator! min faḊlik Ȧtini el-K̇hidma addouwaleeia fi markaz el-bareed.
Would you please give me this number . . . in the U.S.?	Min faḊlik, Ȧtini heza el-raQ̇m fi Amreeka

English	Arabic
With pleasure, Sir.	Bi koll sourour ya sayyedi.
Just a minute.	DaQeeQa faQat.
Your party is on the line.	Man TaTlob houwa Ala el-KhaTT.
Did you finish?	Hal intaheit?
Yes Sir.	NaAam ya sayyidi.
You are so kind.	Anta latif jiddan.
You helped me a lot.	SeAadte ni katheeran (kteer).
I thank you so much for your good and fast service.	Ashkorak jiddan jiddan li-mousaAdatik al-moumtaza wa ssareeAa.
You are welcome!	Ahlan wa sahlan!
This package is for you from America.	Heza Al sondouk laka min Amreeka
Pen.	Qalam.
Candy.	Holwayet (Helou).
Watch.	Sa'a.
Bye bye.	BKhotrek (m'a Assalema)

Shopping

English	Arabic
Would you please tell me where is the grocery store? a clothing shop?	Min faDlak dalleeni wein maKhzan Al-ma'akoolet? maKhzan (doukkan) el-thiab?
the shops?	Addakekeen?
Is there a shopping center?	Hal youjad markaz tijara (matjar)? (shopping center).
No! but there are many shops nearby.	La! wa lekin hounaka Iiddat dakekeen bil-Qorb.
Where is the butcher shop? poultry shop? hairdresser? (barbershop)	Wein dokkan el-leHHam? addajaj? Al-HalleQ?

the Vegetable Market	SouQ el KhoDra
Taxi! please take me to the vegetable market.	Taxi! min faDlak Khodni li-souQ Al-KhoDra.

English	Arabic
Hi!	MarHaban!
How much are the cucumbers?	BikamliKhiar (kam siİrliKhiar)?
eggplants?	batenjan?
potatoes?	baTATA?
tomatoes?	banadoura (TomaT)?
greenbeans?	loubia?
peppers?	fleifla?
olives?	zeitoon?
How much is the lettuce?	Bikam Al-Khass?
squash?	kousa?
oranges?	leimoon?
apples?	touffaH?
bananas?	mawz?
pears?	ijjass?
apricots?	mishmish?
Cucumbers are 5 Riyals a kilo.	Kilo el-Khiar bi-khmsa Riyal.
That's too high, I'd rather not buy.	Ghali, oufaDDil alla ashtari.
Well! for you, 4 Riyals a kilo.	Tayyeb! ilak bi-arba'a Riyal Al-kilou.
But I am your good customer.	Wa leken ana zboun (Tayyeb) mneeH
Please give me two kilos.	Min faDlak İTeeni tnein (zawj)kilo.

Souvenirs and Clothing · DaKekeen AzzouKreiat wa thiab

You have a nice souvenir shop.	İndak dokkan lizzokreiat moumtaza
How much is this ring?	Bikam heze el-Khatim?
Is it made of gold?	Hal houa masnouO min zzahab?
This ring has 20 karate gold.	Heze el-Hhatim fih Ishreen Qeerat mina zzahab.
You have beautiful golden pieces.	İndak QitaA zahabiyya jameela.
Give me a good price.	İTeeni siİr mneeH.

English	Arabic
Do you have carpets?	Hal İndak sajjad.
a small handmade table?	Hal İndak Tawila SaGheera bi-sonĖ el-yadd?
sword?	seif?
air blower?	minfaKh?
coffee maker?	ina'a lilQahawa (rakwa)?
something from Mecca?	shei min Mecca?
something with Arabic scripture?	shei bi-kitaba Ȧrabia?
Arab head dress?	kaffya wa ĖQal?
Do you have a guitar?	Ȯud?
flute?	minjeira (nay)?
drum?	Tabla (dirbakka)?
What else do you suggest as a souvenir from your country?	Shou taQtariH essa kazikr min baladak?
I need to buy some clothes.	Ana biHaja lishir'a baȦD assiab.
Where is a good place?	Eina youjad maHall mleeH (mneeH)?
That shop over there!	Addokkan hounek!
Thank you very much.	Shoukran jazeelan.
Hi!	marİIaban (marİIaba).
How are you?	kifak?
Fine, thank you.	MneeH (Tayyeb), shoukran.
I need pants.	A Htej li-banTaloun.
suit.	bithla.
shirt.	Qamees.
tie.	ȮuQda (Gravate).
socks.	kalsat.
gloves.	kfouf.
undershirt.	broutel.
I need underpants.	AHtej li-kalsoon.
long dress	thob
dress.	fisTan.
blouse.	bloozi.
skirt.	tannoura.
nightgown.	Qamees nawm.
sweater.	kanzi.

English	Arabic
perfume.	riḢa (Iṫr).
lipstick.	Ḣoumra.
powder.	boudra.
glasses.	Ėweinat.
sunglasses.	Ėweinat shams.
shoes.	sibbaT (Ḣeeza'a).
I like this dress.	Heza el-fistan yaĖjibouni.
What size please?	Eyya Ǫias min faDlik?
My U.S. size is 14.	Ǫiasseefi Ameerka houa arbaȦatashar.
We use the European system here.	NaḢnou nastaȦmil el-TareeǪa (el-system) el-ouroppi hina (hona).
I think this will fit you.	Azonn anna heza yeTlaȦ Ȧaleiki.
No! I want it shorter.	La! oureedahou aǪsar.
longer.	aTwal.
smaller.	AsG̣har.
bigger.	akbar.
I prefer blue color.	OufaDDil el-lon el-azraǪ.
red.	aḢmar.
white.	abiaḊ.
brown.	asmar.
black.	aswad.
yellow.	assfar.
green.	aK̇hDar.
gray.	aG̣hrash.
What is the price of this shirt?	Ma houwa siỊr hezihi el-Ǫamees?
This is of the best quality.	hezihi min aḢsan jins.
For you! it is six dollars only.	ilak! sitti doular faǪat.
Oh! No! thank you.	La! shoukran.
That's too expensive for me.	G̣hali kteer ilee.
Well! what would you pay?	Tayyeb! shou btidfaȦ?
Tell me the final price.	Ǫoll li assiỊr annihe'ee.
Okay! five dollars for you.	Tayyeb! K̇hamsi doular ilak.
Bye Bye! I'll be back later.	BK̇hotrek, saarjaȦ baȦdan.
Wait a minute.	Intazir daǪeeǪa.

English	Arabic
Come back!	irjaȦ.
Come on! for you, only four dollars.	TaȦa! ilak, bi-arbaȦa doular faQ̇at.
Last word, I will pay three dollars.	EK̇har kalima, bidfaȦlak thlati doular.
Okay my friend, take it.	Tayyeb ya sadeeQ̇i K̇hozha.
I need many more things.	AḢtaj li-İddat ashei ouK̇hra.
Give me a good price and I will buy them from you.	İteeni siİr mneeḢ li-ashtareehom mink.
You are a good customer; I will give you the best price.	Anta zboon mneeḢ; biİteek aḢsan siİr.
You are a gentleman.	Anta rajol Tayyeb.
Thank you very much.	Shoukran jazeelan.

Oil Business

English	Arabic
What is your company's specialty?	Shou ekḢtisas Sharikatkom?
We specialize in oil refining.	EkḢtisasouna fi tasfiat (takrir) ezzeit.
Your project will be of great service to your country.	MashrouȦkom sayouQ̇addim K̇hidma kabira li-baladikom.
This refinery will cost 100 million dollars.	Hezihi el-misfat satoukallif mi'at malyoun doular.
You could export one third of the production.	Yomkinoukom tasdir tolt el-intaj.
We need five big heat exchangers.	NaḢtaj li-K̇hamsat alat Kibar li-tabdil al-Ḣarara.
We need two distillation towers.	NaḢtaj li-borjein li-ttasfia.
Health insurance is needed for our employees.	NaḢtaj li-ttaameen assoḢḢee liȮmmalina.
Prepayment is essential.	AddafeĖ moQ̇ddaman Ḋarouri.
We should form a common committee.	Yajib an noushakkil lajnah moushtaraka.

English	Arabic
Let us meet again tomorrow.	Linajtamil Ghadan thaneeatan.
It was a fruitful session.	Kenat jalsa moothmira.
Goodbye.	MaA a-ssalama.
Our company is seventy years old.	sharikatna Oomraha sab-Een sana.
All spent in the oil business.	kolla fi tijarat Ezzeit.
We have ten thousand employees.	Endana Ashrat alaaf mowazzaf
We have six hundred engineers.	Endana sitmeeyat mouhandis.
Your project is of the first caliber.	mashrouAakom min awwal daraja.
It will cost ten million dollars.	youkallif Ashrat malayeen doular.
It will be finished in three years.	sayaKhlas fi tlat sanawat.
I am a specialist in refining.	Ana IKhtisasi fi tasfiat (taQteer) Al-petrole.
He is a petroleum engineer.	Houa mouhandis petrole.
Your petroleum crude is of good quality.	Petrolak el-Kham min naweE moumtaz.
You have oil reserves for many years.	Indak zeit iHtiatee li-Iddat sineen.
Petrochemicals are important.	Al-petrokeemiawait mouhimmeen.
Petrochemistry	Petrokeemia
Oil field	HaQl zeit.
Petroleum distillation.	tasfeit (taQteer) el-petrole.
Petroleum gas.	Ghaz Al-petrole.
Petroleum geology.	Geologiat Al-petrole.
Petroleum naphtha	Maphtha el-petrole
We have a basic command of petroleum technology.	Indana maArifa aseela fi-technologiat el-petrole.
How many oil wells do you have?	Kam beer zeit Indakom.
Oil is black gold.	el-zeit houa el-zahab el-aswad.

English	Arabic
Oil consumption in your country is small.	Istihlak el-zeit fi baladikom Qaleel.
Oil distribution should not be a problem.	TawzeeÉ el-zeit (ezzeit) leisa bi-moushkila.
Your oil fields are numerous.	HouQul el-petrole İndakom Aadeeda.
The oil tankers are large.	SheHinat el-zeit kibar.
We need your oil for many years.	NaHtaj li-zeitikom li-seeneen Aadeeda.
We have an energy crisis.	İndana moushkilat TaQa.
The environment should be protected.	Yajib an nouHafiz Aala el-bee'a.
Keep nature beautiful.	IHtafiz Aala jamel a-TTabeeAa.

In Construction

English	Arabic
Are you a civil engineer?	Hal anta mouhandis madani (bina'a)?
Yes.	NaAam.
Are you Mr. Kahtan?	Hal anta e'ssayyed Kahtan?
No.	La.
How many carpenters do you have?	Kam najjar İndak?
How many construction workers do you need?	Anta biHaja Li-kam Aamel bina'a?
My personnel are all specialists.	Koll el-mowazzafeen İndi iKhtisasiyyeen.
I have twenty years' experience.	İndi İshreen sanat Khidma.
We will build as you wish.	Sanabni kama toureed.
Our work will be of the best quality (best type).	ShouGlouna sayakoon min aHsan nawÉ.
We guarantee everything.	Nakfal koll shei.
Construction will be of cement and steel.	el-bina'a saykoon min ismant wa foolaz (Hadeed).
Good construction materials.	Mawad bin'a moumtaza.

English	Arabic
Where is the construction diagram?	Eina mouKhaTTaT elbina'a.
This hotel will be without any constructional defects.	Heza el-otel sayakoun bidoun eyye Khalal bina'ee (insha'ee).
This plant is built to specifications.	Heza el-maAmal mabni Hasab ashshooroot.
We are proud of our work.	naHnou nafKhar bi-shouGhlina.
We hope you are pleased.	Na'amal an takoon masroor.

Conversing and Being Friendly

English	Arabic
Hi! Hello!	MarHaba! (MarHaban!)
Welcome.	Ahlan wa sahlan
How are you?	Kifak?
Sad.	Hazeen
Sorry.	Mouta-assef
Very well, thank you.	Kteer mneeH, shoukran
Good morning.	SabaH el-Kheir
Good day.	Naharak saEed
Good evening.	Masa el-Kheir
Good night.	Leila saEeda (tisbah Ala kheir)
How is your family?	Kif Aoilatak?
How is your wife?	Kif Zawjtak?
How is your daughter?	Kif Bintak?
How is your business?	Kif ShouGhlak?
How is your health?	Kif SoHHatek?
Everything is well.	Koll shee mneeH.
Everything is great.	Koll shee Aazeem.
Everything is very good.	Koll shee moumtaz.
Do you come here often?	Hal taji hina Ghaliban?
Once every month.	Marra koll shahr.
Four times a year.	ArbaAat marrat bi-ssana.
Your job is a good one.	ShouGhlak moumtaz.
What is your profession?	Shou mihentak? (ma heea sonEtak)

English	Arabic
I am a petroleum engineer.	Ana mouhandis petrole.
refinery engineer.	tasfeeiat petrole.
civil engineer.	madani.
chemical engineer.	Keemie-ee.
mechanical engineer.	meekaneekee.
professor.	professawr.
dentist.	tabib asnan.
Doctor of engineering.	Daktour bil-handasa.
lawyer.	mouHamee?
businessman.	rajoul aAmel.
secretary.	Secretaire (masculine).
	Secreteira (feminine)
You are a genius.	Anta AabQaree.
You are intelligent.	Anta zakee.
You are smart.	Anta shatir.
You are well educated.	Anta mouthaQQaf.
I admire American ingenuity.	Ana mouAjab bil-AbQaria
	el-Ameerkia.
I am honored to meet you.	Ana atasharraf bi-miEriftak.
Many thanks (thousand thanks).	Alf shoukr.
If you please.	iEmal maArouf.
With pleasure.	bee-Sourour.
Thanks for the hospitality.	Shoukran li-DDiefa.
You are welcome.	Ahlan wa sahlan.
Please sit down.	Ajlis min faDlak.
Excuse me.	SamiHni.
Give my regards to Najib.	Salamati li-Najib
He is very nice.	Houa latif jiddan.
Tell me about you.	AHbirni Aank.
Pay attention.	Intabih.
Give me a book.	Atini kitab.
Close the door.	Sakkir-el-beb.
Open the window.	IftaH el-shoubbak.
Explain your method.	IshraH tareeQatek.
Wait a minute.	Intathir daQeeQa.
Go fast.	AsriI.
Call a taxi.	Outloub taxi.

English	Arabic
Is this your first visit to Saudi Arabia?	Hal hezihee ziartek el-oula li-Saudia?
Visit us this weekend.	Zourna hezihee el-weekend.
Ok, thank you.	Tayib, shoukran.
What time should I come?	Ayia waQt yajib an ajee.
Anytime!	Ayia waQt ken.
9 o'clock in the morning.	SsaAa tisAa sabaHan.
We will go to the desert.	Sanazhab ila Al-sahra.
beach.	shatt.
sea.	baHer.
village.	Qariat.
Gulf	khalij
restaurant.	el-matAam.
Let us go for a walk.	Linazhab mishwar.
The flowers here are beautiful.	El-zouhour hina jamila.
Goodbye.	mA ssalama (BKhaterkom).

Sightseeing

English	Arabic
I need some information about tourism.	Ana bi-Hoja li-maAloumat An assiyHa.
Ask the hotel clerk.	Isa'al mouwazzaf el-otel.
Sir! do you have some brochures for visitors?	Sayyidi (ya aKhi)! hal Indak baAD el-manshourawt li-zzaeerine (li-zowwar)?
Oh! thank you! That's what I need.	Shoukran! heza ma aHtejou (ouridouh) lah.
How far is the bureau of information from here?	kam yabOod maktab Al-ma'aloumat min hina?
Just one kilometer.	kilometer waHad faQat.
It looks like you have two types of tours.	yazhar annahou Indak nawEein min rraHlat.
One during the day, and one at night.	WaHida Khilal annahar wa waHida fi lleil.
How much does the bus tour cost?	kam toukallif raHlat el-bus (el-bousta).

English	Arabic
How long does it last?	kam hia mouddatouha?
Four hours.	ArbaȦ seȦawt.
That's fine.	MleeḤ.
I would like to see	Oureed an ashouf wasat el-
downtown.	medina.
the museum.	el matḤaf.
the mosque.	jemeĖ.
old arabic style building.	binaya Ȧla TTiraz el-Ȧrabi
	Al-Qadeem
garden.	jouneina.
sand dunes.	tilal raml.
desert.	sahra.
archeological sites.	marawkiz atharia.
industrial sites.	marawkiz seenaİyya.
zoo.	ḤadiQat el-Ḥayiwanat.
Are we allowed to take	Hal yosmaḤ lana bi-aǨhz
pictures?	assouwar.
Yes! But not military sites.	NaȦam! walekin Ġheir el-
	marakiz Al-Harbiyya.
Take pictures of beautiful	Khoz souwar lil-manawzir
scenery.	el-jamila.
I would like to take the night	Oureed an cǨhoz erraḤla
tour also.	elleiliyya eiDan.
Does it cost the same as the	Hal toukallif that assiİr allazi
day tour?	toukallifouhou raḤlat
	annahar?
Yes.	NaȦam.
When does it start?	Eyye meta tabda'a?
It starts at eight P.M.	Tabda'a esseȦa aththemina
	masa'an.
How long does it last?	kam mouddatouha?
It lasts until midnight.	Tadoum Ḥatta mountasaf
	lleil.
First we will see the town.	Sanara el-medina awwalan.
Then we will have some tea.	WabaȦdaha sanashrab shaye.
Are we having dinner?	Hal sanataȦashsha?
Is there an entrance fee?	Hal hounek douǨhouliyya?
No!	La!

English	Arabic
Just five dollars.	K̇hamsat doularat faQaT.
I would like to have a bite.	Oureed loQmat akl.
We had a beautiful evening.	QaDaeina sahra jameela.
We had an interesting evening.	QaDaeina sahra sheiyyQa (moufeeda).
We had a great evening.	QaDaeina sahra Ȧzeema (jameela).
We had a bad evening.	QaDaeina sahra sayyia'a (manH̊ousa).
It is necessary to have some pleasure after good business.	AttafsiH̊ Ȧn annafs Ḋarouri baȦd el-Ȧmal el-jayyid.

Personal Encounters

English	Arabic
My name is Mike.	Ismi Mike.
What is your name?	Shou ismak?
My name is Mohammed.	Ismi Mohammed.
Would you like some Pepsi?	Touṙid pepsi?
I like this music.	OuH̊ib hezihi el-mouseeQa.
You speak good English.	Tatakallam inkleezee jayeed (btiH̊kee inkleezee mneeH̊).
Oh no! just a little.	La! Bass shwayyee.
I will be happy to help you.	Ana bkoon masrour bi-mouseȦdatik.
Let us go to the restaurant.	Li-nazhab ila el-matȦam. (K̇hallina nrouH̊ ila el-matȦam).
beach.	el-shatt.
This country is beautiful.	Heza el-Balad jameel.
The sky is blue and clear.	Assama zarQa wa safia.
You teach me Arabic, and I teach you English.	Ȧllmini Ȧrabi wa ana bȦllmik inkleezee.
Please teach me American English.	Ȧllemni inkleezee-Amirkani min faḊlak (iİmal maȦrouf).

English	Arabic
I will never forget you.	Lan ansaka abadan.
I love you very much.	Ana bHobbik kteer.
Please write to me.	Ktoubili İmil maÀrouf.
Come visit me in America.	zourini fi Amirka.

At the Restaurant

English	Arabic
Welcome!	Ahlan wa sahlan
Hi!	Assalamou Àleikom (marHaba)
We need a table for six people.	NaHnou biHaja li-Tawila li-sittat ashKhos.
Please wait a few minutes.	Min faDlak inTazir baÀD el-daQoeQ.
We like a table with a good view.	Noureed Tawila bi-manthar jamil.
At your service. (Under your command!)	TaHt amrek.
As you wish.	kama toureed.
Would you like a coffee?	Hal toureed Qahwa?
Yes, please.	Na'am, iİmal maÀrouf.
Sorry!	Mouta-assef.
What would you like to eat?	Maza tourid an ta'kol?
What do you suggest for food?	Shou btiQterH lil-akl?
I like to have two fried eggs.	Oureed BiDatein miQleeiatein.
one boiled egg.	BiDa maslouQa.
olives.	zeitoun.
roast beef.	LaHm mishwee.
tomatoes.	Banadoura.
lettuce.	Khass.
cucumber.	Khiar.
bread.	Khobz.
butter.	zibda.
water.	ma'a.

English	Arabic

sugar.
coca cola.
steak.
lamb.
hamburger. (kafta)
    (very good ground meat
    with minced parsley
    and spices cooked on
    skewers)
Meat well done.
    medium.
    rare.
    lamb.
    beef.
Kibbi (very good dish
    made from cracked ,
    wheat ground meat, and
    spices).
Tabbouli (salad made from
    cracked wheat, parsley,
    tomatoes, onion, and
    cucumber).
Peas.
Vegetables.
Rice.
Orange juice.
Glass of milk.
Salt.
Soup.
Shawrba.
Fried Fish.
Onions.
Lemon.
Vinegar.
Cabbage.
Grapeleaves.
Grapes.
Squash.

sokkar.
coca cola.
steak.
LaHm kharoof.
kafta.

LaHm maTbooKh mneeH.
wasaT.
Qalil.
Kharoof.
baQar.
Kibbi.

tabbouli.

bazella.
KhoDra.
rouzz.
Aasir leimoon.
Kobbeit Haleeb.
milH.
Shawrba.
Shawrba.
samak miQli.
Basal.
Leimoon HameD.
Khall.
Malfouf.
WaraQ Inab.
Inab.
Kousa.

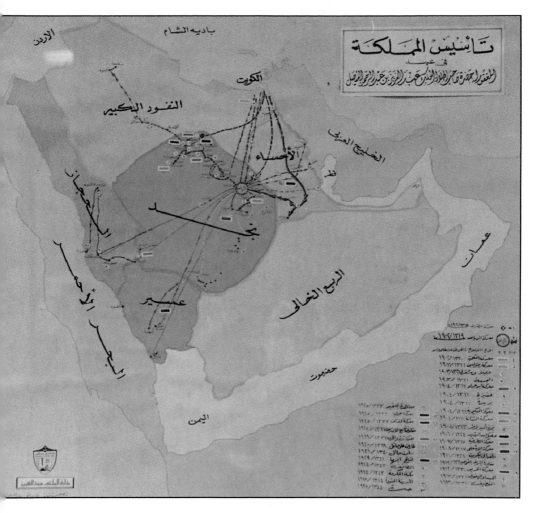

Struggle to unify the Kingdom.

The opening words of the Qur'an—"In the name of God, the Merciful, the Compassionate"—written in flowing thuluth script.

Arabic Numerals

The Arabic numeral system is used throughout much of the world today:

Eastern Symbols: ٩   ٨   ٧   ٦   ٥   ٤   ٣   ٢   ١   ٠

Western Symbols: 9   8   7   6   5   4   3   2   1   0

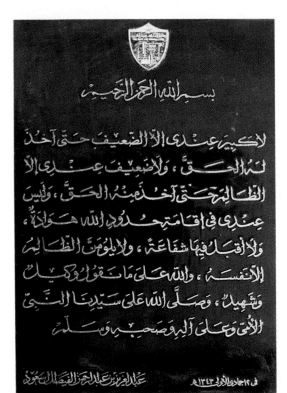

A historic and moving declaration from Abdulaziz (King Ibn Saud) expressing his deep sense of justice.

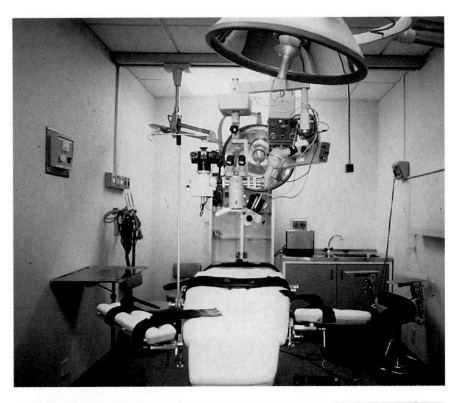

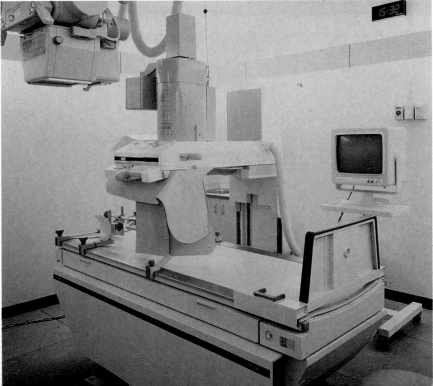

English	Arabic
Garlic.	Toum.
Cucumber.	Khiar.
Corn.	Zora.
Radishes.	Fijl.
Cheese.	Jibna.
Bananas.	Mawz.
Watermelon.	BattiKh.
Apricots.	Mishmish.
Almonds.	Lawz.
Quince.	Safarjal.
Dates.	Seewa.
Figs.	Teen.
Walnuts.	Jawz.
Raisins.	Zbeeb.
I did not order this!	Ana ma Talabt heza.
Could I change this order?	Hal yomkinani taGhieer heza ttalab?
Where is the manager?	Eina el-raees?
I would like to see him.	Oureed an arahou (shoufou).
Would you like to have ice cream?	Hal toureed bouza?
I prefer oranges.	OufaDDel leimoon
apples.	toffaH.
coffee.	Qahwa.
tea.	Shawye.
Get me the bill, please!	Imal maArouf jib el-fatoura. (el-Hisab)
You made a mistake.	Imilt Ghalta.
The price is reasonable.	A-ththaman maQboul.
It is expensive.	Ghali.
Service is poor.	el-Khidma manHousa.
Service is good.	el-Khidma mneeHa.
This is a tip for you.	Heza baKhsheesh lek.
Thank you for the good service.	Shoukran lil Khidma el-mneeHa. (el-moumtaza)
You are welcome.	Ahlan wa sahlan.
Come again (visit us again).	Zourna thaneeatan.

Medical Attention

English	Arabic
I need a doctor.	Ana biHaja li-daktour.
My stomach hurts me.	Miİdati btoujaÀni.
hand.	yadi (the letter *i* indicates possession, meaning my hand).
ear.	outhn (just add *i* and it will become outhni = my ear).
face.	wajeh.
eye.	Àin.
My finger hurts me.	isbaİee bioujaÀni.
foot.	Qadam.
leg.	rijil (Legs = Àrjol).
mouth.	Famm (Fami = my mouth).
neck.	raQba.
shoulder.	ketif.
back.	thahr.
lungs.	ria'tein.
tongue.	lisan.
bruise.	raDDa.
broken bone.	Àthm maksour.
I need a physical exam.	Ana bi-Haja li-faHss toubbi.
She is swollen.	İndaha waram.
Her breathing is bad.	Tanaffousaha manHoos.
She has diarrhea.	İndaha sihel.
She is vomiting.	Innaha testafreGh.
She drank some contaminated water.	Sharibat meeiah (ma'a) moulawwatha.
Does she have cholera?	Hal maÀaha colera?
My blood pressure is high.	DaGht a-ddamm Àali.
low.	waTee.
I have a high temperature.	İndi Harara Àalia.
I have a low temperature.	İndi Harara waTeea.
I have a cold.	İndi rashH.
bad bruise.	raDDa manHoosa.
He is diabetic.	İndahou soukkari.
He is allergic to penicillin.	İndahou Haseseeia lil-bencileen.
Where is the pharmacy?	Eina el-farmasheeia.

English	Arabic
Take these pills.	Khoz hazeehi el-Houboub.
One a day.	Wahida fi el-yom.
One every four hours.	Wahida koll arabaAat ayyem.
You are pregnant.	Anti Hibli.
Congratulations!	Taheneena.
Rest for a few days.	'rtaHee kam yom.
Come and see me after one week.	TaAi shoufini (feminine) baAd ousbO. TaAa shoufni (masculine) baAd ousbO.
Please take me to the hospital.	Khodni lil-mistashfa iImal maAroof.
You are in good health.	Antam bi-soHHa jayyida Anti bi-soHHa jayyida.
You can go home.	Yominak an an tazhab ila el-beit. Yominaki an tazhabi ila el-beit.
How much should I pay you?	Kam yajib an adfaA lak?
Thank you, doctor!	Shoukran ya daktour. (Shoukran ya Hakeem.)
Would you please tell me where is the dentist?	Min faDlak Qol li wein Tabib el-asnan.
He is on the fourth floor.	Howa fi el-TTabeQ el-rabeE.
My teeth hurt me.	Asnanee youjaOoni.
One tooth must be pulled out.	Sin yajib an yoQlaA.
Two teeth should have a filling.	Sinnein biHaja li-Hashwa.
I feel fine.	Ana ashOr mneeH. (Ana bi-soHHa jayyeeda)
Nothing like good health.	La shei mithl assoHHa el-jayyeeda (el-moumtaza).

Emergency

English	Arabic
This is an emergency.	Hezihi Hala Tari'a.
We are in danger.	NaHnou fi Khatar.

English	Arabic
We need help immediately.	NaHnou bi-Haja li-mousaÀada fowran.
I broke my arm and ribs.	Kasart yadi wa aDlouÌi.
I am going to die.	RaH amoot.
I have trouble breathing (my breathing is difficult)	Tanaffousi saÀb.
Call the police.	Nadi el-boulis.
My daughter is lost.	Binti DaÀat.
My son is lost.	Ibni DaÀ.
He is drowning.	Ennahou yaGhraQ.
Stop.	Qif.
Listen.	IsGhee.
Quick.	bi-sorÀa.
Fire.	Nar.
Get a doctor quick.	Jeeb el-Hakim bi-sorÀa.
The house is on fire.	El-beit yaHtareQ.
Watch out.	Intabeh.
This is a big accident.	Heza Hedeth kabir.
I am bleeding.	Dammee yasil (yajri).
We need an ambulance.	NaHnou bi-Haja li-sayyarat el-isÀaf.
What did you say?	Shou Qolt?
A thief took my money.	Liss aKhath foulousee (darahimee).
Is he short?	Hal houwa Qasir?
tall?	Taweel?
man?	rajol?
woman?	imra'a?
You are okay.	Anta mneeH (la b'aass).
Be patient.	kon Tawil el-bel.

Taxi and Car Matters

English	Arabic
Taxi	**Taxi**
Where could I rent a car?	Eina yomkinouni an asta'a jir sayyara?
Here at the airport.	Houna fi el-maTawr.

English	Arabic
How much does it cost?	Kam toukallif?
Oh it's cheaper to take a taxi.	ArKhas an eKhoz (eKhod) taxi.
Or take the bus or train.	Aw e Khoz el-bus (el-bousta) aw tran
Taxi! Please take me to the Hilton hotel.	Taxi! min faDlak Khozni ila otel Hilton.
museum.	el-matHaf.
American Embassy.	saffara el-Ameerkiyya.
Lebanese Embassy.	saffara el-Loubnaniyya.
market.	souQ.
ministry of industry.	wizarat assinaAa.
ministry of petroleum.	wizarat el-petrol.
bus terminal.	markaz el-bousta.
train station.	maHaTTat ettran.
airport.	maTawr.
library.	maktaba.
How far is it?	Kam tabOd min hina?
It is twenty kilometers.	TabOd Ishreen kilometer.
How much does it cost?	Kam toukallif?
About twenty dollars.	Ishreendoular taQriban.
That's too high!	Ghali jiddan.
But these are the rates.	Walekin hezi hai el-asAar.
Please turn the meter on.	Min faDlak shaGhGhil el-Aadded.
I don't have one.	Ma Indi waHad.
Sorry! it doesn't work.	Mouta'assif la yashtaGhil.
Then, I cannot pay more than ten dollars.	Izan la yomkinouni an adfaA akthar min Ashrat doularat.
Step in, you are welcome.	IsAad (oudKhol), ahlan wa sahlan.
Do you agree?	Hal touwafiQ?
No problem!	Ma naKhtalif (mafi moushkila).
I would like to know.	Oureed an AEref.
Okay, my friend, I will take you for fifteen dollars.	Tayyeb ya sadeeQee! eKhozak bi-KhamstaAshar doular.
It is better to agree on a price before taking a taxi.	AfDal el-mouwafaQa Ala asseEir Qabl aKhz attaxi.
They drive fast here.	YasouQoun bisorAa hina.

English	Arabic

Car Matters
QaDaya Ȧssiyyara

I have shipped my car.
Arsalt sayyarati bil-markab.

Where is the port?
Eina el-marfa'a.

Would you take me there, please?
Ḱhozni hounek min faDlak.

I am here as a visitor.
Ana houna ka zaer.

I am here on business.
Ana houna bi-shouĠhl.

Do I have to pay customs?
Hal yajib an adfaȦ jamerik.

No.
La.

Yes! 100 percent.
NaȦm mia bil-mia.

Could I claim it back when I leave the country?
Hal-tarjaȦ li Ȧndama atrok el-balad.

No sir!
La! ya sayyidi (aḰhi).

Our company absorbs the cost.
Sharikatouna tadfaȦ el-masrouf.

Under contract with the government, we are allowed to bring a cart withou paying customs.
Hasab el-ȦQid (el-contra) maȦ el-Ḣoukouma, yousmaḢ lana bijalb sayyara (automobile) bidoun jamerik.

Fill in this application.
Ȧabbi heza TTalab.

Come back in three months for renewal.
IrjaȦ li-ttajdeed baȦd thalathat ashhor.

I have an international driver's license.
Ȧndi shahedat sawQ douwaliyya.

You can use it here.
Yomkinak istiȦmalaha hina.

How could I reach Dhahran from here?
Keifa azhab li-zzahran min hina?

Go through Riyadh.
RouḢ (izhab) bi-TariQ el-ReeyaD.

It is a long way.
TareeQ Taweela.

The road is good.
AttariQ moumtaza.

Is there a gas station nearby?
Hal hounek maḢaTTat benzine bilQorb min hina?

In the next street.
Fi assheriȦ aththani.

Please fill'er up.
Min faDlak Ȧabbiha (fallel)

Please check the oil.
Min faDlak ifḢas el-zeit.

    battery.
    battaria.

    radiator.
    radiater.

    tires.
    daweleeb (Ȧjalet); (kafarat)

English	Arabic
It sure is a good road.	ḤaQQan innaha TariQ moumtaza.
I would like to have some Arabic tea.	Oureed shawyye Ȧrabi.
coffee.	Ǫahwa.
pepsi; miranda	pepsi; miranda
What happened to you?	Meza jara lak? (shou sarlak)
I had an accident.	Hasal li Hawdeth.
I ran over a sand dune blown on the road.	Marart Ȧla tallat raml nafaḰhatha el-riyaḤ Ȧla ttareeǬ.
I hit a sheep.	Ḋarabt khoroof.
My car needs repair.	Sayyarati biḤaja li-ttasliḤ.
Is there a garage nearby?	Hal youjad garage bil-Ǭorb min hina?
In the next town.	Fi el-medina eththania.
Have some tea now, and later I'll push you with the Chevrolet.	Ishrab asshayye el-en (Ḋal Heen) wa baȦdaha sa'ajorr bi-sayyarat ashshavar (chevrolet).
That's very nice of you, sir.	Heza jameelon mink ya aḰhi.
My car has some trouble in the radiator.	Sayyarati fiha ȮTl (Ḱharawb) bi-rradiater.
engine.	el-mooter.
light.	el-Ḋawwe.
carburetor.	carbarater.
automatic transmission.	NaǬl automateeqee.
generator.	dynamo.
brakes.	fremet.
windshield wipers.	misseḤawt.
You have serious engine trouble.	Ȧndak moushkila kabira fi el-mooter
How long would it take to get it fixed?	Kam yaaḰhoz tasliha min el-waǬt?
One week.	OusbouȦ waḤad.
How much will it cost?	Kam toukallif.
About two thousand dollars.	Alfein doular taǬreeban.

English	Arabic
Okay! I'll be back in a week.	Tayyeb! sa'arjaȦ baȦd ousbouḂ.
Hello! Fouad!	MarḢaban ya Fouad.
I am calling you from Dhahran.	Inni outalfin min zzahran.
Is the car going to be ready tomorrow?	Hal takoun assayyara jehiza Ġhadan.
No! We need another week.	La! Innana bi-Ḣaja li-ousbouḂ eK̇har.
We are still looking for parts.	La (ma) nazel, noufattish Ȧla Q̇itaȦ.
We will be getting some from Jidda, Riyad and Dammam.	SanaḢsl Ȧla el-baȦḊ min jadda, el-RiaḊ, wa ddammem.
These parts are very expensive.	Hezihi el-Q̇iTaȦ Ġhalia jiddan.
Please speed up the repairs.	Min faḊlak asreḂ bi-ttasliḢ.
You will have your car "Inshalla" in another week!	Satastalim sayyratak, baȦd ousbouḂ inshalla!
It is ready now.	Innaha jehiza el-en.
It runs good.	Tamshi mneeḢ.
Well! I learned a lesson.	Tayyeb! taȦallamt oumthoola.
An expensive lesson.	Oumthoula Ġhalia.
I wish you good luck.	Atamanna lak Ḣazzan jayyidan (saIeedan).
I need it.	Inni bi-Ḣaja lah.
Thank you.	shoukran.

Appendices

Appendix	Title
A	Conversions You Will Need
B	The Islamic Calendar
C	Glossary Of Useful Words
D	Average Monthly Temperatures For Certain Arab Cities
E	Temperature Conversions
F	Useful Tables
G	References
H	About The Authors
I	Index

Appendix A

Conversions You Will Need

Length
> 1 centimeter = 0.39 inch
> 1 meter = 3.28 feet
> $= 10^6$ microns $= 10^{10}$ angstroms
> 1 kilometer = 1,000 meters
> $= 0.62$ mile
> 1 inch = 2.54 centimeter
> 1 foot = 12 inch = 30.48 cm
> 1 yard = 3 feet
> 100 miles = 161 kilometers
> 1 mile = 5,280 feet
> 1 nautical mile = 1.15 miles

Weights
> 1 gram = 0.04 ounce = 15.4 grains
> 1 kilogram = 1,000 grams
> $= 2.20$ pounds
> 1 metric ton = 1,000 kilograms = 1.10 tons
> 1 pound = 454 grams
> $= 7,000$ grains
> 1 ton = 2,000 pounds

Volume
> 1 liter = 2.11 pints
> $= 1.06$ quarts
> $= 0.26$ gallons (U.S.A.)
> 10 liters = 2.2 imperial gallons = 2.6 gallons (U.S.A.)
> 1 gallon = 3.78 liters
> 1 ft^3 = 7.48 gallons
> 1 ounce = 29.6 milliliter
> 1 barrel = 42 gallons

Force
1 pound force = 4.45×10^5 dynes

Energy and Power
1 watt = 1 Joule/sec.
1 horsepower = 33,000 ft-$lb_{f/min}$.
1 calorie = 4.19 Joules
1 kilocalorie = 1,000 calories
1 kilowatt = 1.34 horsepower
1 calorie/gram = 1.8 British thermal unit/pound mass
$\qquad\qquad\qquad$ = 1.8 Btu/lb_m
1 BTU = 252 calories
$\qquad$ = 778 ft-lb_f

Area
1 sq. mile = 640 acres
1 ft^2 = 144 $in.^2$
1 $in.^2$ = 6.45 cm^2
1 acre = 43,560 ft^2
$\qquad$ = 4,074 m^2
1 hectare = 2.471 acres = 10,000 m^2

Pressure
1 atmosphere = 760 millimeter of mercury
$\qquad\qquad$ = 14.7 lb_{f/in^2}
$\qquad\qquad$ = 14.7 psi
$\qquad\qquad$ = 29.92 ins. of mercury
$\qquad\qquad$ = 33.91 ft. of water
$\qquad\qquad$ = 0.987 bar
$\qquad\qquad$ = 1 Kg_f/cm^2
1 millimeter of mercury = 1 torr
1 bar = 10^5 pascal

Density
1g/cm^3 = 8.34 lb_m/gal
22.4 liters/g-mole at 32°F., 1 atm. = 359 ft^3/lb-mole

Temperature
Degrees centigrade = 5/9 (Degrees Fahrenheit − 32)
Degrees Fahrenheit = 1.8 (Degrees Centigrade) + 32

Degrees Centigrade	Degrees Fahrenheit
0	32 (freezing point of water)
5	41
10	50
20	68
30	86
37	98 (normal human body temperature)
38	100.4
39	102.2
41	105.8
40	104
50	122
60	140
70	158
80	176
90	194
100	212 (normal boiling point of water)

Velocity

Velocity of light in vacuum = 3×10^8 m/sec.
Speed of sound in air = 344m/sec = 1129 ft/sec.
   (at 20° C., 1 atm.)

Viscosity

1 Poise = 1 gram/cm-sec
        = 100 centipoises
Viscosity of water at 20° C. = 1 centipoise
Viscosity of air at 20° C. = 0.018 centipoise
Viscosity of mercury at 20° C. = 1.547 centipoises

Sizes

Ladies	U.S.A.	Arab Countries & Much of Europe
Blouses	32	38
	34	40
	36	42
	38	44
	40	46
	42	48

Sizes (continued)

Ladies	U.S.A.	Arab Countries & Much of Europe
Dresses, suits, skirts		
Junior Miss	9	34
	11	36
	13	38
	15	40
	17	42
Ladies Sizes	10	38
	12	40
	14	42
	16	44
	18	46
	20	48
Sweaters	34	40
	36	42
	38	44
	40	46
	42	48
	44	50
Shoes	6	$37^1/_2$
	$6^1/_2$	38
	7	$38^1/_2$
	$7^1/_2$	39
	8	$39^1/_2$
	$8^1/_2$	40
	9	$40^1/_2$
	$9^1/_2$-10	41-42
Stockings	$8^1/_2$	$8^1/_2$
	9	9
	$9^1/_2$	$9^1/_2$
	10	10
	$10^1/_2$	$10^1/_2$
	11	11

Men	U.S.A.	Arab Countries & Much of Europe
Suits, coats, pajamas	34	44
	36	46
	38	48
	40	50
	42	52
	44	54
	46	56
	48	58
Shirts	14	36
	$14^1/_2$	37
	15	38
	$15^1/_2$	39
	$15^3/_4$	40
	16	41
	$16^1/_2$	42
	17	43
Sweaters	Small	44
	Medium	46–48
	Large	50
	Extra Large	52–54
Hats	$6^5/_8$	53
	$6^3/_4$	54
	$6^7/_8$	55
	7	56
	$7^1/_8$	57
Underwear	Small	5
	Medium	6–7
	Large	8
	Extra-Large	9–10
Shoes	5	38
	6	39
	7	41
	8	42
	$8^1/_2$–9	42–43
	9	43
	$9^1/_2$–10	43–44
	$10^1/_2$–11	44–45
	$11^1/_2$–12	45–46

Sizes (continued)

Men	U.S.A.	Arab Countries & Much of Europe
Socks	5	$9^1/_2$
	$5^1/_2$–6	10
	$6^1/_2$–7	10–$10^1/_2$
	$7^1/_2$–8	$10^1/_2$–11
	$8^1/_2$–9	11
	$9^1/_2$	$11^1/_2$
	$10^1/_2$–11	12
	$11^1/_2$–12	12–$12^1/_2$

Appendix B

The Islamic Calendar

Hijra, or the year the Prophet Mohammed migrated from Mecca to Madina corresponds to July 16, 622 A.D. (Gregorian solar year), or the year 1 A.H. (Anno Hegirae = Hijra year) for the Islamic calendar. It is a lunar year, where one lunar month covers the cycle between two new moons encompassing 29 days, 12 hours, 44 minutes and 2.8 seconds. The lunar year has 354 days and 11/30 of a day; every 30 years, this amounts to 11 days. Assuming that every 32 Gregorian years are equal to 33 Islamic lunar years, the following two equations may be used:

$$\text{A.D.} = \text{Gregorian year} = 622 + \left(\frac{32}{33} \times \text{A.H.}\right)$$

or,
$$\text{A.H.} = \text{Hijra year} = \frac{33}{32} \times (\text{A.D.} - 622)$$

These two equations give the year in which a corresponding year began. Although 1398 A.H. began on December 12, 1977, most of it was in 1978 A.D.

The twelve lunar months of the Hijra year are:

Mouharram	Joumada awwal	Ramadan
Safar	Joumada thani	Shawwal
Rabi' awwal	Rajab	Zul-Qa'dah
Rabi' thani	Sh'aban	Zul-Hijjah

The following are some corresponding years between the Moslem and Christian calendars. The indicated months are the dates on which the Hijra years begin.

A.H. (Hijra Year)	A.D. (Gregorian Year)	A.H. (Hijra Year)	A.D. (Gregorian Year)
1	622 July 16	1348	1929 June 9
150	767 February 6	1349	1930 May 29
500	1106 September 2	1350	1931 May 19
600	1203 September 10	1351	1932 May 7
1000	1591 October 19	1356	1937 March 14
1305	1887 September 19	1357	1938 March 3
1319	1901 April 20	1362	1943 January 8
1320	1902 April 10	1373	1953 September 10
1321	1903 March 30	1382	1962 June 4
1322	1904 March 18	1384	1964 May 13
1323	1905 March 8	1395	1975 January 14
1324	1906 February 25	1396	1976 January 3
1325	1907 February 14	1399	1978 December 2
1326	1908 February 4	1400	1979 November 22
1327	1909 January 23	1401	1980 November 9
1328	1910 January 13	1402	1981 October 30
1329	1911 January 2	1403	1982 October 19
1330	1911 December 22	1404	1983 October 8
1331	1912 December 11	1405	1984 September 27
1332	1913 November 30	1406	1985 September 16
1333	1914 November 19	1407	1986 September 6
1334	1915 November 9	1408	1987 August 26
1335	1916 October 28	1409	1988 August 14
1336	1917 October 17	1410	1989 August 4
1337	1918 October 7	1411	1990 July 24
1338	1919 September 26	1412	1991 July 13
1339	1920 September 15	1413	1992 July 2
1340	1921 September 4	1414	1993 June 21
1341	1922 August 24	1415	1994 June 10
1342	1923 August 14	1416	1995 May 31
1343	1924 August 2	1417	1996 May 19
1344	1925 July 23	1418	1997 May 9
1345	1926 July 12	1419	1998 April 28
1346	1927 July 1	1420	1999 April 17
1347	1928 June 20	1421	2000 April 6

Appendix C

Glossary of Useful Words

English	Arabic
About (talking about)	taQreeban (natakallam Ȧan)
Acceptable	maQboul
Accident	Ḣawdeth
Active	Ḣarik (m), Ḣarika (f)
Address	Ȯunwan
My address is	Ȯunwani
After	baĖd
Afternoon	baĖd ezzohr
Again	marra thania
Against	Ḋidd
Age	Ȯomr
Agree	youwafiQ
Agricultural settlements	Hujar
Air	hawa
Airline	Tayiaran
Airmail	bareed jawwi
Airplane	Tayyara
Airport	maTawr
Alcohol (wine)	Ḳhamr (Kouhoul)
All	koll (jameeȦn)
Allergy	Ḣasaseeia
Allowed	masmouḢ
Almonds	lawz
Alms giving	Zakat
Also	eiḊan
Ambulance	sayyarat isȦaf
American	Ameerkani, Amreekee

English	Arabic
American Embassy	assaffara el-Ameerkiyya
And	wa
Another	eKhar (ouKhra)
Answer	jawab
Anybody	eyye shaKhs
Anyway	Ala eyye Hal (Ala kollin)
Appetizers	meza
Apples	toffaH
Application	Talab
Apologize	yaEtazir
Apricots	mishmish
April	Nisan (Avril)
Arab	Arab
Arab head dress	kaffya wa EQal
Arabic	Arabi
Arabic style building	binaya Ala TTiraz el-Arabi
Archeological sites	marawkiz atharia
Arrival	wousoul
Arrive	yasil
Associate	zameel
Atmosphere	jawwe
Audience (with the)	Majlis
August	Eb (oot)
Authority	solTa
Automatic transmission	naQl automateeqee
Available	jehez (mawjoud)
Avoid	yatajannab
Back (behind)	zahr (wara)
Bad	sayyea'a (manHousa) (f)
Balcony	balcon
Bananas	mawz
Bank	bank
Barber	HalleQ
Base	asas, QoIda
Basket	salli
Bath	Hammem
Bathroom	beit mayye (mirHaD)
Battery	battaria

English	Arabic
Bazaar	souq
Beach	shatt
Beans	fasoulia
Beautiful	jamil
Because	bisabab
Bed	sarir (taKht)
Bedouin	Badawi (Badou)
Beef	baQar (laHm baQar)
Before	Qabl
Began	yabda'a
Best	afDal
Better	aHsan
Big	kabir
Bill	Hisab (fetoura)
Billion	miliar
Birds	Aasafir
Biscuit	bascout
Bite (food)	loQmat
(to bite)	AaDDa
Black	aswad
Blood	damm
Blouse	bloozi
Blow	nafaKha
Blue	azraQ
Body	jism
Book	kitab
Both	el-zawj (kilahoume)
Bottle	annini
Bottled mineral water	Qanninat ma'a maAdani
Box	sondouQ
Boy	walad
Brakes	fremet
Bread	Khobz
Breakfast	fouTour (tarweeQa)
Breathing	tanaffous
Broke	kasara
Brother	aKh
Brotherhood	Ikhwan

English	Arabic
Brown	asmar
Bruise	raDDa
Buick	Bweek
Build	yabni
Bureau	maktab (bureau)
Bus terminal	markaz el-bousta
Business	shouGhl (Aamal)
Businessman	rajoul aAmel
Butcher	leHHam
Butter	zibda (Samn)
Buy	yashtari
By God	Wallahi
Bye Bye	bKhotrek (m) bKhotrik (f)
Cabbage	malfouf
Call	nadi
Call for someone	Ya (ya Allah)
Camel	jamal
Can	yaQdir
Candy	Helou (Holwayet)
Cannot	la aQdir (la youmkin)
Car	sayyara (automobile)
Carburetor	carbaratcr
Carpenter	najjar
Carpets	sajjad
Cat	QiTTa (hirra)
Cedars	arz
Cement	ismant
Cent	centime
Chair	koursi
Change	Ghayyer (baddil)
Charming	seHira
Cheap	raKhees
Cheaper	arKhas
Cheese	Jibna
Chevrolet	shavar (Chevrolet)
Chick peas	hommous
Chicken	dajej (farrouj)
Cholera	colera

English	Arabic
Christian	maseeHee
Cigarettes	sajair (douKhKhan)
City	madina
Clean	nazeef
Clear	safi
Climate	TaQs
Close (to)	sakkir
Clothing	thiab
man's garment	Abaya
Coat	thawb (kabbout)
Coffee	Qahwa
Coin	oumla
Cola	cola
Cold (have a cold)	bard rasheH
Cold	berid
Color	lon
Come	yaji
Come in	tafaDDal (oudKhol)
Come on	taAa
Come back	irjaA
Command	amr
Committee	lajna
Community (believers)	Ummah
Company	sharika
Consulate	Qounsouliyya
Congratulations	taheneena
Construction	bina'a
Consumption	istihlek
Consulate	Qounsouliyya
Contaminated	moulawwath
Copy	nasKha
Corn	zoura (dara)
Correct	SaHeeH (mazbouT)
Cost	youkallif seEr (thaman)
Countries	bouldan
Country	balad
Crisis	moushkila
Cucumber	Khiar

English	Arabic
Cup	finjen
Currency	flous (Òumla)
Customer	zboon
Customs	jamerik
Dagger	Khanjar
Dancer	rawQisa
Dancers	rawQisawt
Danger	Khatar
Date	tẽreekh
Dates	balaH, tamr
Daughter	bint
Day	nahar (during daylight)
	yom (for the whole day)
Days	ayyem
Death	mowt
December	Kanoon awwal (December)
Declaration	tasriH
Defect	Khalal (ÒuTl)
Delicious (ok)	Tayyib
Demand	yaTloub
Dentist	Tabib asnan
Departure	safar (raHeel)
Desert	saHra'a
Dessert	frotto (Helou, gateau)
Destruction	Kharawb
Diagram	mouKhaTTaT
Diarrhea	sihel
Difficult	saÀb
Dinner	Àasha'a
Direction	ittijeh
Direction (for daily prayers)	Qibla
Dirty	wasiKh (mouwasseKh)
Disconnected	maQTouÈ
Distance	masafa
Distillation	taQteer, tasfia
Distribution	tawzeeÈ
Doctor	Hakeem (daktour)

English	Arabic
Doctor of engineering	daktour bil-handasa
Dog	kalb
Dollar	doular
Donkey	Ḣimawr
Door	beb
Down	taḢt
Downtown	wasat el-medina
Dowry	Mahr
Dress	fisTan
Dress (to)	labisa
Drink	mashroub
Drive	yasouQ̇
Driver	se'eQ̇
Drown	yaG̣hraQ̇
Drugs	moukhaddirawt
Drum	tabla (dirbakka)
Duration	mouddat
During	K̇hilal
Each	koll waḢad
Ear	ouzn
Easy	heiyyin
Eat	yakol
Educated	moutha Q̇Q̇af (mitȦallam)
Education	thaQafa
Eggplants	batenjan
Eggs	biḊ (the i is pronounced like
boiled eggs	eye) biḊ maslouQ̇
Egypt	Misr
Egyptian	misriyya (f) misri (m)
Eight	tmanya˙
Eighteen	tminta-Ȧsher
Eighty	tmaneen
Eleven	Ḣda-Ȧsher
Embassy	saffara
Emergency	Ḣala Tari'a
Employees	Ȯmmal
Energy	TaQ̇a

English	Arabic
Engineer	mouhandis
petroleum engineer	mouhandis petrole
refinery engineer	mouhandis tasfeeia
civil engineer	mouhandis madani
chemical engineer	mouhandis keemie-ee
mechanical engineer	mouhandis meekaneekee
Engine	mooter
English	inkleezi
Enough	bass
Entrance	madḰhal
Entrance fee	douḰhouliyya
Environment	bee'a
Equipment	awayil (elet)
Equivalent	yousaywee
Especially	Ḱhousousan
Essential	Ḋarouri
European	ouroupee
Evening	masa
Everyone	koll waHad
Everything	koll shee
Expensive	Ġhali
Excuse me	semilȈni
Experience	Ḱhibra
Explain	ishraH
Export	tasdir
Eye	Ȧin
Eyes	Ȯuyoun
Face	wajeh
Faithful (followers of Islam)	Mou'minoun
Family	Ȯeela
Far	baĖeed
how far?	kam yabȮd?
Farmer	mouzer'e, fallaH
Fast	sareeE
Fasting during Ramadan	sawm
Father	abb
Father of	abou
Fax	fax

English	Arabic
Feast of sacrifice celebrating end of pilgrimage	Eid al-Adha
February	Shbat (Fibrayar)
Feel	yashȮor
Female Moslem making the Hajj	Hajja
Festival for breaking of fast	Eid al-Fitr
Fever	Ḣomma (Ḣarara)
Fifteen	Ḳhams-ta Ȧsher
Fifty	Ḳhamseen
Fighter in Holy War	Moujahid (Moujahideen)
Figs	Teen
Fill	Ȧabbi
Fill'er up	Ȧabbiha (fallel)
Film	feelm
Fine, thank you	mliḢ, shoukran
Finish	Ḳhalas, intaha
Fire	ḢareeQ̇ (nawr)
First	awwal
Fish	samak
Five	Ḳhamsa
Fix	yousalleḢ
Floor	TawbiQ̇
Flowers	zouhour
Flute	minjeira (nay)
Food	akl
Foot	Q̇adam
Forbidden	Harãm (mamnou'e)
Forget	yensa
Fork	shawki (firteiki)
Form	shakl
to form	shakkil
Four	arba-Ȧa
Fourteen	ar ba Ȧ-taȦsher
Forty	arbȦeen
Frankincense	Bakhour
Free (to be free)	Ḣorr
Free	balesh

English	Arabic
Friday	el-jomoÅa
Fried fish	samak miQli
Friend	sadeeQ
Fruits	athmawr
Fruitful	moothmir
Funny	mouDHik
Garage	garage
Garden	jouneina
Garlic	Toum
Gross Domestic Product	GDP
Generator	dynamo
Genius	ÅabQaree
Gentleman	rajol Tayyeb (gentelman)
Get	jeeb
Gift	hadiyya
Girl	Bint
Give	yaÈTee
Give me	A'tinee (Haat)
Glass	zoujej (zoujeja)
Glasses	Èweinat
Gloves	kfouf
Go	izhab, rouH
Goat	miÅaz
God	Allah
in the name of God	Bismillah
God is Great	Allahou akbar
God willing	inshalla
Gold	zahab
Gold (karat)	zahab (Qeerat)
Gold pieces	QitaÅ zahab
Good	mneeH, moumtaz
Goodbye	maÅ a-ssalama
Good day	naharak saÈeed
Good evening	masa el-Kheir
Good morning	sabaH el-Kheir
Good night	leila saÈeeda
Gown worn by men	dishdasha (Thobe)
Gown worn under abaya	Kaftan

English	Arabic
Grapes	İnab
Grapeleaves	waraQ İnab
Gray	aĠhrash
Great	Ȧzeema (f) Ȧzeem (m)
Green	aKhDar
Greenbeans	loubia
Greetings, hello	marHaban, assalamou Ȧalaikom
Grocery	ma'akoulet
Guarantee	kafela
We guarantee	nakfol
Guide	mourshid (daleel)
Guitar	Ȯoud (guitar)
Hair	shaȦer
Half	noss, (nisf)
Hamburger (see kafta)	hamburger
Hand	yadd
Handmade	sonȦ el-yadd
Handsome	jameel
Happen	Hasal (jara)
Happy	masrour (mabsout)
Have	ymlik
I have	İndi
We have	İndana
He	houa
Headcord on head dress	A'ghal
Headdress	koufiyah
He paid	dafaA
He said	Qawla (houa yaQool)
Headache	soudaȦ (wajaȦ ra'as)
Headscarf (man's)	Ghutrah
Health	soHHa
Hear	yasmaȦ
Heart	Qalb
Heat	Harawra
Hello	marhaba (assalamou aleikom)
Help	mousaȦada
Here	hina

English	Arabic
High	Aali
Hilton Hotel	otel Hilton
Hold	yamsik
Holiday	Ieed
Holy Book	Qoran
Holy War	Jihad
Home	beit
Honor	sharaf
I am honored	ana atasharraf
Hope	amal
Hospital	mistashfa
Hospitality	Diefa
Hot	Hawrr (saHina)
Hot water	ma'a soKhn
Hotel	otel, (hotel)
Hour	seAa
House	beit
House of Al-Saud	Beit Al-Saud
How	keef
How much	kam (Qiddeish)
How are you	kifak (for one) kifakom (for plural)
Humid	raTib
Humidity	rouTouba
Hundred	meeya
Hungry	jouAan
Hurry up!	asreE (bisourAa)
Hurt	youjaA
Husband	zawj
My husband	zawjee
Ice cream	bouza
Idea	fikra
If	eza
Ill	mareeD
Imam (Moslem leader in prayer)	Imam
Immediately	fowran
Immigrant	muhajir

English	Arabic
Important	mouhimm
Impossible	moustaHeel
In	fi
Included	Dimm (deKhil)
Individual	fard
Industrial sites	marawkiz seenaIyya
Information	maAloumat
Intelligent	zakee
Interesting	sheiyyQa (moufeeda)
International	douwali
Introduce	yoQaddim
Islam	Moslem (faith)
Islamic law	Shari'a
It	houa (hia)
It does not matter	my khalif
January	kanoun el-theni (Janvieh) (yaneyer)
Jasmine flower	yasmine
Jew	yahoudee
Jewelry	Jawaher
Job	shouGhl (mihna)
Jordan	el-ordon
Judge	Quadi
Juice	Aasir
July	Tammouz (Yolyo)
June	Houzeiran (Jwan)
Kafta (Hamburger)	kafta
Keep	iHtafiz
Key	mifteH
Kibbi	kibbi
Kilometer	kilomitr
Kind	nawE
Kind	laTeef
Kiss	bawsee
Knife	sikkeen
Know	yaErif
Lamb	Kharoof
Language	louGha

English	Arabic
Large	kabir
Last	eKhar (aKheer)
Later	baAden
Law	Qanoon (shariAa)
Lawyer	mouHamee (avoca)
Learn	taAallam
Leather	Jild
Leave	yatrok
Lebanese mountains	jibēl Loubnan
Lebanese Embassy	el-saffara el-Loubnaniyya
Lebanon	Loubnān
Left	shamal
Leg	rijil (legs = Arjol)
Lemon	leimoon HameD
Lentils	a'das
Letter	maktoub (risala)
Lettuce	Khass
Lesson	oumthoula
Library	maktaba
License	roKhsat
License for driving	roKhsat sawQ (shahedat sawQ)
Light	Dawwe
Like (alike)	mithl
Lines	KhouTouT
Lips	shfaf
Lipstick	Houmra
Listen	isGhee
Little	Qaleel
Little bit	shwayye
Little boy	walad saGheer
Long	Taweel
Look	yanzor (yashouf)
Lose	yaKhsar
Lost	DaA
Love	Hobb, Gharawm
Low	waTee

English	Arabic
Luck	Ḥazz
Good luck	Ḥazz saĪeed
Lunch	Ġhaza'a (Ġhada)
Lungs	riatein
Madame	sayyidat (madam)
Made	yasnaȦ (ya Ȧmal)
Magazine	majalla
Maid	sawneĖ (m), sawneȦa (f)
Mail	bareed
Make	yasnaȦ
Man	rajol
Man of religion reminding	Moutawa'a (Moutawwe'e)
populace to pray	
Manager	raees
Many	Ȧddat
March	Ezar (Mars)
Market	souQ̇
Free market	souQ̇ Ḥorra
Materials	mawad
Matters	Q̇aḊaya
May	Ayyar (Mayo)
Me	ana
For me	li (ili)
Meal	waQ̇Ȧa (waleema)
Measure for crude oil	barmeel
Meat	laḤm
Meat balls	kafta
Meat, well done	laḤm maTbooǨh mneeḤ
Medicine	Tobb
Medium	wasaT
Meet	yajtamĖ
Method	TareeQ̇a
Midnight	nisf el-leil
Migration for Moslems	Hijra
Military	Ḥarbi
Military sites	marawkiz Ḥarbiyya
Milk	Ḥaleeb
Million	malioun

English	Arabic
Ministry of industry	wizarat assinaȦa
Minute	daQiQa
Mistake	Ghalta
Monday	El-ithnein
Money	darahim (foulous) floos
Month	shahr
Moon	Qamar (Badr)
More	akthar
Morocco	Marrakesh
Morning	sabaH
Moslem religion	Islam
Mosque	jemeȦ
Mother	omm (umm)
Motor	mouter
Mountain	jabal
Mouth	Famm (Fami = my mouth)
Museum	matHaf
Music	mouseeQa
Musical instrument similar to guitar	Oud
Name	ism
My name	ismi
Your name	ismak
Nature	TabeeȦa
Near	Qareeb
Nearby	bil-Qorb
Necessary	Darouri
Neck	raQba
Need	Haja
Never	abadan
Night	leil
Nightgown	Qamees nawm
Nine	tis-Ȧ
Nineteen	tiseȦta-Asher
Ninety	tis-Ȧen
No	la
Noble (Honorable)	sharif
Noisy	mouDijja (fiha Dajij)

English	Arabic
Non-alcoholic beer	beera bidoon kooHool
Noon	ezzohr
Nothing	la shei
November	tishreen Tani (November)
Now	el-en (dal Heen)
Number	Aadad
Oath (of allegiance to the King)	Bay'ah
October	Tishreen awwal (October)
Off	miTfi (msakkar)
Office	maktab
Often	Ghaliban
Oil	zeit
Crude oil	petrole Kham
Oil field	HaQl zeit
Oil well	beer zeit
O.K.	Tayyib (mneeH)
Olives	zeitoun
Once	marra
One	waHad (waHid)
Onions	basal
Open	iftaH
It is open	maftouH
Operator	operator (standard)
Orange juice	Aasir leimoon
Oranges	leimoon
Order (giving an order)	amr
Order	talab
Original	aslee
Our	yaKhossouna (lana)
Over	Ala
Over there	Hounek
Package	Oulba (soundouQ)
Pants	banTaloun
Parts	QitaA
Passport	passpor
Past	maDi
Patient (from patience)	Tawil el-bel
Patient	mareeD

English	Arabic
Pay	yedfaȦ
Pay attention	intabih
Peace	salam
Peace be upon you	Assalamou alaikom
Pears	ijjass
Peas	bazella
Peasant	falleh
Pen	Ċalam
Penicillin	benċileen
People	shaĖb (nãs)
People (six)	sittat ashḰhass
Peppers	fleifla
Pepsi-cola	pepsi-cola
Perfume	riḢa (Ịtr)
Permit	Tasreeh
Personnel	mowazzafeen
Petroleum	petrole (zeit)
Petroleum geology	geologiat el-petrole
Petroleum gas	Gaz el-petrole
Pharmacy	farmasheeia
Picture	soura
Pictures	souwar
Pig	Ḱhanzeer
Pilgrimage to Mecca	Ḣajj
Pilgrimage (minor form)	Ụmrah
Pillow	miḰhadda
Pills	Ḣouboub
Plan	ḰhoTTa
Plant (industrial)	maȦmal
Plant (agricultural)	nabet
Please	Ịmal maȦrouf (min faḊlak)
Pleasure	sourour
Police	boulees
Police station	markaz al-Shourta (Al-bolees)
Political	siasee (siasa)
Pollution	talawwoth
Poor	faĊeer
Poor (for service)	manḢoos

English	Arabic
Port	el-bor
Position	markaz
Possible (is it?)	hal moumkin?
Post	bareed
Postcard	kart postale
Post office	markaz el-bareed
Potatoes	baTaTa
Poultry	dajaj
Pound	lira
Powder	boudra
Praise	hamd
Praise be to God	alhamdulillah
Prayer	salah
Pregnant	Hibli
Pressure	DaGht
Pretty	Helou
Price	thaman
Prince	Amir
Private	khousousee
Problem (crisis)	moushkila
Production	intej
Profession	mihna
Profession of Moslem Faith	Shahada
Professor	professawr (oustaz)
Profit	ribeH (maksab)
Project	mashrouE
Prompt	Ala el-waQt (promto)
Proud	yaftaKhir
Pyramids	el-Ahram
Quality	nawE
Quality	sifa
Quality (best)	aHsan jins
Quarter	robE
Question	sou'el
Quiet	houdou'e
Quick	sareeE
Quickly	bisorAa
Quince	safarjal

English	Arabic
Radiator	radiater
Radio	radio
Radishes	fijl
Rain	maTar (shita)
Raisins	zbeeb
Ramadan (Holy Moslem month of fasting)	Ramadan
Rare	nedir (Qalil)
Ready	HaDer (jehez)
Reasonable	maQboul
Reception	istiQbel
Recommend	yaQtariH
Red	aHmar
Refining	tasfiat (taQteer) (takrir)
Regards, hello	salamat
Regards (my)	salamati
Relative (related to the family)	Qareeb
Religious man calling for prayer time	Mou'azzin
Religious pronouncement	Fatwa
Renewal	tajdeed
Rent (to rent)	yasta'ajir
Rent	ajawr
Repair	yousalliH (tasleeH)
Represent	yarmoz (youmaththil)
Reservation	Hajz
Resident	mouwaTen
Respect	yaHtarim
Restaurant	matAam (restauran)
Review	yourajeE (mourajaAa)
Ribs	aDloE
Rice	rouzz
Ride	yarkab
Right	saHH (saHeeH)
Ring	Khatim
River bed (dry)	wadi
Riyal (Saudi money)	Riyal
Road	TareeQ

English	Arabic
Roast beef	laHm mishwee
Room	Ghorfa
Sacred building containing the sacred black stone	Ka'aba
Sacred sanctuary	Haram
Sad	Hazeen
Safe	ameen
Salad	salaTa
Salt	milH
Same	shei nafsou
Sand	raml
Sand dunes	tilal raml
Satan	Iblis (sheytan)
Saturday	El-Sabt
Saudi Arabia	assaOudyya el-Arabyya
Kingdom of Saudi Arabia (KSA)	Al-mamlaka Al-Arabyya AssaOudyya
Saudi Riyals	rialat saOudyya
Save	younji (najet)
Say	yaQool
Sayings of the Prophet	Hadith
Scenery	manawzir
Scholars (religious)	Ulama
School	madrasa
Screwdriver	mafrak
Sea	baHr
Seat	maQAad
See	shouf
See you later	min shoufak baAden
Second (time)	Thania
Second	tani (m), tania (f)
Secretary	secretaire (m), secretaira (f)
Send	yoursil (arsala)
September	Eiloul (September)
Service	Khidma
Session	jalsa
Seven	sab-A
Seventeen	sabe Eta-Asher

English	Arabic
Seventy	sab-Een
Shawrba (soup)	shawrba
She	hia
Sheep	Ghanam (Kharouf)
Sheikh (honorable title)	Sheikh
Ship	markab
Shirt	Qamees
Shoes	sibbaT (Heeza'a)
Shop, shops	doukkan, dakekeen
Shoulder	ketif
Short	Qasir
Shower	marashsh
Shi'a	Sect of Islam
Shut	yousakkir
Sick	mareeD
Sightseeing	tanazzoh
Sign	ishara (Aalema)
Silk	hareer
Sir	sayyid
Sister	ouKht
Sit (sit down)	ajlis
Six	sitta
Sixteen	sitta-Asher
Sixty	sitteen
Size	Qias
Skirt	tannoura
Sleep (to sleep)	yanem
Sleep	nawm
Small	saGhir
Smart	shatir
Smell	raw-eeHa
Snow	thalj (talj)
Soap	sawboun
Socks	kalsat
Some	baED
Something	baED esshei
Son	Ibn (Bin)
Son of (Ibn)	Bin

English	Arabic
Soon	Ḣawlan
Sorry	mouta-assef
Soup	shawrba
Souvenir	tazkawr
Speak (I speak)	bi-Ḣki
Speaker	khateeb
Specialty	eK̇htisas
Spoon	milȦaQa
Spring	el-rabiḶ
Squash	kousa
Stamps	TawebeĖ
Start	yabda'a
Station	maḢaTTat
Gas station	maḢaTTat benzine
Steak	steak
Steel	foolaz, Ḣadeed
Stomach	milḷdat
Stop	Q̇if
Store	maK̇hzan
Storm	Ȧasifa
Straight	douĠhri
Street	shereĖ
Study	yadros
Successor (title for	Caliph (khalipha)
Moslem leader)	
Sugar	sokkar
Suggest	yaQtariḢ
Suit	bizla
Suitcase	shanta
Summer	sseif
Sun	shams
Sunday	El-aḢad
Sunglasses	Ȯuweinet shams
Sunset	Maghrib (ghouroub)
Sunni (sect of Islam)	Sunni
Sure	akeed
Surface mail	bareed baḢri
	bareed (arḊi)

English	Arabic
Sweater	kanzi
Sweet	Helou (m), Helwee (f)
Swollen	mawroom (mouarram)
Sword	seif
Sword dance	Ardha
Tabbouli (salad made from cracked wheat, parsley, tomatoes, onion and cucumber).	tabbouli
Table	tawila
Take	Khoz
Talk	kalam
Tall	taweel
Taste	zouQ (yazouQ)
Tax (religious)	Zakat
Taxi	taxi
Tea	shawye
Teach	youAallim
Teacher	mouAallim (m), mouAallima (f)
Teeth	asnan
Telegram	TalleGhrof
Telephone	Talifon
Television	Talvizion
Tell	aHbir
Tell me	aHbirni
Temperature	Harara (darajit el-Harara)
Ten	Ashra
Tent	khayma
Ten thousand	Ashrat alaaf
Thank you	shoukran
Thief	liss
Things	ashye
Think	youfakkir
Thirsty	AaTshen
Thirteen	tlatta-Asher
Thirty	tlateen
This	heza (m), hezeehi (f)
Thousand	alf

English	Arabic
Three	tlata
Three times	tlat marrat
Thursday	el-K̇hamis
Third pillar of Islam	Zakat
Ticket	Tazkara
Tie	QuQ̇da (gravate)
Tires	daweleeb (Ȧjalet); (kafarat)
Time	zaman (waQt)
Times	marrawt
Many times	Ȧddat marrawt
Tip	baK̇hsheesh
Tired	taȦban
Today	el-yom ('lyom, heza el-yom)
Toilet	mirḢaḊ (toilet)
Tomatoes	banadoura (TomaT)
Tomorrow	Ġhadan (Ġhoudwa)
Tongue	lisan
Too large	kteer kabira
Took	aK̇haz
Tooth	sinn
Tour	raḢla
Tourism	siyaḢa
Town	madina
Trade	tijarat
Traditions	a'adẽt (taqaleed)
Traditions	Sunna
(set by the Prophet)	
Train station	maḢaTTat ettran
Transfer	yantaQil (yanQol)
Translator	moutarjim
Trees	ashjor
Trip	raḢla
Trouble	moushkila
Tuesday	El-thoulatha
Turn	yadour (yaloff)
Twelve	Tna-Ȧsher
Twenty	Ėshreen
Twenty-five	K̇hamsa wa Ėshreen

English	Arabic
Twenty-one	waHad wa Eshreen
Twice	marratein
Two	tnain
Two hundred	meetein
Two thousand	alfein
Type	nawE
Typewriter	ela kateeba (dactilo)
Typist	TabbeE (man yaTbA Ala el-ela el-kateeba)
Ugly	bashiI
Underpants	kalsoon
Undershirt	broutel
Understand	yafham
United States of America (U.S.A.)	Al-wilayat al-mouttaHida Al-Amreekiyya (Amreeka)
University	jemeeAa
Until	Hatta
Up	fawQ
Urgent	Tari-a
Urgent case	Hawla Tari-a
Value	Qeemat
Vegetables	KhoDra
Very	kteer
Very cold	berid jiddan
Very well, thank you	kteer mneeH, shoukran
View	manzar
Village	Qariat
Vinegar	Khall
Visit	zeeyara
To visit us	zoorna
Vomiting	yestafriGh
Wait	intazir
Waiter	garsawn
Walk	mishwar
Walnuts	jawz
Want	youreed
War	Harb
Warm	Hawrr

English	Arabic
Watch	sa'Aa
Watch out	intabeh
Water	ma'a
Watermelon	battiH
We	naHnou
Wednesday	el-arbouAa
Week	ousbouE
Weekend	weekend
Welcome	ahlan wa sahlan
Well	mneeH
What?	meza, (shou), (kam)?
What time is it?	kam esseAa?
What is this?	shou heza?
When?	eyye mata (eyyia waQt)?
Where?	eina?
Whiskey	wiskey
White	abiaD
Wife	zawjat
Wind	reeH
Wind (Humid/from East)	Sharqi
Wind (North)	Shamal
Window	shoubbak
Windshield wipers	misseHawt
Wine	Khamr
Winter	El-shita
Wish	irada (raghba)
I wish	ourid (arghab)
You wish	tourid
We wish	nourid
With	maA
Woman	imra'a
Women	Hareem (Nisa)
Wonderful	Azeem (moumtez)
Words	kalem
Work	Aamal (shouGhil)
Worker	Aamel
World	Awlam
Would like	oureed

English	Arabic
Write	yoktob
Year	sana
Years	sanawat
Yellow	assfar
Yes	naAam
Yesterday	al-bariHa
Yogurt	Laban (zabadi)
You	ant (anta)/anti for female
Yours	lak (ilak)
Zero	sifir
Zoo	HadiQat el-Hayiwanat

Appendix D

Average Monthly Temperatures for Certain Arab Cities

City, Country		Jan.	Feb.	Mar.	April	May	June	July	Aug.	Sept.	Oct.	Nov.	Dec.
							Average Monthly Temperature						
Algiers, Algeria Average Humidity 61% Low temperature 40°F. High temperature 87°F. Major Precip. November to March: 20 inches fall. Pleasant climate March–May. Hot and humid in the summer.	°F. °C.	54 12.2	55 12.8	58 14.4	62 16.7	66 18.9	72 22.2	77 25.0	78 25.6	75 23.1	69 20.6	61 16.1	56 13.3
Oran, Algeria	°F. °C.	54.5 12.5			62.6 17			76.1 24.5			67.1 19.5		
Manama, Bahrain Climate is very hot and damp from May to October. Humidity is usually very high. Climate is pleasant from December to March.	°F. °C.	61 16.1	62 16.7	68 20	75 23.9	84 28.9	88 31.1	91 32.8	92 33.3	88 31.1	82 27.8	74 23.3	65 18.3
Cairo, Egypt Hot climate, average humidity 29%; usually very dry. Average yearly precipitation 1 inch. May–August, very hot and dry. November–January, pleasant weather.	°F. °C.	56 13.3	59 15.0	64 17.8	70 21.1	77 25.0	82 27.8	83 28.3	83 28.3	79 26.1	76 24.4	68 20.0	59 15.0
Alexandria, Egypt Max. Temp. 111°F., Min. Temp. 37°F. Average yearly precipitation 7.0 inches.	°F. °C.	58 14.4			67 19.4			79 26.1			76 24.4		
Baghdad, Iraq Hot days & cold nights, April–October. Climate very hot and dry. Average Yearly humidity: 29% November–March, Pleasant weather. Average Yearly precipitation: 6 inches. June–August, very high temperatures (105°–121°F.).	°F. °C.	50 10.0	53 11.7	60 15.6	71 21.7	82 27.8	87 30.6	93 33.9	93 33.9	87 30.6	77 25.0	64 17.8	53 11.7

Average Monthly Temperature

City, Country	Jan.	Feb.	Mar.	April	May	June	July	Aug.	Sept.	Oct.	Nov.	Dec.
Amman, *Jordan*	°F. 47			61			77			69		
	°C. 8.33			16.1			25.0			20.6		
Kuwait, *Kuwait*	°F. 54	58	65	75	85	91	94	96	90	82	71	60
	°C. 12.2	14.4	18.3	23.9	29.4	32.8	34.4	35.5	32.2	27.8	21.7	15.5
Beirut, *Lebanon*	°F. 55.4	56.3	59	63.5	70.7	74.3	77	79.7	77.9	74.3	67.1	59.9
	°C. 13	13.5	15	17.5	21.5	23.5	25	26.5	25.5	23.5	19.5	15.5
Tripoli, *Libya*	°F. 54	56	60	65	69	74	78	79	78	73	65	57
	°C. 12.2	13.3	15.6	18.3	20.6	23.3	25.6	26.1	25.6	22.8	18.3	13.9
Rabat, *Morocco*	°F. 54			62			73			68		
	°C. 12.2			16.7			22.8			20.0		
Casablanca, *Morocco*	°F. 54	55	58	61	64	69	72	74	71	67	61	56
	°C. 12.2	12.8	14.4	15.1	17.8	20.6	22.2	23.3	21.7	19.4	16.1	13.3

Amman, *Jordan*
Maximum Temperature: 109° F. Minimum Temperature: 21° F. Precipitation: yearly 11 inches.

Kuwait, *Kuwait*
Temperature ranges 100° F. from June to September and 122° F. for July and August. Average humidity: 55%. Yearly precipitation 5 inches. Some dust storms.

Beirut, *Lebanon*
Temperate climate throughout the year. Many sunny days and cool nights. It seldom rains in the summer. Topcoat is essential in evenings in the mountains and winter days in Beirut. Average yearly humidity: 64%. Average Precipitation: 35 inches. Summertime the city is hot and humid, but the mountains are very pleasant, just ten miles east of the city and beyond.

Tripoli, *Libya*
Average yearly precipitation: 15 inches. Average yearly humidity: 62%. June–October maximum temp.: 114° F. Dec.–February minimum temp.: 35° F.

Rabat, *Morocco*
Average yearly humidity: 68%. Average yearly precipitation: 16 inches. Normally not very hot. January–March: minimum temperature 33°F.

Casablanca, *Morocco*

City, Country	Average Monthly Temperature											
	Jan.	Feb.	Mar.	April	May	June	July	Aug.	Sept.	Oct.	Nov.	Dec.
Muscat, *Oman* Very hot and dry climate, Average yearly precipitation: 3.9 inches. May–August extremely hot and dry. Maximum temperature: 116° F. Minimum temperature: 51° F.	°F. 72 °C. 22.2	74 23.3	77 25	84 28.9	91 32.8	93 33.9	92 33.3	87 30.6	87 30.6	85 29.4	79 26.1	72 22.2
Doha, *Qatar* Maximum temperature: 105° F. Humidity 40%. May–October hot and humid. November–March moderate climate.	°F. 64 °C. 17.7						81 27.2					
Riyadh, *Saudi Arabia* Hot and dry weather. Average precipitation yearly: 3.2 inches. Maximum temperature: 113° F. Minimum temperature: 19° F. Desert climate, cold nights.	°F. 58 °C. 14.4			77 25.0			93 33.9			78 25.6		
Dhahran, *Saudi Arabia* In the East at Dhahran, Dammam, Ras Tannura, October–January: pleasant. February–May warmer with sand storms. July–September very hot and humid.	°F. 60.8 °C. 16			78.8 26			96.8 36			84.2 29		
Khartoum, *Sudan* Extremely hot and dry climate, Maximum temperature: 118° F. Cold nights, very dry throughout the year. Average Humidity: 21%	°F. 75 °C. 23.9	77 25.0	83 28.3	89 31.7	92 33.3	93 33.9	89 31.7	87 30.6	90 32.2	90 32.2	83 28.3	77 25.0

City, Country		Jan.	Feb.	Mar.	April	May	June	July	Aug.	Sept.	Oct.	Nov.	Dec.
						Average Monthly Temperature							
Damascus, Syria	°F.	45	48	54	62	70	76	80	82	76	68	57	48
	°C.	7.2	8.9	12.2	16.7	21.1	24.4	26.7	27.8	24.4	20.0	13.9	8.9
Tunis, Tunisia	°F.	51	53	56	61	66	74	79	80	77	68	60	52
	°C.	23.9	25.0	28.3	31.7	33.3	33.9	31.7	30.6	32.2	32.2	28.3	25.0
United Arab Emirates													
Abu Dhabi	°F.	63.5			75.2			90.5			81.5		
	°C.	17.5			24			32.5			27.5		
Sharjah	°F.	64			75			91			82		
	°C.	17.7			23.9			32.8			27.8		
Kamaran—I, Yemen	°F.	78			84			92			88		
	°C.	25.6			28.9			33.3			31.1		
Medina al-Shaab, Yemen (*Southern*)	°F.	75						88					
	°C.	23.9											

Damascus, Syria
May–October: hot and dry.
Average yearly humidity: 36%.
Average precipitation: 9 inches. Extreme minimum temperature: 21° F.

Tunis, Tunisia
Average yearly humidity: 54%
Average yearly precipitation: 17 inches.
April–October Maximum temp.: 118° F.
March–May: Pleasant conditions

United Arab Emirates

Abu Dhabi
Mid–Oct. through April temp. range 45° F.–80° F. May to Oct. very hot.

Sharjah
Maximum temperature: 118° F.
Minimum temperature: 37° F.
Yearly precipitation: 4.2 inches.
May–October very hot and humid.

Kamaran—I, Yemen
Usually hot and dry climate.
Average precipitation: 3.4 inches yearly
Maximum temperature: 105° F.
Minimum temperature: 66° F.
Average Humidity: 35–40%

Medina al-Shaab, Yemen (*Southern*)
Maximum temperature: 110° F.
Average humidity: 40%

Appendix E

Temperature Conversions

Boldface numbers indicate the temperature to be converted; they are of the "floating" type, since they could represent degrees Centigrade or degrees Fahrenheit. When converting from degrees Centigrade to degrees Fahrenheit, the answer will be in the right Column, under the °F. heading, while the left Column will give the answer in degrees Centigrade, when converting from °F. to °C.

Example: Under the heading TC
if 25 represents 25° C., the right column gives its equivalent of 77° F. However, if you choose 25 to represent 25 °F., the left column gives its equivalent of −3.9° C.

These formulas may also be used in temperature conversions:

Degrees Centigrade: $°C. = 5/9 \ (°F. -32)$
Degrees Kelvin: $°K. = °C. + 273$
Degrees Fahrenheit: $°F. = 9/5 \ (°C.) +32$
Degrees Rankine: $°R. = °F. +460$

°C	TC	°F	°C	TC	°F
-27.8	**-18**	-0.4	-21.7	**-7**	19.4
-27.2	**-17**	1.4	-21.1	**-6**	21.2
-26.7	**-16**	3.2	-20.6	**-5**	23.0
-26.1	**-15**	5.0	-20.0	**-4**	24.8
-25.6	**-14**	6.8	-19.4	**-3**	26.6
-25.0	**-13**	8.6	-18.9	**-2**	28.4
-24.4	**-12**	10.4	-18.3	**-1**	20.2
-23.9	**-11**	12.2	-17.8	**0**	32.0
-23.3	**-10**	14.0	-17.2	**1**	33.8
-22.8	**-9**	15.8	-16.7	**2**	35.6
-22.2	**-8**	17.6	-16.1	**3**	37.4

°C	TC	°F	°C	TC	°F
-15.6	4	39.2	5.6	42	107.6
-15.0	5	41.0	6.1	43	109.4
-14.4	6	42.8	6.7	44	111.2
-13.9	7	44.6	7.2	45	113.0
-13.3	8	46.4	7.8	46	114.8
-12.8	9	48.2	8.3	47	116.6
-12.2	10	50.0	8.9	48	118.4
-11.7	11	51.8	9.4	49	120.2
-11.1	12	53.6	10.0	50	122.0
-10.6	13	55.4	10.6	51	123.8
-10.0	14	57.2	11.1	52	125.6
-9.4	15	59.0	11.7	53	127.4
-8.9	16	60.8	12.2	54	129.2
-8.3	17	62.6	12.8	55	131.0
-7.8	18	64.4	13.3	56	132.8
-7.2	19	66.2	13.9	57	134.6
-6.7	20	68.0	14.4	58	136.4
-6.1	21	69.8	15.0	59	138.2
-5.6	22	71.6	15.6	60	140.0
-5.0	23	73.4	16.1	61	141.8
-4.4	24	75.2	16.7	62	143.6
-3.9	25	77.0	17.2	63	145.4
-3.3	26	78.8	17.8	64	147.2
-2.8	27	80.6	18.3	65	149.0
-2.2	28	82.4	18.0	66	150.8
-1.7	29	84.2	19.4	67	152.6
-1.1	30	86.0	20.0	68	154.4
-0.6	31	87.8	20.6	69	156.2
0.	32	89.6	21.1	70	158.0
0.6	33	91.4	21.7	71	159.8
1.1	34	93.2	22.2	72	161.6
1.7	35	95.0	22.8	73	163.4
2.2	36	96.8	23.3	74	165.2
2.8	37	98.6	23.9	75	167.0
3.3	38	100.4	24.4	76	168.8
3.9	39	102.2	25.0	77	170.6
4.4	40	104.0	25.6	78	172.4
5.0	41	105.8	26.1	79	174.2

°C	TC	°F	°C	TC	°F
26.7	80	176.0	46.7	116	240.8
27.2	81	177.8	47.2	117	242.6
27.8	82	179.6	47.8	118	244.4
28.3	83	181.4	48.3	119	246.2
28.9	84	183.2	48.9	120	248.0
29.4	85	185.0	49.4	121	249.8
30.0	86	186.8	50.0	122	251.6
30.6	87	188.6	50.6	123	253.4
31.1	88	190.4	51.1	124	255.2
31.7	89	192.2	51.7	125	257.0
32.2	90	194.0	52.2	126	258.8
32.8	91	195.8	52.8	127	260.6
33.3	92	197.6	53.3	128	262.4
33.9	93	199.4	53.9	129	264.2
34.4	94	201.2	54.4	130	266.0
35.0	95	203.0	55.0	131	267.8
35.6	96	204.8	55.6	132	269.6
36.1	97	206.6	56.1	133	271.4
36.7	98	208.4	56.7	134	273.2
37.2	99	210.2	57.2	135	275.0
37.8	100	212.0	57.8	136	276.8
38.3	101	213.8	58.3	137	278.6
38.9	102	215.6	58.9	138	280.4
39.4	103	217.4	59.4	139	282.2
40.0	104	219.2	60.0	140	284.0
40.6	105	221.0	60.6	141	285.8
41.1	106	222.8	61.1	142	287.6
41.7	107	224.6	61.7	143	289.4
42.2	108	226.4	62.2	144	291.2
42.8	109	228.2	62.8	145	293.0
43.3	110	230.0	63.3	146	294.8
43.9	111	231.8	63.9	147	296.6
44.4	112	233.6	64.4	148	298.4
45.0	113	235.4	65.0	149	300.2
45.6	114	237.2	65.6	150	302.0
46.1	115	239.0			

Appendix F
Useful Tables

Commercial Banks' Major Assets & Liabilities (Million Riyals)

	1991 Amount		1991 Change		1992 Amount		1992 Change		1993 Amount		1993 Change	
	31.12.1990	31.12.1991	Absolute	%	31.12.1991	31.12.1992	Absolute	%	31.12.1992	31.3.1993	Absolute	%
Liabilities												
Deposit liabilities	143,662	171,222	+27,560	+19.2	171,222	177,408	+6,186	+3.6	177,408	186,777	+9,269	+5.3
Foreign liabilities	30,172	27,936	−2,236	−7.4	27,936	32,509	+4,573	+16.4	32,509	41,277	+8,768	+27.0
Capital and reserves	17,359	18,783	+1,424	+8.2	18,783	24,457	+5,674	+30.2	24,457	26,564	+2,105	+8.6
Assets												
Bank cash + deposits with SAMA	11,636	12,678	+1,042	+9.0	12,678	10,693	−1,985	−15.7	10,693	11,956	+1,263	+11.8
Claims on private sector	65,295	73,616	+8,321	+12.7	73,616	87,161	+13,545	+18.4	87,161	93,760	+6,599	+7.6
Claims on government sector	19,029	41,768	+22,739	+119.5	41,768	59,292	+17,524	+42.0	59,292	61,245	+1,953	+3.3
Foreign assets	123,467	118,951	−4,516	−3.7	118,951	106,372	−12,579	−10.6	106,372	116,361	+9,989	+9.4

Money Supply
(Million Riyals)

	1991				1992				1993			
	Amount		Change		Amount		Change		Amount		Change	
	31.12.1990	31.12.1991	Absolute	%	31.12.1991	31.12.1992	Absolute	%	31.12.1992	31.3.1993	Absolute	%
Currency in circulation	44,776	44,620	– 156	– 0.3	44,620	43,769	– 851	– 1.9	43,769	46,573	+ 2,804	+ 6.4
Demand deposits	57,488	75,850	+ 18,362	+ 31.9	75,850	84,160	+ 8,310	+ 11.0	84,160	91,553	+ 7,393	+ 8.8
Money supply (M$_1$)	102,264	120,470	+ 18,206	+ 17.8	120,470	127,929	+ 7,459	+ 6.2	127,929	138,126	+ 10,197	+ 8.0
Time & savings deposits	39,281	44,623	+ 5,342	+ 13.6	44,623	46,326	+ 1,703	+ 3.8	46,326	46,102	– 224	– 0.5
Money supply (M$_2$)	141,545	165,093	+ 23,548	+ 16.6	165,093	174,255	+ 9,162	+ 5.5	174,255	184,228	+ 9,973	+ 5.7
Other quasi-monetary deposits	46,893	50,749	+ 3,856	+ 8.2	50,749	46,922	– 3,827	– 7.5	46,922	49,122	+ 2,200	+ 4.7
i) Residents' foreign currency deposits	41,666	45,343	+ 3,677	+ 8.8	45,343	41,179	– 4,164	– 9.2	41,179	43,621	+ 2,442	+ 5.9
ii) For letters of credit	3,593	3,528	– 65	– 1.8	3,528	3,875	+347	+ 9.8	3,875	3,599	– 276	– 7.1
iii) For guarantees	1,634	1,878	+ 244	+ 14.9	1,878	1,868	– 10	– 0.8	1,868	1,902	+ 34	+ 1.8
Money supply (M$_3$)	188,438	215,842	+ 27,404	+ 14.5	215,842	221,177	+ 5,335	+ 2.5	222,177	233,350	+ 12,173	+ 5.5

Source: Sama

Allocation of Gross Domestic Product by Institutional Sector in Producers' Values At Current Prices (Million Riyals)

	1399/1400 1979	1400/01 1980	1401/02 1981	1402/03 1982	1403/04 1983	1404/05 1984	1405/06 1985	1406/07 1986	1407/08 1987	1408/09 1988	1409/10 1989
1. Oil Sector	252,705	360,741	337,884	206,360	157,989	132,555	96,958	67,461	70,443	69,115	90,749
2. Non-Oil Private Sector	74,559	88,520	102,874	117,446	127,816	129,998	130,981	123,686	122,967	126,812	130,045
3. Government Sector	56,325	68,733	81,418	87,992	82,594	84,871	82,092	76,699	78,590	80,981	83,289
4. GDP Excluding Import Duties	383,589	517,994	522,176	411,798	368,399	347,424	310,031	267,846	272,000	276,908	304,083
5. Import Duties	2,217	2,595	2,542	3,433	3,624	3,973	3,910	3,245	3,453	8,236	6,740
6. GDP Including Import Duties	385,806	520,589	524,718	415,231	372,023	351,397	313,941	271,091	275,453	285,144	310,823

Gross Domestic Product by Kind of Economic Activity in Producers' Values At Current Prices (Million Riyals)

	1399/1400 1979	1400/01 1980	1401/02 1981	1402/03 1982	1403/04 1983	1404/05 1984	1405/06 1985	1406/07 1986	1407/08 1987	1408/09 1988	1409/10 1989
A—Industries and Other Producers Except Producers of Government Services:											
1. Agriculture, Forestry & Fishing	4,648	5,572	6,740	8,725	9,611	11,620	13,789	15,861	18,312	20,895	22,650
2. Mining and Quarrying:											
a) Crude Petroleum & Natural Gas	237,218	340,997	323,328	192,874	143,172	120,305	88,286	61,262	63,390	61,711	83,847
b) Other	1,361	1,696	1,969	1,785	1,799	1,864	1,812	1,758	1,723	1,760	1,812
3. Manufacturing:											
a) Petroleum Refining	12,828	18,027	13,260	13,287	14,714	13,824	10,200	5,894	9,902	9,675	9,405
b) Other	6,467	7,721	9,124	10,686	12,224	13,597	14,299	13,828	13,950	14,787	15,822
4. Electricity, Gas and Water	271	395	-429	-850	-66	-586	301	523	681	722	750
5. Construction	43,108	50,348	58,181	54,903	49,956	44,964	38,745	33,989	33,250	32,027	32,475
6. Wholesale & Retail Trade, Restaurants and Hotels	17,760	21,984	25,064	28,088	28,510	30,386	30,222	29,072	27,797	26,802	26,078
7. Transport, Storage & Communication	15,749	17,123	19,871	21,489	23,668	23,844	23,719	22,783	22,087	22,807	23,121
8. Finance, Insurance, Real Estate & Business Services:											
a) Ownership of Dwellings	10,962	11,973	12,562	13,313	13,742	13,117	10,648	7,934	6,528	6,093	6,071
b) Other	7,853	10,352	13,300	16,871	18,940	17,383	16,536	14,524	14,944	16,319	16,998
9. Community, Social & Personal Services	5,260	5,504	6,814	8,408	9,226	9,704	11,033	10,584	10,507	11,107	11,414
10. Less: Imputed Bank Services Charge	-3,279	-3,607	-3,968	-4,364	-4,406	-4,670	-4,529	-4,304	-4,132	-4,104	-4,200
SUB-TOTAL	360,206	488,085	485,816	365,215	321,090	295,352	255,061	213,708	218,939	220,601	246,243
B—Producers of Govt. Services:											
1. Public Administration & Defence	13,545	14,437	18,120	23,861	24,365	26,417	27,757	27,336	26,792	28,432	29,206
2. Other Services	9,839	15,468	18,242	22,725	22,944	25,655	27,214	26,802	26,269	27,876	28,634
SUB-TOTAL	23,384	29,905	36,362	46,586	47,309	52,072	54,971	54,138	53,061	56,308	57,840
Total Except Import Duties	383,590	517,990	522,178	411,801	368,399	347,424	310,032	267,846	272,000	276,909	304,083
Import Duties	2,217	2,595	2,542	3,433	3,624	3,973	3,910	3,245	3,453	8,236	6,740
Gross Domestic Product (GDP)	385,807	520,585	524,720	415,234	372,023	351,397	313,942	271,091	275,453	285,145	310,823

Source: Sama, Ministry of Finance and National Economy, Central Dept. of Statistics

Saudi Banks

The Arab National Bank
P.O. Box 56921, Riyadh 11564
Tel: 402-9000
Fax: 402-7747
Tlx: 402-660

Al-Bank Al-Saudi Al-Hollandi
P.O. Box 1647, Riyadh 11431
Tel: 406-7888/401-0288
Fax: 403-1104
Tlx: 401-488

Bank Al-jazira
P.O. Box 5859, Riyadh 11432
Tel: 403-6344/401-1636
Fax: 403-6344
Tlx: 401-155

Saudi British Bank
P.O. Box 9084, Riyadh 11413
Tel: 405-0677
Fax: 405-0660
Tlx: 402-349

Al-Bank Al-saudi Al-Faransi
P.O. Box 56006, Riyadh 11554
Tel: 402-2222
Fax: 404-2311
Tlx: 407-666

United Saudi Commercial Bank
P.O. Box 25895, Riyadh 11476
Tel: 478-4200/478-8075
Fax: 478-3197
Tlx: 405-461

The National Commerce Bank
P.O. Box 3555, Jeddah
Tel: 644-6644
Fax: 644-6644
Tlx: 605-573

Al-Rajhi Banking Investment Corporation
P.O. Box 28, Riyadh 11511
Tel: 405-4244
Fax: 405-2950
Tlx: 406-317

Saudi American Bank
P.O. Box 833, Riyadh 11421
Tel: 477-4770
Fax: 477-4770
Tlx: 400-195

Riyadh Bank
P.O. Box 229, Riyadh 11411
Tel: 401-4000/402-4011
Fax: 404-2705
Tlx: 400-975

Saudi Cairo Bank
P.O. Box 42647, Riyadh 11551
Tel: 478-9345/476-0281
Fax: 479-1515
Tlx: 401-051

Saudi Investment Bank
P.O. Box 3533, Riyadh 11481
Tel: 477-8433
Fax: 477-6781
Tlx: 401-170

Appendix G

References

1. Abou-Ayyash, A., "Personal Communication," General Manager, Rashid Engineering, Riyadh, 1990–1994.
2. Al-Dayel, A. R., Editor-in-chief, Al-Mubtaath Magazine, Royal Embassy of Saudi Arabia, Cultural Mission, Washington D.C., issues 1985–1994; No. 147, Sept. 1993.
3. Al-Farsy, Fouad, Modernity and Tradition: The Saudi Equation, Kegan Paul International, London, 1990.
4. Al-Faruqi, I. R., Islam, Argus Communications, Niles, Il., 1984.
5. Al-Gosaibi, G., Gulf Crisis: Attempt at Understanding, Dar Al-Saqi, Beirut, London, 1991 (In Arabic).
6. Al-Khuli, M. A., The Light of Islam, Al-Farazdak Press, Riyadh, 1983.
7. Al-Khuli, M. A., The Need For Islam, Al Farazdak Press, Riyadh, 1981.
8. Al-Khuli, M. A., The Translations of The Meanings of Some Traditions of Prophet Muhammad, Al-Farazdak Press, Riyadh, 1984.
9. Al-Mana, M., Arabia Unified: A Portrait of Ibn Saud, Hutchinson Benham, London, 1980.
10. Al-Rihani, Amin, History of Najd & Annexed Territory, and the Story of Abdulaziz, fourth printing, Dar Rihani, Beirut, 1970 (In Arabic).
11. Al-Sha'er, A., The Echoes of the Saudi Position During the Events of the Arab Gulf, Saudi Press Agency, June 13, 1991, (In Arabic and English).
12. Al-Sha'er, A., Kingdom of Saudi Arabia, History, Civilization and Development (60 Years of Progress), Ministry of Information, Riyadh, 1991, (In Arabic).
13. Al-Sweel, A. I. and J. W. Wright, Jr. editors, Saudi Arabia, Tradition and Transition, The Saudi Arabian Cultural Mission, Washington, D.C., Spring, 1993.
14. Arab Urban Development Institute, Riyadh, The City of The Future, King Saud University Press.
15. Aramco, Aramco Exhibit A House of Discovery, Aramco.
16. Aramco, "Science, The Islamic Legacy," Aramco World Magazine, Aramco, Corporation, Washington, D.C., 1986.

17. Aramco World, Saudi Arabia Yesterday and Today, Vol. 43 #7, Saudi Aramco Services Company, Houston, Texas, also Vols. 1986–1994.

18. Aramco World, The Middle East and the Age of Discovery, Vol. 43 #3, Saudi Arabian Oil Co., Dhahran, Saudi Arabia.

19. Azzi, Robert, Saudi Arabian Portfolio, Ministry of Information Dept. of Foreign Information, Fretz Bros., Zurich, 1978.

20. Bassiouni, M. C., Introduction To Islam, Rand McNally & Co., Chicago, Il.

21. Beard, Armand, City Guide To Riyadh, Tihama, Riyadh, Saudi Arabia.

22. Berlitz, S. A., Arabic For Travelers, Artes Graficas, S. A. Bilbao, Spain, 1977.

23. Bureau of Public Affairs, U.S. Department of State, Background Notes on the Countries of the World, April, 1975.

24. Canby, Thomas Y., "After The Storm," National Geographic, Vol. 180, #2, Washington, D.C., August, 1991.

25. Carter, Jimmy, The Blood of Abraham, Houghton Mifflin Co., Boston, MA., 1985.

26. Chaline, Claude and Fares, Adib, The Contemporary Town Planning and Riyadh, Western Countries, 1981.

27. Chubin, Shahram, Editor, Security In The Persian Gulf, Pt. 1: Domestic Political Factors, International Institute for Strategic Studies, 1981.

28. Churchill, Winston, The Second World War, Abridged Edition to Mark the Fiftieth Anniversary of the Outbreak of the War, Cassell, London, 1989.

29. Cleron, J. P., Saudi Arabia 2000: A Strategy for Growth, St. Martin's Press, New York, 1978.

30. Collier's Encyclopedia, "Saudi Arabia," pp. 450–457, 1982.

31. Corcoran, K. R., Editor, Saudi Arabia: Keys to Business Success, McGraw-Hill (UK) Ltd., Maidenhead, England, 1981.

32. Cordesman, A., "Iran-Iraq War and Western Security: 1984–87," Jane's London, 1987.

33. Daghistani, Abdal-Majeed Ismail, Al-Taif, A City In Transition, A Falcon Press Production, Jeddah, 1981.

34. Dahlan, Ahmed H., Politics, Administration Development, Amana Corporation, Brentwood, Md., 1990.

35. David, Peter, Truimph In The Desert, Random House, Inc., New York, 1991.

36. DeGaury, G., Faisal: King of Saudi Arabia, Atthur Barker, London, 1966.

37. Doi, Abdur Rahman, Shariah: The Islamic Law, Taha Publishers, London, 1984.

38. El-Mallakh, Ragaei, Saudi Arabia, Rush to Development, Profile of an Energy Economy and Investment, Johns Hopkins University Press, Baltimore, MD., and Croom Helm, London, 1982.

39. El-Mallakh, Ragaei, Editor, OPEC: Twenty Years and Beyond, Westview Press, Boulder, Colorado, 1982.

40. El-Mallakh, Ragaei, and Kadhim. M., Arab Institutionalized Development Aid: An Evaluation, The Middle East Journal, pp. 478-9, Autumn, 1976.

41. Encyclopedia Americana, "Ibn Saud," Vol. 14, p. 618, American Corporation, New York, 1965.

42. Encyclopedia Americana, "Saudi Arabia," Vol. 24, pp. 316–316b, American Corporation U.S.A., 1965.

43. Farrar, G. L., McCaslin, J., et Al, Staff editors, International Petroleum Encyclopedia, Petroleum Publishing Co., Tulsa, OK., 1986–1994.

44. Farsi, Zaki M. A., National Guide & Atlas of the Kingdom of Saudi Arabia, Al-Madina Printing & Publication Co., Jeddah, Saudi Arabia, 1988.

45. Findley, Paul, They Dare to Speak Out, Lawrence Hill & Co., Westport, Connecticut, 1985.

46. Forbes Magazine, "Saudi Arabia Yesterday and Today," reprinted from the August 7, 1989 issue and "Saudi Business," reprint, March, 1990.

47. Frieddrich, O., Editor and Editors of Time Magazine, Desert Storm–The War in the Persian Gulf, Time Warner Publishing Co., 1991.

48. Friedman, T. L., From Beirut to Jerusalem, Anchor Books Doubleday, New York, August, 1990.

49. Gazzaz, H. H., The Security We Enjoy, Dar Al-Elm Printing & Publishing Co., Saudi Arabia, 1992.

50. Geagea, N., Translated and Edited by Fares, Lawrence, Mary Of The Koran, Philosophical Library, Inc., New York, 1984.

51. Glass, C., Tribes With Flags, The Atlantic Monthly Press, New York, 1990.

52. Goldschmidt, A., Jr., A Concise History of the Middle East, Westview Press, Boulder, Colorado, 1979.

53. Graz, Liesl, The Turbulent Gulf, I. B. Tauris & Co., Ltd., London, 1990.

54. Griffith, William E., The Middle East, 1982: Politics, Revolutionary Islam, and American Policy, Cambridge: Center for International Studies, Massachusetts Institute of Technology, January 20, 1982.

55. Grolier Universal Encyclopedia, "Saudi Arabia," Vol. 9, Grolier Universal Encyclopedia, pp. 119–123, American Book, Stratford Press Inc., New York, 1966.

56. Haig, Alexander, "Saudi Security, Middle East Peace, & U.S.

Interest," (Current Policy Series, No. 323), Department of State, Bureaus of Public Affairs, Washington, October, 1981.

57. Hariri, Rafiq, Personal Communication, President of the Council of Ministers of the Lebanese Republic, Chairman of the Board, Saudi Oger, Riyadh, 1990–1994.

58. Hathloul, Saud, Ibn, History of the Kings of Al-Saud, Madina Printing, Riyadh, 1982 (In Arabic).

59. Helms, C. M., The Cohesion of Saudi Arabia, Johns Hopkins University Press, Baltimore, MD and London, 1981.

60. Hersey, Regina, Editor, Directory of Saudi Arabian Companies, 1984: Saudi Products & Services, Leland Publishing Co., 1983.

61. Hiro, Dilip, Desert Shield to Desert Storm, Paladin, 1992.

62. Higgins, Francis, U.S./Arab Trade and U.S. Export Disincentives, Information Series #2, Bell, Boyd & Lloyd, Chicago, 1978.

63. Hitti, P. K., History of The Arabs, 10th edition, St. Martin's Press, New York, 1974.

64. Holt, P. M. The Age of The Crusades, Longman Group Ltd., London, 1986.

65. Hourani, A., A History of the Arab Peoples, Faber and Faber, Ltd., London, 1991.

66. Howarth, D. A., The Desert King: A Life of Ibn Saud, Collins, London, McGraw-Hill, New York, 1964.

67. Ibrahim, A. Al-Moneef, Transfer of Management Technology to Developing Nations: The Role of Multinational Oil Firms in Saudi Arabia, Brouchey, Stuart, Editors, Ayer Co., 1980.

68. Issa, Seyyed, Economic Development in the Kingdom of Saudi Arabia, Saudi Presses, Riyadh, 1984 (In Arabic).

69. Jawad, Abdul G. M., Investment Climate and Opportunities in the GCC Region, Saudi Cairo Bank, Jeddah, Saudi Arabia, 1990.

70. Johany, Ali D., Berne, Michel & Mixon, J. Wilson Jr., The Saudi Arabian Economy, Croom Helm, London, 1986.

71. Kabadaya, S., Desert Storm, Intl. Saudi Research and Marketing Co., London, January 17–February 28, 1991 (In Arabic).

72. Kelly, J. B., Arabia The Gulf & The West, Basic Books, Inc., New York, 1980.

73. King Fahd Holy Qur-an Printing Complex, The Holy Qur-an, English translation, 1990.

74. Kingdom of Saudi Arabia, The International Humanitarian Role of The Kingdom of Saudi Arabia, National Information Agency, 1990.

75. Knauerhase, Ramon, "Saudi Arabia: Fifty Years of Economic Change," Current History, 82 No. 480 pp. 19–23, January, 1983.

76. Koury, Enver M., The Saudi Decision-Making Body: the House of Saud, Institute of Middle East & North Africa, 1978.

77. Laranteno, M. A., Marvelous Stories from the Life of Muhammad, The Islamic Foundation, 1982.

78. Lawrence, T. E., Seven Pillars of Wisdom, Penguin Books Inc., 1976.

79. Lawton, J., Clark, A., "Foundations: A Decade of Development," Aramco World Magazine, Vol. 33, #6, November–December, 1982.

80. Lebkicher, Roy, Rentz George, Steinke Max, Aramco Handbook, Arabian American Oil Co., (now Saudi Aramco), Netherlands, 1960.

81. Lee, William F., "U.S.-Arab Economic Ties: An Interdependent Relationship," Journal of American-Arab Affairs, pp. 5–13, Winter, 1982–1983.

82. Lees, Brian, A Handbook of the Sa'ud Ruling Family of Saudi Arabia, Royal Genealogics, London, 1980.

83. Linden, F., Wyatt, F., Inst. S.M.M., Arabian Transport Services, 2nd Edition, Anglo-Arabian Publishing, London, 1985.

84. Long, D., The Hajj Today: A Survey of the Contemporary Pilgrimage to Makkah, State University of New York Press, Albany, New York, 1979.

85. Looney, Robert E., Saudi Arabia's Development Potential: Application of An Islamic Growth Model, Lexington Books, 1981.

86. Mansfield, P., Arab World, T. Y. Crowell, 1976.

87. Mechin-Benoist, Ibn Saud, Ou la Naissance d'un Royaume, Editions Albin Michel 1955, translated from the French by Laund, Ramadan, Dar Aswad for Publishing, Beirut, 1976 (In Arabic).

88. Mian, Q. Javed & Lerrick, Alison, Saudi Business & Labour Law: Its Interpretation & Applications, Graham & Trotman, England, 1982.

89. Middle East Institute, The Middle East Between War and Peace, 37th Annual Conference, Washington, Sept. 30–Oct. 1, 1983.

90. Ministry of Agriculture and Water, A Guide to Agricultural Investment In Saudi Arabia, Dept. of Agricultural Development, Riyadh, 1979.

91. Ministry of Agriculture and Water, Agricultural Development in The Kingdom of Saudi Arabia, Riyadh, 1975–1994.

92. Ministry of Finance & National Economy, Cost of Living Index: All Cities and Middle-Income Saudi Populations, Department of Statistics, 1984, 1994.

93. Ministry of Finance & National Economy, Central Dept. of Statistics, Yearbooks, Riyadh, 1986–1994.

94. Ministry of Information, Lapic Allahoma, Dar Al-Ard Publication & Informational Services, Saudi Arabia, 1993.

95. Ministry of Information, This Is Our Country, Kingdom of Saudi Arabia, Interior Information, 1992.

96. Ministry of Information, This Is Our Country, Dar Al-Sahra for Publishing and Distribution, Riyadh, 1991, (1411 A.H.), (In Arabic).

97. Ministry of Information, The Royal Message by the Custodian of the Two Holy Mosques King Fahd Ibn Abdulaziz Al-Saud and H.R.H. Crown Prince Abdullah Ibn Abdulaziz Al-Saud, Deputy Prime Minister and Head of the National Guard, to the Pilgrims to the Holy House of Allah in the Year 1411 A.H. (1991), Printed by Dar Al-Asfahani, Jeddah, 1991.

98. Ministry of Information, Twenty Years of Achievements in Planned Development 1970–1989 (1390–1410 A.H.), Dar Al-Mawsou'a Al-Arabia for Publishing and Distribution, Riyadh, 1991 (1411 A.H.), (In Arabic).

99. Ministry of Information, Victory of Truth, Kingdom of Saudi Arabia, Nebras, 1991 (Also in Arabic).

100. Ministry of Information, Asir, National Offset Printing Press, Riyadh.

101. Ministry of Information Affairs, This Is Our Country, Internal Information, Kingdom of Saudi Arabia, 1988.

102. Ministry of Information, A Decade Of Progress, Kingdom of Saudi Arabia, Obeikan Printing Co., 1985. (In English and Arabic).

103. Ministry of Information, "Meeting of King Fahd With Saudi Students Studying Abroad, Jeddah, Aug. 20, 1984," Yamama Press, Riyadh, 1984 (In Arabic).

104. Ministry of Information, "Frankness and Clarity," Dialogue Between King Fahd and the Faculty & Students at King Faisal University-Hasa, 1984, Mutawwa Press, Dammam, 1984 (In Arabic).

105. Minosa, Tchekof, Najran Desert Garden of Arabia, Scorpio Films Production, Paris, France, 1983.

106. Mostyn, T., Editor, Saudi Arabia: A Meed Practical Guide, Middle East Economic Digest, 1981.

107. Nakhleh, E. A., Arab-American Relations in the Persian Gulf, American Enterprise Institute, Washington, 1975.

108. Nation's Business, Saudi Arabia, reprint, Transnational Association, Washington, D.C., March, 1985.

109. Nawwab, Ismail I., Speers, P. C., & Haye, P. F., Editors, Aramco and Its World: Arabia and the Middle East, Dhahran, 1981.

110. New York Times, "Kingdom Stops Wheat Imports," Vol. 18, issue 875, p. 5, July 25, 1984.

111. Newsweek, Issues relating to the Gulf War, August, 1990–August, 1991.

112. Nyrop, R. F., Editor, Saudi Arabia–A Country Study, Area Handbook Series, American University, Washington, Superintendent of Documents, U.S. Government Printing Office, Washington, 1985.

113. Oil and Gas Journal–L. R. Aalund et Al., "The Role of State Oil Companies," Oil & Gas Journal, PennWell, Tulsa, OK., August, 1993.

114. Pendleton, Madge, Davies, D. L., Davies, Martina S., Snodgrass,

Frances O., The Green Book, Guide For Living In Saudi Arabia, 3rd Edition, Middle East Editorial Associates, Washington, 1980.

115. Pesce, Angelo, Jiddah: Portrait of An Arabian City, Falcon Press, London, 1977.

116. Peterson, J. E., Editor, The Politics of Middle East Oil, Middle East Institute, Washington, 1983.

117. Philby, H., St. John B., Arabian Oil Ventures, Middle East Institute, Washington, 1964.

118. Philby, H., St. John B., "Sa'udi Arabia," World Affairs series National & International Viewpoints, Ayers Co., 1955, (Reprint 1972).

119. Philby, H., St. John B., The Heart of Arabia, Constable, London, 1922.

120. Plastic World, "Saudi Arabia May Soon Replace the U.S. and Japan as One of the Biggest Exporters of Plastics to World Markets," pp 56–57, March 1985.

121. Princeton University Press, The Arabs; A Short History, Princeton University Press, Princeton, New Jersey, 1949.

122. Quandt, W. B., Saudi Arabia In The 1980's, The Brookings Institution, Washington, 1982.

123. Rashid Engineering, Riyadh, 1990–1994.

124. Rashid, N. I. and Shaheen, E. I., Saudi Arabia and the Gulf War, International Institute of Technology, Inc., Joplin, Missouri, U.S.A., 1992.

125. Rashid, N. I. and Shaheen, E. I., King Fahd and Saudi Arabia's Great Evolution, International Institute of Technology, Inc. Joplin, Missouri U.S.A., 1987 and 1991, (In English and Arabic).

126. Rashid, N. I. and Shaheen, E. I., "The Great Academic Evolution in the Kingdom of Saudi Arabia," presented at the Annual meeting of AIChE in New York, U.S.A., Nov. 1987.

127. Rihani, Ameen F., Maker of Modern Arabia, Greenwood, reprint of 1928 Edition, Washington, 1983.

128. Ross, Heather, C., The Art of Bedouin Jewelery, Arabesque Commercial, Switzerland, 1981.

129. Ross, Heather, C., The Art of Arabian Costume: A Saudi Arabian Profile, Arabesque Commercial SA, Switzerland, 1981.

130. Royal Embassy of Saudi Arabia, "Saudi Arabia," Monthly News letter, 1985–1994.

131. Royal Embassy of Saudi Arabia, "Saudi Arabia," Vol. 10, #1, Information Office, Washington, D.C., Spring, 1993.

132. Royal Embassy of Saudi Arabia, "Business, Budgets and the Economy," Information Office, Washington, D.C., 1993.

133. Royal Embassy of Saudi Arabia, The Cultural Mission To The U.S.A., Science and Technology Unit, Washington, D.C., 1992.

134. Royal Embassy of Saudi Arabia, Conversations and Dialogue of the

Custodian of the Two Holy Mosques at Saudi Universities and with Saudi Students Abroad, Cultural Mission, Washington, D.C., 1991.

135. Royal Embassy of Saudi Arabia, "A Guide to Doing Business in the Kingdom of Saudi Arabia, Washington, D.C., 1991, 1993.

136. Royal Embassy of Saudi Arabia, Islam, Information Office, Washington, D.C.

137. Royal Embassy of Saudi Arabia, Islam, A Global Civilization, Islamic Affairs Department, Washington, D.C.

138. Royal Embassy of Saudi Arabia, Understanding Islam and the Muslims, Embassy of Saudi Arabia, Washington, D.C.

139. Salloum, H. I., "Personal Communication," Cultural Mission, Royal Embassy of Saudi Arabia, Washington, D.C., 1992–1994.

140. Saudi Agency for Consulting Services, "Guide to Industrial Investment," sixth printing, Riyadh, 1984 (In Arabic).

141. Saudi Arabia, "The 50th Anniversary of the Kingdom, A Two-Part Survey," International Herald Tribune (entire issue), Paris, July, 1982.

142. Saudi Arabian Airlines, Transitional Information Pertinent To Saudi Arabia, Saudi Arabian Airlines, Kansas City, Missouri, 1978.

143. Saudi Arabian Monetary Agency, Annual Reports, Sama, Research and Statistics Dept., Riyadh, Feb. and Aug. 1993.

144. Saudi Press, "Numerous Articles From Newspapers, Relating to the Gulf War, The Kingdom and King Fahd," Riyadh, 1985–1994, (Mostly in Arabic and some in English).

145. Saudi-Oger Ltd., Riyadh, June, 1980, 1982 and Personal Communication 1994.

146. Saudia, Ahlan Wasahlan, Vol. #17 issue 5 and others, Makkah Adv. Int'l ltd, United Kingdom, May, 1993.

147. Seale, P., Asad: The Struggle for the Middle East, University of California Press, Los Angeles & Berkeley, 1989.

148. Schoellner, Joan, "Living In The Middle East . . . A Wife's View," Chemical Engineering issue June 20, 1977, pp. 125–130, McGraw-Hill, 1977.

149. Shah, Ali Sirdar Ikbar, The Controlling Minds of Asia, Herbert Jenkins ltd., London, 1937.

150. Shaheen, E. I., Technology of Environmental Pollution Control, 2nd Edition, PennWell Books, Tulsa, OK., 1992.

151. Shaheen, E. I., and Rashid, N. I., "The Energy Spectrum," presented at the AIChE Symposium: Energy: Yesterday, Today and Tomorrow, New Orleans, LA., April 6–10, 1986.

152. Shaheen, E. I., Basic Practice of Chemical Engineering, (Houghton Mifflin Co., 1st Edition 1975), International Institute of Technology, Inc., Joplin, MO., 2nd Edition, 1984.

153. Shaheen, E. I., Arabic-English With A Petroleum Accent, Petroleum Publishing Co., Tulsa, OK., 1977.

154. Shaheen, E. I., Energy-Pollution Illustrated Glossary, Engineering Technology, Inc., Mahomet, Il., 1977.

155. Shaheen, E. I., "Surviving Even Thriving Overseas," Chemical Engineering, issue December 6, 1976, McGraw-Hill, 1976.

156. Shaheen, E. I., "The Energy Crisis: Is It Fabrication or Miscalculation?," Vol. 8 #4, Environmental Science and Technology, April, 1974.

157. Shair Management Services, Editors, Business Laws & Practices of Saudi Arabia, Graham Trotman, England, 1979.

158. Sharq Awsat, Saudi Newspaper, 1990–1994.

159. Shaw, John A., and Long, D. E., "Saudi Arabian Modernization: The Impact of Change On Stability," 10, (Washington Papers #89.), Praeger, Center For Strategic and International Studies, Georgetown University, Washington, 1982.

160. Shilling, N. A., A Practical Guide To Living and Traveling In the Arab World, Inter-Crescent Publishing Co., Dallas, Texas, 1978.

161. Sluglett, P., and Sluglett, M. Editors, The Times Guide To The Middle East, Time Books, London, 1991.

162. Smith, R. M., Editor and Editors of Newsweek Magazine, Commemorative Issue, America at War: From the Frenzied Buildup to the Joyous Homecoming, Newsweek, Inc., Spring/Summer, 1991.

163. Stacey International, The Kingdom of Saudi Arabia, Stacey International, London, 1992.

164. Thatcher, M., The Downing Street Years, Harper Collins Publishers, New York, 1993.

165. Troeller, Gary, The Birth of Saudi Arabia: Britain and the Rise of the House of Sa'ud, Cass, London, 1976.

166. Twitchell, K. S., Saudi Arabia, 3rd Edition, Princeton University Press, Princeton, 1958.

167. U.S. Department of Commerce, An Introduction to Contract Procedures In The Near East & North Africa, 3rd Edition, International Trade Administration, Washington, November, 1984.

168. U.S. Department of Defense, Briefings, Interviews and Speeches Relating to the Gulf War, Washington, D.C. and Tampa, Florida U.S.A., August, 1990–August, 1991.

169. U.S. Dept. of State, Background Notes–Saudi Arabia, Bureau of Public Affairs, Washington, Feb., 1983.

170. U.S. Department of State, Bureau of Consular Affairs, Tips For Travelers To Saudi Arabia, Department of State Publications, Department of Foreign Services, September, 1983.

171. U.S. House of Representatives, Foreign Affairs, and National Defense Division, Saudi Arabia and The United States: The New Context in An Evolving "Special Relationship," Congressional Research Service, Library of Congress, August, 1981.

172. U.S. News and World Report, Issues relating to the Gulf War, August, 1990–August, 1991.

173. United Nations, Kuwait Report to the Secretary-General, Issued as Security Council document S/22535, United Nations Department of Public Information, Sept., 1991.

174. United Nations, Global Outlook 2000, United Nations Publications, 1990.

175. Vincett, Betty A.L., Animal Life In Saudi Arabia, Garzanti Editore S.pa, Italy, 1982.

176. Vincett, Betty A.L., Wildflowers of Central Saudi Arabia, Garzanti S.pa, Italy, 1977.

177. Wall Street Journal, "Saudi Arabia: A Strategic Kingdom," July 28, 1989.

178. Walmsley, John, Joint Ventures In Saudi Arabia, Graham & Trotman, England, 1979.

179. Watson, B. W., Military Lessons of the Gulf War, Greenhill Books, London, Presidio Press, California, 1991.

180. Weiss, Leopold, "New Travels In Arabia," from Neue Zurcher Zeitung (Swiss Daily), The Living Age, Vol. 334, pp. 1170–1180, Boston, 1928.

181. Weiss, Leopold, "Trouble In Arabia," The Living Age, Translated from Neue Zurcher Zeitung, Vol. 334, pp. 806–813, Boston, 1928.

182. Weiss, Leopold, "Through Central Arabia: In The Kingdom of Nejd," Living Age, Translated from the Neue Zurcher, Zurich, German-Language Daily, Vol. 337, pp. 427–432, Boston, 1929–30.

183. Wells, H. G., The Outline of History, Vol. 1, Garden City Books, Garden City, N.Y., 1949.

184. White House, Statements and Speeches by President George Bush, Washington, D.C., August, 1990–August, 1991.

185. Winter, E. L., Your Future In Jobs Abroad, Richards Rosen Press, Inc., N.Y., 1968.

186. Witherow, J. and Sullivan, Aidan, The Sun Times War In The Gulf, Sidgwech Jackson, London, 1991.

187. Wolfe, R. G., Editor, The United States, Arabia, and the Gulf, Georgetown University Center For Contemporary Arab Studies, Washington, 1980.

188. Woodward, Bob, The Commanders, Simon & Schuster, New York, 1991.

189. Young, Arthur N., Saudi Arabia: The Making of a Financial Giant, New York University Press, New York, 1983.

190. Zirikli, Khir, al-Din, Arabia Under King Abdul Aziz, 4 Volumes, Beirut, 1985 (In Arabic).

Appendix H

About the Authors

Dr. Nasser I. Rashid

Dr. Nasser I. Rashid was born in Madina in 1939 and was brought up in the best Saudi traditions of Islamic religious beliefs. He studied in the Kingdom, Syria and Lebanon prior to his university education. He excelled as a student; then he won a Saudi government scholarship to study at the University of Texas in Austin, Texas, U.S.A. He joined the university in 1961 and graduated with a Bachelor of Science degree in Civil Engineering in 1965 and earned his Doctor of Philosophy degree in 1970 from the same university.

His great intellect, coupled with his deep rooted Arab background and the position of eminence that he occupies in recent years, were basic qualities which made him uniquely qualified to co-author this book. With his good friend and colleague Dr. Shaheen, he previously co-authored the book entitled: *"King Fahd and Saudi Arabia's Great Evolution," in English and Arabic* and the book entitled *"Saudi Arabia And The Gulf War."* He also has written a number of scholarly articles.

A world-renowned man, he is listed in Who's Who in Saudi Arabia and International Who's Who in the Arab World. He received many educational honors while at the university. Because of his outstanding ability and personal warmth, he became President of the Arab Student Organization. In 1980 he was selected as the Distinguished Graduate of the College of Engineering at the University of Texas, in Austin, Texas, USA. He is a member of many honorary fraternities and he received the Distinguished Leadership Award and the Man of the Year Award for outstanding accomplishments from the American Biographical Institute. He is listed in the International Directory of Distinguished Leadership. Many Islamic foundations granted him honorary awards for his help. His contributions to St. Jude Children's Research Hospital, in Memphis, Tennessee earned him an Award for Humanitarian Efforts and Generous Support. The president of the French Republic, François Mitterrand, has awarded him the Ordre Nationale de la Legion d'Honneur. On October 4, 1991, Dr. Rashid was granted the highly esteemed Distinguished Alumnus Award from the University of Texas, in recognition of his great achievements and vast contributions to society and the world community.

After graduating from the University of Texas, Dr. Rashid joined the King Fahd University of Petroleum and Minerals in Dhahran, Saudi Arabia. While teaching there, he became director of construction and campus development. He later became Dean of Business and then Dean of Engineering at KFUPM. He participated in establishing an accredited program for the College of Engineering and established ties with major American universities.

Dr. Rashid left the university for private business in 1975, when he established his company: Rashid Engineering, a consulting firm based in Riyadh, Saudi Arabia. In 1978, the late King Khaled of Saudi Arabia asked him if it was feasible to build a first class hotel in eight months in a summer resort in the Kingdom. An ingenious plan was devised and the Intercontinental Hotel in Taif was completed in eight months. That is how Rashid Engineering and their team in Saudi Oger became the fast builders in the Kingdom. In the span of the next ten years, the two firms undertook the planning, design, management and construction of over ninety huge projects, each completed in record time. Dr. Rashid was a member of the Contractors Classification Committee, charged with prequalifying and classifying all contractors. He was also on the board of several financial institutions including the Real Estate Development Bank and Investcorp.

He has contributed over one hundred million dollars, involving a wide spectrum of humanitarian organizations. He has supported various programs fighting childhood leukemia. Using about 100 million dollars of his own money, he designed and built the King Fahd Children's Medical Center (KFCMC) in Riyadh.

Dr. Rashid became one of the most loyal confidants of the Custodian of the Two Holy Mosques. At present, he is the Engineering Consultant to King Fahd, the Crown Prince and the Royal Court. Dr. Rashid was not a passive observer of what had been taking place in the Kingdom. He lived and participated actively and most dynamically in the development process that has swept through the Kingdom during its golden decade. His great intellect and logical, methodical approach, along with the vast experience and scholarly achievements of his co-author, all contributed greatly to writing a unique book with a vast wealth of information about Saudi Arabia.

Dr. Esber I. Shaheen

Dr. Esber I. Shaheen is President of the International Institute of Technology, Inc. (IITI). He was born in 1937 in a remote village, Darshmezzine, El-Koura, in North Lebanon. Through his spirit of adventure as a young man with ambition and thirst for knowledge, Dr. Shaheen emigrated to the United States of America where he sought higher learning and opportunity. Working to support himself through college, he first attended the University of Texas in Austin for two years. He earned the Bachelor of Science degree in Chemical Engineering from Oklahoma State University. Later, he studied at the University of Arizona in Tucson and completed his Master of Science degree. He received the Doctor of Philosophy degree from the University of Tennessee in Knoxville.

He has vast experience in writing, technology transfer, training, international consulting and management of international projects. Extensive travel and a wide educational spectrum formulated his forthright views and thoughts. His experience in the Arab world, his frequent travels to the Kingdom of Saudi Arabia, along with the know-how and wide range of technology acquired in America, plus his vast interest and knowledge of history, gives him a unique perspective for efficiently and enthusiastically researching and writing this book.

To gain valuable experience, Dr. Shaheen served as Director of Education Services for the Institute of Gas Technology and Director of International Education Programs for Gas Developments Corporation in Chicago, Illinois, USA. He was a professor and distinguished lecturer at more than six different universities throughout the United States of America and the international community. These included: the University of Tennessee in Knoxville and the Chattanooga campus; the Illinois Institute of Technology in Chicago, Illinois; King Fahd University of Petroleum and Minerals in Dhahran, Saudi Arabia and the University of Wisconsin. Several consulting and training projects, both on the national and international scale, have been designed and managed by Dr. Shaheen. He was formerly senior engineer and manager of education projects at the Algerian Petroleum Institute.

Dr. Shaheen is the co-author with Dr. Rashid of the book entitled: *"Saudi Arabia and the Gulf War,"* and the book *"King Fahd and Saudi Arabia's Great Evolution."* This book was first published in English, then a modified version was published in Arabic. He also authored six other textbooks, amongst them the current *Best Seller* "Technology of Environmental Pollution Control–Second Edition." He has produced more than fifty articles and presentations. He is the author, co-author or editor of nearly twenty training manuals in the fields of gas engineering, energy, environment and petrochemical processing. He has several years of experience in a wide variety of industrial and educational programs. Dr. Shaheen is an orator, a dynamic and inspiring speaker. He received an award of excellence for outstanding professional development. He is listed in American Men of Science, Men of Achievement and Personalities of the West. He is an Honorary Texas citizen and an Outstanding Educator of America. Dr. Shaheen received the Toastmasters International Award for dynamic speaking. He received a Certificate of Appreciation and is listed on the Presidential Commemorative Honor Roll. He was awarded the Medal of Merit from President Ronald Reagan of the United States of America, and the Medal of Merit from His Royal Highness Prince Mohammed Bin Fahd Bin Abdulaziz, Governor of the Eastern Province in the Kingdom of Saudi Arabia.

He taught at King Fahd University of Petroleum and Minerals in Dhahran, Saudi Arabia for two academic years (1970–1972). The interaction was a great learning experience; bringing both Arab and American insights into the learning process. Many years of traveling through the Middle East contributed to his better understanding of the region. Dr. Shaheen returned to the United States of America and continued his education and training career. After several years in the United States, he returned to the Kingdom of Saudi Arabia and was astonished to see the level of progress achieved in a record time.

Being an American of Arab origin, he had a vital interest in the area and kept abreast of current affairs in the Middle East and the Arabian Gulf. With his vast experience in America, exceeding thirty-seven years, he dedicated much of his time, as a public service, to spreading the word of truth and justice about the Gulf Crisis, so that the American public and others would be better informed and more enlightened. During the entire Gulf Crisis, from the Iraqi occupation of Kuwait to the war of liberation and beyond, Dr. Shaheen gave over 150 interviews, lectures and commentaries which were covered by newspapers, television and radio stations across America. His views were received by millions of Americans across the USA.

Index